THE MANUSCRIPTS OF SEDULIUS
A PROVISIONAL HANDLIST

**Transactions of the
American Philosophical Society**
*Held at Philadelphia
For Promoting Useful Knowledge
Vol. 85, Pt. 5*

THE MANUSCRIPTS OF SEDULIUS
A PROVISIONAL HANDLIST

Carl P.E. Springer

American Philosophical Society
Independence Square   Philadelphia
1995

Springer, Carl P.E.

   The Manuscripts of Sedulius
   A Provisional Handbook

1. Sedulius   2. Manuscripts, classical
3. Handlist, manuscripts, Sedulius
4. *Paschale Carmen*

ISBN:0-87169-855-2   94-78523

Uxor tua sicut vitis abundans, in lateribus domus tuae. Filii tui, sicut novellae olivarum, in circuitu mensae tuae. Ecce sic benedicetur homo qui timet Dominum.

Psalm 127.3-4.

TABLE OF CONTENTS

PREFACE

It would not have been possible to bring a project of this nature to this stage of completion without the assistance and encouragement of a large number of individuals and institutions. It would be remiss of me, too, not to mention them explicitly here and express my appreciation for their help and encouragement. My greatest personal debt is recorded indirectly in the dedication to this volume.

My thanks first of all to the National Endowment for the Humanities for a grant in 1988 to support a trip to the Hill Monastic Microfilm Library at St. John's University in Collegeville, Minnesota, and to Julian Plante and Thomas Amos for their assistance and hospitality during my stay there. The Andrew W. Mellon Fellowship Program gave me a grant to study at the Vatican Microfilm Library at St. Louis University in the summer of 1989. A Fulbright-Hays Research Grant in 1990 permitted me to spend a semester at St. Pietersabdij in Brugge. Heartfelt thanks to Father Eligius Dekkers, Roland Demeulenaere, and the Benedictine brothers who helped to make this and subsequent stays at Steenbrugge so rewarding. The Research Group on Manuscript Evidence, especially Raymond Page, Mildred Budny, and Timothy Graham, at the Parker Library of Corpus Christi College, Cambridge, have been most generous in assisting my research on the "Corpus Sedulius" and gracious in their hospitality during my visits to the Parker Library. The American Philosophical Society awarded me a grant in 1992 to study Sedulian manuscripts at the Bibliothèque Nationale in Paris and the Vatican Library in Rome. My thanks to Colette Jeudy and the staff of the Institut de Recherche et d'Histoire des Textes in Paris, who were most helpful in making their resources available to me. I must also mention my appreciation for the generosity of the Alexander von Humboldt Foundation which supported my research at the University of Regensburg in 1993 and 1994. To Jürgen Blusch, Nikolaus Henkel, Klaus Thraede, and Manfred Wacht, all of the University of Regensburg, as well as the courteous staff of the *Monumenta Germaniae Historica* and the Bayerische Staatsbibliothek in Munich, where I spent so many fruitful hours, my thanks for assistance rendered, material and otherwise.

My thanks, too, to the following libraries for permitting me to examine manuscripts *in situ:* Albi, Bibliothèque Municipale; Angers,

Bibliothèque Municipale; Antwerpen, Musaeum Plantin-Moretus; Bamberg, Staatsbibliothek; Berlin, Staatsbibliothek-Preussischer Kulturbesitz; Bern, Burgerbibliothek; Brugge, Stedelijke Openbare Bibliotheek; Bruxelles, Bibliothèque Royale Albert 1er; Cambridge, Corpus Christi College (Parker Library) and University Library; Épinal, Bibliothèque Municipale; Évreux, Bibliothèque Municipale; Firenze, Biblioteca Medicea Laurenziana; Gent, Bibliotheek der Rijksuniversiteit; Laon, Bibliothèque Municipale; London, British Library; München, Bayerische Staatsbibliothek; Orléans, Bibliothèque Municipale; Oxford, Bodleian Library; Padova, Archivio e Biblioteca Capitolare; Paris, Bibliothèque Nationale and Bibliothèque Mazarine; Perugia, Biblioteca Communale Augusta; Praha, Národní Knihovna; Sankt Gallen, Stiftsbibliothek; Torino, Biblioteca Nazionale Universitaria; Trier, Bibliothek des Priesterseminars; the Vatican Library in Rome; and Wolfenbüttel, Herzog August Bibliothek. I should also thank the librarians and manuscript specialists in this country and abroad, who have been most gracious in answering my questions, sometimes expressed only in the most halting way, in person and by mail. These include: Gerard Achten, Bernhard Barth, Ewa Barteczko, Anthony S. Bliss, Carla Guiducci Bonanni, Livia Borghetti, D. Chelot, Helmut Claus, Marvin L. Colker, C. Coppens, Ian Cunningham, Dr. Deeters, F. Déguilly, Felix Ekowski, P.K. Eskreet, Girard Etzkorn, G. Franz, Martin Germann, Miroslava Hejnová, Steffen Hoffmann, C. Husson, Lou Jordan, Martin Kauffmann, Anna Lenzuni, Francine de Nave, Christiane Nicq, Ch. Pollin, J. Pons, Paul Raabe, Gian Albino Ravalli Modoni, Gianfranco Ravasi, Mario Roncetti, Bernhard Schemmel, Bernhard Schmitt, Brigitte Schürmann, Johannes Schwind, Leonardo Selvaggi, Chr. v. Steiger, Martin Steinmann, Louis Torchet, Ursula Winter, and Marian Zwiercán.

    Expressions of gratitude should also be extended to colleagues at Illinois State University who have encouraged me from the beginning, and to the University Research Grant program, which has provided me with a number of summer grants over the last years in support of my research on Sedulius. In particular, I should note the support of Virginia Owen, Dean of the College of Arts and Sciences, and her successor in that position, Paul Schollaert, as well as my colleagues in the Department of Foreign Languages, especially Alice Berry, Mark Johnston, and Diane Urey, who wrote such effective letters of recommendation in support of this project, and Willard Bohn, who tracked down a Sedulian manuscript written in Italy which had wandered far from its original home to settle finally in Berkeley. To my students in the Honors Mentorship Program, including Steve Benner, Brad Churchill, John Semlak, Marcy James, and

Michelle Anderson, my thanks for their many hours of ungrudging labor. To the interlibrary loan staff at Illinois State University and the University of Regensburg who have helped me with unfailing courtesy and efficiency, my warmest appreciation.

To Mildred Budny, Timothy Graham, Nikolaus Henkel, Colette Jeudy, Joseph Laurenti, Michael Roberts, and Klaus Thraede, who read a preliminary draft and made valuable suggestions for its improvement, this monograph owes a great deal. To two of my teachers at the University of Wisconsin-Madison, Fannie J. LeMoine and William Courtenay, who first aroused my interest in the literature of Late Antiquity and manuscript studies respectively, I am still grateful. For all such errors and limitations as remain, the author is, of course, solely responsible. This is, it should be remembered, a "provisional" listing of the manuscripts of Sedulius. There remain, as is well known, many large manuscript collections (e.g., the Vatican Library in Rome and the Ambrosian Library in Milan), as well as smaller libraries in Spain and eastern Europe, which are but poorly or only partially catalogued. There are, doubtless, other Sedulian manuscripts which remain to be discovered. Indeed, it is my hope that by publishing this "Handlist," I may appeal to readers who know of the existence of Sedulian manuscripts which may not be included here, as well as to those who notice mistakes of fact or judgment in my description of the manuscripts and their contents, to lend me their assistance (I am in the process of preparing a new edition of all of Sedulius' works for *Corpus Christianorum, Series Latina*). Whatever its limitations may be, I am convinced, finally, that a list such as this may serve not only as a useful resource for scholars who specialize in the Christian Latin poetry of Late Antiquity or in manuscript studies, but may also help a wider range of students of cultural and intellectual history better to appreciate the impact of this influential author over the course of a millennium of western European history. Corrections, suggestions for improvement, and inquiries may be addressed to the author in care of the Department of Foreign Languages, Illinois State University, Normal, IL 61790-4300, or by electronic mail: cpsprin@rs6000.cmp.ilstu.edu.

LIST OF FREQUENTLY OCCURRING ABBREVIATIONS

AH	*Analecta Hymnica Medii Aevi.*
AJP	*American Journal of Philology.*
ALMA	*Archivum Latinitatis Medii Aevi (Bulletin Du Cange).*
Arevalo	Faustino Arevalo, ed., *Coelius Sedulius* (1794), reprinted in *PL*, vol. 19, cols. 433 ff.
Arntzenius	Hendrik Jan Arntzen, *Coelii Sedulii Carminis Paschalis Libri V et Hymni Duo. Cum Notis Casparis Barthii, Christophori Cellarii, Cornelii Valerii Vonckii, Joannis Friderici Gruneri, Aliorumque. Quibus Adcedunt Thomae Wopkensii Adversaria Emendatoria Maxima ex Parte adhuc Inedita. Curante Henrico Joanne Arntzenio* (Leeuwarden: G. Coulon, 1760, and H.A. de Chalmot, 1761).
APS	American Philosophical Society.
ARSR	*Archivio della Real Società Romana di Storia Patria.*
AST	*Analecta Sacra Tarraconensia.*
Baroffio	B. Baroffio, review of Gamber in *RSCI* 23 (1969), 490-8.
BDA	*Bollettino della Deputazione Abruzzese di Storia Patria.*
Beccaria	Augusto Beccaria, *I codici di medicina del periodo presalernitano (secoli ix, x e xi)* (Roma, 1956).
BECh	*Bibliothèque de l'École des Chartes.*
Beeson	Charles Henry Beeson, *Isidor-Studien* = Quellen und Untersuchungen zur lateinischen Philologie des Mittelalters 4.2 (München, 1913).
Beneventan	E.A. Loew (Lowe), *The Beneventan Script: A History of the South Italian Minuscule*, 2nd rev. ed., Virginia Brown = Sussidi eruditi 33-4 (Roma, 1980).
Bergmann	Rolf Bergmann, *Verzeichnis der althochdeutschen und altsächsischen Glossenhandschriften. Mit Bibliographie der Glosseneditionen, der Handschriftenbeschreibungen und der Dialektbestimmungen* = Arbeiten zur Frühmittelalterforschung 6 (Berlin and New York, 1973).

BIRHT — *Bulletin d'information de l'Institut de Recherche et d'Histoire des Textes.*

Bischoff, *MS* — Bernhard Bischoff, *Mittelalterlichen Studien. Ausgewählte Aufsätze zur Schriftenkunde und Literaturgeschichte* (Stuttgart, 1966-81).

Bischoff, "FHH" — Bernhard Bischoff, "Frühkarolingische Handschriften und ihre Heimat," *Scriptorium* 22 (1968), 306-14.

BM — *British Museum. General Catalogue of Printed Books,* esp. vol. 218 (London, 1964).

BN — *Catalogue général des livres imprimés de la Bibliothèque Nationale,* esp. vol. 169 (Paris, 1946).

Boas — Marcus Boas, *Disticha Catonis* (Amsterdam, 1952).

Brunet — Jacques-Charles Brunet, *Manuel du libraire et de l'amateur de livres,* vol. 5 (Paris, 1864).

Bruckner — Albert Bruckner, *Scriptoria Medii Aevi Helvetica. Denkmäler schweizerischer Schreibkunst des Mittelalters* (multi-volume; Genève, 1935-57).

Bühler — Curt F. Bühler, "The Earliest Spanish Printings of Sedulius," *Gutenberg-Jahrbuch* 1972, pp. 107-9.

Bursill-Hall — G.L. Bursill-Hall, *A Census of Medieval Latin Grammatical Manuscripts* = Grammatica Speculativa: Sprachtheorie und Logik des Mittelalters (Stuttgart, 1981).

Cat. gen. quarto — *Catalogue général des manuscrits des bibliothèques publiques des départements* (Paris, 1849-1885).

Cat. gen. octavo — *Catalogue général des manuscrits des bibliothèques publiques de France. Départements* (Paris, 1886 ff.).

CCSL — *Corpus Christianorum. Series Latina.*

CCCM — *Corpus Christianorum. Continuatio Medievalis.*

Census — S. De Ricci, *Census of Medieval and Renaissance Manuscripts in the United States and Canada,* vols. 1-3 (New York, 1935-40).

Census Suppl. — W.H. Bond and C.U. Faye, *Supplement to the Census of Medieval and Renaissance Manuscripts in the United States and Canada* (New York, 1962).

Chev. — Ulysse Chevalier, *Repertorium Hymnologicum. Catalogue des chants, hymnes, proses, séquences, tropes en usage dans l'église latine depuis les origines jusqu'a nos jours* = Subsidia Hagiographica 4.1-5 (Louvain, 1892-1921).

CLA

E.A. Lowe (Loew), *Codices Latini Antiquiores: A Palaeographical Guide to Latin Manuscripts Prior to the Ninth Century* (Oxford, 1934 ff.).

Contreni

John J. Contreni, *The Cathedral School of Laon from 850 to 930: Its Manuscripts and Masters* = MBMRF 29 (München, 1978).

Copinger

W.A. Copinger, *Supplement to Hain's Repertorium Bibliographicum*, vol. 2 (London, 1902).

CP

Classical Philology.

CPL

Eligius Dekkers, *Clavis Patrum Latinorum* = Sacris Erudiri 3 (2nd ed.; Brugge, 1961).

CQ

Classical Quarterly.

CSEL

Corpus Scriptorum Ecclesiasticorum Latinorum.

DACL

Dictionnaire d'archéologie chrétienne et de liturgie.

Ehrensberger

H. Ehrensberger, *Libri Liturgici Bibliothecae Apostolicae Vaticanae Manu Scripti* (Freiburg, 1897).

EL

Ephemerides Liturgicae.

EHR

English Historical Review.

Esposito

M. Esposito, "A Ninth-Century Commentary on Phocas," *CQ* 13 (1919), 166-9.

Frere

W.H. Frere, et al., *Bibliotheca Musico-Liturgica. A Descriptive Handlist of the Musical and Latin-liturgical MSS. of the Middle Ages Preserved in the Libraries of Great Britain and Ireland* (London, 1901-1932).

Gamber

Klaus Gamber, *Codices Liturgici Latini Antiquiores* = Spicilegii Friburgensis Subsidia 1 (2nd ed.; 2 vols.; Freiburg, 1968) and *Supplementum: Ergänzungs- und Registerband* = Spicilegii Friburgensis Subsidia 1a (Freiburg, 1988).

Glauche

Günter Glauche, *Schullektüre im Mittelalter. Entstehung und Wandlungen des Lektürekanons bis 1200 nach den Quellen dargestellt* = MBMRF 5 (München, 1970).

Gneuss, *Hymnar*

Helmut Gneuss, *Hymnar und Hymnen in englischen Mittelalter. Studien zur Überlieferung, Glossierung und Übersetzung lateinischer Hymnen in England* = Buchreihe der Anglia, Zeitschrift für englische Philologie 12 (Tübingen, 1968).

Gneuss, "List"   Helmut Gneuss, "A Preliminary List of Manuscripts Written or Owned in England up to 1100," *Anglo-Saxon England* 9 (1981), 1-60.

Graesse   Jean George Theodore Graesse, *Trésor de livres rares et précieux ou nouveau dictionaire bibliographique,* vol. 6 (Leipzig and Paris, 1900).

Guaglianone   Anton. Guaglianone, *Aviani Fabulae,* in *Corpus Scriptorum Latinorum Paravianum* (Torino, 1958).

Haebler   Konrad Haebler, *Bibliografía Iberica del Siglo XV* (New York, 1903-17).

Hain   L. Hain, *Repertorium Bibliographicum in Quo Libri Omnes ab Arte Typographica Inventa usque ad Annum MD* (Leipzig and Paris, 1900).

Hauréau, *Notices*   B. Hauréau, *Notices et extraits de quelques manuscrits latins de la Bibliothèque Nationale* (Paris, 1890-3).

Hörmann   Wolfgang Hörmann, *Sancti Aureli Augustini Opera. Sect. I, Pars IV. Soliloquiorum Libri Duo. De Inmortalitate Animae. De Quantitate Animae, CSEL,* vol. 89 (Wien, 1980).

Huemer   Johannes Huemer, *Sedulii Opera Omnia, CSEL,* vol. 10.

Huemer, *De Sedulii*   Johannes Huemer, *De Sedulii Poetae Vita et Scriptis Commentatio* (Wien, 1878).

Huemer, "Glossen"   Johannes Huemer, "Über ein Glossenwerk zum Dichter Sedulius. Zugleich ein Beitrag zu den grammatischen Schriften des Remigius von Auxerre," *Sitz. Wien* 96 (1880), 505-51.

Jeudy, "Priscien"   Colette Jeudy, "L'*Institutio de nomine, pronomine et verbo* de Priscien: Manuscrits et commentaires médiévaux," *RHT* 2 (1972), 73-144.

Jeudy, "Phocas"   Colette Jeudy, "L'*Ars de nomine et verbo* de Phocas: Manuscrits et commentaires médiévaux," *Viator* 5 (1974), 61-156.

Jeudy, "Remi"   Colette Jeudy, "Remigii Autissiodorensis Opera (Clavis)," in *L'École carolingienne d'Auxerre de Murethach à Remi, 830-908* (Paris, 1991), pp. 458 ff.

Jeudy & Riou   Colette Jeudy and Yves-François Riou, *Les Manuscrits classiques latins des bibliothèques publiques de France,* vol. 1 (Paris, 1989).

Jeudy & Riou, "Notes"   Colette Jeudy and Yves-François Riou, "Notes sur *Les Manuscrits classiques latins des bibliothèques publiques de France*," *RHT* 16 (1986), 311-8.

JLW   *Jahrbuch für Liturgiewissenschaft.*

Jullien   Marie-Hélène Jullien, "Les Sources de la tradition ancienne des quatorze *Hymnes* attribuées à Saint Ambroise de Milan," *RHT* 19 (1989), 57-189.

Ker, *Cat.*   N.R. Ker, *Catalogue of Manuscripts Containing Anglo-Saxon* (Oxford, 1957).

Ker, *Med.*   N.R. Ker, *Medieval Libraries of Great Britain. A List of Surviving Books* = Royal Historical Society Guides and Handbooks 3 (2nd ed.; London, 1964), and *Supplement to the Second Edition*, A.G. Watson (London, 1987).

Kristeller   Paul Oskar Kristeller, *Latin Manuscript Books Before 1600. A List of the Printed Catalogues and Unpublished Inventories of Extant Collections* = MGH Hilfsmittel 13 (revised by Sigrid Krämer) (fourth ed.; München, 1993).

Kristeller, *Iter*   Paul Oskar Kristeller, *Iter Italicum: A Finding List of Uncatalogued or Incompletely Catalogued Humanistic Manuscripts of the Renaissance in Italian and Other Libraries* (London and Leiden, 1967 ff.), multi-volume.

Kurz   Rainer Kurz, "Zu Konrads von Hirsau *Dialogus super auctores 590* über das Leben des Sedulius," *MlatJb* 14 (1979), 265-72.

Laistner   M.L.W. Laistner and H.H. King, *A Hand-List of Bede Manuscripts* (Ithaca, 1943).

Lapidge, "Booklists"   Michael Lapidge, "Booklists from Anglo-Saxon England" in *Learning and Literature in Anglo-Saxon England: Studies Presented to Peter Clemoes on the Occasion of his Sixty-fifth Birthday*, ed. Michael Lapidge and Helmut Gneuss (Cambridge, 1985), pp. 33-89.

Lapidge, "Latin Texts"   Michael Lapidge, "The Study of Latin Texts in Late Anglo-Saxon England: The Evidence of Latin Glosses" in *Latin and the Vernacular Languages in Early Medieval Britain: Papers Delivered to the Fifth Annual St. John's House Symposium*, ed. Nicholas Brooks (Leicester, 1982).

Legendre   P. Legendre, *Études tironiennes. Commentaire sur la VIe églogue de Virgile tiré d'un manuscrit de Chartres avec divers appendices et un facsimilé* = Bibl. de l'École des Hautes Études. Sciences historiques et philosophiques 165 (Paris, 1907).

Lehmann	Paul Lehmann, *Erforschung des Mittelalters: ausgewählte Abhandlungen und Aufsätze* (Leipzig and Stuttgart, 1941-62).
Leroquais, *Bréviaires*	Victor Leroquais, *Les Bréviaires manuscrits des bibliothèques publiques de France* (Paris, 1934 ff.).
Leroquais, *Psautiers*	Victor Leroquais, *Les Psautiers manuscrits latins des bibliothèques publiques de France* (Macon, 1940 ff.).
Lesne	Émile Lesne, *Histoire de la propriété ecclésiastique en France, IV: Les Livres, scriptoria, et bibliothèques du commencement du VIIIe à la fin du XIe siècle* = Mémoires et travaux publiés par des professeurs des Facultés Catholiques de Lille 46 (Lille, 1938).
Lokrantz	Margareta Lokrantz, *L'Opera poetica di S. Pier Damiani* = Acta Universitatis Stockholmiensis. Studia Latina Stockholmiensia 12 (Stockholm, Göteborg, Uppsala, 1964).
Ludwig	E. Ludwig, *Sedulii Paschalis Operis Liber Quintus. Nach den zum ersten Male verglichenen besten Handschriften revidirt* (Heilbronn, 1880).
MA	*Le Moyen Âge.*
Mazzatinti	G. Mazzatinti, *Inventari dei manoscritti delle biblioteche d'Italia* (Forlì, 1890 ff.).
MBMRF	Münchener Beiträge zur Mediävistik und Renaissance-Forschung.
McGurk	Patrick McGurk, *Latin Gospel Books from A.D. 400 to A.D. 800* = Les Publications de Scriptorium 5 (Paris, Bruxelles, Antwerpen, Amsterdam, 1961).
McKinlay	Arthur Patch McKinlay, *Arator: The Codices* (Cambridge, Mass., 1942).
MCLBV	*Les Manuscrits classiques latins de la Bibliothèque Vaticane,* ed. Elisabeth Pellegrin, Jeannine Fohlen, Colette Jeudy, Yves-François Riou (Paris, 1975-82).
Mead	Herman Ralph Mead, *Incunabula in the Huntington Library* (San Marino, CA, 1937).
MEFRM	*Mélanges de l'École Française de Rome. Moyen âge-temps moderns.*
Mearns	James Mearns, *Early Latin Hymnaries. An Index of Hymns in Hymnaries before 1100* (Cambridge, 1913).
Meritt	Herbert D. Meritt, *Old English Glosses* (New York, 1945).

MGH AA	*Monumenta Germaniae Historica. Auctores Antiquissimi.*
MGH PLAC	*Monumenta Germaniae Historica. Poetae Latini Medii Aevi, vol. 1, Poetae Latini Aevi Carolini.*
MH	*Museum Helveticum.*
M&H	*Medievalia et Humanistica.*
MlatJb	*Mittellateinisches Jahrbuch.*
Mostert	M. Mostert, *The Library of Fleury: A Provisional List of Manuscripts* (Hilversum, 1989).
MS	*Mediaeval Studies.*
MT	*Museum Tusculanum.*
Munari	Franco Munari, *Mathei Vindocinensis Opera, vol. 1: Catalogo dei manoscritti* = Storia e letteratura. Raccolta di studi e testi 144 (Roma, 1977).
Munk Olsen	Birger Munk Olsen, *L'Étude des auteurs classiques latins aux XIe et XIIe siècles. I-II: Catalogue des manuscrits classiques latins copiés du IXe au XIIe siècle. III.1: Les Classiques dans les bibliothèques médiévales. III.2: Addenda et Corrigenda-Tables* (Paris, 1982-89).
Neues Archiv	*Neues Archiv der Gesellschaft für ältere deutsche Geschichtskunde.*
NKGWG	*Nachrichten von der königlichen Gesellschaft der Wissenschaften zu Göttingen. Philologisch-historische Klasse.*
Norton	F.J. Norton, *A Descriptive Catalogue of Printing in Spain and Portugal 1501-1520* (Cambridge, 1978).
Not. et extr.	*Notices et extraits de manuscrits de la Bibliothèque Nationale et autres bibliothèques.*
NUC	*The National Union Catalog: Pre-1956 Imprints,* esp. vol. 536 (London, 1977).
NYPL	*The New York Public Library Dictionary Catalogue of the Rare Book Division,* esp. vol. 17 (Boston, 1971).
Odriozola	Antonio Odriozola, "La caracola del bibliófilo nebrisense o la casa a cuestas indispensable al amigo de Nebrija para navegar por el proceloso mar de sus obras," *Revista de bibliografía nacional* 7 (1946), fasc. 1a 4, pp. 3-114.
Passalacqua	Marina Passalacqua, *I codici di Prisciano* = Sussidi eruditi 29 (Roma, 1978).

Pellegrin

Elisabeth Pellegrin, *Bibliothèques retrouvées. Manu-scrits, bibliothèques et bibliophiles du Moyen Âge et de la Renaissance* (Paris, 1990). (Contains reprints of many of Pellegrin's articles, published in a wide assortment of journals between 1938 and 1985.)

Piacentini

Paola Scarcia Piacentini, *Saggio di un censimento dei manoscritti contenenti il testo di Persio e gli scoli e i commenti al testo* = Studi su Persio e la scoliastica persiana 3.1: Studi sulla tradizione di Persio e la scoliastica persiana (Roma, 1973).

PL

Patrologia Latina.

Proctor

Robert Proctor, *An Index to the Early Printed Books in the British Museum* (London, 1898).

RB

Revue bénédictine.

REAug

Revue des études augustiniennes.

Reynolds

L.D. Reynolds, ed, *Texts and Transmission. A Survey of the Latin Classics* (Oxford, 1983).

RhM

Rheinisches Museum.

RHT

Revue d'histoire des textes.

RSCI

Rivista di storia della chiesa in Italia.

RSPh

Revue des sciences philosophiques et theologiques.

RTAM

Recherches de théologie ancienne et médiévale.

Salmon

Pierre Salmon, *Les Manuscrits liturgiques latins de la Bibliothèque Vaticane I. Psautiers, antiphonaires, hymnaires, collectaires, bréviaires* = Studi e testi 251 (Vaticano, 1968).

Sanford

Eva Matthews Sanford, "The Use of Classical Latin Authors in the *Libri Manuales*," *TAPA* 55 (1924), 190-248.

Schaller

Dieter Schaller and Ewald Köngsen, *Initia Carminum Latinorum Saeculo Undecimo Antiquiorum. Biblio-graphisches Repertorium für die lateinische Dichtung der Antike und des früheren Mittelalters* (Göttingen, 1977).

Schenkl

Heinrich Schenkl, *Bibliotheca Patrum Latinorum Britannica* (Wien, 1891-8).

SE

Sacris Erudiri.

SFRMP

Société Française de Reproductions de Manuscrits à Peintures.

SIFC	*Studi italiani di filologia classica.*
Sitz. Wien	*Sitzungsberichte der kaiserlichen Akademie der Wissenschaften in Wien. Philosophisch-historische Klasse.*
SL	M. Guidobaldi and F. Pesando, *Scripta Latina. Index Editionum Quae ad Usum Historicum Maxime Adsunt* (Roma, 1993).
Sosa	Guillermo S. Sosa, *Incunabula Iberica. Catalogue of Books Printed in Spain and Portugal in the XVth C.* (Buenos Aires, 1973).
Sottili	Agostino Sottili, *I codici del Petrarca nella Germania Occidentale* = Censimento dei codici Petrarcheschi 4 and 7 (Padova, 1971 and 1978).
Stegmüller	F. Stegmüller, *Repertorium Biblicum Medii Aevi* (Madrid, 1950-80).
Steinmeyer & Sievers	Elias Steinmeyer and Eduard Sievers, *Die althochdeutschen Glossen* (Berlin, 1879-1922).
Stillwell	Margaret Binham Stillwell, *Incunabula in American Libraries* (New York, 1940).
Sum. Cat.	Falconer Madan, H.H.E. Craster, and N. Denholm Young, *A Summary Catalogue of Western Manuscripts in the Bodleian Library at Oxford which have not hitherto been Described in the Quarto Series with References to the Oriental Manuscripts and Papyri* (Oxford, 1859-1953).
TAPA	*Transactions of the American Philological Association.*
TCBS	*Transactions of the Cambridge Bibliographical Society.*
Traube	Ludwig Traube, *Vorlesungen und Abhandlungen* (München, 1909-20).
VC	*Vigiliae Christianae.*
Walther	Hans Walther, *Initia Carminum ac Versuum Medii Aevi Posterioris Latinorum. Alphabetisches Verzeichnis der Versanfänge mittellateinischer Dichtung* = Carmina Medii Aevi Posterioris Latina 1.1 (Göttingen, 1969).
Walpole	A.S. Walpole, *Early Latin Hymns with Introduction and Notes* (Cambridge, 1922).

Wickersheimer

Ernest Wickersheimer, *Les Manuscrits latins de médecine du haut Moyen Âge dans les bibliothéques de France* = Documents, études et répertoires publiés par l'I.R.H.T. 11 (Paris, 1966).

WS

Wiener Studien.

ZOG

Zeitschrift für die österreichischen Gymnasien.

INTRODUCTION

I.

According to one of the versions of a biographical notice found in a number of early manuscripts which contain his works, the Latin poet Sedulius was a layman who studied philosophy in Italy, later taught epic poetry (probably as a *"grammaticus"*), and wrote "his books" in Greece during the reigns of Theodosius II and Valentinian III (i.e., between 425 and 450 AD).[1]

Although his works no longer enjoy the popularity they once did, Sedulius was in vogue for over a thousand years after he lived and wrote.[2] His masterpiece, the *Paschale Carmen*, is one of the earliest examples of what has often been termed "biblical epic," a popular genre from the fourth century to the 17th, of which John Milton's *Paradise Lost* is perhaps the most famous representative in the English language.[3]

---

[1] As it may be found, for example, in Paris, Bibliothèque Nationale, Lat. 18554 (f. 3v): Incipit ars Sedulii poetae qui primo laicus in Italia philosophiam didicit. Postea cum aliis metrorum generibus heroicum metrum Macedonio consulente docuit. In Achaia libros suos scripsit in tempore imperatorum minoris Theodosii filii Arcadii et Valentiniani filii Constantii.
For fuller biographical background on Sedulius, see Carl P.E. Springer, *The Gospel as Epic in Late Antiquity. The Paschale Carmen of Sedulius* = Supplements to Vigiliae Christianae II (Leiden, 1988), esp. chap. 2.

[2] On Sedulius and other "curriculum authors," see the fundamental work of Ernst Robert Curtius, *European Literature and the Latin Middle Ages*, trans. Willard Trask (New York, 1953), pp. 49 ff. Glauche's still valuable investigation of the *"Lektürekanon"* up until 1200 is referred to frequently in the pages below. More recently the subject has been taken up by Birger Munk Olsen, *I classici nel canone scolastico altomedievale* = Quaderni di cultura mediolatina 1 (Spoleto, 1991), esp. pp. 66-8.

[3] See the studies of Reinhart Herzog, *Die Bibelepik der lateinischen Spätantike: Formgeschichte einer erbaulichen Gattung I* = Theorie und Geschichte der Literatur und der schönen Künste 37 (München, 1975); Dieter Kartschoke, *Bibeldichtung. Studien zur Geschichte der epischen Bibelparaphrase von Juvencus bis Otfrid von Weissenburg* (München, 1975); and Wolfgang Kirsch, *Die lateinische Versepik des 4. Jahrhunderts* = Schriften zur Geschichte und Kultur der Antike 28 (Berlin, 1989). Michael Roberts, *Biblical Epic and Rhetorical Paraphrase in Late Antiquity* (Liverpool, 1985), is the best overview of the genre in English.

Of the poem's popularity and influence, Max Manitius declares emphatically:

Das *Carmen Paschale* hat die denkbar grösste Verbreitung gefunden und blieb eines der Hauptvorbilder für die ganze lateinische Poesie des Mittelalters.[4]

In the early Middle Ages, Sedulius' works were read and acclaimed by such important figures as the Venerable Bede, who used Sedulius as one of his principal models in his treatise on metrics, Alcuin, the influential advisor of Charlemagne, and Isidore of Seville, the Spanish churchman whose library included a copy of Sedulius (highly recommended for pious readers who had grown tired of the works of Virgil, Horace, Ovid, Persius and other classical poets).[5] The fifth-century poet continued to be read and praised during the later Middle Ages and the early modern period. The Italian humanist, Petrarch, who could not resist the opportunity to pun on Sedulius' name in his *Bucolicum Carmen* (10.311 ff.),[6] the English divine, John Colet, who recommended the "wisdome with clene and chast laten" of Sedulius' work for students attending St. Paul's School in London, and the German reformer, Martin Luther, who translated one of Sedulius' hymns into the

---

[4]*Geschichte der christlich-lateinischen Poesie bis zur Mitte des 8. Jahrhunderts* (Stuttgart, 1891), p. 309.

[5]I offer here the pertinent lines from the verses on Isidore's library, as found in Beeson, pp. 157-63:

> Si Maro, si Flaccus, si Naso et Persius horret,
> Lucanus si te, Papiniusque tedet,
> pareat eximio dulcis Prudentius ore,
> carminibus variis nobilis ille satis.
> Perlege facundi studiosum carmen Aviti,
> ecce Iuvencus adest, Seduliusque tibi.
> Ambo lingua pares, florentes versibus ambo,
> fonte evangelico pocula larga ferunt.
> Desine gentilibus ergo inservire poetis:
> dum bona tanta potes, quid tibi Calliroen?

[6]I quote from Thomas G. Bergin, *Petrarch's Bucolicum Carmen* (New Haven and London, 1974), p. 172:

> Longe ibi trans fluvium, regum inter busta seorsum,
> unus erat rutilus divini ruris arator
> qui pinguem scabro sulcabat vomere campum.
> Huic comes, hinc prudens, hinc sedulus alter aranti
> certabant rigido glebas confringere rastro.

vernacular and referred to its author as *poeta Christianissimus*-all read Sedulius.[7]

One of the reasons, doubtless, for Sedulius' enduring popularity was the use in medieval schools of his *Paschale Carmen*, a Latin version of the life of Christ in dactylic hexameters, divided into five books, the first of which is devoted to Old Testament miracles prefiguring the *clara miracula Christi* which are the concern of the remaining four books.[8] The Latin Christian epics of Late Antiquity were often employed in the Middle Ages, it appears, to assist schoolboys in mastering the intricacies of Virgilian prosody, without forcing them to agonize over the tragedy of the pagan Dido (as we know from his *Confessions* that Augustine did) or to wrestle with the troubling notion of the existence of deities other than the God of the Bible.[9] Instructors faced with the challenge of introducing their charges to the mysteries of dactylic hexameters without disturbing their Christian faith must have found Sedulius' epic life of Christ an extremely useful means to achieve their pedagogical ends.

There are some scholars, to be sure, who have urged caution in using the term "classbook" to describe such volumes as Cambridge, University Library, Gg. 5. 35.[10]   Based on the fact that the Latin

---

[7]In his treatise, *De Divinitate et Humanitate Christi*, as it is to be found in *D. Martin Luthers Werke. Kritische Gesamtausgabe (Weimarer Ausgabe)*, vol. 39.2, p. 95:

> Sedulius poeta christianissimus canit: Beatus autor seculi servile corpus induit, idque per totam ecclesiam, cum nihil possit magis dici haereticum, quam humanam naturam esse vestem divinitatis. Non enim vestis et corpus constituunt unam personam, sicut Deus et homo constituunt unam personam. Tamen piissime sensisse Sedulium, caetera carmina probant evidentissime.

The reader is referred to the final chapter of my *Gospel as Epic*, see note 1 above, for a more wide-ranging, but by no means exhaustive, account of Sedulius' influence during the early modern period.

[8]See note 56 below for a fuller discussion of the book division of the *Paschale Carmen*.

[9]Virgil, of course, continued to be read throughout the Middle Ages. On medieval attitudes towards classical authors, the reader might consult with profit T.J. Brown's engaging article, "An Historical Introduction to the Use of Classical Latin Authors in the British Isles from the Fifth to the Eleventh Century" in *La culture antica nell'occidente latino dal vii all'xi secolo* = Settimane di studio 22 (1975), 273-99 and R.H. Rouse, "*Florilegia* and Latin Classical Authors in Twelfth- and Thirteenth-Century Orléans," *Viator* 10 (1979), 131-60.

[10]Lapidge, "Latin Texts," p. 126, *contra* A.G. Rigg and G.R. Wieland, "A Canterbury Classbook of the Mid-eleventh Century (the 'Cambridge Songs' Manuscript)," *Anglo-Saxon England* 4 (1975), who suggest (p. 130) that the manuscript was used to provide youthful students in pre-conquest England with a "fundamental literary programme in Christian Latin poetry."

glossing "begins intensively on the first folio or two, peters out over the next few folios, and then usually ceases altogether," Michael Lapidge suggests that the Sedulian manuscripts he has studied may have been used for private monastic reading. It is clear that Sedulius' reputation was not confined to the school room, and, indeed, he seems to have enjoyed a double reception in the Middle Ages, not only as a successful example of Christian appropriation of a Classical literary form, suited for study in the schools, but also as a respected work of biblical interpretation. In Venantius Fortunatus, *Carm.* 8.1.59, Sedulius alone of the canonical Christian poets (see the list in Fortunatus' *Vita Martini* 1.14-25), is included in the company of such ecclesiastical authorities as Gregory, Basil, Athanasius, Hilary, Ambrose, Jerome, Augustine, Orosius, and Caesarius of Arles. Although modern critics like Ernst Robert Curtius have often dismissed Sedulius as little more than a "grandiloquent" rhetor who had "nothing to say," Sedulius' medieval readers apparently felt that *what* this "most Christian poet" wrote as well as *how* he wrote it was important. His words were not only praised for their elegance in the Middle Ages, but also used by churchmen from Hincmar of Reims to Martin Luther to illustrate doctrinal positions and even to settle theological controversies.[11]

Not all of the manuscripts listed below may have been written for use in schools, but some certainly were. Gernot Wieland has argued persuasively that at least two Sedulian manuscripts (Oxford, Bodleian Library, Lat. Th. C. 4 and Cambridge, University Library, Gg. 5. 35), were "clearly designed for teachers for use in the classroom."[12] It is indeed difficult to imagine why so many glosses on the *Paschale Carmen* would be devoted to matters of stylistics (e.g., identifying figures of speech) and why so few devotional or edifying glosses would be included in manuscripts which were being used primarily for spiritual edification

---

[11]See, for example, Hincmar's treatise *De Una et Non Trina Deitate* (directed against Gottschalk, who also cites Sedulius), *PL,* vol. 125, col. 564:

    Nam et quod venerandus Sedulius sicut coactus metri necessitate, trinam fidem et in eodem Paschali opere posuit, dicens: Quod simplex triplicet, quodque est triplicabile simplet.

The quote from Sedulius is followed by a citation from the sixth book of Augustine's *De Trinitate.* On Venantius Fortunatus' regard for Sedulius, see Michael Roberts, "The Description of Landscape in the Poetry of Venantius Fortunatus: The Moselle Poems," *Traditio* 49 (1994), 2.

[12]"The Glossed Manuscript: Classbook or Library Book?" *Anglo-Saxon England* 14 (1985), 173.

and not for the sake of grammatical instruction in schools.[13] There are other explanations for the "petering out" of glossing after the first leaves. Some teachers may have needed only to explain a phenomenon once (at least if they had gifted students) and not every time it recurred in a text. Another possibility is that only the first part of the *Paschale Carmen* was read in certain schools (perhaps there was not time enough to read more). A glance through Huemer's *"Index scriptorum qui vel citaverunt vel imitati sunt Sedulium"* (*CSEL*, vol. 10, pp. 361-71) suggests that the first lines of the *Paschale Carmen* were far more familiar to medieval readers than the rest of the poem.

It is certainly no accident that the *Paschale Carmen* is so often found in the company of other texts which were used in medieval schools: "Cato's" *Distichs*, the epigrams of Prosper, and the fables of Avianus, as well as more theoretical treatises on grammar and style such as Bede's *De Arte Metrica* and *De Schematibus et Tropis* and Priscian's *Institutio de Nomine et Pronomine et Verbo*. It seems clear, too, that the *Paschale Carmen* was used as a school text in the early modern period. The prefaces to many of the early printed editions make it quite clear that their editors (and commentators) expected this author to be used in schools. Aldus Manutius in Italy, John Colet in England, Georg Fabricius in Germany, and Antonio Nebrija in Spain-all obviously believed that the *Paschale Carmen* offered the most salutary kind of pedagogical benefits for Christian school children.[14]

Of the authors of the Latin biblical epics written in Late Antiquity who were often included in the medieval curriculum, especially Juvencus, who wrote his *Evangeliorum Libri Quattuor* during the reign of Constantine, and the sixth-century Arator, whose *Historia Apostolica* is heavily indebted to the author of the *Paschale Carmen*, Sedulius appears to have enjoyed the widest circulation and most consistent popularity over the years.[15] Manitius' listing of medieval collections

---

[13]For figures of speech and thought identified in marginal glosses, see, e.g., Biblioteca Apostolica Vaticana, Reg. Lat. 333, where in the short space of four leaves (ff. 108v-111r), we find anaphora, apostrophe, zeugma, prolepsis, catacresis, metonomy, hyperbole, hypallage, and allegory identified in the margins.

[14]On Sedulius as a school text in early sixteenth-century Spain, see F.J. Norton, *Printing in Spain 1501-1520* (Cambridge, 1966), p. 127. For other references the reader is referred to *The Gospel as Epic* (see note 1 above), pp. 135 ff.

[15]On Sedulius' influence on Arator, see Neil Wright, "Arator's Use of Caelius Sedulius: A Re-examination," *Eranos* 87 (1989), 51-64. Neither Juvencus nor Arator seem to have enjoyed the kind of popularity that Sedulius did in the later Middle Ages. On the waning

which owned at least one copy of Sedulius (the list, which includes 100 references to the author of the *Paschale Carmen*, is by no means complete) reveals the extent of the fifth-century poet's popularity. Other early Latin Christian poets such as Avitus, "Cyprianus Gallus," Dracontius, Juvencus, Proba, and Venantius Fortunatus appear to be less well represented. Indeed, of the "patristic poets," only Prudentius can be said to rival Sedulius' popularity. Although Sedulius was never to regain the kind of stature he obviously enjoyed during the Carolingian Age, there are over 80 manuscripts of the *Paschale Carmen* (not including fragments) dating from the thirteenth to the sixteenth centuries which are still extant. The flood of early printed editions, beginning already in the 1470s, which contain his works (see the appendix below) will give the reader some indication of how popular Sedulius continued to be after the invention of the printing press. From England in the north to Italy in the south, from Spain in the west to Austria in the east, the *Paschale Carmen* was popular reading in Europe for over a thousand years after its composition.[16]

---

interest in Juvencus after the eleventh century, see Glauche, p. 124, n. 43 and Reinhart Herzog, *Restauration und Erneuerung. Die lateinische Literatur von 284 bis 374 n. Chr.* = Handbuch der lateinischen Literatur der Antike, vol. 5, ed. R. Herzog and P.L. Schmidt (München, 1989), p. 336. Of Arator's popularity in the later Middle Ages, Arthur Patch McKinlay remarks in *Scriptorium* 6 (1962), 151: "the interest falls off markedly after the Thirteenth Century." The distribution of manuscripts (not including fragments) of the *Paschale Carmen* by century is as follows: s. vii: 1; s. viii: 2; s. viii-ix: 1; s. ix: 19; s. ix-x: 4; s. x: 13; s. x-xi: 1; s. xi: 20; s. xi-xii: 3; s. xii: 23; s. xii-xiii: 3; s. xiii: 11; s. xiii-xiv: 1; s. xiv: 14; s. xv: 49; s. xv-xvi: 2; s. xvi: 8.

[16]Max Manitius (ed. Karl. Manitius), *Handschriften antiker Autoren in mittelalterlichen Bibliothekskatalogen* = Zentralblatt für Bibliothekswesen 67 (Leipzig, 1935), pp. 268 ff. We find copies of Sedulius, according to Manitius, in the following medieval book collections in German-speaking areas of Europe: Köln, Freising, S. Gallen, Lorsch, Murbach, Reichenau, Weissenburg, Passau, Regensburg (S. Emmeram), Salzburg (Dom), Minden, Benediktbeuern, Egmond, Blaubeuren, Füssen, Gorze, Reisbach, Toul, Bamberg, Pfävers, Frowin von Engelberg, Halberstadt, Muri, Oberaltaich, Rastede, Wessobrunn, Wigrad, Lisborn, Neumünster, Schlettstadt, Arnstein, Hamersleven, Klosterneuburg, Marienfelde, Pegau, Rolduc, Fürstenfeld, Prüll, Amplonius (Erfurt), Wien, Melk, Bordesholm, Prague, Fulda, and Trier (S. Eucharius-Matthias). Medieval booklists in France which mention Sedulius, according to Manitius, include those of S. Wandrille, S. Riquier, Nevers, Adso abbas, Fleury, Arras, Massay, Puy, Robert de Galone, Cluny, S. Amand, Anchin, S. Bertin, Corbie, Limoges, Marseilles, S. Maur de Fossés, Rouen, Tournai, S. Pons de Tomières, S. André de Villeneuve, Paris (S. Geneviève), Chartres, and Avignon. In Italy and Spain Manitius mentions copies of Sedulius' works in collections at Cremona, Bobbio, Monte Cassino, Urbino, Pistoia and at Oviedo, Ripoll, and Oña.

While space prevents us here from offering a detailed consideration of Sedulius' reception in all of these countries throughout all of these centuries, we may consider briefly for the sake of illustration how well known the *Paschale Carmen* was in just one geographical region, namely England, both before and immediately following the Norman Conquest. A number of manuscripts from the pre-conquest period have come down to us. The earliest of these is Cambridge, Corpus Christi College, 173 (8th century). Almost as hoary in their antiquity are London, British Library, Royal 15 B. XIX (second half of the 10th century), a fragmentary manuscript, Oxford, Bodleian Library, Lat. Th. C. 4, dated to the same period, and Cambridge, University Library, Gg. 5. 35 (middle of the 11th century). Three manuscripts which were certainly written in Anglo-Saxon England, but whose specific origins have not been identified are: Edinburgh, National Library of Scotland, Adv. 18. 7. 7 (end of the 10th century); Paris, Bibliothèque Nationale, Lat. 8092 (first half of the 11th century); and Paris, Bibliothèque Sainte-Geneviève, 2410 (end of the 10th century). Early Sedulian manuscripts with possible Anglo-Saxon connections include: Antwerpen, Musaeum Plantin-Muretus, M. 17. 4 (9th century), one of the few illustrated manuscripts of the *Paschale Carmen*; Basel, Universitätsbibliothek, O. IV. 17 (8-9th century), possibly written in Fulda under Anglo-Saxon influence; and Gotha, Forschungs- und Landesbibliothek, MBR. I. 75 (8th century), which may well have been written in the south of England or on the continent at an Anglo-Saxon center. There are also two manuscripts of the period in England which contain commentaries on the *Paschale Carmen*: Cambridge, Gonville and Caius College, 144/194 (9th/10th century) and Salisbury, Cathedral Library, 134 (c. 1000).

The early English churchmen, Aldhelm and Bede, quote from Sedulius often and at length-indeed, their indirect witness to the text of Sedulius, coming as early as it does, must be taken into serious account by the textual critic. The fifth-century poet was also well known by Alcuin.[17] It comes as no surprise, either, to discover that this popular

---

[17]On Sedulius' impact on Aldhelm and Bede, see Max Manitius, "Zu Aldhelm und Baeda," *Sitz. Wien* 112 (1886), 575-9 and 621-2. For Aldhelm's debt to Sedulius, see now Andy Orchard, *The Poetic Art of Aldhelm* = Cambridge Studies in Anglo-Saxon England 8 (Cambridge, 1994), pp. 164-6 and 233-5. On Alcuin's familiarity with Sedulius, see Peter Godman, *Alcuin: The Bishops, Kings, and Saints of York* (Oxford, 1982), pp. lxix-lxxii and p. 151. The Welshman Asser (bishop of Sherborne until 909), who played a major role in Alfred's educational program, quotes from the first book of the *Paschale Carmen*, mistaking Geta (mentioned in line 19) for an ancestor of Alfred's. See the edition of William Henry Stevenson, *Asser's Life of King Alfred together with the Annals of Saint*

author is mentioned so frequently (at least six times) in that "valuable index of what books were available in Anglo-Saxon England," namely, the surviving booklists and inventories of Anglo-Saxon libraries.[18] Alcuin's catalogue of the books given to him by the archbishop of York in 778, for example, places the author of the *Paschale Carmen* at the head of a list that includes other popular Christian Latin poets such as Juvencus, Prudentius, and Arator:

> quid quoque Sedulius vel quid canit ipse Iuvencus,
> Alcimus et Clemens, Prosper, Paulinus, Arator,
> quid Fortunatus vel quid Lactantius edunt....[19]

The list of books given by Sæwold, abbot of the monastery of S. Peter in Bath, to the church of S. Vaast in Arras shortly after the Norman Conquest, also includes a reference to the author of the *Paschale Carmen*: *Iuvencus, Sedulius in uno volumine.*[20] We know from an inventory of his bequest that Bishop Leofric procured a copy of "Sedulies boc" for the church at Exeter sometime during the third quarter of the eleventh century.[21] In the late eleventh century Sedulius' name appears along with other school authors in a list of books which appear mainly to have been used in a schoolroom, written on the empty folios at the end of Oxford, Bodleian Library, Tanner 3. This list, which was in Worcester by the second half of the twelfth century, mentions Sedulius' name twice and Remigius' commentary on Sedulius once among the first fifteen entries:

> Daniel propheta, Orosius, Sedulius, Dialogus, Glosarius, Marti-
> anus, Persius, Prosper, Terrentium, Sedulius, Sychomagia,

Neots (Oxford, 1904), p. 3. The reader may also wish to consult my entry on "Sedulius" forthcoming in *Sources of Anglo-Saxon Literary Culture*, ed. Paul E. Szarmach, Center for Medieval and Early Renaissance Studies, SUNY-Binghamton, which covers some of this same material.

[18]Lapidge, "Booklists," p. 34.

[19]See Lapidge, "Booklists," p. 46 and Godman, note 17 above, pp. 122-7.

[20]I follow the text of Lapidge, "Booklists," p. 60. See also the commentary on the list by Philip Grierson, "Les Livres de l'Abbé Seiwold de Bath," *RB* 52 (1940), 96-116.

[21]See Lapidge, "Booklists," p. 66. See also the discussion of the list in the introduction to *The Exeter Book of Old English Poetry*, ed. R.W. Chambers, M. Förster, and R. Flower (London, 1933), pp. 25-30.

Boetius, Lucanus, Commentum Remigii super Sedulium....[22]

It is possible that the author of the *Paschale Carmen* is even better represented in these documents than has heretofore been supposed. In the last of the booklists mentioned above, there is a puzzling entry, the 38th item on the list (following *"Apollonius"* and preceding *"Boetius super Perhiermenias"*), which refers to *"Ars Sedulii."*[23] Most recently, in his thoroughgoing analysis of "Booklists from Anglo-Saxon England," Michael Lapidge has taken this to be a reference to "one of the grammatical commentaries of Sedulius Scottus," the ninth-century poet and exegete who wrote commentaries on Donatus, Priscian, and Eutyches.[24] Although it is most unlikely that the fifth-century poet ever intended any of his works to be described as *Ars Sedulii* (the designation is not found in the earliest manuscripts), we do know that this title was assigned to one of his works by medieval scribes. A prefatory note contained in a number of Sedulian manuscripts contemporary with our booklist or earlier, including Chartres, Bibliothèque Municipale, 110; Évreux, Bibliothèque Municipale, 43; Paris, Bibliothèque Nationale, Lat. 18554; Biblioteca Apostolica Vaticana, Ottob. Lat. 35; and Wolfenbüttel, Herzog August Bibliothek, 79 Gud. Lat. 2°,[25] refers to the dedicatory epistle which Sedulius wrote to Macedonius as *"Ars Sedulii."* Perhaps some scribe or glossator saw broad similarities between the theoretical remarks on writing poetry in Sedulius' letter to Macedonius and such classic treatises on the subject as Horace's *Ars Poetica*, which was also written in epistolary form (addressed to a Piso and his two sons) or

---

[22]I use the text provided by Lapidge, "Booklists," p. 70.

[23]Although he does not comment explicitly on what this *"Ars"* might be, H.M. Bannister, "Bishop Roger of Worcester and the Church of Keynsham, with a List of Vestments and Books possibly belonging to Worcester," *EHR* 32 (1917), 387-93, groups it with the other references to the fifth-century poet in his discussion of the booklists. J.D.A. Ogilvy, *Books Known to the English, 597-1066* (Cambridge, Mass., 1967), p. 239, does not venture even to guess as to what this item might refer: "What the *Ars* apparently attributed to him in that list is, I do not know."

[24]Lapidge, "Booklists," p. 73, n. 38.

[25]London, British Library, Harley 4092 also includes the reference to the Epistle to Macedonius as *"Ars Sedulii."* The Chartres manuscript was destroyed in World War II. Interestingly, the preface to Juvencus' *Evangeliorum Libri Quattuor* is also described as *"Ars Juvenci"* in Cambridge, University Library, Gg. 5. 35.

Aldhelm's *Epistola ad Acircium*,[26] and decided that Sedulius' epistle ought to be described as an *Ars*, too.[27] However inaccurate or inadequate the designation may be, we do know of at least one manuscript, Paris, Bibliothèque Sainte-Geneviève, 2410, which not only describes the epistle to Macedonius as *Ars Sedulii*, but was also "certainly written in late Anglo-Saxon England" (second half of the tenth century).[28] If the compiler of our booklist had this manuscript, or another like it, before him and glanced at the first three words of the text (*"Incipit ars Sedulii"*), we could understand if he failed to read the rest of the text carefully and simply recorded the entry as *Ars Sedulii* (even though the letter to Macedonius may very well have been followed, as it is in most Sedulian manuscripts, by the *Paschale Carmen*).[29] If we note, too, that Sedulius Scottus is not mentioned elsewhere in the booklists, it seems more likely that the *"Ars Sedulii"* in the list in Oxford, Bodleian Library,

---

[26]An excerpt follows Sedulius in Paris, Bibliothèque Sainte-Geneviève, 2410. In a number of codices Sedulius' works are also found side by side with Bede, *De Arte Metrica* (e.g., Angers, Bibliothèque Municipale, 522; Orléans, Bibliothèque Municipale, 302; and Orléans, Bibliothèque Municipale, 318).

[27]Certainly Sedulius' epistle to Macedonius is more than a simple prefatory puff. The poet uses the epistle to make an extensive apology for his literary undertaking and to set forth his distinctively Christian poetic programme. Sedulius is well aware of what a challenging project he has undertaken:

   qui nulla veteris scientiae praerogativa suffultus tam inmensum paschalis pelagus
   maiestatis et viris quoque peritissimis formidandum parva tiro lintre cucurrerim.

Anticipating objections, the Christian poet defends his use of meter (it is more attractive and easier to memorize):

   Cur autem metrica voluerim haec ratione conponere, non differam breviter
   expedire. Raro, pater optime, sicut vestra quoque peritia lectionis adsiduitate
   cognoscit, divinae munera potestatis stilo quisquam huius modulationis aptavit, et
   multi sunt quos studiorum saecularium disciplina per poeticas magis delicias et
   carminum voluptates oblectat. Hi quicquid rhetoricae facundiae perlegunt,
   neglegentius adsequuntur, quoniam illud haud diligunt: quod autem versuum
   viderint blandimento mellitum, tanta cordis aviditate suscipiunt, ut in alta memoria
   saepius haec iterando constituant et reponant.

Sedulius also explains to Macedonius how he has abbreviated and arranged his biblical subject matter:

   Quattuor igitur mirabilium divinorum libellos, quos ex pluribus pauca conplexus
   usque ad passionem et resurrectionem ascensionemque Domini nostri Iesu Christi
   quattuor evangeliorum dicta congregans ordinavi....

[28]Lapidge, "Latin Texts" p. 114.

[29]The first epistle to Macedonius was sometimes separated from the rest of Sedulius' works and may even have circulated independently (cf., e.g., Bern, Burgerbibliothek, AA 90).

Tanner 3 refers to the epistle to Macedonius written by the Sedulius who appears with such frequency in the booklists assembled by Lapidge and not to one of the grammatical commentaries written by his ninth-century namesake.[30]

II.

Although Sedulius is probably best known for his *Paschale Carmen*, his other works, including the *Paschale Opus*, a prose paraphrase of his famous verse composition, were also well known during the Middle Ages. (Both of these titles, which he assigns the works in prefatory letters written to the presbyter Macedonius, are Sedulius' own; in later manuscripts and early printed editions the adjective and noun are often reversed.)

The *Paschale Opus* never enjoyed the same degree of popularity as Sedulius' verse version. We have only a handful of manuscripts which contain the work more or less in its entirety (Berlin, Staatsbibliothek zu Berlin-Preussischer Kulturbesitz, Phillipps 1727; Bruxelles, Bibliothèque Royale Albert 1er, 5649-5667; Épinal, Bibliothèque Municipale, 74; London, British Library, Harley 3012; Orléans, Bibliothèque Municipale, 303; Paris, Bibliothèque Nationale, Lat. 12279; and Zürich, Zentralbibliothek, Rh. 77). Three manuscripts (Paris, Bibliothèque Nationale, Lat. 8094; Sankt Gallen, Stiftsbibliothek, 877; and Cambridge, Corpus Christi College, 173) contain the second

---

[30]The two Sedulii have often been confused. Johannes Trithemius, the fifteenth-century Benedictine scholar, evidently confusing the author of the *Paschale Carmen* with Sedulius Scottus, tells of how Sedulius left the British isles, travelled through France, Asia, and Greece, and finally ended up in Rome. There is no reliable early evidence that the first Sedulius ever left the Mediterranean area. The confusion has persisted into the 20th century. George Sigerson simply assumed that Sedulius, "the first scholar-saint of Erinn," as he designated the author of the *Paschale Carmen* in the title of his *The Easter Song: Being the First Epic of Christendom by Sedulius, the First Scholar-Saint of Erinn* (Dublin, 1922), came from Ireland. More recently the two have been confused by Tony Hunt, *Teaching and Learning Latin in Thirteenth-Century England* (Cambridge, 1990), where references to the author of the *Paschale Carmen* and the *Comm. in Eutychem* are both listed in the index under Sedulius Scottus (vol. 1, p. 453). We do know that the Carolingian poet was aware of his fifth-century namesake. In his commentary on the Gospel of Matthew he praises the author of the *Paschale Carmen* (*Hinc Sedulius egregie versibus describit dicens....*) and quotes approvingly from PC 2.279-81. See Bengt Löfstedt, *Sedulius Scottus, Kommentar zum Evangelium nach Matthäus* = Vetus Latina. Die Reste der altlateinischen Bibel. Aus der Geschichte der lateinischen Bibel, vols. 14 and 19 (Freiburg, 1989-91), vol. 1, p. 203.

dedicatory epistle to Macedonius but nothing (or little) of the *Paschale Opus* itself.

Several factors may have contributed to the failure of the *Paschale Opus* to achieve such a wide and sustained popularity as the *Paschale Carmen*. It is longer, in the first place, and one suspects that it would have been more tedious for the average student to read than the *carmen*. If Sedulius' life of Christ was used in schools, furthermore, as an exercise in learning the art of reading and writing Latin dactylic hexameters, the verse version of the work, naturally, would have been of far greater pedagogic value than the prose version. More striking than the intrinsic literary merit of this paraphrase, doubtless, is the precedent which Sedulius' "double work" (the *Paschale Carmen* in verse and the *Paschale Opus* in prose) set, especially for Anglo-Latin authors. In his *Historia Ecclesiastica Gentis Anglorum* (5.18), Bede specifically mentions Sedulius' *opus geminatum* as the inspiration for Aldhelm's treatise on virginity, of which he wrote a prose as well as a verse version. At least indirectly Sedulius' example must also have influenced Bede himself and Alcuin, who wrote such *opera geminata* as well.[31]

Sedulius also wrote two hymns. Of these, one is an invitation in 110 lines to praise Christ, beginning *Cantemus, socii, Domino*, written in elegiac distichs in epanaleptic form (sometimes described as *versus serpentini* or *reciproci* in the manuscripts, as, e.g., in München, Bayerische Staatsbibliothek, Clm 18628, f. 68v), while the other, beginning *A solis ortus cardine*, is an alphabetic composition in iambic dimeter quatrains, the hymnic form popularized by Ambrose, recounting in 23 stanzas the life of Christ from birth to ascension-or, if you like, from A to Z. Despite his relatively modest accomplishments as a hymnwriter, Sedulius was often included in the same distinguished company as Ambrose, Prudentius, and Gregory as one of the "four principal authors" of hymns in the early church. In a notice commonly found in a number of manuscripts of the *Liber hymnorum* or *Expositio hymnorum* (as, e.g., in Cambridge, Gonville and Caius College, 136; Dublin, Trinity College Library, 270; London, British Library, Harley 4967; München, Bayerische Staatsbibliothek, Clm 5594; Napoli, Biblioteca Nazionale, V. H. 16; Oxford, Bodleian Library, Laud Misc.

---

[31]Peter Godman, "The Anglo-Latin *Opus Geminatum* from Aldhelm to Alcuin," *Medium Aevum* 50 (1981), 215-29 and Gernot Wieland, "*Geminus Stilus*: Studies in Anglo-Latin Hagiography" in *Insular Latin Studies. Papers on Latin Texts and Manuscripts of the British Isles: 550-1066*, ed. Michael W. Herren = Papers in Medieval Studies 1 (Toronto, 1981), pp. 113-33.

40; Paris, Bibliothèque Nationale, Lat. 3371; and Rouen, Bibliothèque Municipale 56), we read versions of the following:

> Iste liber dicitur hymnorum. Hymnus est laus Dei cum cantico facta. Quattuor fuerunt principales auctores hymnorum qui hymnos consuerunt [or composuerunt], scilicet Gregorius, Prudentius, Ambrosius, Sedulius, sed quidam vir prudens nomine Hilarius videns eos multos composuisse hymnos, placuit ei quosdam in unum colligere et compendiosum opus facere....[32]

Cantemus, socii, Domino was widely known during the Middle Ages and also appear to have been read in schools (it is heavily glossed in some manuscripts). When Dunstan, Archbishop of Canterbury from 959 to 988, was blessed with an ecstatic vision of a chorus of virgins in the church of S. Mary (close to S. Augustine's Abbey in Canterbury), the heavenly music that he heard them singing was *Cantemus, socii, Domino*.[33]

Sedulius' other hymn was even more popular. Alcuin quotes it in its entirety in *Off. per Fer.* 609-11. This alphabetical composition was especially well known because of the wide-spread use of its first stanzas

---

[32]I follow the transcription (with a few minor orthographical variations) of Marvin L. Colker, *Trinity College Library Dublin: Descriptive Catalogue of the Medieval and Renaissance Latin Manuscripts* (Dublin, 1991), vol. 1, p. 493. See also Gneuss, *Hymnar*, p. 200.

[33]See William Stubbs' Rolls series volume *Memorials of St. Dunstan* (1874), pp. 48-9. The text follows:

> Huic igitur dum in propria praesulatus sui civitate commanebat, sanctae consuetudinis inter caetera sublimitatum studia fuit, ut in secretis noctium temporibus sancta loca, propter multimodam populorum ad se venientium inhaesionem vel etiam aliorum multorum occupationem, sancta semper psalmodia decantando lustraret. Et venit hac lege religionis innexus ad almi patris Augustini aediculam, nocturnis ut dixi temporibus oraturus; et dum se sacris inibi suppleret orationibus, processit ad orientalem Dei puerperae aecclesiam tantumdem precaturus. Cumque ad hanc propinquando psallendoque venisset, forte ex insperato noctis eventu audierat insolitas sonoritarum voces, subtili modulamine in hac eadem basilica concrepantes. At ille continuo per quendam patuli foraminis hiatum inspiciens, vidit praelocutam ecclesiam omni esse fulgida luce perfusam, et virgineas turmas in choro gyranti hymnum hunc poetae Sedulii cursitando cantentes, "Cantemus, socii, Domino, etc." Itemque perpendit easdem post versum et versum voce reciproca, quasi in circuitionis suae concentu, primum versiculum eiusdem hymniculi more humanarum virginum repsallere, dicentes; "Cantemus, socii, Domino cantemus honorem; Dulcis amor Christi personet ore pio," et caetera.

during the Christmas and Epiphany seasons. The first seven stanzas (stanzas A-G) were excerpted for use during the Christmas season as an independent hymn, often with a final doxology appended. The stanzas immediately following, beginning with the words *Hostis Herodes impie*, were frequently used as an Epiphany hymn.[34] The entire hymn appears in some of the earliest manuscripts of the *Paschale Carmen* and is present in shortened form in hymnaries as early as the late 10th century.[35] Lines 65-68 of the hymn (describing Jesus' healing of the woman with an issue of blood) were evidently used as a charm against bloodletting (cf. London, British Library, Royal 2 A. XX, f. 16v):

> Rivos cruoris torridi
> Contacta vestis obstruit,
> Fletu rigante supplicis
> Arent fluenta sanguinis.

The opening words of this hymn were so well known that medieval poets could expect their audience to recognize them when they were used to introduce other serious works or even for the sake of parody. See, e.g., the first stanza of the anonymous lament for Charlemagne: *A solis ortu usque ad occidua/littora maris planctus pulsat pectora*.[36] From a later date, we have a parody directed against the Hussites that begins: *A solis ortus cardine precessit solis radius*, etc.[37] Selections from the hymn (in

---

[34]One of the stanzas was also sung on the Feast of the Holy Innocents (*Katerva matrum personat...*). In Paris, Bibliothèque Nationale, Lat. 103, for instance, the rubric *De Innocentibus* immediately precedes lines 37-40. The stanza is followed by the rubric *De Epiphania* and lines 33-36, 41-44, and 49-53 of the hymn. The entire 23-stanza composition appears to have been used in the Spanish liturgy, but as six separate hymns (cf. London, British Library, Add. 30851). See Chev. 2662, 2682-3, 5491, 6096, 8072-3, 10573-5, and 14198.

[35]See Gneuss, *Hymnar*, p. 36, n. 48.

[36]*MGH PLAC*, vol. 1, pp. 435-6. Found in Bruxelles, Bibliothèque Royale Albert 1er, 8860-8867, ff. 39-40.

[37]Walther, *Initia* 88. For another example of parody involving *A Solis Ortus Cardine* (as well as the first lines of other famous Latin hymns), see the macaronic drinking song, *Jubilus Bibulorum*, ed. by Hermann Ühlein and Elisabeth Gensler, in "Liturgie und Parodie: Tagzeitengesänge in feucht-fröhlicher Runde" in *Liturgie und Dichtung: Ein interdisziplinäres Kompendium*, ed. H. Becker and R. Kaczynski (St. Ottilien, 1983), vol. 1, pp. 642-4. For a full range of variations following the initial four words of Sedulius' hymn, see Chev. 21-38. Ford Madox Ford used them as the title for a poem on World War I, which begins: "Oh, quiet peoples sleeping bed by bed/Beneath grey roof-trees in

translation, naturally) are included in Anglican (or Episcopalian), Roman Catholic, and Lutheran hymnals to this day.[38] As *Christum wir sollen loben schon,* the German version of *A Solis Ortus Cardine* has been immortalized in settings by Johann Sebastian Bach and other Lutheran musicians.[39]

Among the works which are sometimes attributed to Sedulius in medieval manuscripts, but which most scholars agree are not genuine, we find the short cento often referred to as *De Verbi Incarnatione,* in Paris, Bibliothèque Nationale, Lat. 13047, as well as a preface to the Virgilian cento of Proba, which begins *Romulidum ductor clari lux altera solis,* as it does, for example, in Roma, Biblioteca Angelica, 1515 (V. 3. 22), f. 30v.[40] Versions of the popular hymn beginning *Salve festa dies*

---

the glimmering West,/We who can see the silver grey and red/Rise over No Man's land-salute your rest."

[38]See my article, "Sedulius' *A Solis Ortus Cardine:* The Hymn and Its Tradition," *EL* 101 (1987), 69-75, for a general discussion of the hymn's structure and a brief review of its later history. Martin Luther's German translation of the first seven stanzas with a doxology appeared in the *Erfurt Enchiridion,* published in the summer of 1524. The translation of stanzas 8, 9, 11, and 13 did not appear until much later (1541). Johannes Hutt, an Anabaptist from Augsburg, had produced a less literal translation of the first stanzas shortly before Luther's, but there were a number of other German versions long before his; see, e.g., Philipp Wackernagel, *Das deutsche Kirchenlied von der ältesten Zeit bis zu Anfang des XVII. Jahrhunderts* (Leipzig, 1867), vol. 2, no. 562 and 756; Günther Bärnthaler, *Übersetzungen im deutschen Spätmittelalter. Der Mönch von Salzburg, Heinrich Laufenberg und Oswald von Wolkenstein als Übersetzer lateinischer Hymnen und Sequenzen* = Göppinger Arbeiten zur Germanistik 371 (Göppingen, 1983); and Nikolaus Henkel, *Deutsche Übersetzungen lateinischer Schultexte. Ihre Verbreitung und Funktion im Mittelalter und in der frühen Neuzeit* = Münchener Texte und Untersuchungen zur deutschen Literatur des Mittelalters 90 (München, 1988), pp. 141-2. See Otto Schliszke, *Handbuch der Lutherlieder* (Göttingen, 1948), p. 53, for a reference to Luther's particular devotion to this hymn:

Ich wurde einmal heftig angefochten. Am Lavendelbaum im Garten hab ich das Lied gesungen: 'Christum wir sollen loben schon....' Sonst wäre ich vergangen.

[39]Bach's most famous setting is in the Cantata for the second day of Christmas [BWV, 121], but the hymn is also included in *Orgelbüchlein* [BWV, 611], and *Choralbearbeitungen in Kirnbergers Sammlung* [BWV, 696]. The hymn in Latin was also set to music by Palestrina, Orlando di Lasso, and Johann Josef Fux.

[40]As described in H. Narducci, *Catalogus Codicum Manuscriptorum,* vol. 1 (Roma, 1892), p. 654. The dedication is often found in conjunction with Sedulius' works in manuscripts which do not contain Proba's cento itself, as, for instance, in Antwerpen, Musaeum Plantin-Moretus, M. 17. 4; Evreux, Bibliothèque Municipale, 43; Leiden, Bibliotheek der Rijksuniversiteit, B.P.L. 175; München, Bayerische Staatsbibliothek, Clm 18628; Paris, Bibliothèque Nationale, Lat. 15148 and 18553; Biblioteca Apostolica Vaticana, Barb. Lat. 429; Vendôme, Bibliothèque Municipale 165; Venezia, Biblioteca

(adapted from a poem by Venantius Fortunatus) are also attributed to Sedulius in a number of manuscripts.[41] Perhaps Sedulius' reputation as one of the four great Latin hymnwriters (Fortunatus is not in the list) as well as his popularity as a "curriculum author" helped to convince scribes who were in doubt about the authenticity of these compositions to attribute them to Sedulius.

Compositions frequently attached to the *Paschale Carmen* in the manuscripts, but which were certainly not written by Sedulius, include two laudatory acrostic (and telestic) poems, attributed in many manuscripts to a certain Bellesarius and the equally obscure Liberatus, whose initial and final letters spell out the words *Sedulius Antistes*. These are included in Huemer's edition (pp. 307-10), although not in the order in which they are to be found in many manuscripts. A short epigram found in some manuscripts (e.g., Firenze, Biblioteca Medicea Laurenziana, Plut. 24, Sin. 12; Holkham Hall, Library of the Earls of Leicester, 419; Biblioteca Apostolica Vaticana, Vat. Lat. 1665) may well be the work of a devout scribe:

> Haec tua perpetuae quae scripsi dogmata vitae,
> Corde, rogo, facias, Christe, manere meo:
> Ut, tibi quae placeant, tete faciente, requirens,
> Gaudia coelorum, te duce, Christe, metam. [*PL* 19, 771-2]

Another epigram in praise of Sedulius which is included in some manuscripts (e.g., Edinburgh, National Library of Scotland, Adv. 18. 7. 7, f. 41v) begins:

> Qualiter affixus ligno iam Christus in alto

Marciana, Lat. XII. 7; Wolfenbüttel, Herzog August Bibliothek, 79 Gud. Lat. 2°, etc. There is a possible connection here (worth exploring further) with the biographical detail which surfaces only in the ninth century, namely, that Sedulius wrote his works during the reign of Theodosius, son of Arcadius (mentioned in lines 13-14 of the dedication: ...*tradasque minori/Arcadio*).

[41]E. Jørgensen's catalogue of the Kongelige Bibliotek in København (København, 1923), p. 304 attributes the *"Versus paschales"* in Ny Kgl. S. 55b fol. to Sedulius, but in fact it is the hymn which begins *Salve festa dies, toto venerabilis aevo/qua Deus infernum vicit et astra tenet.* See also similar attributions in Glasgow, University Library, Hunter. T. 2. 14 and Paris, Bibliothèque Nationale, Lat. 15159. The common version of the hymn found in many Sedulian manuscripts is excerpted from Venantius Fortunatus, *Carm.* 3.9.1, but we know of a number of different medieval hymns for various festive occasions which begin: *Salve festa dies....* [see Chev. 17931 ff. and Walpole, pp. 181 ff.].

Sedulius cecinit totum complecteret orbem
Seu demonstraret pro toto pendere mundo
Versibus his mundo Christo miserante salutem....

followed by six lines taken directly from the *Paschale Carmen* (5.190-5).
In a manuscript in the Ambrosian Library in Milano (I. 35 Sup.) there
is yet another short poem in praise of Sedulius, following the epistle to
Macedonius (f. 4r):

> Scripsit Sedulius carmine nobili
> Laudes, Christe, tuas gestaque caelica
> Lucani similis versibus arduis.
> Iam cedant veteres: nam superat novus
> Hic, hic Sedulius carmine nobili,
> Dum te, Christe, canit, optime, maxime,
> Qui cum patre tenes regna perennia,
> Cum sancto pariter flamine iugiter,
> Cui sit laus et honor saecla per omnia.[42]

In the great Bobbio codex of Sedulius now in the Biblioteca
Nazionale Universitaria at Torino (E. IV. 42), we find a subscription
which explains the role of the Roman consul of 494, Turcius Rufius
Apronianus Asterius, in restoring the work of Sedulius after its author's
death:

> Robeo [of uncertain meaning]. Incipit sacrum opus, id est ex
> vetere testamento liber primus, et ex novo quattuor, quod Sedulius
> inter cartulas suas sparsas reliquit, et recollecti adunatique sunt a
> Turcio Rufio Asterio v.c. et exconsule ordinario atque patricio,
> supra scriptorum editore librorum. [*CSEL*, vol. 10, p. vii]

This subscription in a number of permutations is found in many Sedulian
manuscripts, often beginning *Hoc opus Sedulius inter cartulas*.... A late
variation (as edited from Wien, Nationalbibliothek, 85) is:

> Moriens ergo indigestum dereliquit hoc opus in cartulis scriptum.
> Sed postea Turcius Asterius vir clarissimus ad omnem elegantiam
> illud ordinavit, ad legentium utilitatem publicavit.

---

[42]Huemer, *De Sedulii*, p. 8.

It is often followed by a verse preface written (presumably) by Asterius and included by Huemer in his edition (*CSEL*, vol. 10, p. 307):

> Sume sacer meritis veracis dicta poetae,
> Quae sine figmenti condita sunt vitio.
> Quo caret alma fides, quo sancti gratia Christi,
> Per quam iustus ait talia Sedulius.
> Asteriique tui semper meminisse debeto
> Cuius ope et cura edita sunt populis.
> Quem quamvis summi celebrent per saecula fastus
> Plus tamen ad meritum est si viget ore tuo.

Not infrequently a prose preface follows (here as edited from Paris, Bibliothèque Nationale, Lat. 18554):

> Sedulius epistola Macedonio praemissa presbytero sedecim dehinc versuum prologo lecturos invitans paupertatem exilis ingenii holerum conparat vilitati. Ex cuius carmine de singulis utriusque testamenti miraculis haec sunt capitula praenotata.

Also appearing in many manuscripts are countless variations on a biographical notice which sometimes takes a question-and-answer form, as it does, for instance, in this *accessus* in Paris, Bibliothèque Nationale, Lat. 18554, f. 3r:

> Videlicet quis fecit? Sedulius. Quid fecit? Paschale carmen de veteri et novo testamento. Cur fecit? Quia videbat quod pauci essent qui de humanitate et incarnatione salvatoris metrico opere aliquod opus facerent. Quomodo fecit? Metrico stilo non prosaico. Quando fecit? Tempore Theodosii et Valentiani imperatorum. Ubi fecit? In Achaia. Quibus facultatibus vel unde? De facultatibus eorum quos imitatus est.

The same manuscript contains what is essentially the same information in several different formats (beginning, for example, with *Incipit ars Sedulii....* as in note 1 above) and also as an entry in "Jerome's catalogue:"

> Sicut sanctus Hieronimus dicit in catalogo virorum illustriorum: iste Sedulius primo laicus fuit et in Achaia docuit seculares disciplinas. Postea vero totum se ad dominum contulit et omnem

studium quod antea habuerat in illis saecularibus disciplinis convertit ad divinas scripturas. Scripsit ergo librum hunc de vetere et novo testamento propositis convenientibus praefationibus. Hanc autem epistulam scripsit ad Macedonium tunc temporis presbyterum, ut huius auctoritate librum suum roboraretur. Consuetudo enim erat ut sapientes viri scripturas suas viris prudentibus traderent quatinus eorum favore auctorarentur.[43]

III.

The last complete edition of Sedulius' works by Johannes Huemer in *CSEL*, vol. 10 (Wien, 1885) is over a hundred years old and, although it is still the authoritative edition of Sedulius' works, it can no longer be deemed adequate in view of the large number of early manuscripts which Huemer failed to consult.[44] Faustino Arevalo's edition of 1794, which was later reprinted in the nineteenth volume of J.P. Migne's *Patrologia Latina*, was even less satisfactory, based, as it was, almost exclusively on manuscripts to be found in the Vatican Library.[45] Just six years

---

[43]On some of the permutations of these biographical notices, see Johannes Huemer, "Zur Bestimmung der Abfassungszeit und Herausgabe des *Carmen Paschale* des Sedulius," *ZOG* 27 (1876), 500-5. On the *accessus* in general, see Denis van Berchem, "Poètes et grammairiens. Recherche sur la tradition scolaire d'explication des auteurs," *MH* 9 (1952), 79-87; Edwin A. Quain, "The Medieval *Accessus ad Auctores*," *Traditio* 3 (1945), 215-64; and H. Silvestre, "Le Schéma 'moderne' des *accessus*," *Latomus* 16 (1957), 684-9. See also R.B.C. Huygens, *Accessus ad Auctores, Bernard d'Utrecht, Conrad d'Hirsau, Dialogus super Auctores* (Leiden, 1970). On Conrad of Hirsau in particular, see in addition to the study of Kurz, Leslie G. Whitbread, "Conrad of Hirsau as Literary Critic," *Speculum* 47 (1972), 234-45 and T.O. Tunberg, "Conrad of Hirsau and His Approach to the *Auctores*," *M&H* 15 (1987), 65-94.

[44]It should be said, in all fairness, that Huemer's edition represents a decided improvement upon its predecessors and that its virtues were recognized by his contemporaries (see, e.g., Candel's description of the work in *Revue de philologie* 28 (1904), 281, as *"un chef-d'oeuvre de science et de sagacité"*). For specific criticisms and emendations, see the studies of E. Ludwig, "Präpositionales Retro," *Archiv für lateinische Lexicographie und Grammatik* 8 (1893), 294; Carl Weyman, *Beiträge zur Geschichte der christlich-lateinischen Poesie* (München, 1926), pp. 121 ff.; and Carlo Tibiletti, "Note al testo del *Paschale Carmen* di Sedulio" in *Forma Futuri. Studi in onore del Cardinale Michele Pellegrino* (Torino, 1975), pp. 778-85.

[45]Other editions preceding Huemer's include the following (I have marked those which I have seen with my own eyes with an asterisk):
    -Marguerin de La Bigne, in *Magna Bibliotheca Veterum Patrum et Antiquorum Scriptorum Ecclesiasticorum* (Köln, 1618-22; reprinted in 1644, 1654, 1677 (also includes the *Paschale Opus*) [*NUC*, vol. 310, pp. 79-80].

before Huemer's edition appeared, J. Looshorn had published an edition, *Sedulii Opera, Recensita ad Fidem Codicum Manuscriptorum Monacensium* (München, 1879), but it was based on an extremely limited number of manuscripts. Also appearing in print shortly before the publication of Huemer's edition was E. Ludwig's edition of the fifth book of the *Paschale Opus, Sedulii Paschalis Operis Liber Quintus. Nach den zum ersten Male verglichenen Handschriften revidirt* (Heilbronn, 1880), but Ludwig used two manuscripts only (Zürich, Zentralbibliothek, Rh. 77 and London, British Library, Harley 3012) to edit what is only a small part of the fifth-century poet's corpus. The flurry of scholarly interest in editing Sedulius at the end of the 19th century has unfortunately not recurred in our own. Most critics and commentators have reproduced Huemer's text with little or no criticism. Francesco Corsaro's edition of the poem which appeared with an Italian translation in 1956 was simply

---

-John Forrest, *Coelii Sedulii Scoti Poemata Sacra denuo Recognita, Collata et Brevibus Notis Illustrata* (Edinburgh: A. Anderson, 1701) [Graesse, p. 339; *NUC,* vol. 536, p. 219].*

-No editor's name given, *Coelii Sedulii Poemata Sacra, denuo Recognita, Collata et Notis Selectioribus Illustrata* (London: G. Strahan, 1702) [=Arntzenius' *Edinburgiensis* or *Scota; NUC,* vol. 536, p. 220].

-Chr. Cellarius, *Coelii Sedulii, Poetae inter Christianos Veteres Elegantissimi, Mirabilium Divinorum Libri, Paschale Carmen Dicti, et Hymni Duo* (Halle, 1704; 2nd ed. 1739) [*BM,* vol. 218, col. 296; Graesse, p. 339; *NUC,* vol. 536, p. 219].*

-M. Maittaire, in *Opera et Fragmenta Veterum Poetarum Latinorum Profanorum et Ecclesiasticorum* (London, 1713) [*BM,* vol. 150, col. 813; *NUC,* vol. 356, p. 526].

-Johann Friedrich Gruner, *Coelii Sedulii Mirabilium Divinorum Libri V, sive Carmen Paschale* (Leipzig, 1740 and 1747) [Graesse, p. 339; *NUC,* vol. 536, p. 219].*

-J.A. Fabricius, *Coelii Sedulii Presbyteri Carmen de Verbi Incarnatione ex Ms. Codice Corbejensi ante Annos Nongentos Exarato* in *Bibliotheca Latina Mediae et Infimae Aetatis,* vol. 6 (Padova, 1754), pp. 335-39 [*NUC,* vol. 536, p. 218].

-Hendrik Jan Arntzen, *Coelii Sedulii Carminis Paschalis Libri V et Hymni Duo. Cum Notis Casparis Barthii, Christophori Cellarii, Cornelii Valerii Vonckii, Joannis Friderici Gruneri, Aliorumque. Quibus Adcedunt Thomae Wopkensii Adversaria Emendatoria, Maxima ex Parte adhuc Inedita* (Leeuwarden: G. Coulon, 1760 and H.A. de Chalmot, 1761) [*NUC,* vol. 536, p. 218].*

-Pasquale Amati in *Collectio Pisaurensis Omnium Poematum, Carminum Fragmentorum Latinorum a Prima Latinae Linguae Aetate ad Sextum usque Christianum Seculum et Longobardorum in Italiam Adventum Pertinens* (Pisauri, 1766) [*BM,* vol. 4, col. 468].

-Andreas Galland in *Bibliotheca Veterum Patrum Antiquorumque Scriptorum Ecclesiasticorum,* vol. 9 (Venezia, 1765-81) [*NUC,* vol. 189, p. 433].

-A.F. Hurez in *Poètes ecclesiastiques latins,* vol. 4 (Cambrai, 1826).

-Hugo Hurter in *Sanctorum Patrum Opuscula Selecta* (Innsbruck, 1868-85), vol. 33 [*NUC,* vol. 261, p. 515].*

a reprinting of Huemer's text.[46] Since Huemer's time several commentaries have appeared, including that of Nicholaas Scheps, *Sedulius' Paschale Carmen, Boek I en II: Ingeleid, Vertaald en Toegelicht* (Delft, 1938), which, while useful, includes only the first two books of the *Paschale Carmen* and does not offer a new text. More recently, P.W.A.Th. van der Laan has published his doctoral dissertation, *Sedulius Carmen Paschale Boek 4. Inleidung, Vertaling, Commentaer* (Oud-Beijerland, 1990), but his study, valuable as it is, breaks little new significant textual ground.[47]

Most obvious among the deficiencies of Huemer's edition is his failure (despite his claim to have used "the oldest and best" codices) to consider a number of early and important Sedulian manuscripts.[48] The most glaring omission is that of the 8th-century manuscript, Cambridge, Corpus Christi College, 173, one of the most complete of the earliest Sedulian manuscripts. Huemer must have known of its existence, since he used its text of both of Sedulius' hymns.[49] The 1885 edition of Sedulius relies heavily on the seventh-century manuscript of Sedulius written in Bobbio (mentioned above), Torino, Biblioteca Nazionale Universitaria, E. IV. 42.[50] While this is certainly the single most

---

[46]Francesco Corsaro, *Sedulio poeta* = Pubblicazioni dell'Istituto Universitario di Magistero di Catania, serie letteraria, no. 2 (Catania, 1956). Among other editions which have appeared in this century, we might mention Guido Maria Dreves' text of Sedulius' two hymns in *AH*, vol. 50: *Hymnographi Latini. Lateinische Hymnendichter des Mittelalters*, zweite Folge (Leipzig, 1907), pp. 53-60. Walther Bulst, *Hymni Latini Antiquissimi LXXV, Psalmi III* (Heidelberg, 1956), includes an edition of H2 (pp. 71-3 and 187). Perhaps the most singular publication of Sedulius appeared in this country in 1955: excerpts from PC 1 in American uncial type with woodcuts of the four evangelists by Victor Hammer were printed by Carolyn Reading for the Anvil Press in Lexington, Kentucky (*NUC*, vol. 536, p. 218).

[47]*Sedulius, Carmen Paschale, Buch III. Ein Kommentar* (Basel, 1995) has recently been prepared for publication by Michael Mazzega (doctoral dissertation at the University of Münster), but I have not yet been able to obtain a copy.

[48]In tanta codicum multitudine ad Sedulii opera recensenda antiquissimi et optimi hi sunt selecti (*CSEL*, vol. 10, p. iv).

[49]Henry Bradshaw collated the two hymns for Huemer (see *CSEL*, vol. 10, p. xlvii).

[50]The Torino manuscript (which Huemer refers to in his edition as E. IV. 44), was one whose readings Huemer obviously took some care in recording. Still, a random check *(in situ)* of some passages in the second book of the *Paschale Carmen* revealed that Huemer occasionally missed some fairly obvious (and possibly important) variant readings (e.g. *urbem* rather than *orbem* in PC 2.187 and *suos* instead of *tuos* at PC 2.296). As the earliest and most complete of the Sedulian manuscripts, with many unique and "better" readings, this manuscript will doubtless always hold pride of place in any consideration of

important Sedulian manuscript,[51] there are a number of other early (and interesting) manuscripts in addition to the "Corpus Sedulius," to which Huemer could not gain access, or of which he was simply ignorant, including the manuscript of Sedulius in the Plantin-Moretus Museum in Antwerp, containing a number of splendid miniatures and dated to the ninth century,[52] as well as the earliest witness to the *Paschale Opus*,

---

the textual evidence for reconstructing the work of Sedulius. One reason, no doubt, for Huemer's reliance on the Bobbio manuscripts (the fragmentary manuscript now in the Ambrosian library in Milano, R. 57. Sup, was also written in Bobbio) is the fact that *contaminatio* in the textual tradition of the *Paschale Carmen* is rampant, making it virtually impossible to set up the kind of neat *stemma codicum* that one can construct for the *Paschale Opus*, which has a much less complicated manuscript tradition. Indeed, Huemer used what might be called a modified "optimist" approach, relying on a *codex optimus* supplemented by readings from other manuscripts when his favorite manuscript failed him. See the discussion by Leonard E. Boyle, "Optimist and Recensionist: 'Common Errors' or 'Common Variants,'" in *Latin Script and Letters A.D. 400-900. Festschrift Presented to Ludwig Bieler on the Occasion of his 70th Birthday*, ed. John J. O'Meara and Bernd Naumann (Leiden, 1976), pp. 264 ff. It is easy to fault Huemer's decision, but it must have been far more difficult to obtain and study the manuscript evidence for an author like Sedulius in the 1880s than it is today.

[51]One might comment also on Huemer's curiously inconsistent orthography (wavering between *postquam* and *posquam*, *thesaurus* and *thensaurus*, *quattuor* and *quatuor*, etc.), an indecision which is largely due to what might be termed over-zealous dedication to the Bobbio manuscripts. On p. xxxiiii he declares:

In orthographia carminum constituenda libros in universum secutus sum, at ex formis vulgaribus eas recepi quae cum aevo Seduliano convenire videbantur. Quae ex posterioribus saeculis inrepserunt tantum non omnia excussi, cum ex libris vetustissimis iisque sermone vulgari scriptis minima quaeque in notis adposuerim, ut tandem aliquando vera imago exprimi posset orthographiae quam dicunt per saeculum V et VI usitatae.

The result is a cluttered critical apparatus which is sometimes hardly intelligible.

[52]Although the Antwerpen manuscript has been described as the "only surviving, illustrated, manuscript version" of the *Paschale Carmen* (see Carol Lewine's 1970 Columbia dissertation, p. 1), the assertion needs to be at least partially qualified. There are other Sedulian manuscripts which contain illustrations, some of them quite elaborate. München, Bayerische Staatsbibliothek, Clm 18628, for example, has a seated figure depicted on f. 16v. On f. 147v, Paris, Bibliothèque Nationale, Lat. 242 has a nice illustration of a seated figure with a cross in his left hand pointing to the words: *pastor bonus tibi commendo spiritum meum*. Above, there appears a lion or panther carrying its prey in its mouth. (*Probationes pennae* on the same page include a complaint typical of scribes: *scribere qui nescit nullum putat esse laborem*.) Udine, Biblioteca Arcivescovile, Qt. 10. I. 23 has an illustration of the crucifixion which takes up nearly a full page (f. 31r). Wolfenbüttel, Herzog August Bibliothek, 404. 1 (6) Novi, a fourteenth-century fragment of only 2 leaves (PC 1.97-125, 173-205), contains a number of illustrations: on the recto there are illustrations of a bearded man (Sedulius?) sitting on a bench between two trees

Berlin, Staatsbibliothek zu Berlin-Preussischer Kulturbesitz, Phillipps 1727.[53] Indeed, Huemer only consulted some 30 manuscripts in total and several of these he knew only second-hand.[54] Of manuscripts not used by Huemer, a number are quite early, dating to the ninth or tenth centuries, for example: Albi, Bibliothèque Municipale, 98; Angers, Bibliothèque Municipale, 522; Barcelona, Archivo de la Corona de Aragón, 106; Edinburgh, University Library, Adv. 18. 7. 7; Épinal, Bibliothèque Municipale, 74; London, British Library, Harley 3072 and Royal 15 B. XIX; Orléans, Bibliothèque Municipale, 295, 302 (two copies of the *Paschale Carmen*), 303 (contains the *Paschale Carmen* and the *Paschale Opus*), and 318; Paris, Bibliothèque Nationale, Lat. 242, 8093, 8094, 10307, 18553, 18554; Paris, Bibliothèque Sainte-Geneviève, 2410; and Wolfenbüttel, Herzog August Bibliothek, 191 Gud. Lat. 4°.

The following pages list over 400 manuscripts which contain some or all of the works of Sedulius. This represents a considerable improvement on Huemer's relatively brief list (*CSEL*, vol. 10, pp. iv-xxiv and xxxvi-xxxviii), of whose limitations the Austrian editor was himself aware:

De reliquiis codicibus per Germaniam Franciam Brittaniam Italiam

---

with his hand extended towards one of them (cf. PC 1.97-8) and the sacrifice of Isaac; on the verso we find depicted the destruction of Sodom (Lot's wife has been turned into a pillar of salt); the lengthening of Hezekiah's life; and the story of Jonah. There is a particularly nice portrayal of Jonah's foot in the mouth of the great fish. (It is unclear whether he is in the process of being swallowed or is just emerging after his 3-day ordeal.)

[53]Of the manuscripts which Huemer collated, the readings of the Berlin manuscript of the *Paschale Opus* most often correspond with Paris, Bibliothèque Nationale, Lat. 12279 and Zürich, Zentralbibliothek, Rh. 77 (as opposed to Bruxelles, Bibliothèque Royale Albert 1er, 5649-5667, and London, British Library, Harley 3012).

[54]For the eight Vatican manuscripts included in his edition, Huemer simply adopted the readings of Arevalo's 1794 edition. Unfortunately for Huemer (and for us) Arevalo himself was not always as painstaking as he might have been. It is interesting, for instance, to note that Huemer records two readings from Biblioteca Apostolica Vaticana, Reg. Lat. 333 for H1. In fact Reg. 333 contains neither of Sedulius' hymns and they are now to be found in Leiden, Universiteit Bibliotheek, Voss. Lat. Q. 86. As Grace Frank and E.K. Rand were able to prove, Voss. Lat. Q. 86 and Reg. 333 at one time constituted one codex. When the volume was split apart (by Alexander Petau), the two hymns of Sedulius were separated from the rest of his works and they have been in the Leiden University Library since the death of Isaac Vossius (1689). Oddly enough, Arevalo includes readings from Reg. 333 for H1 and Huemer simply follows his lead. Huemer also lists readings for the hymns from Voss. Lat. Q. 86 in the critical apparatus, but they do not agree with the imaginary readings of Reg. 333. Such are the perils of "second-hand" citations!

Hispaniam diffusis, quos aut consulto sprevi aut in tanta copia librorum adire non potui, dubito, num magna de iis possint sperari (p. xxxiv).

Huemer's observations on the manuscripts are frequently incorrect and the alert reader will be quick to note the differences between his descriptions of the manuscripts and their Sedulian contents and my own, although I have not pointed out these discrepancies in every case.

This said, it would be most misleading, on the other hand, to suggest that the present list of Sedulian manuscripts is itself complete. As mentioned above, there are a number of manuscript libraries in Europe which have still to be adequately catalogued (or whose catalogues I have been unable to see). Many of them undoubtedly possess manuscripts containing the works of Sedulius or *"Seduliana"* which are waiting to be discovered. Even when modern catalogues of manuscript collections are available, it is altogether possible that Sedulian materials may have slipped through the cataloguer's (or indexer's) net, and, consequently, through my own as well. In a number of instances, I have not been able to see the manuscripts (particularly those listed in the second section) with my own eyes, or to obtain copies. To some extent, therefore, I have been forced to submit myself to the vagaries of catalogue descriptions.[55] That the select bibliography offered for each

---

[55]Even the most careful cataloguer, of course, can commit egregious errors. McKinlay, p. 30, for instance, declares that Frankfurt, Stadtbibliothek, 139 contains Sedulius on ff. 46r-70r. The latest catalogue of the collection, however, G. Powitz and H. Buck, *Kataloge der Stadt- und Universitätsbibliothek Frankfurt am Main, 3.2: Die Handschriften der Bartholomaeussstifts und des Karmeliterklosters in Frankfurt am Main*, in *Die Handschriften der Stadt- und Universitätsbibliothek Frankfurt am Main* (Frankfurt, 1974), pp. 318-9, indicates that it is Prosper and not Sedulius whose works occupy ff. 46r-70r. Some catalogue entries are exasperatingly vague (e.g., *"Sedulii carmina"* or *"ses poésies"*) or just plain wrong. Even the great Delisle "nods" on more than one occasion. One thinks, for example, of his description of Paris, Bibliothèque Nationale, Lat. 10307 as containing *"la préface de Sedulius."* Delisle was evidently confused by the appearance on f. 2r of Juvencus, *Evangeliorum Libri Quattuor*, written in alternating columns with Sedulius' *Paschale Carmen*. Indexers, too, make mistakes. For example, in the index to volume 6 (p. 320) of *Cat. gen. octavo* a reference to Sedulius is made to Douai, Bibliothèque Municipale, 532 (13th century), but I was unable to find Sedulius on the catalogue page cited. Conversely, there is no reference under "Sedulius" in the index of *Cat. gen. octavo*, vol. 12, p. 406, to Orléans, Bibliothèque Municipale, 307, a Sedulian manuscript which consequently escaped my notice for some time. It need hardly be said that in the case of manuscripts of which I have no copy or have not seen in person, my own precision is limited by the exactitude of the descriptions in secondary sources which I have been able to consult. I have, accordingly, indicated which manuscripts I have seen in person and/or

manuscript may, furthermore, better reflect the sporadic character of my own reading than serve as a systematic listing of all relevant sources, I am fully aware. The scholarly literature devoted to manuscript studies is not only enormous in its sheer quantity, but also appears in some of the most unlikely (and obscure) journals. Incomplete though they are, however, such references will doubtless be of assistance in directing the eager student to other (and possibly more complete) descriptive sources.

In the first section of the list that follows I have cited those manuscripts which contain either the *Paschale Carmen* or the *Paschale Opus* (or, in a few instances, both). Wherever possible, I have tried to identify the specific nature of the "Sedulian" material each manuscript contains. Abbreviations frequently used in the entries below include the following:

-**E1:** Sedulius' first epistle to Macedonius, prefatory to the *Paschale Carmen* (*CSEL*, vol. 10, pp. 1-13).

-**E2:** Sedulius' second epistle to Macedonius, prefatory to the *Paschale Opus* (*CSEL*, vol. 10, pp. 171-4).

-**PC:** Sedulius' biblical epic, the *Paschale Carmen* (*CSEL*, vol. 10, pp. 14-146).

-**PO:** Sedulius' prose paraphrase of the *Paschale Carmen*, the *Paschale Opus* (*CSEL*, vol. 10, pp. 175-303).

-**H1:** Sedulius' hymn beginning *Cantemus, socii, Domino* (*CSEL*, vol. 10, pp. 155-62).

-**H2:** Sedulius' hymn beginning *A solis ortus cardine* (*CSEL*, vol. 10, pp. 163-8).

-**A Solis Ortus Cardine:** the first stanzas of H2 (usually A-G).

-**Hostis Herodes:** the subsequent stanzas of H2 (often H-N).

-**Accessus:** standardized account of Sedulius' life in question-and-answer format, often beginning: *Videlicet quis fecit? Sedulius.*

-**Acrostic poems:** two poems spelling out *Sedulius Antistes* with the initial and final letters of their 16 lines, beginning *Sedulius Christi miracula versibus edens* (attributed to Bellesarius) and *Sedulius Domini per culta novalia pergens* (attributed to Liberatus) respectively (*CSEL*, vol. 10, pp. 307-10).

-**Asterius' epigram:** 8-line epigram beginning: *Sume, sacer meritis, veracis dicta poetae* (*Anth. Lat.* 491; *CSEL*, vol. 10, p. 307).

-**Biographical notice:** brief account of Sedulius' career, often

---

of which I have acquired copies (in most instances only of the leaves with Sedulian contents).

beginning *Incipit ars Sedulii*, or *Sedulius versificus*, or *Sedulius primo laicus* (see *CSEL*, vol. 10, p. viii).

-**Dedicatory preface to Proba's cento:**   15-line dedication beginning *Romulidum ductor, clari lux altera solis* (*CSEL*, vol. 16, p. 568; *Anth. Lat.* 719d).

-**Prose preface:**   often follows Asterius' epigram; usually beginning *Sedulius epistola Macedonio praemissa presbytero.*

-**Subscription:**   notice on the revision of Sedulius' works by the consul Turcius Rufius Apronianus Asterius, often beginning *Hoc opus Sedulius inter cartulas dispersum reliquit* (*CSEL*, vol. 10, p. vii).

Under many of the entries in the first section of the handlist I have indicated the number of books into which the *Paschale Carmen* and the *Paschale Opus* have been divided,[56] as well as commenting on glossing, illustration, and other physical features of the manuscript in question. In most cases I have also tried to provide the reader with a general idea of what other works, if any, may be found on the leaves preceding and following Sedulius' works, although my descriptions of these authors and their works are little more than abbreviated summaries of the standard catalogue descriptions. In some instances, of course, the materials bound together into one volume may have been combined only at a date much later than their original composition. For the sake of consistency and ease of reference the names of authors and works are

---

[56]The number of books into which the *Paschale Carmen* is divided varies widely. A few later manuscripts (e.g., Paris, Bibliothèque Nationale, Lat. 8313) simply divide the poem into two books: the first for the Old Testament; the second for the New. Only slightly more common is the division of the poem into three books, as follows: PC 1-2=Book 1; PC 3-4=Book 2; and PC 5=Book 3 (cf. Isidore's description in *De Viris Inlustribus* 20), as, for example, in Barcelona, Archivo de la Corona de Aragón, Ripoll 106; Gotha, Forschungs- und Landesbibliothek, MBR. I. 75; Paris, Bibliothèque Nationale, Lat. 8093; and Sankt Gallen, Stiftsbibliothek, 197. Other manuscripts are divided into four continuous books, with no break between what are the third and fourth books in Huemer's edition. The most common system of book division divides the *Paschale Carmen* into five books, with the second book described as "the first book concerning the New Testament" (abbreviated in the list below as "1+4"). Other manuscripts simply divide the *Paschale Carmen* into five continuous books. Still others divide the *Paschale Carmen* into six books, often with PC 5.261-438 as the final book. These manuscripts, too, frequently make a distinction between books dedicated to the Old and New Testaments respectively. Some manuscripts are not divided into books at all, as, for example, those at Trinity College, Cambridge (O. 3. 41), the University of Gent (615), the University of Freiburg (370), the University of Graz (1585), et al. Given the wide variety of systems of book division, one can certainly understand how a scribe working with two or more divergent exemplars might have ended up with an inconsistent book division (which is frequently the case), or simply have abandoned the notion of book division altogether.

usually standardized according to generally accepted conventions (e.g., *Clavis Patrum Latinorum, Oxford Classical Dictionary,* Walther's *Initia,* etc.) and do not reflect the idiosyncracies of the manuscript tradition.

In the second section of the handlist I have cited a goodly sampling of manuscripts which contain less substantial portions of Sedulius' works or *Seduliana.* The descriptions of these manuscripts and their contents are not so detailed as in the first section. I provide no more than a very summary account of the material (other than the works of Sedulius) which each manuscript in this section contains. These manuscripts differ widely among each other. Some are *florilegia.* There are a number of individual passages from the *Paschale Carmen* which proved to be especially popular to medieval readers. One thinks, for example, of Sedulius' famous description of the four evangelists (PC 1.355-8), as found in Cambridge, Corpus Christi College 286, "the Canterbury Gospels," or his well known lines in praise of Mary, the mother of God (PC 2.63 ff.),[57] or the description of the cross, whose peculiar shape moves Sedulius to contemplate the universality of the significance of the crucifixion (PC 5.188 ff.). Other manuscripts are truly fragmentary, e.g., Leiden, Bibliotheek der Rijksuniversiteit, Voss. Q. Lat. 86, which was originally connected with the Vatican manuscript, Reg. Lat. 333, or Reg. Lat. 166, which was once part of Orléans, Bibliothèque Municipale, 307. Other entries are hymnaries (of which my list, I am sure, includes only a sampling) containing one or more excerpts from Sedulius' second hymn. Still other manuscripts simply contain one or more of the versions of the medieval *accessus* to Sedulius or glosses and commentaries on his works. The most famous medieval commentary on Sedulius was written by Remigius of Auxerre (c. 840-908), whose work serves as the basis for many medieval glosses on the *Paschale Carmen,* but there are other glosses in Anglo-Saxon, Old High German, and Latin which may or may not be connected with Remigius'

---

[57]See Antoon A.R. Bastiaensen, "L'Antienne *Genuit puerpera regem:* Adaption liturgique d'un passage du *Paschale Carmen* de Sedulius," *RB* 83 (1973), 388-97, for the transformation of PC 2.63-9 for use in the liturgy. The first lines were adapted as the Introit for the Common of feasts of Mary and the last line was used in the Magnificat antiphon on the feast of the Presentation of Mary. The second antiphon of Christmas Lauds includes lines 67-8. See Joseph Connelly, *Hymns of the Roman Liturgy* (New York, 1957), p. 57, for a fuller discussion. For manuscripts containing such antiphons, see the edition of R.-J. Hesbert, *Corpus Antiphonalium Officii,* vol. 1-3 = Rerum Ecclesiasticarum Documenta. Series Maior. Fontes 7-9 (Roma, 1963-8), passim.

commentary.[58]

My primary intention here has been to list Sedulian manuscripts and to delineate as precisely as possible the Sedulian works or relevant incidental material which they contain. Of less importance, at least for my purposes, is the description of the manuscripts themselves, and I have included only a few details which may help the reader to appreciate the physical circumstances in which these witnesses to the text of Sedulius' works are to be found. In addition to the location of the manuscript by city and library (I have generally followed Kristeller's nomenclature) and number or shelf-mark, each entry contains one or more of the following: an indication of the manuscript's date (usually by century), the number of leaves or pages (usually those numbered), the approximate size of the book block (usually in millimeters), and a brief indication of the manuscript's provenance. In those (relatively few) instances in which manuscripts are written on paper rather than parchment or vellum, I have so noted. For many of these details I have relied on the expertise of paleographers and cataloguers whose contributions the reader will find listed in the "Bibliography" which accompanies each entry. Where there are discrepancies between or among these descriptions, I have generally followed the most recent (or authoritative) source cited. The reader should also be advised that when quoting from manuscripts or printed editions, I have made minor orthographical

---

[58]For the numerous Old English glosses in Cambridge, Corpus Christi College, 173, see H. Meritt, *Old English Glosses (A Collection)* (London, 1945), pp. 29-38 and R.I. Page, "The Study of Latin Texts in Late Anglo-Saxon England [II]: The Evidence of English Glosses" in *Latin and the Vernacular Languages in Early Medieval Britain: Papers Delivered to the Fifth Annual St. John's House Symposium,* ed. Nicholas Brooks (Leicester, 1982), pp. 154 ff. Edinburgh, National Library of Scotland, Adv. 18. 7. 7 has substantial sections glossed in Old English and Latin; see H. Meritt, "Old English Sedulius Glosses," *AJP* 57 (1936), 140-50. See also Merritt, same as above, pp. 38-9, for the OE glosses in Royal MS. 15 B. XIX. For glossing in Cambridge University Library, Gg. 5. 35, see Arthur S. Napier, *Old English Glosses Chiefly Unpublished* (Oxford, 1900), p. 217. On the glossing in Paris, Bibliothèque Nationale, Lat. 8092, see Michael Lapidge, "Some Old English Sedulius Glosses from BN Lat. 8092," *Anglia* 100 (1982), 1-17, which should be supplemented by P.P. O'Neill, "Further Old English Glosses on Sedulius in BN Lat. 8092," *Anglia* 107 (1989), 415. For general comments and extensive bibliography on Latin and vernacular glossing, see the first chapter of Tony Hunt, *Teaching and Learning Latin in Thirteenth-Century England*, vol. 1 (Cambridge, 1991), pp. 3 ff. Sedulian manuscripts with Old High German glosses have been considered by Klaus Siewert, *Glossenfunde. Volkssprachiges zu lateinischen Autoren der Antike und des Mittelalters* = Studien zum Althochdeutschen 11 (Göttingen, 1989), pp. 56-60. A partial edition of Remigius of Auxerre's commentary appeared in Huemer's edition in *CSEL*, vol. 10, pp. 316 ff. Colette Jeudy is currently editing the complete work.

adjustments and have expanded abbreviations for the sake of greater consistency and ease of reading. All references to the works of Sedulius (including page numbers in the prose works), unless otherwise indicated, are based on Huemer's edition.

I. MANUSCRIPTS CONTAINING THE *PASCHALE CARMEN* AND/OR *PASCHALE OPUS*

ADMONT, Stiftsbibliothek, 472
s. xii; 36 leaves; folio.

Contents: On ff. 3r-36r: E1, PC (missing original leaves between ff. 24v and 25r [=3.166 to 4.189]; 5.368-429 out of order on f. 35r-v), H1, H2. *Accessus* beginning *In capite uniuscuiusque libri septem periochae;* biographical notice *(Qui primo laicus in Italia philosophiam didicit...);* subscription; Asterius' epigram; and biographical notice *(Sedulius versificus primo....)* on ff. 1r-2v.
Other information: PC divided into four or five books. Used by Huemer (a). Heavily glossed with extensive marginal commentary. Microfilm acquired.
Bibliography: *CSEL,* vol. 10, p. xxiii; Jakob Wichner, *Catalogus Codicum Manu Scriptorum Admontensis* (Admont, 1888-9), p. 202.

ALBI, Bibliothèque Municipale, 98 (108)
s. ix$^{3/3}$; 36 leaves; 254 x 178 mm.; written in southern France; owned by a monastery or cathedral in south-eastern France, perhaps Albi.

Contents: On ff. 5r-35v: E1, PC (5.332 ff. in a more recent hand), H1. Preceded by *Disticha Catonis* (ff. 1r-3v); Eugenius of Toledo, *Carm.* 16, 18, 19 (f. 4r); et al. Subscription and Asterius' epigram on f. 4v.
Other information: Last leaves (ff. 33-36) date to s. xii. Present volume separated from Albi, Bibliothèque Municipale, 30 (115), a copy of Ps.-Isidore Mercator, *Decretales,* in 1984. PC divided into five books (1+4). Extensive interlinear and marginal glossing. Seen in person. Microfilm acquired.
Bibliography: *Cat. gen. quarto,* vol. 1, p. 498; Jeudy & Riou, pp. 14-6; Jeudy & Riou, "Notes," 313; Munk Olsen, vol. 3.2, p. 190; Schafer Williams, *Codices Pseudo-Isidoriani: A Palaeographico-historical Study* = Monumenta Iuris Canonici, Series C: Subsidia, vol. 3 (New York, 1971), pp. 3-4.

ANGERS, Bibliothèque Municipale, 522 (502)
s. ix-x; 90 leaves; 263 x 180-190 mm.; probably written in western
France; prov. S. Aubin, Angers.

Contents: On ff. 37v-88r: E1, PC, H1, H2. *Accessus* (beginning *His
ita notandum quia septem periochae*) on f. 41r. Preceded by Bede, *De
Arte Metrica* (ff. 1r-26v) and an excerpt from *De Schematibus et Tropis*
(ff. 26v-35v); *De Metris* (f. 36r); and miscellaneous verses, including
excerpts from the epigrams of Martial and Alcuin, *Carm.* 111 (ff. 36v-
37r). Followed by a fragment of Priscian, *Institutio de Nomine et
Pronomine et Verbo* (ff. 88v-90v).
Other information: Some leaves written somewhat later (ff. 36-37=s.
xi; ff. 88v-90v=s. x²). PC divided into six books (last book, *"Liber
quintus de passione Christi,"* begins with PC 5.261). Extensive
interlinear glossing and marginal commentary (Remigius'), beginning on
f. 37v. Some of the marginalia is written so as to form triangular
designs (as, e.g., on f. 64v). Seen in person. Microfilm acquired.
Bibliography: *Cat. gen. octavo*, vol. 31, p. 359; S. Gavinelli, "Un
manuale scolastico carolingio: Il codice Bolognese 797," *Aevum* 59
(1985), 187; Colette Jeudy, "Le *Carmen* 111 d'Alcuin et l'anthologie de
Martial du manuscrit 522 (502) de la Bibliothèque Municipale d'Angers"
in *Scire Litteras. Forschungen zum mittelalterlichen Geistesleben.
Festschrift Bernhard Bischoff zu seinem 80. Geburtstag* = Abhandlungen
der Bayerischen Akademie der Wissenschaften, Phil.-hist. Klasse, n. F.,
99 (München, 1988), pp. 221-6; Jeudy, "Priscien," 89; Jeudy, "Remi,"
p. 496; Jeudy & Riou, pp. 75-8; C.B. Kendall and M.H. King, *Bedae
Venerabilis Opera. Pars VI. Opera Didascalia I, CCSL*, vol. 123A, pp.
62 and 78; Laistner, p. 134; Munk Olsen, vol. 3.2, p. 191; Passalacqua,
p. 5.

**ANTWERPEN, Musaeum Plantin-Moretus Bibliotheek, M. 17. 4
(126)**
s. ix*in.*; 76 leaves; 250 x 170 mm.; written at the cathedral scriptorium
of Liège; later at S. Jacques, Liège.

Contents: On ff. 1r-41r: E1, PC (missing two original leaves after f.
34 [=5.145-253]; also missing two original leaves after f. 19 [=3.9-
103], replaced in s. xii), H1. Dedicatory preface to Proba's cento and
acrostic poem in praise of Sedulius (Bellesarius') on f. 41r. Acrostic
poem of Liberatus follows E1 on f. 5v. Followed by Prosper's epigrams
(ff. 41v-68v) and miscellaneous verses on ff. 68v-69v (including poems

beginning *Haec Augustini ex sacris; Crede ratem ventis; Virgo parens hac luce;* and Alcuin, *Carm.* 104), as well as a dialogue attributed to Bede. Another text of Prosper's epigrams (s. xiii) in a smaller format follows on ff. 70r-76r.

Other information: Manuscript may be connected with Heiric of Auxerre (died after 875); the name Ericus appears on the frontispiece near the head of Christ. See also the reference to Cuthwine on f. 68v. According to Henderson, the Sedulius text "may represent a Carolingian copy of an English copy of a late fifth-century exemplar." Used by Th. Poelman for his edition of the epigrams of Prosper (1560). Not used by Huemer, but Caesar (see below) made a selective collation of the manuscript against Huemer's oldest manuscripts (text is closer to the Bobbio manuscripts than to Basel, Universitätsbibliothek, O. IV. 17). PC divided into five books (1+4). Contains 16 miniatures. Extensive interlinear glossing in Latin and Old High German. Seen in person. Microfilm acquired.

Bibliography: J.J.G. Alexander, *Insular Manuscripts: 6th to the 9th Century* = A Survey of Manuscripts Illuminated in the British Isles, vol. 1 (London, 1978), p. 83; Bergmann, p. 2; idem, *Mittelfränkische Glossen. Studien zu ihrer Ermittlung und sprachgeographischen Einordnung* = Rheinisches Archiv 61 (2nd ed.; Bonn, 1977), pp. 228-33 [s. x-xi]; Bischoff, "FHH," 306; Bischoff, *MS,* vol. 3, p. 9; C. Caesar, "Die Antwerpener Handschrift des Sedulius," *RhM* 56 (1901), 247-71; Albert S. Cook, "Bishop Cuthwini of Leicester (680-691), Amateur of Illustrated Manuscripts," *Speculum* 2 (1927), 253-7; J. Denucé, *Musaeum Plantin-Moretus. Catalogue des manuscrits* (Antwerpen, 1927), pp. 135-7; George Henderson, "Emulation and Invention in Carolingian Art" in *Carolingian Culture: Emulation and Innovation,* ed. Rosamond McKitterick (Cambridge, 1994), pp. 253-4; Jeudy, "Remi," p. 496 [s. xi]; W. Köhler, "Die Denkmäler der karolingischen Kunst in Belgien" in *Belgische Kunstdenkmäler,* ed. Paul Clemen (München, 1923); Kurz, 267 ff.; Lehmann, vol. 3, pp. 40 and 186; Lesne, p. 683; W. Levinson, *England and the Continent in the Eighth Century* (Oxford, 1946), pp. 133-4; Carol Lewine, "The Miniatures of the Antwerp Sedulius Manuscript: The Early Christian Models and their Transformations," Dissertation, Columbia University, 1970, passim; eadem, "*Vulpes Fossa Habent* or the Miracle of the Bent Woman in the Gospels of St. Augustine, Corpus Christi College, Cambridge, Ms. 286," *The Art Bulletin* 56 (1974), 497-8; Otto Pächt, *The Rise of Pictorial Narrative in Twelfth-Century England* (Oxford, 1962), pp. 19-20; Peter Pauly, *Die althochdeutschen Glossen der Handschriften Pommersfelden 2671 und*

Antwerpen 17.4.　Untersuchungen zu ihrem Lautstand = Rheinisches Archiv 67 (Bonn, 1968), passim; Steinmeyer & Sievers, vol. 2, pp. 616-7 and vol. 4, p. 376; Traube, vol. 3, pp. 239-41; David H. Wright, "The Codex Millenarius and Its Model," *Münchener Jahrbuch der bildenden Kunst* 15 (1964), 46.

ANTWERPEN, Musaeum Plantin-Moretus Bibliotheek, M. 212 (125)
s. xiv; 41 leaves; 206 x 145 mm.

Contents:　On ff. 1r-41r:　PC, H1.　On verso of last leaf:　letter of a certain Wilts (Wilhelmus?) to a John *"logicalibus scientiis vacantem."*
Other information:　PC divided into five books.　Interlinear and marginal glossing.　Given to Th. Poelman by Chr. Plantin in 1500.　Seen in person.　Microfilm acquired.
Bibliography:　Denucé, same as above, pp. 102-3.

ANTWERPEN, Musaeum Plantin-Moretus Bibliotheek, M. 374 (23)
s. xi; 72 leaves; 177 x 108 mm.

Contents:　On ff. 2r-36v:　E1 (s. xv), PC, H1, H2.　Subscription and Asterius' epigram on f. 5v; biographical notes, including *accessus*, on ff. 36v-37r.　Followed by the epigrams of Prosper (ff. 37r-59v); the fables of Avianus (ff. 59v-69v); and notes on Latin grammar (ff. 70r-73v).
Other information:　PC divided into six books (last book begins with PC 5.261).　Seen in person.　Microfilm acquired.
Bibliography:　Denucé, same as above, pp. 74-5; Glauche, p. 51; Jeudy, "Remi," p. 496.

BARCELONA, Archivo de la Corona de Aragón, Ripoll 106
s. ix/x; 140 leaves; 265 x 225 mm.; S. Maria, Ripoll.

Contents:　On ff. 58v-75v:　E1, PC (om. PC 5.104-176), H1.　Preceded by Bede, *De Arte Metrica* and *De Schematibus et Tropis* (ff. 9v-25v); Augustine, *Soliloquia* (ff. 27v-50r); *Disticha Catonis* (ff. 50r-53v); et al. Followed by *Geometria Gisemundi* (ff. 75v-89r); works of Boethius ("*Opuscula Sacra*" 1-4) (ff. 102v-114v); the beginning of Jerome's commentary on Daniel (ff. 121v-122r); et al. (For a full description of the contents, see García below.)
Other information:　First eight leaves of volume (epigrams of Prosper) date to s. xii.　PC divided into three books (no division between PC 2 and 3 or between PC 4 and 5).　Text of PC not divided into poetic lines.

Text is very close to that of the Bobbio manuscripts. Microfilm acquired.

Bibliography: S. Corbin, "Le *Cantus Sibyllae:* Origine et premiers texts," *Revue de musicologie* 31-2 (1952), 1-20, esp. 5; A. Cordoliani, "Los manuscritos de cómputo ecclesiástico en las bibliotecas de Barcelona," *AST* 23 (1950), 107-10; Lisardo Rubio Fernández, *Catálogo de los manuscritos clásicos latinos existentes en España* (Madrid, 1984), p. 36; Zacharias García, "Bibliotheca Patrum Latinorum Hispaniensis II.1," *Sitz. Wien* 169.2 (1915), pp. 56-8; Henry A. Grubbs, *A Supplement to the Manuscript Book Collections of Spain and Portugal* = A Union World Catalog of Manuscript Books: Preliminary Studies in Method 5 (New York, 1935), p. 93 [s. x]; Hörmann, pp. xix-xx [s. ix^2]; Munk Olsen, vol. 3.1, p. 210 and vol. 3.2, p. 8; Reynolds, p. 5; Carl Thulin, *Zur Überlieferungsgeschichte des Corpus Agrimensorum. Excerptenhandschriften und Kompendien* = Göteborgs Kungl. Vetenskaps-och Vitterhets-Samhälles Handlingar 4.14-15 (Göteborg, 1911), pp. 55-66; Lucio Toneatto, "Note sulla tradizione del *Corpus Agrimensorum Romanorum* I. Contenuti e struttura dell'*Ars Gromatica* di Gisemundus (ix sec.)," *MEFRM* 94 (1982), 197 ff.

BASEL, Universitätsbibliothek (Öffentliche Bibliothek der Universität Basel), O. IV. 17
s. viii-ix; 64 leaves; 148 x 166 mm.; possibly written at Fulda.

Contents: On ff. 11r-64v: E1, PC 1.1 to 5.227. Preceded by Ps.-Sulpicius Severus, *Epist.* 3 (missing beginning) on ff. 1r-5v; Gregory of Tours, *Historiarum Libri Decem (History of the Franks)* 1.48 (description of S. Martin of Tours) on ff. 5v-7v; and by the same author, *De Virtutibus S. Martini* 1.4-5 (ff. 7v-10r).

Other information: According to Lowe, written "in a German centre under Anglo-Saxon influence, possibly at Fulda with which its later history is connected." PC divided into five books (1+4). Text of PC not divided into poetic lines. Used by Huemer (A) who (wrongly) suggests: *"nunc tantum f. 11-64 extant."* Corrected by an eleventh-century hand. Owned by Remigius Faesch, professor at Basel (died in 1667). Microfilm acquired.

Bibliography: *CLA,* vol. 7, p. 5, no. 853; *CSEL,* vol. 10, pp. ix-x; Martin Steinmann, *Die Handschriften der Universitätsbibliothek Basel. Register zu den Abteilungen AI-AXVI und O* = Publikationen der Universitätsbibliothek Basel 4 (Basel, 1982), p. 528.

BERKELEY, University of California Library, MS UCB 68
s. xiv[1]; 49 leaves; 270 x 159 mm.; written in north-eastern Italy
(Veneto).

Contents: On ff. 1r-49r: PC. Preceded by subscription and prose
preface.
Other information: Palimpsest. Lower text is an account book which
mentions various crops such as wheat, barley, oats, spelt, panic, millet,
beans, and chicory as well as *"bestias"* and *"duas vachas."* No book
divisions in PC (121 chapters). Owned by the Rev. Henry Drury and Sir
Thomas Phillipps (9252). Marginal and interlinear commentary on first
18 leaves.
Bibliography: Census Suppl., p. 4; Schenkl, no. 1792.

**BERLIN, Staatsbibliothek zu Berlin-Preussischer Kulturbesitz, Diez.
C Fol. 1**
s. xv (1494) (ff. 1-120); 380 leaves; 315 x 215 mm.; Leipzig; paper.

Contents: On ff. 1r-44r: PC. Followed by Pius II (Aeneas Silvius
Piccolomini), *De Passione Christi* (f. 47r-v); Hieronymus de Vallibus
Paduanus, *Jesuida* (ff. 48r-58v); and Boethius, *Philosophiae Consolatio*
(ff. 59v-119r).
Other information: Miscellany volume consisting of nine separate parts
(s. xv-xvi). Commentary in margin. PC 1.280 ff. = *"Prologus secundi
libri."* On f. 44r: *"Carmen paschale Sedulii clerici explicit feliciter."*
Bibliography: Kristeller, *Iter,* vol. 3, p. 359; Ursula Winter, *Die
europäischen Handschriften der Bibliothek Diez. Dritter Teil, Die
Manuscripta Dieziana C* (Wiesbaden, 1994), pp. 7-11; eadem, "Mittel-
lateinische Texte in Handschriften der Bibliothek Diez," *MlatJb* 19
(1984), 219-20.

**BERLIN, Staatsbibliothek zu Berlin-Preussischer Kulturbesitz,
Hamilton 602**
s. xii[1]; 32 leaves; 200 x 130 mm.

Contents: On ff. 1v-32r: E1 (beginning *Sedulius mittit epistulam ad
Macedonium),* PC. Biographical notice *(Sedulius versificus primo
laicus....)* on f. 32r.
Other information: Listed in the catalogue of Pietro Antonio Crevenna
of 1789. PC apparently divided into three books (no book divisions
between PC 2 and 3 or between PC 4 and 5). Probably written by

several very similar hands. Occasional interlinear glossing and some marginalia. Microfilm acquired.

Bibliography: Helmut Boese, *Die lateinischen Handschriften der Sammlung Hamilton zu Berlin* (Wiesbaden, 1966), pp. 286-7.

BERLIN, Staatsbibliothek zu Berlin-Preussischer Kulturbesitz, Phillipps 1727
s. viii-ix; 63 leaves; 232 x 140 mm.; written in Verona; later at S. Aubin, Angers.

Contents: On ff. 1r-63v: PO (missing first part; begins with p. 185, line 8). [References here and elsewhere to the text of the PO are to Huemer's edition in *CSEL,* vol. 10, pp. 171 ff.] Subscription on f. 63v.
Other information: Formerly bound with the "Commodianus" (Phillipps 1825). Written by several scribes in an "early Caroline minuscule of Veronese type." Corrections may have been made by the archdeacon Pacificus (776-846 A.D.). Divided into five continuously numbered books. Includes indices. Seen in person. Microfilm acquired.
Bibliography: *CLA,* vol. 8, p. 11, no. 1058; Valentin Rose, *Verzeichniss der lateinischen Handschriften der königlichen Bibliothek zu Berlin* (Berlin, 1893-1919), vol. 1, *Die Meerman-Handschriften des Sir Thomas Phillipps* (1893), p. 387; Jean Vezin, *Les Scriptoria d'Angers au XIe siècle* = Bibliothèque de l'École des Hautes Études, IVe Section, Sciences historiques et philologiques 322 (Paris, 1974), pp. 62-3.

BERLIN, Staatsbibliothek zu Berlin-Preussischer Kulturbesitz, Lat. 8° 147
s. xii²; 121 leaves; 170 x 124 mm.; written in France?

Contents: On ff. 70r-121r: PC, H1 (1-12 only; written in another hand). On f. 121v: *Amen dico tibi tu remanebis ibi.* Preceded by Arator, *Historia Apostolica* (ff. 2r-69r).
Other information: PC divided into four or five continuously numbered books (no division between PC 2 and 3; but last book is described as the fifth). Interlinear glossing and marginal notes. Microfilm acquired.
Bibliography: McKinlay, p. 28.

BERLIN, Staatsbibliothek zu Berlin-Preussischer Kulturbesitz, Lat. 8° 156 (formerly Phillipps 25146)
s. xii; 94 leaves; octavo; written in Germany.

Contents: On ff. 1r-41v: E1, PC, H1, H2. Acrostic poems in praise of Sedulius (in the reverse of Huemer's order) on ff. 41v-42r. Remigius' commentary on Sedulius on ff. 42v-94v.

Other information: PC divided into six (or seven) books. Book divisions at PC 1.103 and at PC 5.261. Microfiche acquired.

Bibliography: Esposito, 169; Jeudy, "Remi," p. 496; Kristeller, *Iter,* vol. 3, p. 480; Schenkl, no. 2130.

BERN, Burgerbibliothek, 267

s. x$^{3/4}$; 33 leaves; quarto; written at Fleury.

Contents: On ff. 1r-33v: PC (incomplete; contains 1.339-368; 2.1-25 and 102-177; 3.189-339; 4 [*in toto*]; 5.1-56 and 95-438), H1, H2 (followed by doxology).

Other information: PC apparently divided into five books (1+4). Extensive interlinear glossing especially in first two books. Writing on first 18 leaves has faded badly. Used by Huemer (B). Seen in person. Microfilm acquired.

Bibliography: CSEL, vol. 10, p. xvii; H. Hagen, *Catalogus Codicum Bernensium (Bibliotheca Bongarsiana)* (Bern, 1875), p. 300; K. Halm, "Verzeichniss der älteren Handschriften lateinischer Kirchenväter in den Bibliotheken der Schweiz," *Sitz. Wien* 50 (1865), 157; Jeudy, "Remi," p. 496; H. Leclercq in *DACL* 5.2 (Paris, 1923), col. 1759; Lesne, pp. 552 and 555; Mostert, p. 69.

BERN, Burgerbibliothek, 286

s. xi$^{in.}$; 89 leaves; 272 x 198 mm.; written in France; prov. Fleury.

Contents: On ff. 4r-41v: E1, PC, H1, H2 (first stanza only on f. 41v; remainder on f. 35r-v). Subscription, prose preface, Asterius' epigram, and biographical notice *(Sedulius versificus....)* on f. 3r. Preceded by a short Latin glossary (f. 2r) and the first two lines of *Ilias Latina* (f. 2v). Followed by Arator, *Historia Apostolica* (ff. 42r-89r) and the first four lines of Ovid, *Metamorphoses* on f. 89v.

Other information: Ascribed to Fleury (by Cuissard), because it contains Greek. PC apparently divided into five books (1+4). Some glossing. Used by Huemer (b). Seen in person. Microfilm acquired.

Bibliography: CSEL, vol. 10, p. xxii; Ch. Cuissard, "L'Étude du grec à Orléans depuis le IXe siècle jusqua'au milieu du XVIIIe siècle," *Mémoires de la Société Archéologique et Historique de l'Orléanais* 19 (1883), 645-840, esp. 684; Ettore Cuzzi, "I tre codici ambrosiani di

Aratore," *Rendiconti del Reale Istituto Lombardo di Scienze e Lettere* 59 (1936), 6-10; Glauche, pp. 67-8; Hagen, same as above, pp. 308-9; Halm, same as above, 157; Huemer, *De Sedulii,* p. 32; Kurz, 266; McKinlay, pp. 60-1; Mostert, p. 70; Munk Olsen, vol. 1, p. 415 and vol. 2, pp. 128 and 881; M. Scaffai, "Tradizione manoscritta dell'*Ilias latina*" in *In verbis verum amare. Miscellanea dell'Istituto di Filologia Latina e Medioevale dell'Università di Bologna,* ed. Paulo Serra Zanetti (Firenze, 1980), p. 242.

BRUGGE, Stedelijke Openbare Bibliotheek, 168
s. xii/xiii; 55 leaves; 220 x 145 mm.; Notre-Dame des Dunes (near Brugge).

Contents: On ff. 24r-54r: E1, PC, H1. Acrostic poems in praise of Sedulius on f. 26r (Liberatus') and f. 52r (Bellesarius') respectively; biographical notice *(Sedulius primo laicus in Italia didicit philoso-phiam....)* on ff. 54r-55v. Preceded by the epigrams of Prosper (ff. 1r-22r) and Ps.-Prosper, *Poema Coniugis ad Uxorem* (ff. 22r-23v).
Other information: PC divided into four continuously numbered books (no break between PC 3 and 4). Interlinear glossing and marginal commentary (Remigius'). Seen in person.
Bibliography: A. De Poorter, *Catalogue des manuscrits de la Biblio-thèque Publique de la Ville de Bruges,* vol. 2 in *Catalogue général des manuscrits des bibliothèques de Belgique* (Gembloux and Paris, 1934), pp. 215-6; Esposito, 169; Marie-Thérèse Isaac, *Les Livres manuscrits de l'Abbaye des Dunes d'après le catalogue du XVIIe siècle* = Livre-Ideés-Société 4 (Aubel, 1984), pp. 148-9; Jeudy, "Remi," p. 496.

BRUXELLES, Bibliothèque Royale Albert 1er, 2766-2770
s. xv; 181 leaves; 220 x 150 mm.; S. Maria in Bethlehem (near Leuven); paper and parchment.

Contents: On ff. 2r-37r: E1, PC, H1, H2. Subscription, Asterius' epigram, biographical notice, and Gelasian decree on f. 4v. Acrostic poem (Bellesarius') in praise of Sedulius on f. 36r-v. Hymn beginning *Salve festa dies* (f. 37r-v) attributed to Sedulius. Followed by Thomas Aquinas, *De Perfectione Spiritualis Vitae* (ff. 38r-79v) and *Quaestio Disputata de Ingressu Puerorum* (ff. 79v-92v); Anselm of Canterbury, *De Libertate Arbitrii* (ff. 98r-105r); Henricus ex Pomerio, *Pomerium Spirituale Fratris* (ff. 110r-126r); and a number of sermons (ff. 130r-181r).

Other information: PC divided into five books (1+4). Seen in person. Microfilm acquired.

Bibliography: H.F. Dondaine and H.V. Shooner, *Codices Manuscripti Operum Thomae de Aquino* = Editiones Operum Sancti Thomae de Aquino 2 (Roma, 1967), vol. 1, p. 156; Joseph van den Gheyn, et al., *Catalogue des manuscrits de la Bibliothèque Royale de Belgique* (Bruxelles, 1901-48), vol. 2 (1902), pp. 193-4.

BRUXELLES, Bibliothèque Royale Albert 1er, 5649-5667
s. ix^2 (ff. 166-208); 229 leaves; 207 x 148 mm.; Gembloux.

Contents: On ff. 166r-183v: PO (starting with Huemer's page 212, line 11). On ff. 183v-185r: glosses on E1. *"Incipit ars...."* on bottom of f. 185r. Other explanatory notes on Sedulius on ff. 185v-186r. Followed by a letter of Colmán on the text of Sedulius (ff. 186r-187v); Eutyches, *Ars de Verbo* (ff. 188v-207v); the sequence *Dominus caeli rex*; and an excerpt from Martianus Capella, *De Nuptiis Philologiae et Mercurii* [Schaller 14743] on f. 208v. (Quintus Serenus, *Liber Medicinalis,* on ff. 121-151.)

Other information: Composite volume with some elements dating as late as s. xiv. Of the six manuscripts bound together, ours (ff. 166-208) is the fifth. Used by Huemer (B), who dates it to s. xi (collated for Huemer by P. Schroeder). Seen in person. Microfilm acquired.

Bibliography: Beccaria, pp. 117-8; Bischoff, *MS,* vol. 1, p. 199; *Catalogus Codicum Hagiographicorum Bibliothecae Regiae Bruxellensis. Pars I. Codices Latini Membranei,* vol. 1 (Bruxelles, 1886), pp. 595-601; *CSEL,* vol. 10, p. xxxviii; Esposito, 169; Colette Jeudy, "Les Manuscrits de l'*Ars de verbo* d'Eutychès et le commentaire de Rémi d'Auxerre" in *Études de civilization médiévale (IXe-XIIe siècles). Mélanges offerts à Edmond-René Labande* (Poitiers, 1965), pp. 423-4; Marie-Rose Lapière, *La Lettre ornée dans les manuscrits mosans d'origine bénédictine (XIe-XIIe siècles)* = Bibliothèque de la Faculté de Philosophie et Lettres de l'Université de Liège 229 (Paris, 1981), p. 365; Lesne, p. 684; Munk Olsen, vol. 2, pp. 477-8; Baron Fréderic de Reiffenberg, "Paléographie-histoire littéraire," *Bulletin de l'Académie Royale des Sciences et des Belles-lettres de Bruxelles* 10 (1843), 362-81; Sanford, 205; Richard Sharpe, "An Irish Textual Critic and the *Carmen paschale* of Sedulius. Colmán's Letter to Feradach," *Journal of Medieval Latin* 2 (1992), 44-54; H. Silvestre, "Un second témoin manuscrit de la séquence *Dominus caeli rex,*" *RB* 91 (1981), 169-71; Paul Thomas, *Catalogue des manuscrits de classiques latins de la*

Bibliothèque Royale de Bruxelles = Université de Gand. Recueil de travaux publiés par la Faculté de Philosophie et Lettres 18 (Gent, 1896), pp. 26-8.

BRUXELLES, Bibliothèque Royale Albert 1er, 9964-9966
s. xi; 104 leaves; 205 x 135 mm.; S. Jacques, Liège.

Contents: On ff. 1r-42r: PC, H1, H2. Subscription, prose preface, and Asterius' epigram on ff. 3v-4r. Acrostic poems in praise of Sedulius (in Huemer's order; Liberatus' poem is missing last six lines) on f. 42v. Followed by Juvencus, *Evangeliorum Libri Quattuor* (ff. 43r-104r).
Other information: PC divided into five continuously numbered books. There is an interesting doodle (of a bird-like animal) on f. 41r. Seen in person. Microfilm acquired.
Bibliography: D. De Bruyne, "Un feuillet oncial d'une règle de moniales," *RB* 35 (1923), 126-8; van den Gheyn, *Catalogue,* same as above, vol. 2, pp. 192-3; Lehmann, vol. 3, p. 40; Lesne, p. 683.

BUDAPEST, Eötvös Loránd Tudomány Egyetem Könyvtára (University Library), 64
s. xv*med.*; 326 leaves; 213 x 145 mm.; written in Poland; paper.

Contents: On ff. 273r-319r: PC. Preceded by miscellaneous sermons (ff. 1r-13r); a sermon on true friendship (ff. 14r-18v); a life of S. Burchardus (ff. 19r-20r); chronological tables (1444-1519) (ff. 21v-33v); Ps.-Bernard, *Carmen Paraeneticum ad Rainaldum* (ff. 34r-57v); Julianus Pomerius, *De Vita Contemplativa* (ff. 58r-77r); Ps.-Ovid, *De Vetula* (ff. 78r-137r); *Palaestra de Victoria Christi* (ff. 137v-142v); Johannes de Fonte, *Compendium Sententiarum Petri Lombardi* (ff. 143r-213r); sermons of Marcus Bonifilius (ff. 213v-235v); Paulus Piczkowski on the immaculate conception (ff. 236r-264r); the same author's sequence on the same theme (ff. 264r ff.); and miscellaneous sermons (ff. 267v-271v).
Other information: Written by Wenceslaus B.A. Cracoviensis. *"Primus liber"* begins with PC 1.103. Heavily glossed. Index on f. 272r-v. Microfilm acquired.
Bibliography: Ladislaus Mezey and Agnes Bolgár, *Codices Latini Medii Aevi Bibliothecae Universitatis Budapestinensis* (Budapest, 1961), pp. 105-10.

CAMBRIDGE, Corpus Christi College, 173

s. viii² (ff. 59-83); 83 leaves; 280 x 212 mm.; written in southern England, probably Kent; later at Christ Church, Canterbury.

Contents: On ff. 57r-82v: E1 (ff. 57-58 dated to s. ix), PC, H2, E2, H1. Bound with "The Parker Chronicle and Laws" (ff. 1-56=s. ix-xi). E2 followed by Pope Damasus' epigram on S. Paul (*Carm.* 7). H1 followed by extract from Augustine, *De Civitate Dei* 18.23.

Other information: PC divided into six books. Last book begins with 5.261. Given by Archbishop Parker (died 1575) to Corpus Christi College. Name of Frithestan, Bishop of Winchester (910-931) found at top of f. 57r. Extensive glossing in Latin and Old English. Used by Huemer (X) for the hymns only (collated for Huemer by Bradshaw). Seen in person. Microfilm acquired.

Bibliography: T.A.M. Bishop, "An Early Example of the Square Minuscule," *TCBS* 4.3 (1966), 246-52; *CLA*, vol. 2 (2nd ed.), p. 3, no. 123; *CSEL*, vol. 10, pp. xlvii and 155; Gneuss, *Hymnar*, pp. 103, 117, and 122; Gneuss, "List," no. 53; Montague Rhodes James, *A Descriptive Catalogue of the Manuscripts in the Library of Corpus Christi College Cambridge,* vol. 1 (Cambridge, 1912), pp. 395-40; Ker, *Cat.,* pp. 57-9; Ker, *Med.,* p. 199; Lapidge, "Latin Texts," p. 113 and n. 78; G.R. Manton, "The Cambridge Manuscript of Sedulius's *Carmen Paschale,*" *Journal of Theological Studies* 40 (1939), 365-70; Meritt, pp. 29-38; Andy Orchard, *The Poetic Art of Aldhelm* = Cambridge Studies in Anglo-Saxon England 8 (Cambridge, 1994), p. 164; R.I. Page, "The Study of Latin Texts in Late Anglo-Saxon England [II]: The Evidence of English Glosses" in *Latin and the Vernacular Languages in Early Medieval Britain: Papers Delivered to the Fifth Annual St. John's House Symposium,* ed. Nicholas Brooks (Leicester, 1982), pp. 141-65; M.B. Parkes, "The Palaeography of the Parker Manuscript of the *Chronicle,* Laws and Sedulius, and Historiography at Winchester in the Late Ninth and Tenth Centuries," *Anglo-Saxon England* 5 (1976), 149-71.

CAMBRIDGE, Trinity College, O. 3. 41 (1213)
s. xii; 71 leaves; 235 x 152 mm.; Reading?

Contents: On ff. 34r-69v: PC (missing ending: 5.283 ff.). Preceded by the epigrams of Prosper (ff. 1r-30v) and Ps.-Prosper, *Poema Coniugis ad Uxorem* (ff. 30v-33r). Devotional notes (s. xii-xiii) follow.

Other information: No book divisions. Microfilm acquired.

Bibliography: Montague Rhodes James, *The Western Manuscripts in the Library of Trinity College, Cambridge: A Descriptive Catalogue* (4 vols.; Cambridge, 1900-4), vol. 3, pp. 222-3; Ker, *Med.*, p. 158 [rejects Reading provenance]; Schenkl, no. 2412.

CAMBRIDGE, University Library, Ee. 6. 38 (1130)
s. xv; 75 leaves; quarto (small).

Contents: On ff. 1r-42v: E1, PC, H1, H2. Subscription, Asterius' epigram, and dedicatory preface to Proba's cento on f. 1r. On ff. 5r-6v: a dialogue between Thomas Skylman and Laurentius Wychygham about Sedulius. Followed by Alexander Neckham, *De Vita Monachorum* (ff. 43r-55r); *"Liber Cleri Delicie"* (ff. 55v-68v); verses on the months of the year (f. 69r); Prudentius, *Dittochaeon* (ff. 70r-73v); Tranquillus Physicus, *De Duodecim Ventis* (f. 74r); and a hymn in honor of the Virgin Mary (f. 75r-v), beginning *Alme parentis merita*, on the feast of circumcision (the first lines of each stanza of H2 are "worked into" this acrostic hymn).

Other information: *"Liber primus"* ends with 1.290. Some glossing at beginning. Seen in person. Microfilm acquired.

Bibliography: *A Catalogue of the Manuscripts Preserved in the Library of the University of Cambridge* (Cambridge, 1856-67), vol. 2 (1857), pp. 274-6.

CAMBRIDGE, University Library, Gg. 5. 35 (1567)
s. xi; 454 leaves; quarto; S. Augustine's, Canterbury.

Contents: On ff. 53r-84r: PC, H1, H2. Asterius' epigram on f. 53r; acrostic poems in praise of Sedulius (in the reverse of Huemer's order) on f. 84r-v. Preceded by Juvencus, *Evangeliorum Libri Quattuor* (ff. 1r-53r). Followed by Arator, *Historia Apostolica* (ff. 84v-126r); the epigrams of Prosper (ff. 126v-146r); Ps.-Prosper, *Poema Coniugis ad Uxorem* (ff. 146r-148r); Prudentius, *Psychomachia* (ff. 148r-164r) and *Dittochaeon* (ff. 164r-167r); Lactantius, *De Ave Phoenice* (ff. 167r-169v); Boethius, *Philosophiae Consolatio* (ff. 170r-209v); Hrabanus Maurus, *De Laudibus Sanctae Crucis* (ff. 209v-262r); and a musical treatise attributed to Hucbald (ff. 263r-276r). In the second and third parts of this composite volume are found: Aldhelm, *De Virginitate* (ff. 280r-327r); Milo Monachus, *De Sobrietate* (ff. 327r-362r); *Versus de XII Lapidibus Pretiosis* (f. 362r-v); alphabetical hymns on All Saints (ff. 362v-363v); Abbo of S. Germain, *Bella Parisiacae Urbis,* Book 3 (ff. 363v-365v); two hymns, beginning *O Dee cunctipotens* and *Omnipotens solus regnas* respectively (ff. 365v-367r); Hucbald of S. Amand, *De*

Laude Calvorum (ff. 367r-369r); *De Filomela* (f. 369r); Eugenius of Toledo, *Carm.* 37 (f. 369r-v); Eusebius, *Aenigmata* (ff. 370r-374v); Tatwine, *Aenigmata* (ff. 374v-377v); Alcuin (Smaragdus), *Dogmata ad Carolum Imperatorem* (ff. 378r-379v); *Disticha ad Eundem Regem* (ff. 379v-381r); *Versus Cuiusdam Scoti de Alfabeto* (ff. 381r-382r); Boniface, *Aenigmata* (ff. 382r-388v); hymn beginning *Sancte sator* (f. 388v); Alcuin's epitaph (ff. 388v-389r); Symphosius, *Aenigmata* (ff. 389r-394r); Aldhelm, *Aenigmata* (ff. 394r-407r); *Disticha Catonis* (ff. 407r-412v); Alcuin, *Praecepta Vivendi* (attr. Columban) (ff. 412v-416r); Bede, *De Die Iudicii* (ff. 416r-418v); riddles attributed to Bede (f. 418v); hymns, prayers, et al. (some in Greek) (ff. 419v-423v); *Bibliotheca Magnifica* (ff. 423v-425r); a medical treatise (ff. 425v-431v); "Cambridge Songs" (ff. 432r-441v); miscellaneous verses (ff. 442r ff.); et al.

Other information: Volume consists of three contemporaneous parts, of which ours is the first (ff. 1-276). PC divided into six books. "*Liber veteris testamenti*" begins with 1.103 and ends with 1.354. PC 1.355-368 = "*De quattuor evangelistis.*" Last book *("quintus")* begins with 5.261. Frequent glosses. Neums in first two lines of H2. Text similar to Huemer's *Cant.* (p. xxiv), but not identical. Seen in person. Microfilm acquired.

Bibliography: Beccaria, pp. 237-9; Karl Breul, *The Cambridge Songs. A Goliard's Song Book of the XIth Century* (Cambridge, 1915); *A Catalogue of the Manuscripts Preserved in the Library of the University of Cambridge* (Cambridge, 1856-67), vol. 3 (1858), pp. 201-5; *CCSL*, vols. 133 and 133A, passim; Glauche, pp. 67-8 and 100; Gneuss, *Hymnar,* pp. 97 and 117; Gneuss, "List," no. 12; Michael W. Herren, *The Hisperica Famina: II. Related Poems. A Critical Edition with English Translation and Philological Commentary* = Studies and Texts 85 (Toronto, 1987), p. 18; Jeudy, "Remi," p. 496; Ker, *Cat.,* pp. 21-2; Ker, *Med,* p. 40; Laistner, p. 127; Lapidge, "Latin Texts," pp. 113-6 and n. 81; McKinlay, pp. 39-41; Nicolò Messina, *Pseudo-Eugenio di Toledo, Speculum per un nobile Visigoto* = Monografias de la Universidad de Santiago de Compostela 85 (Santiago de Compostela, 1984), p. 19; Munk Olsen, vol. 1, pp. 67-8 and vol. 3.1, p. 65; Arthur S. Napier, *Old English Glosses Chiefly Unpublished* (Oxford, 1900), p. 217; Andy Orchard, *The Poetic Art of Aldhelm* = Cambridge Studies in Anglo-Saxon England 8 (Cambridge, 1994), p. 164; A.G. Rigg, "Medieval Latin Poetic Anthologies (I)," *MS* 39 (1977), 282; A.G. Rigg and Gernot R. Wieland, "A Canterbury Classbook of the Mid-eleventh Century (the 'Cambridge Songs' Manuscript)," *Anglo-Saxon England* 4 (1975), 113-30; Sanford, 216; Karl Strecker, *Die Cambridger Lieder* = *MGH*

Scriptores Rerum Germanicarum in Usum Scholarum Separatim Editi 40 (2nd ed.; Berlin, 1955); Gernot R. Wieland, *The Latin Glosses on Arator and Prudentius in Cambridge University Library, Ms Gg.5.35* = Studies and Texts 61 (Toronto, 1983), *passim.*

CHÂLONS-SUR-MARNE, Bibliothèque Municipale, 8 (9)
s. xi-xii; 120 leaves; 241 x 165 mm.; S. Pierre-au-Mont, Châlons.

Contents: On ff. 27r-70r: E1, PC, H1, H2. Prose preface and index for first two books on ff. 30v-31v. Biographical notice *(Sedulius versificus primo laicus in Italia...),* subscription, and Asterius' epigram on f. 70r-v. Preceded by the epigrams of Prosper (ff. 1r-26r) and followed by Arator, *Historia Apostolica* (ff. 71r-119r) and an account of the last minutes of Gregory VII (f. 119v).
Other information: Interlinear and marginal glosses through PC 3. Book division of PC unclear. Microfilm copy acquired.
Bibliography: Cat. gen. octavo, vol. 3, pp. 4-5 [s. xi]; Glauche, p. 124, n. 43 [s. xii]; McKinlay, pp. 6-7; G.L. Perugi, *Aratore: De actibus apostolorum* (Venezia, 1909), 69-70; G. Waitz, "Reise nach dem südlichen Frankreich von August bis November 1837," *Archiv der Gesellschaft für ältere deutsche Geschichtskunde* 7 (1839), 220-1.

CHANTILLY, Musée Condé, 454 (997)
s. xv; 37 leaves; 193 x 135 mm.

Contents: On ff. 1r-37r: PC. Includes PC 3.176-181 (otherwise found only in early printed editions).
Other information: PC not divided into books. Some interlinear and marginal glosses. Manuscript decorated with arms and monogram of Antoine de Chourses and Catherine de Coëtivy. Microfilm acquired.
Bibliography: Catalogue général des manuscrits des bibliothèques publiques de France. Paris. Bibliothèques de l'Institut. Musée Condé à Chantilly (Paris, 1928), p. 98.

CHARLEVILLE-MÉZIÈRES, Bibliothèque Municipale, 103
s. xii-xiii; 345 pages; 228 x 159 mm.; Signy.

Contents: On pp. 1-94: E1, PC, H1, H2 (with doxology). Subscription, Asterius' epigram, prose preface, and biographical notice *(In primo laicus in Italia....)* on pp. 9-10. Acrostic poems in praise of Sedulius (in Huemer's order) on pp. 95-96. Followed by Juvencus, *Evangeliorum*

Libri Quattuor (pp. 96-236) and Arator, *Historia Apostolica* (pp. 237-345).

Other information: PC divided into four books (no break between PC 2 and 3). Some interlinear glossing at beginning of PC 1. Microfilm copy acquired.

Bibliography: Cat. gen. quarto, vol. 5, pp. 594-6; Glauche, pp. 67-8; McKinlay, p. 7.

CHARLOTTESVILLE, University of Virginia, Personal Library of Marvin L. Colker, 9
s. xv; 37 leaves; 200 x 120 mm.; Italy; paper.

Contents: On ff. 1r-36v: PC, H1, H2. On ff. 34v-35v: *Conflictus Veris et Hiemis.*

Other information: PC not divided into books. Purchased in 1944 by Professor Colker from Maggs.

Bibliography: Census Suppl., p. 517.

DIJON, Bibliothèque Municipale, 497 (288)
s. xiii$^{ex.}$; 267 leaves; 447 x 340 mm.; written in northern France; prov. Notre-Dame, Cîteaux.

Contents: On ff. 251v-257r: PC, H1 (1-88). Preceded by Statius, *Thebaid, Achilleid* (ff. 2r-36v); Virgil, *Eclogues, Georgics, Aeneid* (ff. 36v-78v); Horace, *Odes, Ars Poetica, Epodes, Carmen Saeculare, Epistles, Sermones* (ff. 78v-103v); Lucan, *Bellum Civile* (ff. 104r-129v); Persius, *Satires* (ff. 129v-132r); Juvenal, *Satires* (ff. 132r-144r); Ovid, *Fasti* (ff. 144r-159r); miscellaneous verses including Ps.-Priscian, *De Sideribus* (f. 159v); Ovid, *Metamorphoses, Amores, Tristia, Epistulae ex Ponto, Ibis, Remedia Amoris, Ars Amatoria, Heroides* (ff. 160r-244r); Ps.-Ovid, *De Nuce, De Lupo, De Pulice* (ff. 244r-245r); the fables of Avianus (ff. 245v-247v); *Disticha Catonis* (ff. 247v-248v); and *Ilias Latina* (ff. 248v-251v). Followed by the epigrams of Prosper (ff. 257r-261r); Prudentius, *Psychomachia* (to line 765) (ff. 261r-263v); and Donatus, *Ars Minor* (ff. 264r-267r).

Other information: PC divided into three or four books ("*Incipit expositio*" at beginning of second book; no division between PC 3 and 4). Written in triple columns on each page. Microfiche acquired.

Bibliography: J. Boussard, "Le Classement des manuscrits de la Thébaïde de Stace," *REL* 30 (1952), 228; *Cat. gen. quarto,* vol. 5, pp. 117-23; Glauche, p. 127, n. 53; Guaglianone, p. xix; Jeudy & Riou, pp.

503-10; E.J. Kenney, "The Manuscript Tradition of Ovid's *Amores, Ars Amatoria* and *Remedia Amoris,*" *CQ* (n.s.) 12 (1962), 3; Antonio La Penna, *Publi Ovidi Nasonis Ibis. Prolegomeni, testo, apparato critico e comm.* = Biblioteca di studi superiori 34. Filiologia latina (Firenze, 1957), pp. xcv-xcvi; Domenico Lassandro, "Note sugli Epigrammi di Prospero d'Aquitania," *Vetera Christianorum* 8 (1971), 211-24; Friedrich Walter Lenz, "Bemerkungen zu dem pseudo-ovidischen Gedicht *De Lupo,*" *Orpheus* 10 (1963), 23; idem, *"De Pulice Libellus,"* *Maia* (n.s.) 14 (1962), 306; idem, "Ovids *Remedia* und der *Codex Iureti,*" *SIFC* (n.s.) 31 (1959), 169-74; idem, *P. Ovidi Nasonis Remedia Amoris, Medicamina Faciei*, in *Corpus Scriptorum Latinorum Paravianum* (Torino, 1965), p. xxxviii; Franco Munari, "Sugli *Amores* di Ovidio," *SIFC* (n.s.) 23 (1949), 148; idem, *Catalogue of the Manuscripts of Ovid's Metamorphoses* = University of London, Institute of Classical Studies, Bulletin Supplement 4 (London, 1957), p. 19; H. Omont, *Description du corpus poetarum de Dijon* (Paris, 1883), pp. 39-49; Piacentini, p. 22; Reynolds, pp. 193, 260, 265, and 274; Sanford, 231; M. Scaffai, "Tradizione manoscritta dell'*Ilias latina*" in *In verbis verum amare. Miscellanea dell'Istituto di Filologia Latina e Medioevale dell'Università di Bologna*, ed. Paulo Serra Zanetti (Firenze, 1980), pp. 232-4.

DUBLIN, Trinity College Library, 2100
s. xv-xvi; 254 leaves; 211 x 142 mm. (ff. 85-122); written in Italy; paper.

Contents: On ff. 85r-122v (s. xv^2): PC, H1, H2 (beginning *O [sic] solis ortus cardine)*. Preceded by Ludolph of Saxony, *Vita Christi* (ff. 1r-78r); meditations, prayers, and hymns (ff. 78r-84v); and followed by *Quaedam Notabilia de Passione Christi* (ff. 123r-135v); Giulio Camillo (Delminio), *Theologica Disciplina* (ff. 137r-174v); Theobaldus' *Physiologus* (ff. 177r-192v); Prudentius, *Dittochaeon* (ff. 193v-197r); *Liber Quinque Clavium Sapientiae* (ff. 197r-204r); and Robertus de Tumbalena, *In Cantica Canticorum* (ff. 207r-252v).
Other information: One of about a thousand codices belonging to Matteo Luigi Canonici (1727-1805) of Venezia, bought by the Rev. Walter Sneyd (1809-88). PC not divided into books. Microfilm acquired.
Bibliography: Bursill-Hall, p. 60; idem, "Johannes de Garlandia-Forgotten Grammarian and the Manuscript Tradition," *Historiographica Linguistica* 3 (1976), 159 and 174; Marvin L. Colker, *Trinity College*

Library Dublin: Descriptive Catalogue of the Medieval and Renaissance Latin Manuscripts (Dublin, 1991), vol. 2, pp. 1272-9; Eugenio Garin, *La cultura filosofica del rinascimento italiano* (Firenze, 1961), p. 154.

EDINBURGH, National Library of Scotland, Adv. 18. 4. 7
s. xv; 42 leaves; 250 x 160 mm.; written in Italy, possibly Firenze.

Contents: On ff. 1r-40r: PC, H1, H2. Acrostic poems in praise of Sedulius (in the reverse of Huemer's order) on ff. 40v-41r. Also includes (on f. 41r) a short epigram on Sedulius (10 lines), beginning *Qualiter affixus ligno iam Christus in alto* (as in Vat. Ottob. Lat. 36).
Other information: PC divided into six books (1+5); *"liber primus"* begins with 1.103 and the last book *("liber quintus et ultimus")* begins with 5.261. PC is entitled *De Actibus Prophetarum et Toto Christi Salvatoris Cursu* (as in Vat. Ottob. Lat. 36 and an untraced manuscript of the 15th century, Coislin, Lat. 203 (S. Germain-des-Prés MS. 1456). Little glossing. Microfilm acquired.
Bibliography: Ian C. Cunningham, "Latin Classical Manuscripts in the National Library of Scotland," *Scriptorium* 27 (1973), 75; Schenkl, no. 3007; Elspeth D. Yeo and Ian C. Cunningham, *Summary Catalogue of the Advocates' Manuscripts, National Library of Scotland* (Edinburgh, 1971), p. 105.

EDINBURGH, National Library of Scotland, Adv. 18. 7. 7
s. x$^{ex.}$; 41 leaves; 200 x 125 mm.; Thorney.

Contents: On ff. 1v-40v: E1, PC, H1, H2. Subscription, Asterius' epigram, and biographical notice *(Sedulius versificus primo....)* on f. 1r. Acrostic poems in praise of Sedulius (in the reverse of Huemer's order); verses on Sedulius beginning *Qualiter adfixus ligno iam Christus in alto* (see above); and *Anth. Lat.* 392 on ff. 40v-41v.
Other information: PC divided into five books (1+4). Contains glosses in Latin and Old English. In library of Henry Savile of Banke (1568-1617). Used for Edinburgh edition of 1701. Microfilm acquired.
Bibliography: Cunningham, "Latin Classical Manuscripts," same as above, 87-8; Glauche, p. 100; Gneuss, "List," no. 253; Ker, *Cat.,* p. 150; N.R. Ker, "A Palimpsest in the National Library of Scotland. Early Fragments of Augustine's *De Trinitate,* the *Passio S. Laurentii* and Other Texts," *Edinburgh Bibliographical Society Transactions* 3 (1956), 171-8; Lapidge, "Latin Texts," p. 114 and n. 83; Meritt, pp. 39-42; Andy Orchard, *The Poetic Art of Aldhelm* = Cambridge Studies in

Anglo-Saxon England 8 (Cambridge, 1994), p. 164; Schenkl, no. 3033; A. Vernet, "Notice et extraits d'un manuscrit d'Édimbourg," *BECh* 107 (1948), 33-51; Andrew G. Watson, *The Manuscripts of Henry Savile of Banke* (London, 1969), p. 18; Yeo and Cunningham, *Summary Catalogue,* same as above, p. 100.

ÉPINAL, Bibliothèque Municipale, 74 (161)

s. ix$^{2/3}$; 139 leaves; 255 x 195 mm.; written in eastern France; owned by priory at S.-Mont; later at Moyenmoutier.

Contents: On ff. 3r-73r: E1, PC, H1, H2 (with doxology), E2, PO (after f. 58 missing a number of original leaves = Huemer's page 215, line 5 to page 262, line 17). Biographical notice *(Sedulius versificus primo....* [attr. Jerome]) and acrostic poems in praise of Sedulius (in Huemer's order) on f. 37r-v. Between the hymns (on ff. 39v-40r): Ps.-Cato, *Monosticha* (1-14 and 17-35). Subscription and Asterius' epigram on f. 73v. Followed by poem beginning *Has mea mens fidei iures sanctique timoris*; Juvencus, *Evangeliorum Libri Quattuor* (up to 3.687) (ff. 74r-106v); Adrevaldus of Fleury, *De Benedictionibus Patriarcharum* (ff. 107r-119r); *Disticha Catonis* (ff. 119r-125v); Eugenius of Toledo, *Carm.* 6, 2, 7 (ff. 125v-126v); Alcuin, *Carm.* 62 (ff. 126v-130v); and *Sibylla Theodola* (ff. 130v-138v). On f. 2v: "*commemorationes fratrum.*"

Other information: PC divided into three (see Jeudy & Riou, p. 614, n. 4), or more likely, four books (no break between PC 3 and 4). Many interlinear and marginal glosses. PO divided into five books. Includes indices. Seen in person. Microfilm acquired.

Bibliography: Bernhard Bischoff, "*Sibylla Theodola,* eine Beschreibung des Paradieses (Achtes Jahrhundert?)" in *Anecdota Novissima. Texte des vierten bis sechzehnten Jahrhunderts* = Quellen und Untersuchungen zur lateinischen Philologie des Mittelalters 7 (Stuttgart, 1984), pp. 57-79, esp. p. 61; *Cat. gen. quarto,* vol. 3, p. 430 [s. x]; Huemer, *De Sedulii,* p. 38; Jeudy & Riou, pp. 614-7; Munk Olsen, vol. 1, p. 68.

ÉVREUX, Bibliothèque Municipale, 43

s. xi; 61 leaves; 195 x 150 mm.; Lyre.

Contents: On ff. 1v-59r: E1, PC, H1, H2. Dedicatory preface to Proba's cento and biographical notice *(Incipit ars....)* on f. 1r-v.

Other information: PC divided into six books. "*Liber Sedulii de miraculis veteris testamenti*" begins with PC 1.103; final book begins

with 5.261.   PC 1.355-68 = *"Prologus quattuor evangelistarum."*
Includes indices. Seen in person. Microfiche acquired.
Bibliography: Cat. gen. octavo, vol. 2, pp. 426-7 [s. ix]; Geneviève
Nortier, *Les Bibliothèques médiévales des abbayes bénédictines de
Normandie* (Caen, 1966), pp. 124 and 140.

FIRENZE, Biblioteca Medicea Laurenziana, Conv. Soppr. 22
s. xv; 46 leaves (last two blank); 198 x 133 mm.; Badia Fiorentina.

Contents: On ff. 1r-44r: PC, H1. *Titulus* for the latter: *incipit
paracterium carmen, id est repercussorium, eo quod unus uni repercu-
tiatur ad alterum.*
Other information: No glossing. PC divided into four continuously
numbered books (no division between PC 3 and 4). Seen in person.
Bibliography: Franciscus de Furia, *Catalogus Codicum Manuscriptorum
Graecorum, Latinorum, Italicorum, Qui a Saeculo XVIII Exeunte usque
ad Annum MDCCCXLVI Saeculi Insequentis in Bibliothecam Mediceam
Laurentianam Translati Sunt, Supplementum Alterum ad Catalogum,* vol.
1, ff. 967r-968r.

FIRENZE, Biblioteca Medicea Laurenziana, Conv. Soppr. 252
s. xiv; 95 leaves; 276 x 168 mm.; S. Maria Novella.

Contents: On ff. 1r-33r: E1, H2, PC, H1. After H2: *qui nos in recto
faciat persistere calle ut sibi servitium valeamus reddere dignum.* On ff.
3v-4r: subscription; scribal dedication *(Deo et Domino nostro Iesu
Christo, redemptori humani generis, sit infinita laus, qui me peccatorem,
famulum suum, evangelicam doctrinam quam beatus Sedulius per versus
ordinavit scribendo finire permisit, qui vivit et regnat cum Deo Patre in
unitate Spiritus Sancti, Deus per infinita saecula saeculorum, Amen.);*
and *accessus.* Followed by Prosper's epigrams (ff. 34r-55r); Arator,
Historia Apostolica (ff. 55v-92v); fragment of grammar (third declen-
sion) (ff. 93r-95v). On f. 33v: beginning of alphabetical list of Biblical
names (Adam-Asael).
Other information: PC divided into five books (1+4). Index for Book
2. Some glossing. Seen in person.
Bibliography: Catalogus Codicum, same as above, vol. 2, ff. 453r-455r.

FIRENZE, Biblioteca Medicea Laurenziana, Conv. Soppr. 518
s. xv; 45 leaves (last two blank); 214 x 144 mm.; Camaldoli.

Contents: On ff. 1r-43v: PC, H1. Same title for H1 as in Conv. Soppr. 22 (above).
Other information: PC divided into four books (no division between PC 3 and 4). *"Liber secundus"* begins with PC 1.334. Little glossing. Seen in person.
Bibliography: *Catalogus Codicum,* same as above, vol. 3, f. 244r.

FIRENZE, Biblioteca Medicea Laurenziana, Plut. 23. 15
s. xv (1484-9); 320 leaves; 316 x 200 mm.; written in Firenze.

Contents: On ff. 231r-272v: E1, H2, PC, H1. Subscription, *accessus,* et al. on ff. 235v-236v (after H2). Includes biographical notice *(Denique ipse Sedulius primum laicus in Italia philologium didicit....)* on f. 236r. At end of H2 (f. 235v): *qui nos in recto faciat persistere calle ut sibi servitium valeamus reddere dignum.* Preceded by works of Prudentius (ff. 1r-160v); Juvencus, *Evangeliorum Libri Quattuor* (ff. 161r-219r); and Proba's cento (ff. 219v-231v). Followed by Arator, *Historia Apostolica* (ff. 273r-320r).
Other information: PC divided into five books (1+4). Index for second book on ff. 243v-244r. Used by Huemer (l2). Seen in person. Microfilm acquired.
Bibliography: Angelus Maria Bandinius, *Catalogus Codicum Latinorum Bibliothecae Mediceae Laurentianae* (Firenze, 1774-78), vol. 1, pp. 720-4; Huemer, *De Sedulii,* pp. 5, 15, 21, 32-33, 38-9, 41, 43, and 47.

FIRENZE, Biblioteca Medicea Laurenziana, Plut. 24, Sin. 12
s. xi-xii; 91 leaves; 185 x 135 mm.; S. Croce.

Contents: On ff. 1r-47v (s. xi): PC, H1, H2, E1 (initial words only). Epigram beginning *Haec tua perpetuae* between the hymns. Followed by Statius, *Achilleid* (incomplete) (ff. 49r-69v) and Claudian, *De Raptu Proserpinae* (ff. 70r-91v).
Other information: PC divided into four books (no division between PC 3 and 4). Some glossing. Used by Huemer (l). Seen in person. Microfilm acquired.
Bibliography: Bandinius, same as above, vol. 4, p. 178; *CSEL,* vol. 10, p. xxiii; Huemer, *De Sedulii,* pp. 36 and 46; *PL,* vol. 19, col. 474.

FIRENZE, Biblioteca Nazionale Centrale, Magl. VII. 1133 (56)
s. xvi; 48 leaves; 156 x 116 mm.

Contents: On ff. 1r-47r: PC (title: *"Sedulius de mysteriis Iesu Christi"*).

Other information: On f. 2r (written in a more recent hand): *"Monasterii angelorum Petrus Candidus."* Once part of the Strozzi collection. PC divided into five books (no division between PC 3 and 4; *"liber quintus"* begins with PC 5.315). Microfilm acquired.

Bibliography: Aloysius Galante, "Index Codicum Classicorum Latinorum Qui Florentiae in Bybliotheca Magliabechiana Adservantur," *SIFC* 15 (1907), 132.

FIRENZE, Biblioteca Nazionale Centrale, Magl. VII. 1135 (58)
s. xv; 91 leaves; 206 x 142 mm.; paper.

Contents: On ff. 1r-35r: PC, H1. Followed (on ff. 36r ff.) by epistles, et al., of Marsilio Ficino (written in another hand).

Other information: Once part of the Strozzi collection. PC divided into five books. Microfilm acquired.

Bibliography: Galante, "Index," same as above, 133; Kristeller, *Iter,* vol. 1, p. 131.

FREIBURG (BREISGAU), Universitätsbibliothek, 103
s. xv (c. 1478-81); 86 leaves; 210 x 145 mm.; paper.

Contents: On ff. 4v-44v: E1, PC (5.366-376 missing on f. 43r but added on f. 44v). Followed by a sequence on S. Laurence by Adam of S. Victor (f. 46r-v).

Other information: Some leaves blank, e.g., ff. 1r-3v and ff. 47r-86v. PC divided into four books (no original division between PC 3 and 4). Numerous interlinear glosses and marginalia in the scribe's hand. Microfilm acquired.

Bibliography: Winfried Hagenmaier, *Die lateinischen mittelalterlichen Handschriften der Universitätsbibliothek Freiburg im Breisgau (Hss. 1-230),* in *Kataloge der Universitätsbibliothek Freiburg im Breisgau: Die Handschriften der Universitätsbibliothek und anderer öffentlicher Sammlungen in Freiburg und Umgebung,* vol. 1.1 (Wiesbaden, 1974), pp. 86-7.

FREIBURG (BREISGAU), Universitätsbibliothek, 370
s. xv[1]; 30 leaves; 220 x 155 mm.; written in Italy.

Contents: On ff. 1r-29v: PC, H1, H2. Missing PC 2.249 and 5.93,

318-319, 354-355. Also missing H1.39 and H2.85-88.

Other information: PC not divided into books. Contains many eccentric readings. Microfilm acquired.

Bibliography: Hagenmaier, same as above, vol. 3 (1980), pp. 106-7.

GENT, Bibliotheek der Rijksuniversiteit, 17
s. xv/xvi; 283 leaves; 410 x 290 mm.; S. Baafsabdij, Gent.

Contents: On ff. 1r-12v: PC, H1. Followed by Juvencus, *Evangeliorum Libri Quattuor* (ff. 13r-34r); John Gerson, *Monotessaron* (ff. 35r-87r); and an anonymous commentary on the same (ff. 90r-273v). Lives of saints, et al., on ff. 273v-283r.

Other information: PC divided into four books (no division between PC 1 and 2; 1.1-102 = *"Praefatio"*). Owned by Raphael de Marcatellis (abbot of S. Baafsabdij). Seen in person. Microfilm acquired.

Bibliography: Albert Derolez, "L'*Editio Mercatelliana* du *Monotessaron* de Gerson" in *Hommages à André Boutemy* = Collection Latomus 145 (Bruxelles, 1976), pp. 43-54; idem, *Inventaris van de Handschriften in de Universiteitsbibliotheek te Gent* (Gent, 1977), p. 2; idem, *The Library of Raphael de Marcatellis* (Gent, 1979), pp. 218-27; Baron Jules de Saint-Genois, *Catalogue méthodique et raisonné des manuscrits de la Bibliothèque de la Ville et de l'Université de Gand* (Gent, 1849-52), pp. 340-1.

GENT, Bibliotheek der Rijksuniversiteit, 246
s. xi-xii; 98 leaves; 252 x 170 mm.; S. Pietersabdij, Gent.

Contents: On ff. 52v-95r: E1, PC, H2, H1. Biographical notice *(Sedulius primo laicus in Italia....)* on f. 52r; prose preface on f. 55v; acrostic poems (in the reverse of Huemer's order) on f. 95r-v. Preceded by Aldhelm, *De Virginitate* on the first 51 leaves. Originally followed by Juvencus (see f. 95v at bottom). One back fly leaf (f. 96) is from a liturgical manuscript of the tenth century, while two others (ff. 97-98), written in half-uncial (s. vi-vii), contain Jerome, *Epist.* 147 (frag.).

Other information: PC divided into five books (1+4). Indices at beginning of PC 1 and 2. PC 1.355-368 = *"Prologus de quattuor evangelistis."* On f. 1r there is a note by Prof. J.H. Bormans of Liège (written in 1839):

Hic codex a me cum Lovaniensi et duobus Bruxellens. et Arntzeniana Sedulii edit. collatus, nonnullas bonas lectiones, easque singulares obtulit, procul dubio daturus plures, nisi passim malam correctoris manum expertus esset. Antiquior est Bruxellensibus, solo Lovaniensi recentior, sed is geminam ingentem lacunam habet; alterum ex Bruxellensi et Lovaniensem qui olim Leodiensis fuerunt monasterii Sancti Jacobi, et hunc Gandavensem Theod. Pulmannus iam contulerat, ineunte saeculo XVI, plurima tamen praeterierat. Eius manum mihi agnoscere visus sum, fol. 93 verso, in duabus vocibus suppletis.

Interlinear glossing. Seen in person. Microfilm acquired.
Bibliography: *CLA,* vol. 10, p. 34, no. 1556; Derolez, same as above, p. 21; Joseph van den Gheyn, "Les Feuillets de garde du manuscrit no. 246 de la Bibliothèque de l'Université de Gand," *Revue des bibliothèques et archives de Belgique* 5 (1907), 415-9; Saint-Genois, same as above, pp. 250-1.

GENT, Bibliotheek der Rijksuniversiteit, 615
s. xii; 178 pages; 12°; Parkabdij, Gent.

Contents: On pp. 61-127: PC, H1. Acrostic poem in praise of Sedulius (Bellesarius') on p. 127. Preceded by epigrams of Prosper (pp. 1-61) and followed by Prudentius, *Psychomachia* (pp. 128-164); *"Cato Novus"* (pp. 165-176); and hymn beginning *Alma serena pia* (pp. 176-178).
Other information: PC not divided into books. Seen in person. Microfilm acquired.
Bibliography: Derolez, same as above, p. 52; Saint-Genois, same as above, pp. 454-5.

GLASGOW, University Library, Hunterian T. 2. 15 (57)
s. x-xi; 26 leaves (originally 42); 298 x 197 mm.; S. Adalbert, Egmond.

Contents: On ff. 1v-26r: E1, PC (missing 16 original leaves after f. 8 [=1.198 to 4.12]), H1, H2. Subscription, Asterius' epigram, and biographical notice *(Sedulius versificus primo laicus....)* on f. 4v. Acrostic poem in praise of Sedulius (Bellesarius') on f. 25r-v. Following H2 is hymn beginning *Salve festa dies.*
Other information: PC divided into five books. Interlinear and marginal glossing. Microfilm acquired.
Bibliography: Glauche, p. 97 [refers to the manuscript as 62, confusing its catalogue number with its page number in the catalogue of Young and

Aitken]; John Young and P. Henderson Aitken, *A Catalogue of the Manuscripts in the Library of the Hunterian Museum in the University of Glasgow* (Glasgow, 1908), pp. 62-3.

GOTHA, Forschungs- und Landesbibliothek, MBR. I. 75
s. viii; 122 leaves; 240 x 160 mm.; written in southern England or at an Anglo-Saxon continental center; later at Murbach.

Contents: On ff. 1v-25r: PC (1.164-302; 2.42-207 [missing original leaves after f. 3v and f. 6v]; 4.138 to 5.438), H2 (followed by doxology in another hand), H1 (ff. 23v-25r=s. ix$^{in.}$). Biographical notice *(Sedulius versificus primo laicus....)* on f. 20r. Acrostic poem in praise of Sedulius (Bellesarius') on f. 23r (s. ix$^{in.}$). On ff. 20v-22v: three rhythmical poems from the circle of Alcuin: *De Trinitate et de Incarnatione Christi; Deprecatio;* and verses against heretics (Arius and Sabellius, Manichaeus and Photinus, Nestorius and Eutyches). On f. 23r: hymn (frag.) beginning *Hymnum dicat turba fratrum.* Followed by Aldhelm, *De Virginitate* (ff. 25r-69r); *De Ventis* (f. 69v); Victorius, *Cursus Paschalis* (ff. 70r-106r); Dionysius Exiguus, *Codex Canonum Ecclesiasticorum* (ff. 106v-122v): *Canones Apostolorum* (ff. 107r-113v); *Canones Concilii Nicaeni* (ff. 113v-119r); and *Canones Concilii Ancyrani* (incomplete) (ff. 119v-122v).
Other information: Volume made up of three parts (ff. 1-22 [s. viii$^{ex.}$]; 23-69 [s. viii]; and 70-122 [s. viii$^{in.}$]). PC divided into three (or four) books. Includes index for final book on ff. 9v-10v. Some glossing. Bought by Duke Ernest II of Gotha-Altenburg from J.B. Maugérard in 1795. Used by Huemer (Γ), whose description of the Sedulian contents of the manuscript is quite misleading. Photostatic copy acquired.
Bibliography: Bischoff, "FHH," 308; *CLA*, vol. 8, p. 51, no. 1206; *CSEL*, vol. 10, pp. vii-viii; Bruno Krusch, "Über eine Handschrift des Victurius," *Neues Archiv* 9 (1884), 271-81; Kurz, 266; G.R. Manton, "The Cambridge Manuscript of Sedulius's *Carmen Paschale,*" *Journal of Theological Studies* 40 (1939), 366, n. 4; Wilhelm Meyer, "Drei Gothaer Rhythmen aus dem Kreise des Alkuin," *NKGWG* 5 (1916), 644-72; Renate Schipke, *Die Maugérard-Handschriften der Forschungsbibliothek Gotha* = Veröffentlichungen der Forschungsbibliothek Gotha 15 (Gotha, 1972), pp. 51-2; Ernst Heinrich Zimmermann, *Vorkarolingische Miniaturen* (Berlin, 1919 ff.), *Textbd.,* pp. 79-80, 214 and *Tafelbd.,* pp. 2, 129-30.

GRAZ, Universitätsbibliothek, 1585 (42/7)

s. xii; 39 leaves; 150 x 100 mm.; Seckau.

Contents: On ff. 1r-39r: E1, PC, H1 (missing first 13 lines), H2 (ff. 35v-36r blank). Biographical notice *(Sedulius primo in Italia didicit philosophiam...),* subscription (beginning *Hoc autem opus),* and Asterius' epigram on f. 3v. Verse description of four evangelists (anonymous preface to Juvencus, *Evangeliorum Libri Quattuor)* and dedicatory preface to Proba's cento (beginning *Romulidum lector)* on f. 35r.

Other information: No book division for PC originally; five-book format (continuously numbered) added by second hand in margins. Used by Huemer (g). Collated for Huemer by M. Petschenig. Curious scribal note on bottom of f. 3v: *Non laudo qui vilem reddit odorem.* Microfilm acquired.

Bibliography: CSEL, vol. 10, p. xxiii; Anton Kern, *Die Handschriften der Universitätsbibliothek Graz, Handschriftenverzeichnisse österreichischer Bibliotheken,* vol. 2 (Wien, 1956), p. 365.

GRENOBLE, Bibliothèque Municipale, 859
s. xii; 153 leaves; 348 x 258 mm.; Chartreux.

Contents: On ff. 28r-44v: E1, PC, H1, H2. Biographical notice *(Sedulius primo laicus....)* on f. 44v. Preceded by Juvencus, *Evangeliorum Libri Quattuor* (ff. 2r ff.). Followed by Arator, *Historia Apostolica* (ff. 44v-63r); Prudentius, *Psychomachia, Apotheosis, Hamartigenia, Contra Symmachum, Peristephanon, Cathemerinon, Dittochaeon* (ff. 63r-132r); and Alcimus Avitus, *De Spiritalis Historiae Gestis* (ff. 132 ff.), with the sixth book, *"De Virginitate,"* incomplete.

Other information: Manuscript completed by Grenoble, Bibliothèque Municipale, 246 (34 leaves). PC divided into four books (no break between PC 4 and 5). Double columns. Microfiche acquired.

Bibliography: Cat. gen. octavo, vol. 7, p. 256; Glauche, p. 124; McKinlay, p. 9; G.L. Perugi, *Aratore: De actibus apostolorum* (Venezia, 1909), pp. 67-8.

HANNOVER, Niedersächsische Landesbibliothek, IV 506a
s. xiv; 24 leaves; 260 x 190 mm.

Contents: On ff. 11r-24v: E1, PC, H1. Preceded by a treatise on the virtues and vices (ff. 1r-4r) and Prudentius, *Psychomachia* (ff. 4r-10r).

Other information: PC divided into four continuously numbered books (second book begins with PC 1.351; no break between PC 3 and 4).

Microfilm acquired.

Bibliography: Eduard Bodemann, *Die Handschriften der königlichen öffentlichen Bibliothek zu Hannover* (Hannover, 1867), pp. 621-2; Helmar Härtel and Felix Ekowski, *Handschriften der Niedersächsischen Landesbibliothek Hannover. Zweiter Teil: Ms I 176a-Ms Noviss. 64 =* Mittelalterliche Handschriften in Niedersachsen 6 (Wiesbaden, 1982), p. 148.

HOLKHAM HALL (Norfolk), Library of the Earls of Leicester (now of Viscount Coke), 419

s. xi; octavo; S. Giovanni in Viridario, Padova.

Contents: E1, PC. Also includes poem beginning *Haec tua perpetuae;* subscription; and *accessus* beginning *In capite uniuscuiusque libri octo periochae.*

Other information: Given by Pietro da Montagnana to the Canons of S. Giovanni in 1478. PC divided into three books. Includes glosses (Remigius' commentary?).

Bibliography: Seymour De Ricci, *A Handlist of Manuscripts in the Library of the Earl of Leicester at Holkham Hall =* Supplements to the Bibliographical Society's Transactions 7 (Oxford, 1932), p. 36; Esposito, 169; Jeudy, "Remi," p. 497; Kristeller, *Iter,* vol. 4, p. 44; Schenkl, no. 3586.

KARLSRUHE, Badische Landesbibliothek, Aug. 217

s. ix$^{ex.}$ and x; 169 leaves; 241 x 167 mm.; Reichenau.

Contents: On ff. 40r-67v: E1, PC, H1, H2. Subscription and Asterius' epigram on ff. 41v-42r. Acrostic poems in praise of Sedulius (in Huemer's order) on ff. 43v-44r. Biographical notice *(Sedulius versificus primo laicus....)* on f. 44r (followed by Jerome's entry on Juvencus in *De Viris Inlustribus).* Preceded by Juvencus, *Evangeliorum Libri Quattuor* (ff. 1r-40r). On ff. 125v-157v: another text of PC. Preceded by Juvencus, *Evangeliorum Libri Quattuor* (ff. 68r-125v) and followed by Proba's cento, with dedicatory preface *(Romuli ductor....)* (ff. 158r-169v).

Other information: Volume consists of two manuscripts joined together. First text of PC divided into five books (1+4). Glosses and scholia (some in Old High German). Index on ff. 42r-43v. Used by Huemer (K). Second text of PC divided into five continuously numbered books (changed to three-book format by another hand). Includes glosses (some

in Old High German). Interesting sketch on f. 67v. Used by Huemer
(L). Microfilm acquired.
Bibliography: *CSEL,* vol. 10, pp. xi-xii; Alfred Holder, *Die Reich-
enauer Handschriften I: Die Pergamenthandschriften* (rev. ed.; Wies-
baden, 1970), vol. 5 in *Die Handschriften der Badischen Hof- und
Landesbibliothek in Karlsruhe* (12 vols.; Karlsruhe, 1891-1987), pp. 493-
8; Kurz, 266 ff.; Steinmeyer & Sievers, vol. 2, pp. 618, 620-1 and vol.
4, p. 407.

KÖLN, Historisches Archiv der Stadt, W 350 (XIII 4)
s. xv (c. 1480-90); 36 leaves; 205 x 140 mm.; paper.

Contents: On ff. 1r-35v: PC, H1.
Other information: PC divided into four books (no division between PC
1 and 2). PC 1.1-102 = *"Praefatio;"* first book begins with 1.103. Title
of H1: *Repetitio libri et conclusio.* Microfilm acquired.
Bibliography: Joachim Vennebusch, *Die theologischen Handschriften
des Stadtarchivs Köln, Teil 4. Handschriften der Sammlung Wallraf =
Mitteilungen aus dem Stadtarchiv von Köln 4* (Köln-Wien, 1986), p.
173.

KÖLN, Historisches Archiv der Stadt, W 382
s. xvi (c. 1500); 47 leaves; 210 x 145 mm.; paper.

Contents: On ff. 1r-30r: PC (missing 4.2 ff.). Followed by miscella-
neous excerpts on ff. 31v-32r: Ovid, *Ars Amatoria* 3.59-60; Ps.-
Ausonius, *Septem Sapientium Sententiae* 7; Aulus Gellius, *Noctes Atticae*
(12.11); the prefatory letter of Georg Witzel to *Sylvula* (printed in Mainz
in 1544) (ff. 32v-34r); *Oiketes, sive de Officio Famulorum,* by Gilbert
Cousin (printed in Paris, 1535) (ff. 34v-41r); and 17 distichs on the
relics of S. Anna in Düren (f. 47v).
Other information: Second part of volume (ff. 31v ff.) inserted later (s.
xvi^2). Leaves 25-47 (ff. 41v-47r blank) separated in the 19th century and
only rejoined in 1985. Owned by Joannes Remagensis in 1544 (f. 30v).
Text of PC apparently follows a five-book format (1+4). Marginal and
interlinear glosses up to PC 1.153. Microfilm acquired.
Bibliography: Vennebusch, *Die theologischen Handschriften,* same as
above, p. 184.

KRAKÓW, Biblioteka Jagiellońska, 1571 (DD 7. 5)
s. xiv^{ex}.; 223 leaves; 285 x 204 mm.; Praha; paper.

Contents: On ff. 102v-113v: PC, H1. Commentary on PC (breaks off at end of page in the pericope 5.182-195) on ff. 178r-223v. PC preceded by Prudentius, *Psychomachia* (ff. 1r-8r); *Liber Decem Praeceptorum* (ff. 8r-14r); Matthew of Vendôme, *Tobias* (ff. 14v-28v); Alan of Lille, *Liber Parabolarum* (ff. 28v-32v); the epigrams of Prosper (ff. 84v-102r); et al. Followed by Arator, *Historia Apostolica* (ff. 113v-126v) and *Summa de Redemptione Animarum S. Patrum* (ff. 128r-177r).
Other information: Manuscript written by different hands, many of them belonging to students at the university of Praha. PC apparently divided into five books. Written in double columns and heavily glossed with marginal notation up to 4.94. Microfilm acquired.
Bibliography: McKinlay, pp. 59-60; Munari, pp. 57-8; Władysław Wisłocki, *Catalogus Codicum Manuscriptorum Bibliothecae Universitatis Jagellonicae Cracoviensis* (Kraków, 1877-81), vol. 1, pp. 381-2.

KRAKÓW, Biblioteka Jagiellońska, 1607 (DD 6. 16)
s. xv (1434-7); 752 and 143 pages; paper.

Contents: On pp. 1-397: *"Sedulius De Opere Pascali."* Followed by Prudentius, *Dittochaeon* (pp. 411-460); *Speculum Humanae Salvationis* (pp. 462-545); *Physiologus* (pp. 655-708); *Summa Sententiarum Petri Lombardi* (pp. 709-739); *Aesopus* (pp. 1-95); et al. For a fuller description of the contents, see Wisłocki, below.
Other information: Colophon reads as follows:

> Explicit Sedulius per manus cuiusdam Nicolaii, presbiteri de Slupnikii, et est finitus tunc temporis, cum idem fuit vicarius in Gostcza, et finivit ipsum die Mercurii post Epiphaniam, quae fuit dominico die sub anno nativitatis Domini 1437. Quidquid conspexi in hoc libro, quod intellexi, multum delectabar scribendoque speculabar; in hoc libro toto laus sit et gloria Christo.

Bibliography: Wisłocki, same as above, vol. 1, pp. 388-9.

LEIDEN, Bibliotheek der Rijksuniversiteit, B.P.L. 174
s. xii; 20 leaves; 175 x 80 mm.

Contents: On ff. 1r-20r: E1, PC, H1. Biographical notice (beginning *Sedulius primo in Italia*) and notes on first lines of PC (in another hand) on f. 20r.
Other information: PC divided into five continuously numbered books.

Interlinear and marginal glossing. Microfilm acquired.
Bibliography: Arntzenius, *praef.* p. 19; *Bibliotheca Universitatis Leidensis. Codices Manuscripti* (multi-volume; Leiden, 1910-75), *Codices Bibliothecae Publicae Latini III* (1912), p. 87.

LEIDEN, Bibliotheek der Rijksuniversiteit, B.P.L. 175
s. xiii; 42 leaves (f. 41 blank); 170 x 60 mm.

Contents: On ff. 3r-27r: PC, H1. Dedicatory preface to Proba's cento and acrostic poems in praise of Sedulius (in the reverse of Huemer's order) on f. 27r-v. Followed by Peter Riga, *Aurora* (Acts of the Apostles) on ff. 29r-40v.
Other information: Leaves 1-2 and 41 are paper. *"Fuit P. Hespiels curati de Rodelghem, 1486."* Afterwards belonged to F. Nansius, whose name is found on f. 3. Same as Arntzenius' *Cod. C.* PC divided into five books. Interlinear and marginal glossing. Microfilm acquired.
Bibliography: Arntzenius, same as above, p. 19; *Codices Manuscripti,* same as above, pp. 87-8; Stegmüller, vol. 1, p. 381.

LEIDEN, Bibliotheek der Rijksuniversiteit, B.P.L. 176
s. xiv; 30 leaves; 130 x 105 mm.

Contents: On ff. 1r-30v: E1, PC, H1 (first 34 lines only). Asterius' epigram on f. 3v.
Other information: Once belonged to Janus Rutgersius (see f. 30v). PC divided into five books (1+4). Microfilm acquired.
Bibliography: *Codices Manuscripti,* same as above, p. 88.

LEIDEN, Bibliotheek der Rijksuniversiteit, B.P.L. 185
s. xiv; 32 leaves; 135 x 65 mm.

Contents: On ff. 1r-31r: PC, H1 (first six lines).
Other information: On f. 32v: *Liber Walteri Cok monachi.* Once belonged to F. Nansius (f. 1r). Microfilm acquired.
Bibliography: Arntzenius, *praef.,* p. 19; *Codices Manuscripti,* same as above, p. 90.

LEIPZIG, Universitätsbibliothek, 112
s. xiii; 109 leaves; 265 x 180 mm.

Contents: On ff. 85r-94v: E1, PC. On f. 86r: *accessus* beginning *In principio huius libri sex inquiruntur* (section on Sedulius' life begins *Laicus fuit gentilis sed in Italia philosophiam ... didicit)*; acrostic poem in praise of Sedulius (Liberatus'); and Asterius' epigram. Preceded by Peter Riga, *Aurora* (ff. 1r-84v). Followed by Macer Floridus, *De Herbis* (ff. 95r-104v); a hymn to Christ, Mary, and the saints, beginning *Ave Iesu fili Dei* (ff. 105r-106v); and *De Evangeliis,* verses on the Gospel lessons for the Sundays after Trinity (ff. 107r-109r).

Other information: Probably the manuscript used by Cellarius for his edition and cited indirectly by Arevalo and Huemer *(cod. Lips.).* PC divided into five books. Microfilm acquired.

Bibliography: Rudolf Helssig, *Katalog der lateinischen und deutschen Handschriften der Universitätsbibliothek zu Leipzig,* vol. 1, part 1, *Die theologische Handschriften,* in *Katalog der Handschriften der Universitätsbibliothek zu Leipzig* 4 (Leipzig, 1926-35), pp. 123-4.

LIÈGE, Bibliothèque de l'Université, 667

s. xv; 50 leaves; quarto; Huy (Couvent des Croisiers).

Contents: On ff. 1r-50v: PC, H1 (first three lines only).

Other information: Contains some interlinear glosses and extensive marginal commentary. Microfilm copy acquired.

Bibliography: M. Grandjean, *Bibliothèque de l'Université de Liège: Catalogue des manuscrits* (Liège, 1875), vol. 2, p. 332.

LONDON, British Library, Burney 246

s. xii; 58 pages; "*in folio minori;*" Thame.

Contents: On pp. 1-58: E1, PC, H1. Subscription and Asterius' epigram on p. 5.

Other information: PC divided into four or five books (no break between PC 3 and 4; last book, however, is designated as fifth). Extensive interlinear and marginal glossing. Belonged to William Forrest, Catholic priest and poet, who was vicar of Bledlow, near Thame, in 1556. Seen in person. Microfilm acquired.

Bibliography: J. Forshall, *Catalogue of Manuscripts in The British Museum,* new series, part 2 (London, 1840), p. 64; N.R. Ker, "British Museum, Burney 246, 285, 295, 341, 344, 357," *British Museum Quarterly* 12 (1938), 134-5; Ker, *Med.,* p. 188.

LONDON, British Library, Burney 247

s. xv (1464); 380 pages; quarto; Marcoussis; paper.

Contents: On pp. 1-86: E1, PC, H1, H2. Followed by works of Prudentius (pp. 87-370); Marbod of Rennes, *Passio Sanctorum Martyrum Felicis et Adaucti* (pp. 371 ff.); and Ps.-Hilary, *Epistula ad Abram Filiam* (pp. 377 ff.).

Other information: Seen in person. H2 title reads:

> Hymnus Sedulii episcopi, a beato Ieronimo annumerati in catha-
> logo virorum illustrium, super totum evangelium, per litteras
> alfabeti, in metro iambico dimetro acathalectico; floruit autem ipse
> eodem tempore quo et Ieronimus, imperante Theodosio.

Bibliography: Forshall, same as above, p. 64.

LONDON, British Library, Cotton Vesp. D. XXI
s. xii?; 71 leaves; octavo.

Contents: On ff. 41r-71r: PC, H1, H2. Preceded by Nennius, *Historia Brittonum* and prose version of the life of S. Guthlac in Old English (ff. 18-40).

Other information: First seventeen leaves of codex come from Cathedral priory of S. Andrew's, Rochester. PC divided into five books (1+4). Occasional glossing. Seen in person. Microfilm acquired.

Bibliography: British Museum. Guide to the Exhibited Manuscripts, part 2 (London, 1923), pp. 49-50; Paul Gonser, *Das angelsächsische Prosa-Leben des hl. Guthlac* = Anglistische Forschungen 27 (Amsterdam, 1907; reprint 1966), pp. 31-3; Ker, *Med.* p. 161; Theodor Mommsen, *Chronica Minora Saec. IV, V, VI, VII,* vol. 3, *Historia Brittonum cum Additamentis Nennii, MGH AA,* vol. 13, p. 119; Munk Olsen, vol. 2, p. 501; J. Planta, *A Catalogue of the Manuscripts in the Cottonian Library Deposited in the British Museum* (London, 1802), p. 478.

LONDON, British Library, Harley 2772
s. xii (ff. 28-43); 90 leaves; 198 x 119 mm. (part 4); written in Germany.

Contents: On ff. 28r-43v: PC 1.198 to 4.12. Preceded by selections from Virgil, *Aeneid* 7-12 (ff. 1r-15v) and Juvenal, *Satires* 11.154 to 14.160 (ff. 16r-25v) and 13.234 to 14.110 (ff. 26r-27v). Followed by Macrobius' commentary on *Somnium Scipionis* 1.2.2 to 2.15.8 (ff. 44r-74v) and commentary on and paraphrase of Juvenal (s. xi) (ff. 75r-90r).

Other information: Volume consists of 7 fragmentary parts (s. x-xii) of which ours (ff. 28-43) is the fourth. PC divided into five books? Seen in person.

Bibliography: Munk Olsen, vol. 2, p. 732; R. Nares, et al., *A Catalogue of the Harleian Manuscripts in the British Museum* (4 vols.; London, 1808-12), vol. 2 (1808), p. 711; Reynolds, pp. 225 and 228; E.M. Sanford, "Juvenalis, Decimus Junius" in *Catalogus Translationum et Commentariorum: Medieval and Renaissance Latin Translations and Commentaries,* ed. P.O. Kristeller, vol. 1 (Washington, 1960), p. 183; Herbert Thoma, "Altdeutsches aus Londoner Handschriften," *Beiträge zur Geschichte der deutschen Sprache und Literatur* 73 (1951), 197-271, esp. 251; R.D. Williams and T.S. Pattie, *Virgil. His Poetry through the Ages* (London, 1982), pp. 134-5; Karl Zangemeister, *Bericht über die im Auftrage der Kirchenväter-Commission unternommene Durchforschung der Bibliotheken Englands* (Wien, 1877), p. 11.

LONDON, British Library, Harley 3012

s. ix$^{med.}$; 84 leaves; 225 x 180 mm.; written at Tours; later at S. Martin, Wiblingen.

Contents: On ff. 33r-70v: PO, E2. Preceded by Augustine, *De Quantitate Animae* (ff. 1r-32v) and followed by a commentary on the Apocalypse (attr. Jerome) (ff. 71v-84r).

Other information: PO divided into five books. Includes indices. Used by Ludwig (h) and Huemer (H). Collated for Huemer by H. Sedlmeyer and H. Schenkl. Seen in person. Microfilm acquired.

Bibliography: CSEL, vol. 10, pp. xxxvii-viii; Hörmann, pp. xxiv-xxv; Ludwig, pp. 3-4; Nares, *Catalogue*, same as above, vol. 2, p. 724; Zangemeister, same as above, pp. 12-3.

LONDON, British Library, Harley 3072

s. x (ff. 3-87); 103 leaves; 255 x 174 mm.

Contents: On ff. 3r-42r: E1, PC, H1, H2. Subscription follows E1. Preceded by Virgil, *Eclogues* (ff. 1r-2v) and followed by Arator, *Historia Apostolica* (ff. 43r-87r); sermons (ff. 87r-90v); selections from Prudentius, *Cathemerinon* (ff. 91r-93v); Priscian, *Institutio de Nomine et Pronomine et Verbo* (frag.) (ff. 95r-102v); and Servius' commentary on *Georgics* 1.56-63, 70-93, 186-218 (f. 94r-v and f. 103r-v).

Other information: Volume consists of three parts (s. ix-xi), of which ours (ff. 3-87) is the second. "Continental manuscript of unknown origin," according to Lapidge. PC divided into five books (1+4).

Extensive interlinear glossing. Some elaborate initials (e.g., f. 19r and f. 21r). Seen in person. Microfilm acquired.
Bibliography: Jeudy, "Priscien," 106-7; Lapidge, "Latin Texts," p. 137, n. 93; McKinlay, pp. 44-5; Munk Olsen, vol. 2, p. 810; Nares, *Catalogue,* same as above, vol. 2, p. 733; Passalacqua, pp. 144-5; Williams and Pattie, *Virgil,* same as above, p. 135.

LONDON, British Library, Harley 3093
s. xi; 69 leaves; 278 x 197 mm.; written in southern France.

Contents: On ff. 53v-69v: E1, PC, H1, H2 (1-17). Biographical notice *(Primo laicus in Italia....)* on f. 53v. Preceded by Juvencus, *Evangeliorum Libri Quattuor* (ff. 1v-19v); Prudentius, *Psychomachia* (ff. 20r-25v); the epigrams of Prosper (ff. 26r-34r); *Ecloga Theoduli* (ff. 34r-36r); Theobaldus' *Physiologus* (ff. 36r-38r); and Arator, *Historia Apostolica* (ff. 38r-53v).
Other information: No book divisions after end of PC 1. Seen in person. Microfilm acquired.
Bibliography: P.T. Eden, *Theobaldi Physiologus* = Mittellateinische Studien und Texte 6 (Leiden, 1972), pp. 5-9; Glauche, pp. 100 and 111; McKinlay, p. 45; Richard Morris, *An Old English Miscellany Containing a Bestiary, Kentish Sermons, Proverbs of Alfred, Religious Poems of the Thirteenth Century* = Early English Text Society 49 (London, 1872), Appendix I, pp. 201-9; Nares, *Catalogue,* same as above, vol. 2, pp. 734-5; E.O. Winstedt, "Notes on the Manuscripts of Prudentius," *Journal of Philology* 29 (1904), 168.

LONDON, British Library, Harley 4092
s. xiii; 200 x 135 mm.

Contents: On ff. 3r-37v: E1, PC, H1, H2. Biographical notice *(Incipit ars....)* on f. 3r. Acrostic poems in praise of Sedulius (in the reverse of Huemer's order) on ff. 37v-38r. Preceded by Prudentius, *Psychomachia* (last part only) on first two leaves. Followed by Bernard of Cluny, *De Contemptu Mundi;* hymn beginning *Qui sua dat cunctis;* and Boethius, *Philosophiae Consolatio.*
Other information: PC divided into five books. Occasional marginal notes. Microfilm acquired.
Bibliography: C. D'Evelyn, "A Lost Manuscript of the *De Contemptu Mundi,*" *Speculum* 6 (1931), 132-3; Nares, *Catalogue,* same as above, vol. 3, p. 114 [s. xii].

LONDON, British Library, Royal 15 B. XIX
s. x (late) (ff. 1-35); 205 leaves; 260 x 159 mm.; Christ Church, Canterbury.

Contents: On ff. 1r-34v: PC, H1. Acrostic poems in praise of Sedulius (in the reverse of Huemer's order) on ff. 34v-35r. Persius, Bede, et al. on ff. 36-199; riddles of Symphosius and Boniface on ff. 200-205 (s. xi-xii).
Other information: This volume consists of three manuscripts (s. ix-xii) which were not bound together before the time of Charles II. Ours, the first of these, was written by the same scribe who wrote Harley 110. PC divided into six books (1+5). Last book begins with PC 5.261. Includes some Old English glosses. Text of acrostic poems used by Huemer (R'). Seen in person. Microfilm acquired.
Bibliography: T.A.M. Bishop, "Notes on Cambridge Manuscripts, Part VII," *TCBS* 3.5 (1963), 413-23; *CSEL,* vol. 10, p. 309; Glauche, pp. 54 and 65; Gneuss, "List," no. 491; Huemer, *De Sedulii,* pp. 41 and 51; Ker, *Cat.,* pp. 334-5; Ker, *Med.,* p. 171; G. Kölblinger, "*Versus Panos und De rustico,*" *MlatJb* 8 (1973), 19; Laistner, pp. 127 and 149; Lapidge, "Latin Texts," p. 113 and n. 80; Meritt, pp. 38-9; Munk Olsen, vol. 3.1, p. 206; Reynolds, p. xxxii; George F. Warner and Julius P. Gilson, *Catalogue of Western Manuscripts in the Old Royal and King's Collections* (London, 1921), vol. 2, pp. 159 ff.; Williams and Pattie, *Virgil,* same as above, pp. 140-1; Zangemeister, same as above, pp. 31-5.

MILANO, Biblioteca Ambrosiana, C. 64 Sup.
s. xv[2]; 160 leaves; 250 x 180 mm.; written in northern Italy; prov. S. Maria Incoronata, Milano; paper.

Contents: On ff. 91r-131r: PC, H1, H2. Preceded by Augustinus of Ancona's treatises on the resurrection (ff. 1r-35r) and the love of the Holy Spirit (ff. 35r-88v). Followed by Ps.-Cyprian, *De Cruce (De Ligno Vitae)* (ff. 131r-132v); Francesco Filelfo, *Carmen et Epistula ad Nicolaum Arcimboldum* (ff. 133r-136r); Maffeo Vegio's verses on the Virgin Mary [Walther 20491] (ff. 136v-137v); hymn beginning *Salve festa dies* (ff. 137v-139v); Lactantius, *De Ave Phoenice* (ff. 139v-142v); *Versus Avium* (ff. 143r-144r); excerpts from Horace's *Epistles* (ff. 144v-147r); and various short poems by Antonio Panormita, Petrarch, et al. Volume concludes with Ps.-Claudian, *Carmen Paschale* (f. 161v). For

a full description of the contents, see Jordan and Wool, below.
Other information: Given to Card. Federico Borromeo in 1607.
Microfilm seen.
Bibliography: Mirella Ferrari, "Un bibliotecario milanese del quattro-
cento: Francesco della Croce," *Archivio ambrosiano* 42 (1981), 232;
Huemer, *De Sedulii,* pp. 35 and 43; *Inventario Ceruti dei manoscritti
della Biblioteca Ambrosiana,* vol. 3 (Trezzano, 1977), pp. 169-72; Louis
Jordan and Susan Wool, *Inventory of Western Manuscripts in the
Biblioteca Ambrosiana,* part 2 = Publications in Medieval Studies 22.2
(Notre Dame, 1986), pp. 91-6; Paul Klopsch, *"Carmen de Philomela"*
in *Literatur und Sprache im europäischen Mittelalter. Festschrift für
Karl Langosch* (Darmstadt, 1973), p. 175; Kristeller, *Iter,* vol. 1, p.
329; Angelo Roncoroni, "Pseudo-Cipriano, *De ligno crucis,* testo e
osservazione," *Rivista di storia e letteratura religiosa* 12 (1976), 381.

MILANO, Biblioteca Ambrosiana, G. 39 Sup.
s. xv; 34 leaves; 230 x 160 mm.

Contents: On ff. 1r-34v: PC, H1, H2.
Other information: Elaborate initials. Microfilm seen.
Bibliography: Renata Cipriani, *Codici miniati dell'Ambrosiana.
Contributo a un catalogo* = Fontes ambrosiani 40 (Milano, 1968), p. 53;
Inventario Ceruti, same as above, vol. 3, pp. 544-5.

MILANO, Biblioteca Ambrosiana, H. 80 Sup.
s. xv (1436); 91 leaves; 255 x 175 mm.

Contents: On ff. 55r-91v: PC, H1. Preceded by Juvencus, *Evangeli-
orum Libri Quattuor* (ff. 1r-54v).
Other information: Copied by Dominicus Nicolai de Pollinis. Came to
the Ambrosian Library in 1603. PC divided into four books (no division
between PC 3 and 4). Microfilm seen.
Bibliography: Cipriani, same as above, p. 64; Albert Derolez,
Codicologie des manuscrits en écriture humanistique sur parchemin =
Bibliologia 6 (Turnhout, 1984), vol. 2, p. 78; *Inventario Ceruti,* same
as above, vol. 3, pp. 634-5.

MILANO, Biblioteca Ambrosiana, I. 35 Sup.
s. xv; 40 leaves; 210 x 150 mm.; paper.

Contents: On ff. 1r-40v: E1, PC, H1. Isidore's notice on Sedulius (*De

Viris Inlustribus 20) on f. 40v.

Other information: PC divided into 4 books. Interlinear and marginal glossing. Microfilm seen.

Bibliography: *Inventario Ceruti*, same as above, vol. 3, pp. 680-1.

MILANO, Biblioteca Ambrosiana, R. 46 Sup.
s. xv$^{med.}$; 41 leaves; 262 x 185 mm.; S. Maria Incoronata, Milano.

Contents: On ff. 2r-38r: PC, H1, H2.

Other information: No glossing. Microfilm seen.

Bibliography: Annalisa Belloni and Mirella Ferrari, *La biblioteca capitolare di Monza* = Medioevo e umanesimo 21 (Padova, 1974), p. lxxix; Renata Cipriani, *Codici miniati dell'Ambrosiana. Contributo a un catalogo* = Fontes ambrosiani 40 (Milano, 1968), p. 112; M. Ferrari, "Un bibliotecario milanese," *Archivio ambrosiano* 42 (1981), 249; *Inventario Ceruti*, same as above, vol. 4 (1978), p. 647.

MONTPELLIER, Bibliothèque de la Faculté de Médecine, H 362
s. ix$^{4/4}$; 267 leaves; quarto; written in France; prov. Oratorium of Troyes.

Contents: On ff. 1r-38v: E1, PC, H1, H2. Prose preface, acrostic poem in praise of Sedulius (Bellesarius'), subscription, Asterius' epigram, and prose preface on ff. 4v-5r. Acrostic poems in praise of Sedulius (in the reverse of Huemer's order) on ff. 38v-39r. Followed by Juvencus, *Evangeliorum Libri Quattuor* (ff. 39r-93v) and Lucan, *Bellum Civile* (ff. 94r-267r).

Other information: Volume consists of two distinct but contemporaneous parts (ff. 1-93 and ff. 94-267). Leaves 5-7 were added later (s. xiv). PC divided into five books (1+4). Index before first book. Heavily glossed. Used by Huemer (E). Microfilm acquired.

Bibliography: *Cat. gen. quarto*, vol. 1, pp. 430-2; *CSEL*, vol. 10, p. xiv; Harold C. Gotoff, *The Transmission of the Text of Lucan in the Ninth Century* (Cambridge, Mass., 1971), pp. 16-8; Huemer, *De Sedulii*, p. 32; G. Libri, "Notice des manuscrits de quelques bibliothèques des départements," *Journal des savants*, 1842, 39-55; Munk Olsen, vol. 2, p. 49; Reynolds, pp. 216-7; Sanford, 206; Wickersheimer, p. 49.

MONTPELLIER, Bibliothèque de la Faculté de Médecine, H 434
s. xv; 47 leaves; octavo; *"Bibliothèque Albani"* (no. 2032).

Contents: On ff. 1r-46v: PC, H1, H2.
Other information: PC divided into four books (no division between PC 4 and 5). Used by Huemer *(Montep.)*. Microfilm acquired.
Bibliography: Cat. gen. quarto, vol. 1, p. 457; C. Nicq, G. Cames, G. Velay, *Les Manuscrits de l'École de Médecine de Montpellier* (Montpellier, 1994), p. 24.

MÜNCHEN, Bayerische Staatsbibliothek, Clm 2623
s. xiii; 113 leaves; 145 x 105 mm.; Aldersbach.

Contents: On ff. 57r-93v: PC. Preceded by *Exhortationes,* beginning *Karissimi, cum sitis oves Domini* (ff. 1r-24r), and examples demonstrating vowel quantity (including excerpts from Sedulius) (ff. 25r-56r). Followed by sermons (ff. 94r-113r).
Other information: PC divided into two books (division at end of PC 1). Seen in person. Microfilm acquired.
Bibliography: Glauche, p. 105; C. Halm, G. Laubmann, et al., *Catalogus Codicum Latinorum Bibliothecae Regiae Monacensis* (München, 1868 ff.), vol. 1.2 (2nd ed., 1894), p. 21.

MÜNCHEN, Bayerische Staatsbibliothek, Clm 4410
s. xv; 53 leaves; 215 x 162 mm.; S. Ulrich and Afra, Augsburg.

Contents: On ff. 2r-53r: PC. Preceded by biographical notice *(Sedulius primo laicus....)* on f. 1v.
Other information: PC divided into five books. Interlinear glossing and marginal commentary. Seen in person.
Bibliography: Halm, *Catalogus,* same as above, vol. 1.2, p. 191.

MÜNCHEN, Bayerische Staatsbibliothek, Clm 7784
s. xiii-xiv; 104 leaves; 183 x 125 mm. (ff. 49 ff. = 143 x 108 mm.); Indersdorf.

Contents: On ff. 79r-93r: PC. Preceded by a summary of the articles of faith (ff. 2r ff.); a prose treatise on cases which a priest ought to send to the bishop (ff. 16v ff.); hymn beginning *Ut queant laxis* with commentary (ff. 30v ff.); *Liber Lapidarius* (ff. 51r ff.); Henry of Settimello, *Elegia de Diversitate Fortunae et Philosophiae Consolatione* (ff. 62r ff.). Followed by the miracles of Otto, bishop of Bamberg (ff. 93v ff.); *De Arithmetica* (ff. 96r ff.); and Alexander of Villa Dei, *Algorismus* (ff. 101r ff.).

Other information: Miscellany volume. PC written in double columns. Book divisions not noted after PC 3. Interlinear glossing. Seen in person.
Bibliography: Halm, *Catalogus,* same as above, vol. 1.3 (1873), p. 198.

MÜNCHEN, Bayerische Staatsbibliothek, Clm 13241

s. xvi (1519 and 1521); 402 leaves; 220 x 162 mm.; Stadtamhof (Regensburg); paper.

Contents: On ff. 2r-61v: E1, PC, H1, H2. On f. 1r-v: verses on Sedulius and Johannes Trithemius' biography of the poet. Followed by Prudentius, *Praefatio, Cathemerinon, Peristephanon, Dittochaeon, Apotheosis, Hamartigenia, Contra Symmachum* (ff. 62r-324v); Macarius Mutius, *De Triumpho Christi* (ff. 325r-330r); Jacobus Goudanus, *Elegia de Salutifera Mortis Recordatione* and *"eiusdem carmen"* (ff. 330r-334r); hymn beginning *Salve festa dies* (ff. 334r-336v); Johannes Scultetus, *Carmen contra Pestem* (f. 339r); verses of Petrarch to the Virgin Mary, translated by Filippo Beroaldo into Latin (ff. 340r-342v); Filippo Beroaldo, *Carmen de Passione Domini* (ff. 342v-346r); Pius II (Aeneas Silvius Piccolomini), *Carmen de Passione Domini* (ff. 346v-348r); Maffeo Vegio, *Epigramma in Laudem Monicae;* Petrarch, *Carmen de Maria Magdalena* and excerpt from Alan of Lille, *Anticlaudianus* (ff. 348r-351v); and Horace, *Epistles* and *Ars poetica* (ff. 352v-402v).
Other information: PC divided into four books (no division between PC 1 and 2). Some interlinear glossing. Seen in person.
Bibliography: Halm, *Catalogus,* same as above, vol. 2.2 (1876), p. 108; Sottili, vol. 1, pp. 441-5.

MÜNCHEN, Bayerische Staatsbibliothek, Clm 14569

s. xi; 142 leaves; 205 x 145 mm.; S. Emmeram, Regensburg.

Contents: On ff. 33r-72v: PC (begins with 1.32; contains a portion of E1 on an unnumbered fragmentary leaf between ff. 32 and 33), H1, H2. Subscription and Asterius' epigram on f. 72v. Preceded by Virgil, *Aeneid* 7.478-504 and 508-534 (f. 1v); an ecclesiastical calendar (1016-1055) (ff. 2r ff.); computistic texts (ff. 16v ff.); and *"S. Columbanus de Saltu Lunae"* (ff. 26r-28r). Epitaph for Hincmar on f. 72v. Followed by the epigrams of Prosper and Ps.-Prosper, *Poema Coniugis ad Uxorem* (first six lines only) on ff. 73r-98v and various theological treatises (ff. 99r-141v), including one on the Antichrist (ff. 135r-139v).

Other information: PC divided into five books (1+4; first book begins with PC 1.103). PC 1.355-368 = "*Prologus de quattuor evangelistis.*" Extensive interlinear and marginal glossing. Indices. Used by Huemer (e). Seen in person. Microfilm acquired.

Bibliography: Bergmann, p. 70; *CSEL,* vol. 10, p. xxiii; Halm, *Catalogus,* same as above, vol. 2.2 (1876), pp. 194-5; Huemer, *De Sedulii,* pp. 32 and 41; O. Lottin, "Nouveaux fragments théologiques de l'école d'Anselme de Laon," *RTAM* 14 (1947), 172; Steinmeyer & Sievers, vol. 2, p. 621 and vol. 4, pp. 543-4; D. Verhelst, *Adso Dervensis, De Ortu et Tempore Antichristi, CCCM,* vol. 45, p. 95; Heinrich Weisweiler, "L'École d'Anselme de Laon et de Guillaume de Champeaux: Nouveaux documents," *RTAM* 4 (1932), 240-8; idem, *Das Schrifttum der Schule Anselms von Laon und Wilhelms von Champeaux in deutschen Bibliotheken: Ein Beitrag zur Geschichte der Verbreitung der ältesten scholastischen Schule in deutscher Landen* = Beiträge zur Geschichte der Philosophie und Theologie des Mittelalters 33 (Münster, 1936), pp. 9, 12, 26, 50, 92, and 111; idem, "Le Recueil des sentences *Deus de cuius principio et fine tacetur* et son remaniement," *RTAM* 5 (1933), 245-6.

MÜNCHEN, Bayerische Staatsbibliothek, Clm 14693
s. xi (ff. 57-117); 117 leaves; 200 x 155 mm.; S. Emmeram, Regensburg.

Contents: On ff. 57r-111r: E1, PC, H1, H2. Acrostic poem in praise of Sedulius (Liberatus') on f. 62r. Preceded by Horace, *Ars Poetica* (ff. 1v-14v) and *Epistles* (ff. 14v-54v). Followed by *Physiologus* (ff. 111r-116v).

Other information: Volume consists of two parts of which the first (ff. 1-56) dates to s. xii. PC divided into five books (1+4). Used by Huemer (f). Some glossing in first book. Splendid initial P in first line of PC. Two Old High German glosses in H1. Seen in person. Microfilm acquired.

Bibliography: Bergmann, p. 71; Halm, *Catalogus,* same as above, vol. 2.2 (1876), p. 219; Huemer, p. xxiii; Munk Olsen, vol. 1, p. 470 and vol. 3.1, p. 198; Klaus Siewert, *Die althochdeutsche Horazglossierung* = Studien zum Althochdeutschen 8 (Göttingen, 1986), pp. 390-4; Steinmeyer & Sievers, vol. 2, p. 622 and vol. 4, p. 549.

MÜNCHEN, Bayerische Staatsbibliothek, Clm 15147
s. xvi (1501); 314 leaves; 300 x 205 mm.; Rebdorf; paper.

Contents: On ff. 270r-272v: H1 (with a Middle High German verse translation for the first half); and on ff. 278r-314r: PC. On f. 273r: *De Modo Studendi.* Preceded by Virgil, *Eclogues, Georgics,* and *Aeneid* (ff. 1r-151r ff.); Horace, *Epistles* (ff. 160r-192v); and Seneca, *Epistulae Morales* (addressed to Lucilius) (ff. 197r-267v).

Other information: PC divided into four books (no division between PC 3 and 4). Interlinear glossing and marginal notation. On f. 192v: *Scriptum ... in Zwickavia.* On f. 314v: *Sedulii poetae Christianissimi atque celeberrimi Pascalis Carminis opus explicit feliciter.* Seen in person.

Bibliography: Halm, *Catalogus,* same as above, vol. 2.3 (1878), pp. 4-5; Nikolaus Henkel, *Deutsche Übersetzungen lateinischer Schultexte. Ihre Verbreitung und Funktion im Mittelalter und in der frühen Neuzeit* = Münchener Texte und Untersuchungen zur deutschen Literatur des Mittelalters 90 (München, 1988), pp. 263-4.

MÜNCHEN, Bayerische Staatsbibliothek, Clm 18628

s. x^2; 118 leaves; 221 x 175 mm.; Tegernsee.

Contents: On ff. 17r-70r: E1, PC (3.39 to 4.21 dislocated on ff. 32r-39v), H1 (described as *paractericum carmen* and *reciprocum carmen*), H2. Acrostic poem in praise of Sedulius (Liberatus') on f. 16r; biographical notice (Remigius') on f. 17r. Subscription and Asterius' epigram (first three lines) on f. 70r; dedicatory preface to Proba's cento (beginning with seventh line) and acrostic poem in praise of Sedulius (Bellesarius') on f. 70v. Preceded by a passion of Peter and Paul with a preface to Pope Leo (ff. 1r-11r); epigrams on Peter (ff. 11r-12v); *Vita S. Verenae* in verse (ff. 13r-15v); and *Quae Sit Optima Carminis Forma* (f. 15v). Followed by Walafrid Strabo, *Visio Wettini* (ff. 71r-92r); Eugenius of Toledo, *Carm.* 38 (on the ten plagues); "Alcuin's Epitaph;" *De Origine Protoplasti et Eius Reparatione;* et al. (ff. 93r-104v); geographical chart with the names of the winds; treatise on the letters of the alphabet; the Greek and Hebrew alphabets set to verse; et al. (ff. 105r-109r); a passion of S. Mauricius in verse (ff. 109r ff.); and a short chronicle (ff. 111r-117v).

Other information: PC apparently divided into four books (1+3; no division between PC 3 and 4). PC 1.103 ff. = *"Liber primus."* Extensive interlinear glossing in Latin and Old High German. Marginal notes. Illustration of seated figure with book on f. 16v. Used by Huemer (Y). Seen in person. Microfilm acquired.

Bibliography: Bergmann, p. 77; *CSEL,* vol. 10, p. xviiii; Peter Dronke,

Medieval Latin and the Rise of European Love Lyric (2nd ed.; Oxford, 1968), vol. 2, *Medieval Latin Love-Poetry,* p. 566; Ernst Dümmler, "Aus Handschriften," *Neues Archiv* 5 (1879), 630-1; idem, "Die handschriftliche Überlieferung der lateinischen Dichtungen aus der Zeit der Karolinger," *Neues Archiv* 4 (1879), 278; Christine Elisabeth Eder, *Die Schule des Klosters Tegernsee im frühen Mittelalter im Spiegel der Tegernseer Handschriften* (München, 1972), pp. 143-4; Glauche, p. 111; Halm, *Catalogus,* same as above, vol. 2.3 (1878), pp. 191-2; Wilhelm Harster, *Novem Vitae Sanctorum Metricae ex Codicibus Monacensibus, Parisiensibus, Bruxellensi, Hagensi, Saec. IX-XII* (Leipzig, 1887), p. vi; Laistner, p. 147; Legendre, p. 60; Paul Lehmann, *Die Parodie im Mittelalter* (Stuttgart, 1963), p. 223; G. Müller and Th. Frings, *Germania Romana II. Dreissig Jahre Forschung. Romanische Wörter* = Mittelhochdeutsche Studien 19.2 (1968), p. 89; Steinmeyer & Sievers, vol. 2, pp. 617-8 and vol. 4, p. 566; David A. Traill, *Walafrid Strabo's Visio Wettini: Text, Translation, and Commentary* (Frankfurt and Bern, 1974), p. 19; F. Vollmer, *Fl. Merobaudis Reliquiae, Blossii Aemilii Dracontii Carmina, Eugenii Toletani Episcopi Carmina et Epistulae, MGH AA,* vol. 14, p. xlii.

MÜNCHEN, Bayerische Staatsbibliothek, Clm 19455
s. xii; 24 leaves; 200 x 100 mm.; Tegernsee.

Contents: On ff. 1r-24v: PC, H1.
Other information: No book divisions in PC (but five-book format added by later hand). Heavily glossed (interlinear and marginal). Seen in person. Microfilm acquired.
Bibliography: Bergmann, p. 79; Halm, *Catalogus,* same as above, vol. 2.3 (1878), p. 247.

MÜNCHEN, Bayerische Staatsbibliothek, Clm 22125
s. xvi; 40 leaves; 210 x 142 mm.; Wessobrunn; paper.

Contents: On ff. 3r-31v: PC. Preface of Janus Parrhasius (Aulo Ciano Parrasio) on ff. 2r-3r. Notes on Sedulius and Prudentius by the same on ff. 32r-35v. Followed by Hucbald of S. Amand, *De Laude Calvorum* (ff. 36r-38v). Leaves 39 and 40 are blank.
Other information: PC not divided into books. Seen in person.
Bibliography: Halm, *Catalogus,* same as above, vol. 2.4 (1881), p. 27.

NEW HAVEN, Yale University Library, Marston MS 98

s. xv (1473); 61 leaves (misnumbered as 62); 186 x 137 mm.; written in northern Italy; prov. Chiaravalle, Milano; paper.

Contents: On ff. 23r-61r: PC, H1. Preceded by Prudentius, *Praefatio* and *Psychomachia* (ff. 1r-19v); Francesco Filelfo, *Satyrarum Hecatostichon Septima Decas, Hecatosticha Quinta* (final verses) (f. 20r); Franciscus de Fiano, *Deprecacio Pulcherrima ad Gloriosissimam Matrem* (ff. 20v-21v); and hymn beginning *Salve festa dies* (attr. Lactantius) on ff. 21v-23r. Followed by 8-line poem beginning *Ista tibi Antoni* and *Elegia de XII Gradibus Humilitatis* on f. 61r-v.

Other information: Written in a Cistercian monastery. Very similar to Roma, Biblioteca Angelica, 970. Belonged to Gustavo Cammillo Galletti of Firenze (1805-68) and later in the collection of Baron Horace de Landau (1824-1903). Purchased in 1956 from L.C. Witten by Thomas E. Marston. Microfilm copy acquired.

Bibliography: *Census suppl.*, pp. 75-6; Franz Roediger, *Catalogue des livres manuscrits et imprimés composant la Bibliothèque de M. Horace de Landau* (Firenze, 1885-90), vol. 2, p. 104; Barbara A. Shailor, *Catalogue of Medieval and Renaissance Manuscripts in the Beinecke Rare Book and Manuscript Library, Yale University, Vol. III: Marston Manuscripts* (Binghamton, 1992), pp. 188-91.

ORLÉANS, Bibliothèque Municipale, 295 (248 bis)

s. ix$^{3/4}$; 84 leaves (168 pages); 354 x 255 mm.; written in Reims; later at Fleury.

Contents: On pp. 73-99: PC (missing first line), H1, H2 (followed by doxology). Preceded by Donatus, *Ars Maior* and *Ars Minor* (pp. 1-42); Priscian, *Institutio de Nomine et Pronomine et Verbo* (pp. 43-51); Servius, *De Finalibus* (pp. 51-54); Bede, *De Arte Metrica* (pp. 54-64) and *De Schematibus et Tropis* (pp. 65-69); and *Disticha Catonis* (pp. 70-72). Followed by Juvencus, *Evangeliorum Libri Quattuor* (pp. 99-141) and Arator, *Historia Apostolica* (incomplete) (pp. 142-168).

Other information: Manuscript completed by Leiden, Bibliotheek der Rijksuniversiteit, Voss. Lat. F. 12. PC apparently divided into four books. Extensive glossing. Seen in person. Microfilm acquired.

Bibliography: Bischoff, *MS*, vol. 2, p. 55; *Cat. gen. octavo*, vol. 12, pp. 146-7; Glauche, pp. 33 and 35; L. Holtz, *Muretach, In Donati Artem Maiorem = Grammatici Hibernici Carolini Aevi, Pars I, CCCM*, vol. 40, pp. xxxix-xli; idem, "Sur trois commentaires irlandais de l'*Art majeur* de Donat au IXe siècle," *RHT* 2 (1972), 46-7; idem, "La

Typologie des manuscrits grammaticaux latins," *RHT* 7 (1977), 261-2; Jeudy, "Priscien," 113-4; C.B. Kendall and M.H. King, *Bedae Venerabilis Opera, Pars VI. Opera Didascalia I, CCSL,* vol. 123A, p. 68; Lesne, p. 554; McKinlay, p. 11; idem, "Studies in Arator I: The Manuscript Tradition of the *Capitula* and *Tituli,*" *Harvard Studies in Classical Philology* 43 (1932), 123-66; idem, *"Membra Disiecta* of Manuscripts of Arator,"* Speculum* 15 (1940), 95-8; idem, "Latin Commentaries on Arator," *Scriptorium* 6 (1952), 151-3; Mostert, p. 167; Munk Olsen, vol. 1, p. 72 and vol. 3.1, p. 108; Passalacqua, pp. 197-8; Pellegrin, pp. 200-2, 208, 287-8, and 346; Reynolds, p. 203; Sanford, 211; Charles Thurot, "Notices et extraits de divers manuscrits latins pour servir à l'histoire des doctrines grammaticales au Moyen Âge," *Not. et extr.* 22.2 (Paris, 1868), 6.

ORLÉANS, Bibliothèque Municipale, 302 (255)
s. ix$^{in.}$ and s. x; 201 pages; 192 x 172 mm.; Fleury.

Contents: On pp. 2-82 (written in Brittany; s. ix$^{in.}$): E1, PC, H1 (first 25 lines; lines 26-73 are now out of place on pp. 33-34). Subscription on p. 1. Followed by Bede, *De Arte Metrica* (pp. 83-136) and *De Schematibus et Tropis* (pp. 137-150). Works of Sedulius are also found on pp. 151-199 (s. x; written at Fleury?): E1, PC 1.1 to 3.241. On pp. 200-201: *De Sacra Scriptura.*
Other information: First text of PC apparently divided into five books (1+4). Interlinear glossing. Seen in person. Microfilm acquired.
Bibliography: Bischoff, "FHH," 311; Bischoff, *MS,* vol. 3, p. 15; idem, *Paläographie des römischen Altertums und des abendländischen Mittelalters* = Grundlagen der Germanistik 24 (2nd ed.; Berlin, 1986), p. 122; *Cat. gen. octavo,* vol. 12, pp. 150-1; C.B. Kendall and M.H. King, *Bedae Venerabilis Opera, Pars VI. Opera Didascalia I, CCSL,* vol. 123A, pp. 68 and 78; Laistner, p. 133; Lesne, pp. 550-5; J. Loth, "Gloses bretonnes inédites du IXe siècle," *Revue celtique* 33 (1912), 417-31; Mostert, p. 171.

ORLÉANS, Bibliothèque Municipale, 303 (256)
s. x^2; 223 pages; 185 x 192 mm.; written at Fleury.

Contents: On pp. 1-143: E1, PC, H1, H2. Subscription on p. 8; acrostic poems in praise of Sedulius (in Huemer's order) on pp. 9-10; biographical notice *(Sedulius primo laicus....)* on p. 10. Another copy (incomplete) of acrostic poem of Bellesarius on p. 143. Followed by a treatise on grammar (pp. 145-148). Sedulius' works continue on pp. 149-223; E2, PO (incomplete at end; missing material after Huemer's page 302, line 1). Includes indices. Subscription, Asterius' epigram, and prose preface on p. 151.

Other information: PC and PO both divided into five continuously numbered books. Extensive interlinear and marginal glossing in E1 and PC. Candel collated the text of PO against Huemer's edition. Seen in person. Microfilm acquired.

Bibliography: Jules Candel, "Un nouveau manuscrit de l'*Opus paschale* de Sedulius," *Revue de philologie* 28 (1904), 283-92; idem, *De Clausulis a Sedulio in Eis Libris Qui Inscribuntur Paschale Opus Adhibitis* (Toulouse, 1904); *Cat. gen. octavo*, vol. 12, pp. 151-2; S. Corbin, *Paléographie musicale* in *École Pratique des Hautes Études, IVe Section, Sciences historiques et philologiques* (Paris, 1973), 391; Lesne, p. 555; Mostert, pp. 171-2; Ch. Samaran and R. Marichal, *Catalogue des manuscrits en écriture latine portant des indications de date, de lieu ou de copiste* (Paris, 1959-84), vol. 7, p. xxxviii.

ORLÉANS, Bibliothèque Municipale, 307 (260)

s. xi$^{in.}$; 243 pages; 185 x 130 mm.; probably writtten at Fleury.

Contents: On pp. 2-83: PC 1.1 to 5.312. On p. 34: a prayer for one suffering from fever. Followed by Prudentius, *Psychomachia* and excerpts from the *Cathemerinon* (pp. 83-120); miscellaneous poetry, including Petronius, *Satyricon*, frag. 28 (on King Midas) (p. 120); miscellaneous verse and excerpts (pp. 121-6); *De Locutionibus Sanctae Scripturae* (pp. 127-212); and Bede, *De Arte Metrica* (incomplete) (pp. 212-243).

Other information: Originally connected with Vat. Reg. Lat. 166, ff. 42-55. PC apparently divided into five books. Heavily glossed. Seen in person. Microfilm acquired.

Bibliography: *Cat. gen. octavo*, vol. 12, pp. 155-6; S. Corbin, *Paléographie musicale* in *École Pratique des Hautes Études, IVe Section, Sciences historiques et philologiques* (Paris, 1973), 385-92; Edward Courtney, *The Poems of Petronius* (Atlanta, 1991), p. 60; Glauche, p. 68; C.B. Kendall and M.H. King, *Bedae Venerabilis Opera. Pars VI. Opera Didascalia I, CCSL*, vol. 123A, p. 68; Lesne, pp. 552 and 555; *MCLBV*, vol. 2.1, p. 41; Mostert, p. 173; Munk Olsen, vol. 2, p. 224 and vol. 3.1, p. 109; Pellegrin, p. 260.

ORLÉANS, Bibliothèque Municipale, 318 (270)

s. x^2; 180 pages; 240 x 180 mm.; written at Fleury?

Contents: On pp. 5-100: E1, PC, H1, H2. Acrostic poem in praise of Sedulius (Bellesarius') (first nine lines only) on p. 100. Followed by Bede, *De Arte Metrica* and *De Schematibus et Tropis* (pp. 101-181); hymn beginning *Scrutator bene valde* (p. 182); hymn beginning *Eia salutifero pangamus* (p. 183); and treatise on the first declension (p. 184).

Other information: First four pages of manuscript, containing a fragment of the fifth book of Cassiodorus' *Chronica*, are now in Paris, Bibliothèque Nationale, Nouv. Acq. Lat. 1630. PC apparently divided into five books (1+4). Extensive interlinear and marginal glossing. Seen in person. Microfilm acquired.

Bibliography: *Cat. gen. octavo,* vol. 12, pp. 165-6; Corbin, *Paléographie,* same as above, p. 391; Léopold Victor Delisle, "Notices sur plusieurs manuscrits de la Bibliothèque d'Orléans," *Not. et extr.* 31.1 (1884), 401-2 [s. xi]; C.B. Kendall and M.H. King, *Bedae Venerabilis Opera. Pars VI. Opera Didascalia I, CCSL,* vol. 123A, pp. 68 and 78 [s. xi]; M.H. King, "The Glosses in Six Manuscripts of Bede's *De Arte Metrica,*" Dissertation, University of California, 1967; Laistner, p. 133 [s. xi]; Lesne, pp. 552 and 555; Mostert, p. 176; Pellegrin, pp. 163, 170, and 352.

OXFORD, Bodleian Library, Add. B. 119 (SC 29635)
s. xv; 47 leaves; 200 x 146 mm.; written in Italy; parchment and paper.

Contents: On ff. 5r-33r: E1, PC, H1 (subscription and Asterius' epigram follow E1 on f. 6v). Followed by Augustine, *Sermo de Disciplina Christiana* (ff. 34r-40v). Leaves 1-4 and 41-47 are blank.

Other information: PC not divided into books. Seen in person. Microfilm acquired.

Bibliography: Schenkl, no. 386; *Sum. Cat.,* vol. 5, pp. 661-2.

OXFORD, Bodleian Library, Auct. F. 1. 17 (SC 2506)
s. xiv^1; 305 leaves; 345 x 240 mm.; written in England.

Contents: On ff. 283r-295r: PC, H1. Preceded by Alan of Lille, *Liber Parabolarum* (ff. 1r-4v); Matthew of Vendôme, *Tobias* (ff. 5r-18v); Virgil, *Eclogues* and *Georgics* (ff. 19r-38r); Marbod of Rennes, *Epigrams* (ff. 38r-39r); poems from the "Virgilian Appendix" (ff. 39r-46v); Virgil, *Aeneid* (incomplete) (ff. 46v-108v); Geoffrey of Vinsauf,

Poetria Nova (ff. 109r-121v); and works of Ovid: *Heroides, Epistulae ex Ponto, Amores, Ars Amatoria, Tristia, Metamorphoses* (ff. 121v-283r). Followed by Prudentius, *Psychomachia* (ff. 295r-301v).
Other information: Virgilian text used by John Martyn for his edition of the *Georgics* (1741 and 1755). PC divided into five books (1+4). PC 1.350-368 = *"Prologus quattuor evangelistarum."* No break between PC 4 and 5; last book begins with PC 5.315. Extra line (309) at end of PC 4. Written in double columns. Seen in person. Microfilm copy acquired.
Bibliography: F.W. Lenz, "Die Wiedergewinnung der von Heinsius benutzten Ovidhandschriften II," *Eranos* 61 (1963), 108; Munari, pp. 73-4; idem, *Catalogue of the Manuscripts of Ovid's Metamorphoses* = University of London, Institute of Classical Studies, Bulletin Supplement 4 (London, 1957), p. 45; idem, "Sugli *Amores* di Ovidio," *SIFC* (n.s.) 23 (1948), 148, n. 1; S.G. Owen, *P. Ovidii Nasonis Tristium Libri V* (Oxford, 1989), p. xxx; Sanford, pp. 238-9; Jürgen Stohlmann, *"Deidamia Achilli.* Eine Ovid-Imitation aus dem 11. Jahrhundert" in *Literatur und Sprache im europäischen Mittelalter. Festschrift für Karl Langosch zum 70. Geburtstag* (Darmstadt, 1973), pp. 221-2; Schenkl, no. 808; *Sum. Cat.,* same as above, vol. 2, part 1 (1922), pp. 401-2.

PADOVA, Archivio e Biblioteca Capitolare, C. 74

s. xv (1469); 154 leaves (last blank); 234 x 170 mm.; paper.

Contents: On ff. 1r-41v: E1, PC, H1. On f. 39r (after PC) epigram beginning *Haec tua perpetuae.* Followed by Juvencus, *Evangeliorum Libri Quattuor* (ff. 42r-105v) (preceded by Jerome's notice in *De Viris Inlustribus)* and Arator, *Historia Apostolica* (ff. 106r-153v).
Other information: Written (in fifteen days) by Petrus Barrocius, bishop of Padova, who also copied Lucretius (C. 75). His defence of the latter project is interesting:

> Oro te, lector, per eum quem Christiani deum colimus, ne aliena mihi errata innocenti ascribas, namque in his cartis cum pleraeque sententiae, tum versus manci sunt, aut imperfecti, non mea, mehercule, sed exemplaris culpa est factum, quod ex his quae in versuum principiis feci.

PC divided into five continuously numbered books. Some marginal notes. Seen in person.
Bibliography: *Index Codicum Manuscriptorum Qui in Bibliotheca*

Reverendissimi Capituli Cathedralis Ecclesiae Patavianae Asservantur, by Ferdinandus Com. Maldura (1830), p. 143; Kristeller, *Iter,* vol. 2, p. 5.

PARIS, Bibliothèque Nationale, Lat. 242
s. ix² (ff. 95-173); 173 leaves; 170 x 110 mm.; written in France.

Contents: On ff. 133r-173v: PC 1.44 to 5.419 (missing leaves after f. 138v [=1.297-338] and after f. 169v [=5.253-337]), H2. Index on f. 132r-v. Hymn beginning *Haec est dies* (Paulinus of Aquileia, *Carm.* 9) on f. 163r-v. Antiphon beginning *Tibi Christe referimus* and hymn beginning *Audite vobis omnes* on f. 172r-v. Preceded by Ps.-Cicero, *Synonyma* (excerpt) (ff. 95r-104v); Fulgentius, *Expositio Sermonum Antiquorum* (ff. 104v-112r); miscellaneous verses (ff. 112r-115r); a fragment of Priscian, *Institutio de Nomine et Pronomine et Verbo* (ff. 115r-126v); and Servius, *De Centum Metris* (ff. 126v-131r). Hymn beginning *Adorate omnes gentes* on f. 131r-v.
Other information: Volume consists of three manuscripts (s. ix²-xi), of which ours (ff. 95-173) is the third, bound together. PC apparently divided into five books (1+4). Some glossing. Seen in person. Microfilm acquired.
Bibliography: L. Galmes, *Tradición manuscrita y fuentes de los Antikeimenon libri II de San Julián de Toledo* (Berlin, 1961), p. 50, n. 1; Gamber, vol. 1, p. 170, no. 229b; Jeudy, "Priscien," 118-9; Philippe Lauer, *Bibliothèque Nationale. Catalogue général des manuscrits latins,* vol. 1 (Paris, 1939), pp. 89-90; Munk Olsen, vol. 1, p. 346; Dag Norberg, *L'Oeuvre poétique de Paulin d'Aquilée. Édition critique avec introduction et commentaire* (Stockholm, 1979), p. 86; Passalacqua, pp. 215-6; E. Pellegrin, "Essai d'identification de fragments dispersés dans des manuscrits de bibliothèques de Berne et de Paris," *BIRHT* 9 (1960), 29; *PL,* vol. 19, col. 476; H. Silvestre, "Le Culte de Marie Madeleine en Occident," *Scriptorium* 15 (1961), 92; Karl Strecker, "Zu den Gedichtsammlungen der Pariser Handschriften 8812 und 242," *ALMA* 17 (1942), 46-9; idem, *Die Cambridger Lieder = MGH Scriptores Rerum Germanicarum in Usum Scholarum Separatim Editi* 40 (2nd ed.; Berlin, 1955), p. 17; André Wilmart, "Mètres et rythmes carolingiens," *ALMA* 15 (1940), 204-11.

PARIS, Bibliothèque Nationale, Lat. 8092
s. xi¹; 84 leaves; 290 x 205 mm.; written in England.

Contents: On ff. 1r-37v: E1, PC (missing original leaves after f. 32v [=5.101-255] and after f. 34v [=5.354 ff.]), H1 (beginning with line 17), H2. Acrostic poems in praise of Sedulius (in the reverse of Huemer's order) on ff. 37v-38r; biographical notice on f. 1r. Followed by Silvius, *De Cognomentis Salvatoris,* and octosyllables beginning *Tu corda nostra dirige* (f. 38r); Alcuin, *Carm.* 62 *(Praecepta Vivendi;* attr. Columbanus) (ff. 38v-42r); Bede, *De Die Iudicii* (ff. 42r-45r); and Arator, *Historia Apostolica* (ff. 45v-84v).

Other information: Lapidge suggests that this manuscript may have travelled to France "soon after the Norman Conquest." PC divided into six books (1+5). First book begins with 1.103; 1.351-368 = "*Prologus quattuor evangelistarum.*" Last book begins with line 315. Includes indices. Contains a number of glosses in Old English and at least three in Old French. Glossing confined mostly to first twelve folios. Seen in person. Microfilm acquired.

Bibliography: Ernst Dümmler in *MGH PLAC,* vol. 1, p. 275; Gneuss, "List," no. 890; Laistner, p. 128; Lapidge, "Latin Texts," p. 114 and n. 84; idem, "Some Old English Sedulius Glosses from BN Lat. 8092," *Anglia* 100 (1982), 1-17; Max Manitius, *Geschichte der lateinischen Literatur des Mittelalters,* in *Handbuch der Altertumswissenschaft* 9.2 (München, 1911 ff.), vol. 1, p. 185; McKinlay, pp. 14-5; Patrick P. O'Neill, "Further Old English Glosses on Sedulius in BN Lat. 8092," *Anglia* 107 (1989), 415; Andy Orchard, *The Poetic Art of Aldhelm* = Cambridge Studies in Anglo-Saxon England 8 (Cambridge, 1994), p. 164; *PL,* vol. 19, col. 476; Jean Vezin, "Manuscrits de dixième et onzième siècles copiés en Angleterre en minuscule caroline et conservés à la Bibliothèque Nationale de Paris" in *Humanisme actif: Mélanges d'art et de littérature offerts à Julien Cain* (Paris, 1968), vol. 2, pp. 294-5; L. Whitbread, "After Bede: The Influence and Dissemination of his Doomsday Verses," *Archiv für das Studium der neueren Sprachen und Literaturen* 204 (1967), 263.

PARIS, Bibliothèque Nationale, Lat. 8093
s. ix^{1/4} (ff. 1-38); 150 leaves; 277 x 200 mm.; first section written at the cathedral of Lyon.

Contents: On ff. 1r-15v: E1 (to page 7, line 2), PC (om. 5.104-176), H1. Followed by *Carmina* of Eugenius of Toledo (ff. 16v-20r and 24v); *Disticha Catonis* (ff. 20r-23v); hymn beginning *Salve festa dies* (f. 23v); Eugenius, *Hexaemeron* (excerpted from Dracontius, *De Laudibus Dei*) (ff. 25r-32r); Martin of Braga, *Inscriptiones* (f. 32r-v); Damasus' epigram on the Apostle Paul (*Carm.* 7) (f. 32v); Theodulf of Orléans, *Carm.* 41 (ff. 33r-35v); *Versus Sibyllae* (Augustine, *De Civitate Dei* 18.23) (ff. 35v-36r); Julian of Toledo, *Versus ad Modoenum* and Isidore's verses on his library (f. 36v); Phocas' life of Virgil (f. 37r-v); Agrestius, *Versus de Fide ad Avitum Episcopum* (f. 38r); and Paulinus of Nola, *Carm.* 6.256-330 (f. 38r-v).

Other information: Volume consists of nine unrelated parts dating from the ninth to the fourteenth centuries. First part of volume (ff. 1-38) originally connected with Voss. Lat. F. 111. Written by two or three Visigothic scribes. *"Wichtigstes Denkmal der 'spanischen Kolonie' in Lyon, "* according to Bischoff. PC may have been originally divided into three books. Seen in person. Microfilm copy acquired.

Bibliography: Claude W. Barlow, *Martini Episcopi Bracarensis Opera Omnia* = Papers and Monographs of the American Academy in Rome 12 (New Haven, 1950), p. 278; Beeson, pp. 141-2; Bischoff, *MS,* vol. 1, p. 292 and vol. 3, pp. 19-20, n. 64; Bischoff, "FHH," 311; idem, "Ein Brief Julians von Toledo über Rhythmen, metrische Dichtung und Prosa," *Hermes* 87 (1959), 247-256, esp. 250; Boas, pp. xlvii and lx; *Catalogus Codicum Hagiographicorum Latinorum Antiquiorum Saeculo XVI Qui Asservantur in Bibliotheca Nationali Parisiensi,* vol. 2 (Paris, 1890), pp. 555-6; Francesco Della Corte, "L'ordinamento degli *opuscula* di Ausonio," *Rivista di cultura classica e medioevale* 2 (1960), 21; Guaglianone, pp. ix-x; J.N. Hillgarth, "Towards a Critical Edition of the Works of St. Julian of Toledo," *Studia Patristica 1* = Texte und Untersuchungen zur Geschichte der altchristlichen Literatur 63 (Berlin, 1957), 39; Gerald Kölblinger, *"Versus Panos* und *De rustico,"* *MlatJb* 8 (1973), 20; Joseph T. Lienhard, "Textual Notes on Paulinus of Nola, *Carm.* 6, 256-330," *VC* 31 (1977), 53-4; Agustín Millares Carlo, "Manuscritos visigóticos: Notas bibliográficas," *Hispania Sacra* 14 (1961), 399-400; Mostert, p. 224; Munk Olsen, vol. 1, pp. 74-5 and vol. 3.1, p. 127; Pellegrin, p. 283; *PL,* vol. 19, col. 476; Reynolds, pp. xviii-xix, 26-8, and 30-1; Alexander Riese, *Anthologia Latina sive Poesis Latinae Supplementum, Pars Prior: Carmina in Codicibus Scriptis 2* (Leipzig, 1870), pp. xxi f.; Sanford, 207; Feliciano Speranza, *Blossi Aemili Draconti Satisfactio una cum Eugeni Recensione* = Biblioteca di Helikon. Rivista di tradizione e cultura classica dell'Università di Messina. Testi e studi 9 (Roma, 1978), p. xviii; S. Tafel, "Die vordere, bisher verloren geglaubte Hälfte des Vossianischen Ausonius-Kodex," *RhM* 69 (1913), 630-41; Zacharias García Villada, *Paleografía española* (Madrid, 1923), vol. 1, p. 117; F. Vollmer, *Fl. Merobaudis Reliquiae, Blossii Aemilii Dracontii Carmina, Eugenii Toletani Episcopi Carmina et Epistulae, MGH AA,* vol. 14, pp. xix-xx.

PARIS, Bibliothèque Nationale, Lat. 8094

s. x (ff. 1-57); 107 leaves; 252 x 165 mm.; written in France?

Contents: On ff. 1r-33r: E1, PC, H1, H2. Subscription, Asterius' epigram, and prose preface on ff. 2v-3r. Biographical notice *(Sedulius versificatus primo laicus....)* on f. 34r; acrostic poems in praise of Sedulius (in Huemer's order) on f. 34r-v. E2 on ff. 34v-35r, preceded by Paulinus of Nola, *Carm.* 25 *(Epithalamium Iuliani et Titiae)* on f. 33r-v. Followed by the epigrams of Prosper (ff. 35v-57r) and Boethius, *In Librum Aristotelis Peri Hermeneias Commentarii Editio Duplex* (ff. 58r-107r).

Other information: Volume consists of three parts (s. ix-xi), of which ours is the first. PC originally divided into three books (no break between PC 1 and 2 or between PC 3 and 4). Glossing throughout. Includes indices. Used by Huemer for the acrostic poems only (P'). Seen in person. Microfilm copy acquired.

Bibliography: J.A. Bouma, *Het Epithalamium van Paulinus van Nola, Carmen XXV met Inleidung, Vertaling, en Commentaar* (Assen, 1968), pp. 18-21; C. Caesar, "Die Antwerpener Handschrift des Sedulius," *RhM* 56 (1901), 249 and 264; D.M. Cappuyns, "Le Premier représentant de l'Augustinisme médiéval, Prosper d'Aquitaine," *RTAM* 1 (1929), 335, n. 79; Émile Chatelain, *Notice sur les manuscrits des poésies de Paulin de Nole* (Paris, 1880), pp. 39-40; *CSEL,* vol. 10, p. 307; Wilhelm von Hartel, *Sancti Pontii Meropii Paulini Nolani Carmina, CSEL,* vol. 30, p. xxi; Huemer, *De Sedulii,* p. 32; Gerald Kölblinger, *"Versus Panos und De rustico,"* *MlatJb* 8 (1973), 9; G. Lacombe, *Aristoteles Latinus* (Roma, 1939), vol. 1, p. 532; Munk Olsen, vol. 2, p. 158; *PL,* vol. 19, col. 476; Alexander Riese, *Anthologia Latina sive Poesis Latinae Supplementum, Pars Prior: Carmina in Codicibus Scripta 2* (Leipzig, 1870), pp. xi-xii.

PARIS, Bibliothèque Nationale, Lat. 8313

s. xiii; 33 leaves; 185 x 130 mm.

Contents: On ff. 1r-33v: PC, H1 (incomplete at bottom of page; missing last five lines).

Other information: PC divided into two books *("Explicit liber primus. Incipit liber secundus"* at the end of PC 1; *"Explicit liber novi testamenti"* at the end of PC 5). Some glossing. Seen in person. Microfilm acquired.

Bibliography: Catalogus Codicum Manuscriptorum Bibliothecae Regiae (four volumes; Paris, 1739-44), vol. 4 (1744), p. 447; *PL,* vol. 19, col. 476.

PARIS, Bibliothèque Nationale, Lat. 8314
s. xiii-xv; 100 leaves; 198 x 125 mm.

Contents: On ff. 1r-33r: PC, H1, H2 (ff. 23r ff. in a later hand). Followed by Macer Floridus, *De Herbis;* a fragment of Macrobius' commentary on *Somnium Scipionis;* a short work on rhetoric; a short work on using proverbs in composition; excerpts from Vegetius Renatus, *Epitoma Rei Militaris;* and a treatise on grammar.
Other information: PC divided into four books (no break between PC 2 and 3). Little glossing. Elaborate initials. Microfilm acquired.
Bibliography: Bursill-Hall, p. 196; *Cat. Cod.,* same as above, p. 447; *PL,* vol. 19, col. 476; Charles R. Schrader, "The Ownership and Distribution of Manuscripts of the *De Re Militari* of Flavius Vegetius Renatus before the Year 1300," Dissertation, Columbia, 1976, p. 301; Charles Thurot, "Notices et extraits de divers manuscrits latins pour servir à l'histoire des doctrines grammaticales au Moyen Âge," *Not. et extr.* 22.2 (Paris, 1868), 50; Charles Vulliez, "Un nouveau manuscrit 'parisien' de la *Summa dictaminis* de Bernard de Meung et sa place dans la tradition manuscrite du texte," *RHT* 7 (1977), 140, n. 1.

PARIS, Bibliothèque Nationale, Lat. 8315
s. xv (1457); 235 leaves; 198 x 153 mm.; written in Brescia; paper.

Contents: On ff. 2r-34r: H1, E1, PC. Subscription on f. 2r. Followed by excerpt from Boethius, *Philosophiae Consolatio* 3 *(Carm.* 9) (ff. 34v-35v); *Facetus* (ff. 41r-50r); satire beginning *Phoebe alios mores* (ff. 52r-63r); verses of Antonio Partenio (ff. 65r-69v); selections from Virgil, *Georgics* (ff. 75r-86v); verses of Aurelio Lippo Brandolini (ff. 89r-97r); Giovanni Mario Filelfo, *De Laudibus Agri Veronensis* (ff. 99r-142r); Pietro dei Crescenzi, *Ruralium Commodorum Liber* (ff. 150r-173r); two speeches of Pius II at Mantua (ff. 179r-188v); *Orthographia est Scientia* (ff. 191r-195r); and Priscian, *Partitiones XII Versuum Aeneidos Principalium* (ff. 201r-229r); et al.
Other information: PC divided into four books (no break between PC 3 and 4). No glossing. Note on f. 34r: *Ego dominus Hieronymus de Cavallis manu propria scripsi Brixiae.* Seen in person. Microfilm

acquired.
Bibliography: Bursill-Hall, p. 196; *Cat. Cod.*, same as above, p. 447; *Catalogus Codicum Hagiographicorum Latinorum Antiquiorum Saeculo XVI Qui Asservantur in Bibliotheca Nationali Parisiensi,* vol. 2 (Paris, 1890), p. 556 [misnumbered as "8316"]; "Inventaire sommaire des manuscrits relatifs à l'histoire et à la géographie de l'orient latin I," *Archives de l'orient latin* 2 (1884), 140; G. Mardersteig, "Tre epigrammi di Gian Mario Filelfo a Felice Feliciano" in *Classical, Medieval and Renaissance Studies in Honor of B.L. Ullman,* ed. C. Henderson, Jr. (Roma, 1964), vol. 2, p. 376, n. 3; Alfred Morel-Fatio, "Mélanges de littérature catalane," *Romania* 15 (1886), 224; Passalacqua, pp. 239-40; *PL,* vol. 19, col. 476.

PARIS, Bibliothèque Nationale, Lat. 8316
s. xv; 56 leaves; 213 x 140 mm.; paper.

Contents: On ff. 1r-55r: E1, PC, H1. Subscription, Asterius' epigram, and prose preface on f. 5r-v.
Other information: PC divided into five books (1+4). Seen in person. Microfilm acquired.
Bibliography: *Cat. Cod.*, same as above, pp. 447-8; *PL,* vol. 19, col. 476.

PARIS, Bibliothèque Nationale, Lat. 8317
s. xv; 114 leaves; 208 x 138 mm.

Contents: On ff. 1r-38r: E1, PC, H1, H2. Acrostic poem of Belle-sarius on f. 37r-v. Subscription, Asterius' epigram, and biographical notice on f. 3r-v. Hymn beginning *Salve festa dies* on f. 38v. Followed by Proba, *Cento* (ff. 39r-57r); *Scholium de Forma Scribendarum Epistolarum* (ff. 59r-62r); John of Garland, *Cornutus (Distigium)* (ff. 62v-63v); *De Contemptu Mundi* (ff. 63v-66r); *Poenitentiarius* (ff. 66v-69v); *Speculum Puerorum* (ff. 70r-81v); *Rudium Doctrina* (ff. 82r-90v); and *Liber de Computo* (ff. 93r-114v).
Other information: Heavily glossed (interlinear and marginal). Seen in person. Microfilm acquired.
Bibliography: *Cat. Cod.*, same as above, p. 448; B. Hauréau, *Initia Operum Latinorum* (Turnhout, Brepols reprint without date), vol. 4, p. 256a; idem, "Notices sur les oeuvres authentiques ou supposées de Jean de Garlande," *Not. et extr.* 27.2 (Paris, 1879), pp. 28 ff.; Pellegrin, p. 311, n. 5; *PL,* vol. 19, col. 476.

PARIS, Bibliothèque Nationale, Lat. 9347
s. ix[1]; 135 leaves (ff. 61-66 and 129 are missing); 368 x 256 mm.;
written in Reims, probably at the Abbey of S. Remigius.

Contents: On ff. 2v-17r: H2, E1, PC, H1. Subscription and Asterius'
epigram on f. 4r. Acrostic poems in praise of Sedulius (in Huemer's
order) on f. 17v; biographical notice *(Sedulius versificus primo....* [attr.
Jerome]) on f. 17r-v. *Accessus* and commentary on first book of PC on
f. 1v. Followed by Ps.-Cato, *Monosticha* (ff. 17v-18r); Juvencus,
Evangeliorum Libri Quattuor (ff. 18r-39r); the epigrams of Prosper (ff.
39r-48v); Sylvius, *De Cognomentis Salvatoris* (f. 48v); epitaph for Pope
Adrian II (attr. Charlemagne) (f. 49r); Quintus Serenus, *Liber Medici-*
nalis (ff. 49r-57r); verses on the Roman emperors from Julius Caesar to
Vespasian (f. 57r-v); Arator, *Historia Apostolica* (ff. 57v-76v); and
Venantius Fortunatus, *Carmina* (ff. 76r-135v).
Other information: PC divided into five books (1+4). Heavily glossed
throughout. Used by Huemer (F). Seen in person. Microfilm acquired.
Bibliography: Emil Baehrens, *Poetae Latini Minores,* vol. 3 (Leipzig,
1881), p. 106; Beccaria, pp. 159-60; Boas, p. xviii; idem, "De Parisina
Quadam Sententiarum Catonianarum Sylloga," *Mnemosyne* 43 (1915),
286-318; F.M. Carey, "The Scriptorium of Reims during the Archbish-
opric of Hincmar (854-882 AD)" in *Classical and Medieval Studies in*
Honor of E.K. Rand (New York, 1938), pp. 45 and 58; Émile Chatelain,
Introduction à la lecture des notes tironiennes (Paris, 1900), p. 141;
CSEL, vol. 10, pp. xiv-xv; Léopold Victor Delisle, "Inventaire des
manuscrits conservés à la Bibliothèque Impériale sous les nos. 8823-
11503," *BECh* 23 (1862), 306; Ernst Dümmler, "Die handschriftliche
Überlieferung der lateinischen Dichtungen aus der Zeit der Karolinger,"
Neues Archiv 4 (1878-9), 120; Huemer, *De Sedulii,* p. 10, 22, 32, 38,
41, 43, and 51; idem, "Zu *Anthologia Latina* 716 R," *WS* 4 (1882), 170-
2; Kurz, 266; Legendre, p. 62; F. Leo, *Venanti Honori Clementiani*
Fortunati Presbyteri Italici Opera Poetica, MGH AA, vol. 4.1, p. vii;
McKinlay, pp. 18-19; Wilhelm Meyer, "Rhythmische Paraphrase des
Sedulius von einem Iren," *NKGWG,* 1917, 594-6; Munk Olsen, vol. 2,
p. 482 and vol. 3.1, p. 206; Reynolds, p. 383; G. Waitz, "Pariser
Handschriften," *Neues Archiv* 6 (1880-1), 478; Wickersheimer, p. 93.

PARIS, Bibliothèque Nationale, Lat. 10307
s. ix[4/4]; 246 leaves; 345 x 260 mm.; written in eastern France (Lor-
raine?).

Contents: On ff. 1r-34r: E1, PC, H1, H2. Subscription, Asterius' epigram, and prose preface on f. 2r-v. Acrostic poems in praise of Sedulius (in the reverse of Huemer's order) on f. 33r-v. Text of Sedulius written in alternating columns (starting on f. 2r) with Juvencus, *Evangeliorum Libri Quattuor.* Followed by the works of Virgil (along with Servius' commentary): *Eclogues* (ff. 50v-63r), *Georgics* (ff. 63r-96r), and *Aeneid* (ff. 97v-245v).

Other information: Volume consists of two contemporaneous parts (ff. 1-43 and ff. 44-246). PC divided into five books. Indices for first three books. Some glossing in H1. Seen in person. Microfilm copy acquired.

Bibliography: Contreni, pp. 89-90, 119-20, 139-41, and passim; idem, "A propos de quelques manuscrits de l'école de Laon au IXe siècle: Découvertes et problèmes," *MA* 78 (1972), 29 ff.; Delisle, "Inventaire," same as above, 506; Dümmler, same as above, pp. 120-1; Louis Holtz, "Les Manuscrits latins à gloses et à commentaires de l'antiquité à l'époque carolingienne" in *Atti del convegno internazionale: Il libro e il testo* (Urbino, 1984), pp. 164-5; Huemer, *De Sedulii,* pp. 32 and 39; Munk Olsen, vol. 2, pp. 764-5; Sanford, 214; J.J.H. Savage, "The Manuscripts of Servius's Commentary on Virgil," *HSCP* 45 (1934), 189; E. Thomas, *Scoliastes de Virgile: Essai sur Servius et son commentaire sur Virgile* (Paris, 1880), pp. 304-5.

PARIS, Bibliothèque Nationale, Lat. 12279

s. ix*med.*; 147 leaves; 311 x 252 mm.; written at Corbie; later at S. Germain-des-Prés, Paris.

Contents: On ff. 47r-58v: E2, PO (missing ending; breaks off at Huemer's page 287, line 3, at bottom of page). Preceded by a short explanation of the Gospel of John and fragments of Gregory (ff. 1r-10v) as well as Bede, *In Marci Evangelium Expositio* (ff. 11r-46v). Followed by Alcuin's commentary on the Gospel of John (ff. 59r ff.); Bede, *In Librum Patris Tobiae Allegorica Expositio* (ff. 120v-124r); Bede, *Chronica Maiora;* et al. (ff. 124r ff.); Theodulf of Orléans, *De Ordine Baptismi* (ff. 127r-131v); and excerpts from the church fathers on the mass (ff. 131v-147v).

Other information: According to Laistner, manuscript "shows traces of an Insular exemplar." Text of PO divided into five continuously numbered books. Includes indices. Used by Huemer (P). Seen in person. Microfilm acquired.

Bibliography: *CSEL,* vol. 10, p. xxxvi; Léopold Victor Delisle,

"Inventaire des manuscrits latins de Saint-Germain-des-Prés," *BECh* 28 (1867), 358; Laistner, pp. 54, 81, and 153; idem, "Source-Marks in Bede Manuscripts," *Journal of Theological Studies* 34 (1933), 351.

PARIS, Bibliothèque Nationale, Lat. 13377

s. ix (ff. 1-15=s. xii-xiii); 149 leaves; 212 x 136 mm.; written at Corbie; later at S. Germain-des-Prés, Paris.

Contents: On ff. 16r-55v: E1, PC, H1, H2 (with neums). The hymns are separated by the acrostic poems in praise of Sedulius (in Huemer's order) on f. 54r-v and biographical notice *(Sedulius versificus primo laicus....* [attr. Jerome]). Subscription, Asterius' epigram, and prose preface on f. 18r-v. Preceded by sermons of Augustine and the passion of S. Demetrius (ff. 1r ff.). Followed by the epigrams of Prosper (ff. 56v ff.); Bede, *De Arte Metrica* (ff. 83r-101r) and *De Schematibus et Tropis* (ff. 101r-106v); Alcuin, *De Grammatica* (ff. 107r ff.); Bede, *De Orthographia* (ff. 135r ff.); *Exempla de Communibus Syllabis* (f. 149r); and Eugenius of Toledo, *Carm. 1 (Rex Deus immensus....)* (f. 149v). There is a life of Bede on f. 82v.

Other information: PC divided into three books (no break between PC 1 and 2 or between PC 3 and 4). Includes indices. Extensive glossing. Written in the Maurdramnus script. Used by Huemer (H). Seen in person. Microfilm acquired.

Bibliography: Bischoff, *MS*, vol. 2, p. 26; *CSEL*, vol. 10, p. xvi; Léopold Victor Delisle, "Inventaire des manuscrits latins de Saint-Germain-des-Prés," *BECh* 29 (1868), 228; David Ganz, *Corbie in the Carolingian Renaissance* = Beihefte der Francia 20 (Sigmaringen, 1990), p. 138; Huemer, *De Sedulii*, pp. 22, 32, 39, and 51; C.B. Kendall and M.H. King, *Bedae Venerabilis Opera, Pars VI. Opera Didascalia I, CCSL*, vol. 123A, p. 64; Kurz, 266; Laistner, p. 134; Christian de Mérindol, *La Production des livres peints à l'Abbaye de Corbie au XIIe siècle*, vol. 2 (Lille, 1976), pp. 966-9; F. Vollmer, *Fl. Merobaudis Reliquiae, Blossii Aemilii Dracontii Carmina, Eugenii Toletani Episcopi Carmina et Epistulae, MGH AA*, vol. 14, p. 232.

PARIS, Bibliothèque Nationale, Lat. 14143

s. ix; 71 leaves in first part (82 leaves *in toto*); 210 x 145 mm. (cut down); written at Corbie; later at S. Germain-des-Prés, Paris.

Contents: On ff. 3r-55v: E1 (missing beginning; starts at Huemer's page 4, line 1), PC, H1, H2. *Accessus* and *Incipit ars....* on f. 2v.

Biographical notice *(Iste Sedulius primo laicus fuit....* [attr. Jerome]) in margin on f. 2v. Subscription, Asterius' epigram, and prose preface on f. 6r. Acrostic poems in praise of Sedulius (in Huemer's order) between H1 and H2 on ff. 53v-54r. H2 followed by a biographical notice *(Sedulius versificus primo laicus...).* Preceded by hymn beginning *Benedicamus Domino* with neums and lines (f. 1r). Followed by Paul the Deacon, *Carmen de S. Benedicto* (ff. 55v-59v); "Einhard," *Rhythmus de Passione Christi Martyrum Marcellini et Petri* (ff. 60r-68v); *De Gradibus Sacerdotum et Clericorum et Episcoporum* (ff. 68v-70r); *De Libris Divini Auctoritatis* (ff. 70r-71v); and *Carmen de S. Quintino* (ff. 72r ff.).

Other information: PC divided into five continuously numbered books. Glossed extensively in several hands. Used by Huemer (G). Seen in person. Microfilm acquired.

Bibliography: *Catalogus Codicum Hagiographicorum Latinorum Antiquiorum Saeculo XVI Qui Asservantur in Bibliotheca Nationali Parisiensi,* vol. 3 (Paris, 1893), pp. 221-2; *CSEL,* vol. 10, pp. xv-xvi; Delisle, "Inventaire," same as above, 257; idem, *Le Cabinet des manuscrits de la Bibliothèque Nationale,* vol. 2 (Paris, 1874), p. 432, no. 282; Ganz, same as above, p. 148; Wilhelm Harster, *Novem Vitae Sanctorum Metricae ex Codicibus Monacensibus, Parisiensibus, Bruxellensi, Hagensi, Saec. IX-XII* (Leipzig, 1887), p. vi; Huemer, *De Sedulii,* pp. 9-10, 21-22, 35, 38, 41, 43, and 51; Kurz, 266.

PARIS, Bibliothèque Nationale, Lat. 15148

s. xiii; 91 leaves (now missing leaves 2-43); 227 x 147 mm.; S. Victor, Paris.

Contents: On ff. 45r-88v: E1, PC, H1, H2. Prose preface on f. 48r. Dedicatory preface to Proba's cento (starting with second line) and the acrostic poems in praise of Sedulius (in the reverse of Huemer's order) on ff. 88v-89r. Originally preceded by John of Hauville, *Architrenius* (now missing).

Other information: PC divided into five books. First book ends with line 350; 1.351-368 = *"Prologus quattuor evangeliorum."* Index before first book. Heavily glossed. Seen in person. Microfilm acquired.

Bibliography: Léopold Victor Delisle, "Inventaire des manuscrits latins de Saint-Victor conservés à la Bibliothèque Impériale sous les numéros 14232-15175," *BECh* 30 (1869), 76; Gilbert Ouy, et al., *Le Catalogue de la Bibliothèque de l'Abbaye de Saint-Victor de Paris de Claude de Grandrue 1514* (Paris, 1983), p. 368.

PARIS, Bibliothèque Nationale, Lat. 15149
s. xii (ff. 145 ff.); 192 leaves; 208 x 132 mm.; S. Victor, Paris.

Contents: On ff. 145r-192r: E1, PC, H1, H2 (both hymns in another, earlier, hand). Subscription on f. 148r; biographical notice *(Sedulius versificus primordio laicus....)* and other introductory material on f. 192r-v. Preceded by Hildebert of Lavardin, *De Mysterio Missae* (ff. 1r ff.); Odo's life of S. Geraldus (ff. 17r ff.); a passion of S. Catherina (ff. 46r-65v); works attributed to Jerome including *De Viris Inlustribus* (ff. 66r ff.); and a catalogue of the popes (ff. 137r ff.).

Other information: Miscellany volume (s. xii-xiv). PC divided into five books (1+4). Interlinear and marginal glossing. Some fine initials (especially p's). Seen in person. Microfilm acquired.

Bibliography: *Catalogus Codicum Hagiographicorum Latinorum Antiquiorum Saeculo XVI Qui Asservantur in Bibliotheca Nationali Parisiensi,* vol. 3 (Paris, 1893), p. 302; *Cat. de la Bibl. de l'Abbaye de Saint-Victor,* same as above, p. 295; Delisle, "Inventaire," same as above, 76; L. van Acker, *Petri Pictoris Carmina, CCCM,* vol. 25, p. cviii.

PARIS, Bibliothèque Nationale, Lat. 15159
s. xv (1490); 229 leaves; 203 x 140 mm.; S. Victor, Paris; paper.

Contents: On ff. 48r-122v: E1, PC, H1, H2. Subscription, Asterius' epigram, and biographical notice on f. 50r-v. Acrostic poem of Bellesarius between hymns (ff. 120v-121r). Hymn beginning *Salve festa dies* (attr. Sedulius) on ff. 122v-123r. Preceded by *Libellus de Articulis Fidei* (ff. 1r-8r); *Disticha Catonis* (ff. 9v-25r); *Ecloga Theoduli* (ff. 25v-37r); *Memoriale Nominum* (ff. 38r-46v). Followed by John of Garland, *Poenitentiarius* (ff. 124r-127v and ff. 192r-201r); Horace, *Epistles* (ff. 134r-183v); a calendar (ff. 184r-189v); and the *computus* of Anianus (ff. 204r-220v).

Other information: PC divided into five books. Heavily glossed. Seen in person. Microfilm acquired.

Bibliography: Delisle, "Inventaire," same as above, 77; B. Hauréau, "Notices sur les oeuvres authentiques ou supposées de Jean de Garlande," *Not. et extr.* 27.2 (Paris, 1879), 12.

PARIS, Bibliothèque Nationale, Lat. 16669
s. xv; 209 leaves; 216 x 148 mm.; written in Italy; prov. Sorbonne; paper.

Contents: On ff. 78r-125v: PC. Preceded by works of Terentianus Maurus, Alexander of Villa Dei, et al. (ff. 1r ff.). Followed by excerpts from the *Aeneid* (ff. 126r ff.); *Ad Herennium* (ff. 144r ff.); and *Paradoxa* (ff. 200v ff.).

Other information: Owned by Cardinal Richelieu. On f. 1r: *Armando Richelio Cardinale literatissimo atque eloquentissimo Io. Iacobus Buccardus.* Some glossing. PC divided into five continuously numbered books. Seen in person. Microfilm acquired.

Bibliography: Léopold Victor Delisle, "Inventaire des manuscrits latins de la Sorbonne, conservés à la Bibliothèque Impériale sous les nos. 15176-16178 du fonds latin," *BECh* 31 (1870), 73; Olga Rozhdestven-skaia, *Les Poésies des Goliards groupées et traduites avec le texte latin* = Les Textes du Christianisme 9 (Paris, 1931), p. 63; Charles Thurot, "Notices et extraits de divers manuscrits latins pour servir à l'histoire des doctrines grammaticales au Moyen Âge," *Not. et extr.* 22.2 (Paris, 1868), 58.

PARIS, Bibliothèque Nationale, Lat. 16699
s. xii/xiii; 179 leaves; 225 x 148 mm.; written in northern France; prov. Notre-Dame-du-Pré (Amiens).

Contents: On ff. 3r-37r: PC, H1. Followed by Arator, *Historia Apostolica* (ff. 37v-76v); *Hymni de Sancta Maria* (f. 77r); Peter Comestor, *Figura de Partu Virginis Matris* (f. 77r-v); the epigrams of Prosper and Ps.-Prosper, *Poema Coniugis ad Uxorem Suam* (ff. 77v-111v); Arnulf of Lisieux, *De Nativitate Domini* (ff. 112r-117v); Serlo of Wilton, *Carm.* 2 (ff. 117v-120r); Marbod, *Liber Lapidum* (ff. 120r-125v); passions of Laurentius and Vincentius (ff. 125v-127v); excerpts from Virgil, *Eclogues* and *Georgics* (ff. 128r-130v); excerpts from Juvenal, *Satires* (ff. 130v-133r); excerpts from Ovid, *Remedia Amoris* (ff. 133r-135r); excerpts from Lucan, *Bellum Civile* and Persius, *Satires* (f. 135r); Serlo of Wilton, *Carm.* 81-3 (f. 135v); sermons of Peter Comestor (ff. 136r-149r); letters of Pope Urban II and Ivo of Chartres (ff. 149v-151v); a treatment of Anselm's *Cur Deus Homo* (ff. 152r-159v); excerpts from Gregory (ff. 159v-160v); Isidore, *De Fide Catholica contra Judaeos* (ff. 160v-172r); miscellaneous verses (ff. 172r-181v), including poems of Peter the Painter, on ff. 172r-173v.

Other information: PC divided into six books (1+5). Last book begins with 5.261. Little glossing. Seen in person. Microfilm copy acquired.

Bibliography: *Catalogus Codicum Hagiographicorum Latinorum Antiquiorum Saeculo XVI Qui Asservantur in Bibliotheca Nationali*

Parisiensi, vol. 3 (Paris, 1893), pp. 339-40; Delisle, "Inventaire," same as above, 75; Peter Dronke, *Medieval Latin and the Rise of European Love Lyric* (2nd ed.; Oxford, 1968), vol. 2, *Medieval Latin Love-Poetry,* p. 574; Hauréau, *Notices,* vol. 5, pp. 202 ff.; Artur M. Landgraf, *Einführung in die Geschichte der theologischen Literatur der Frühscholastik unter dem Gesichtspunkte der Schulenbildung* (Regensburg, 1948), p. 53; McKinlay, pp. 22-3; Munk Olsen, vol. 2, pp. 864-5; idem, "Les Classiques latins dans les florilèges médiévaux antérieurs au XIIIe siècle I," *RHT* 9 (1979), 120-1; idem, "Vergil i middelalderen. Vergilhåndskrifter og Vergil-florilegier fra det 9. til begyndelsen af det 13. århundrede," *MT* 32-33 (1978), 110-11; Jan Öberg, *Serlon de Wilton, poèmes latins* = Acta Universitatis Stockholmiensis. Studia Latina Stockholmiensia 14 (Stockholm, 1965), pp. 29-30; Sanford, 227; Thurot, "Extraits," same as above, 26; L. van Acker, *Petri Pictoris Carmina, CCCM,* vol. 25, pp. lxxxv-vi.

PARIS, Bibliothèque Nationale, Lat. 18553
s. ix; 109 leaves; 245 x 155 mm.; Notre-Dame, Paris.

Contents: On ff. 2r-43v: E1, PC, H1, H2. Dedicatory preface to Proba's cento on ff. 43v-44r. Followed by Juvencus, *Evangeliorum Libri Quattuor* (ff. 44v ff.).
Other information: PC divided into five books (1+4; *"Liber primus"* begins with line 103; 1.355-68 = *"Prologus de quattuor evangelistarum"*). Extensive interlinear glossing and marginal notation throughout. Includes indices. Seen in person. Microfilm copy acquired.
Bibliography: Léopold Victor Delisle, "Inventaire des manuscrits latins de Notre-Dame et d'autres fonds conservés a la Bibliothèque Nationale sous les numéros 16719-18613," *BECh* 31 (1870), 562.

PARIS, Bibliothèque Nationale, Lat. 18554
s. ix[2]; 168 leaves; 241 x 180 mm.; probably written at S. Denis, Paris, except for last part of MS (Prudentius); later at Notre-Dame.

Contents: On ff. 4r-55v: E1, PC, H1, H2. *Accessus* and biographical notices *(Iste Sedulius primo laicus fuit....* [attr. Jerome] and *Incipit ars....)* on f. 3r-v. Subscription, Asterius' epigram, and prose preface on ff. 7v-8r. Biographical notice *(Sedulius versificus primo....)* on f. 53v; acrostic poems in praise of Sedulius (in Huemer's order) on ff. 53v-54r. Followed by Arator, *Historia Apostolica* (ff. 55v-111v); the epigrams of Prosper (ff. 112r-138v); and Prudentius, *Psychomachia* (s.

xi), with German interlinear and marginal glosses (ff. 140r-168r).
Other information: PC divided into five books (1 + 4). Interlinear and
marginal glossing. Rand suggests (see McKinlay, p. 25) that the
manuscript shows "the influence of Tours." Neums in first stanzas of
H1. Manuscript belonged to Antoine Loisel and later to Claude Joly.
Seen in person. Microfilm copy acquired.

Bibliography: Bergmann, p. 91; Émile Chatelain, *Introduction à la
lecture des notes tironiennes* (Paris, 1900), p. 135; Léopold Victor
Delisle, *Le Cabinet des manuscrits de la Bibliothèque Imperiale,* vol. 1
(Paris, 1868), p. 431, n. 3; idem, "Inventaire," same as above, 562;
Hermann Garke, *Prothese und Aphaerese des H im Althochdeutschen =*
Quellen und Forschungen zur Sprach- und Culturgeschichte der
germanischen Völker 69 (Strassburg, 1891), 71; Glauche, p. 35;
Legendre, p. 163; Lesne, p. 590, note 8; McKinlay, pp. 24-5; Donatella
Nebbiai-Dalla Guarda, *La Bibliothèque de l'Abbaye de Saint Denis en
France* (Paris, 1985), pp. 308-9; Steinmeyer & Sievers, vol. 4, p. 599;
R. Stettiner, *Die illustrierten Prudentius Handschriften* (Berlin, 1895), p.
54; Jean Vezin, "Le Point d'interrogation, un élément de datation et de
localisation des manuscrits. L'Exemple de Saint-Denis au IXe siècle,"
Scriptorium 34 (1980), 193-4; Elis Wadstein, "Kleinere altsächsische
Sprachdenkmäler mit Anmerkungen und Glossar," *Niederdeutsche
Denkmäler* 6 (1899), 148-9.

PARIS, Bibliothèque Nationale, Nouv. Acq. Lat. 474

s. xv; 46 leaves; 210 mm. x 146 mm.; paper.

Contents: On ff. 1r-45v: E1, PC, H1, H2. Subscription, Asterius'
epigram, and prose preface on f. 3v. Epigram of Bellesarius between
hymns (f. 44v). Hymn beginning *Salve festa dies* (attributed to Sedulius)
on ff. 45v-46r.
Other information: PC divided into five books (1 + 4). Owned by Don
de M. le marquis de Queux de Saint-Hilaire. Seen in person. Microfilm
acquired.
Bibliography: Léopold Victor Delisle, *Bibliothèque Nationale.
Manuscrits latins et français ajoutés aux fonds des nouvelles acquisitions
pendant les années 1875-1891. Inventaire alphabétique,* vol. 2 (Paris,
1891), pp. 606-7.

PARIS, Bibliothèque de Sainte-Geneviève, 2410

s. x^2 (ff. 122-173); 229 leaves; 260-265 x 185-190 mm.; written in
England.

Contents: On ff. 122r-169v: E1, PC, H1, H2. Biographical notice *(Incipit ars....)* on f. 122r; acrostic poems in praise of Sedulius (in the reverse of Huemer's order) on ff. 169v-170r. Preceded by Juvencus, *Evangeliorum Libri Quattuor* (ff. 1r-70r) and a commentary on Matthew's Gospel (ff. 71r-117r), as well as two bifolia dating to s. xi[1] containing Greek prayers and *Rubisca* (ff. 118r-121v). Followed by excerpt from Aldhelm, *Epistula ad Acircium.* Leaves 174-229 contain Odo of Cluny, *Occupatio* (breaks off at the beginning of Book 7); completed by Paris, Bibliothèque de l'Arsénal, 903.

Other information: Composite manuscript (s. x-xi) written by a number of English scribes, of which ours (ff. 122-173) is part 4 (s. x[2]). PC divided into six books (first book begins at 1.103; final book division at 5.261). Includes indices. Glossed throughout. From Christ Church, Canterbury? As donated to the library in the 18th century, this manuscript consisted of two volumes, 2409 and 2410 respectively. The former contains Flodoard of Reims, *De Triumphis Christi.* Microfilm acquired.

Bibliography: Gneuss, "List," no. 903; Michael W. Herren, *The Hisperica Famina: II. Related Poems. A Critical Edition with English Translation and Philological Commentary* = Studies and Texts 85 (Toronto, 1987), p. 18; P.C. Jacobsen, *Flodoard von Reims: Sein Leben und seine Dichtung De Triumphis Christi* = Mittellateinische Studien und Texte 10 (Leiden, 1978); Ch. Kohler, *Catalogue des manuscrits de la Bibliothèque Saint-Geneviève* in *Catalogue général des manuscrits des bibliothèques publiques de France. Paris* (1893-6), vol. 2, pp. 340-4; Lapidge, "Latin Texts," p. 114 and n. 65; Andy Orchard, *The Poetic Art of Aldhelm* = Cambridge Studies in Anglo-Saxon England 8 (Cambridge, 1994), p. 164.

PARIS, Private Collection
s. xi (c. 1000); 44 leaves; 208 x 154 mm.; written in northern Italy; prov. S. Severino, Napoli.

Contents: On ff. 12v-40v: E1, PC, H1, H2. Subscription, Asterius' epigram, and prose preface on f. 14v. Preceded by Muretach (Muridach), *In Donati Artem Maiorem* (ff. 1r-11r).

Other information: No foliation or pagination. Written by three hands. PC division into books inconsistent. Extensive glossing. Neums in first lines of H2.

Bibliography: Louis Holtz, "La Main de Franciscellus Mancinus et le fonds ancien de San Severino e Sossio de Naples," *Scriptorium* 44

(1990), 217-258; Jeudy, "Remi," p. 497.

PERUGIA, Biblioteca Communale Augusta, I. 56 (661)
s. xv (1492); 137 leaves; written at S. Pietro, Perugia; paper.

Contents: On ff. 2r-29v: PC (missing several leaves after f. 2 [=1.45 to 2.242]; 2.156-241 on ff. 16r-17v), H1. Followed by elegies of Marcus Antonius Sabellicus (ff. 30r-42v); Franciscus Aretinus, *Phalaris;* et al. (ff. 43r-123v); *Epigramma Romae Inventum in Templo Fauni* (f. 124r); and *Aesopus* (ff. 131v-136r).
Other information: On f. 124: *Hil. Vercellensis scripsit hoc opus in monasterio S. Petri de Perusio.* PC not divided into books. Microfilm acquired.
Bibliography: Kristeller, *Iter,* vol. 2, p. 59; Mazzatinti, vol. 5 (1895), pp. 172-3.

PERUGIA, Biblioteca Communale Augusta, I. 122 (728)
s. xi; 40 leaves; 213 x 153 mm.

Contents: On ff. 1r-40v: PC, H1 (1-36 only).
Other information: Divided into six books (1+5; last book begins with PC 5.261). Extensive glossing. Seen in person. Microfilm acquired.
Bibliography: Mazzatinti, vol. 5 (1895), p. 186.

PHILADELPHIA, University of Pennsylvania Library, Lat. 99
s. xv²; 66 leaves; 140 x 100 mm.; written in Germany; paper.

Contents: On ff. 1r-47r: PC, H1. Followed by miscellaneous verses (ff. 47r-51v); "notes on the order of liturgy and verses in praise of monastic life, especially the Carthusian order" (ff. 59r-65v); and an account of the transfiguration (f. 66r-v). Leaves 52-58 are blank.
Other information: PC divided into four books (no break between PC 1 and 2). Some interlinear glossing and marginal notes. Microfilm copy acquired.
Bibliography: Norman P. Zacour and Rudolf Hirsch, *Catalogue of Manuscripts in the Libraries of the University of Pennsylvania to 1800* (Philadelphia, 1965), p. 22.

POMMERSFELDEN, Gräflich Schönbornsche Bibliothek, 12 (2671)
s. xii (ff. 1-52); 238 leaves; 208 x 146 mm.; Erfurt.

Contents: On ff. 1v-52v: E1, PC, H1. Subscription on bottom of f. 1v. Followed by *Ysengrimus* on ff. 1r-127v (s. xiv[1]) and *Disticha Catonis; Theoduli Ecloga; Aesopus;* the fables of Avianus; et al. on ff. 1r-51v (s. xiv[ex.]).

Other information: Volume consists of three parts, independently foliated, of which ours (ff. 1-52) is the first. Once in the collection of Amplonius (no. 26) in Erfurt. PC divided into five books (1+4). At PC 1.354: *Finit liber Sedulii de miraculis veteris testamenti. Incipit de quattuor evangelistis.* Interlinear and marginal glossing, including many (over 130) Old High German glosses. Microfilm copy acquired.

Bibliography: Rolf Bergmann, *Mittelfränkische Glossen. Studien zu ihrer Ermittlung und sprachgeographischen Einordnung* = Rheinisches Archiv 61 (2nd ed.; Bonn, 1977), pp. 245-7; Guaglianone, p. xxi; Peter Pauly, *Die althochdeutschen Glossen der Handschriften Pommersfelden 2671 und Antwerpen 17.4. Untersuchungen zu ihrem Lautstand* = Rheinisches Archiv 67 (Bonn, 1968), passim; Steinmeyer & Sievers, vol. 2, pp. 614-6 and vol. 4, p. 602; Ernst Voigt, *Ysengrimus* (Halle, 1884), pp. vi-viii.

PRAHA, Národní Knihovna, III. G. 20 (545)
s. xiv[ex.]; 39 leaves; 225 x 155 mm.; paper.

Contents: On ff. 1r-29v: PC, H1. Followed by Hugo of Trimberg, *Laurea Sanctorum* (ff. 29v-35r) and the fables of Avianus (ff. 35v-39r). Includes extra line (309) at end of PC 4 as do the other Prague manuscripts.

Other information: PC not divided into books. Some glossing, especially in first book. Seen in person.

Bibliography: Guaglianone, p. xxiii; J. Truhlář, *Catalogus Codicum Manu Scriptorum Latinorum Qui in C.R. Bibliotheca Publica atque Universitatis Pragensis Asservantur* (Praha, 1905-6), part 1, p. 223.

PRAHA, Národní Knihovna, VIII. H. 23 (1641)
s. xv[in.]; 149 leaves (last blank); 220 x 150 mm.; paper.

Contents: On ff. 37r-75v: PC. Preceded by the epigrams of Prosper (ff. 1r-34r) and Prudentius, *Dittochaeon* (ff. 34v-36v). Followed by Arator, *Historia Apostolica* (ff. 76r-126r); Johannes Turonensis, *Expositio Missae* in verse (ff. 127v-137r); and John of Garland, *De Mysteriis Ecclesiae* (ff. 138r-148v).

Other information: PC not divided into books. Heavily glossed until

PC 4.149. At the end of PC: *"Explicit ... per manus Stephani de
...awia finitus a.d. 1402."* Seen in person.
Bibliography: McKinlay, p. 64; Truhlář, same as above, p. 608.

PRAHA, Národní Knihovna, XIV. F. 18 (2603)
s. xv; 70 leaves; 205 x 150 mm.; paper.

Contents: On ff. 25r-69r: PC. Preceded by a treatise on studying and
memorization (ff. 2r-12v); *Thesaurus Philosophicus* (ff. 13r-21v); and
excerpts from Aristotle in Latin (ff. 21v-24v). Followed by *Rhetorica
Deutsch* (f. 70r-v).
Other information: At end of PC: *Finis adest operis; mercedem postulo
laboris. Scriptus in Slagwyerd in fornace dicentes. Explicit Sedulius.
Finitus die dominico ante festum S. Martini....* Seen in person.
Bibliography: Truhlář, same as above, part 2, pp. 326-7.

PRAHA, Národní Knihovna, XXIII. F. 137 (Lobk. 499)
s. xii; 48 leaves (unnumbered); 210 x 149 mm.; written in Germany;
prov. Weissenau.

Contents: On ff. 1v-48r: E1 *("prosa Sedulii")*, PC, H1, H2 (om. 1-28
and includes doxology). Subscription, Asterius' epigram, and prose
preface on f. 4r-v. Between the hymns (ff. 46v-47v): dedication
beginning *Haec tibi unanime papa;* anonymous description of four
evangelists (preface to Juvencus, *Evangeliorum Libri Quattuor*);
dedicatory preface to Proba's cento (beginning *Romulidum rector...*); and
acrostic poems in praise of Sedulius (in the reverse of Huemer's order).
On f. 48r-v: subscription and Asterius' epigram.
Other information: PC divided into six books (1+5; last book begins
with 5.261). Two interlinear German glosses on f. 7v. Names of King
Philip of Schwaben (died 1208) and his wife Irene on f. 6r. Includes
some illustrative sketches (dry-point) in margins. Seen in person.
Microfilm acquired.
Bibliography: Lehmann, vol. 4, p. 62.

PRINCETON, University Library, Garrett 69
s. xv (1455); 81 pages; 200 x 130 mm.; written in Italy.

Contents: On pp. 1-81: E1, PC, H1.
Other information: PC divided into four books (no division between PC
4 and 5). No glossing. Written by "Mart. Ri" and dated 10 April,

1455. Obtained from W.M. Voynich in 1928. Microfilm acquired.
Bibliography: Census, vol. 1, p. 877.

REIMS, Bibliothèque Municipale, 1277 (J. 749)
s. xv; 185 leaves; 209 x 145 mm.; paper.

Contents: On ff. 36r-89v: PC, H1, E1. H1 followed by acrostic poem
of Bellesarius; E1 followed by acrostic poem of Liberatus. Preceded by
Hildebert of Lavardin, *Vita Beatae Mariae Aegyptiacae* (ff. 13 ff.) and
followed by a letter of Leonardo Bruni to Pope Pius II (Aeneas Silvius
Piccolomini) on a translation of the *Ethics* of Aristotle (ff. 90 ff.) and
Arator, *Historia Apostolica* (ff. 96-162). On f. 185 three epitaphs.
Leaves 3-11 and 162-184 are blank.
Bibliography: Cat. gen. octavo, vol. 39, part 1, pp. 440-7.

ROMA, Biblioteca Angelica, 970 (R. 5. 21)
s. xv (1473); 82 leaves; 125 x 90 mm.; Chiaravalle, Milano; paper.

Contents: On ff. 31r-80r: PC, H1. Preceded by Prudentius, *Praefatio,*
and *Psychomachia* (ff. 1r-26r); Francesco Filelfo, *Satyrarum Hecatosti-
chon Septima Decas, Hecatosticha Quinta* (final verses) (ff. 26v-27r);
Franciscus de Fiano, *Deprecacio Pulcherrima ad Gloriosissimam Matrem*
(ff. 27r-28r); and hymn beginning *Salve festa dies* (attr. Lactantius) (ff.
28r-30v). Followed (on ff. 80r-82v) by eight-line poem beginning *Ista
tibi Antoni; Elegia de XII Gradibus Humilitatis*; an epigram for the writer
of the codex; and an elegiac poem beginning *Virgo decus caeli.*
Other information: Very similar to New Haven, Yale University
Library, Marston MS 98. PC divided into four books (no division
between PC 3 and 4). Colophon reads: *"Est Mon. Carevallis Mediola-
nensis ordinis Cystercensis. Concessus et scriptus per N. Benignum."*
Used by Arevalo *(Ang.).* Microfilm copy acquired.
Bibliography: F. Di Cesare, *Catalogo dei manoscritti in scrittura latina
datati....* (Torino, 1982), 124-5; Enrico Narducci, *Catalogus Codicum
Manuscriptorum praeter Graecos et Orientales in Bibliotheca Angelica
olim Coenobii S. Augustini de Urbe,* vol. 1 (Roma, 1893), p. 408; *PL,*
vol. 19, col. 471.

**ROMA, Biblioteca Nazionale Centrale, Fondo Vittorio Emmanuele
952 (262)**
s. xv; 153 leaves; 200 x 140 mm.; S. Giorgio Maggiore, Venezia;
paper.

Contents: On ff. 113r-152v: PC. Preceded by Arator, *Historia Apostolica* (ff. 1r-52r); Damasus' epigram on S. Paul *(Carm. 7)* (f. 53r-v); Franciscus Patricius, *Ecloga de Christi Natali* (ff. 54r-56v); and Juvencus, *Evangeliorum Libri Quattuor* (ff. 61r-110v).
Other information: Used by Arevalo *(Rom.)*.
Bibliography: Kristeller, *Iter,* vol. 2, p. 122; José Gómez Pérez, *Manuscritos españoles en la Biblioteca Nacional Central de Roma. Catálogo* (Madrid, 1956), p. 122; *PL,* vol. 19, col. 30.

SALAMANCA, Biblioteca Universitaria, 135
s. xv; 100 leaves.

Contents: On ff. 62r-100r: PC, H1. Preceded by *Liber Sacrificiorum* (ff. 1r ff.); the epigrams of Prosper (ff. 14r ff.); and Prudentius, *Psychomachia* (ff. 42v ff.). On f. 100r: epigram beginning *Haec tuae perpetuae.*
Other information: PC divided into six books (last book begins with 5.261). Microfilm copy acquired.
Bibliography: Anselm M. Olivar, "Los manuscritos patrísticos y litúrgicos latinos de la Universidad de Salamanca," *AST* 22 (1949), 85-6.

SANKT GALLEN, Stiftsbibliothek, 197
s. ix-x; 398 pages; 255 x 185 mm.; S. Gallen.

Contents: On pp. 368-397: E1, PC, H1 (only first two verses; at bottom of p. 397). Subscription, Asterius' epigram, and prose preface on p. 371. Preceded by Dictys Cretensis, *Ephemeris Belli Troiani* (pp. 1-87); *Epistulae Senecae ad Paulum et Pauli ad Senecam* (pp. 87-91); Dares Phrygius, *De Excidio Troiae* (pp. 93-120); Alcimus Avitus, *De Spiritalis Historiae Gestis* (pp. 124-280); various Latin poems (pp. 281-328); and Juvencus, *Evangeliorum Libri Quattuor* (pp. 330-368).
Other information: Five manuscripts have been bound together to form this volume. Pages 329 ff. constitute the fifth manuscript. PC divided into three books (no division between PC 1 and 2 or between PC 3 and 4). Written in double columns. Includes indices. Used by Huemer (R). Seen in person. Microfilm acquired.
Bibliography: Claude W. Barlow, *Epistolae Senecae ad Paulum et Pauli ad Senecam (Quae Vocantur)* (Roma, 1938), p. 20; Bischoff, *MS,* vol. 3, p. 197, n. 55; Heinrich Brauer, "Die Bücherei von St. Gallen und das althochdeutsche Schrifttum," *Hermaea* 17 (1926), 48, 58, and 86; Bruckner, vol. 3, pp. 80-1; *CSEL,* vol. 10, p. xviii; W. Eisenhut, *Dictys*

Cretensis, Ephemeridos Belli Troiani Libri a Lucio Septimio ex Graeco in Latinum Sermonem Translati (Leipzig, 1958), pp. xiii-xv; K. Halm, "Verzeichniss der älteren Handschriften lateinischer Kirchenväter in den Bibliotheken der Schweiz," *Sitz. Wien* 50 (1865), 157; Munk Olsen, vol. 1, pp. 381-2; Giovanni Muzzioli, "Due nuovi codici autografi di Pomponio Leto. Contributo allo studio della scrittura umanistica," *Italia medioevale e umanistica* 2 (1959), 341; Gustav Scherrer, *Verzeichniss der Handschriften der Stiftsbibliothek von St. Gallen* (Halle, 1875), pp. 72-4; Steinmeyer & Sievers, vol. 4, p. 445.

SANKT GALLEN, Stiftsbibliothek, 242
s. x; 272 pages; 243 x 185 mm.; written in northern Italy.

Contents: On pp. 168-247 [s. x]: E1, PC, H1. (Pages 202-4 appear to have been written by another hand.) Preceded by hymns of Notker Balbulus and Notker Labeo, *De Musica* (pp. 3-16); *Passio S. Apollinaris* (incomplete) (pp. 17-20); Aldhelm, *Aenigmata* (pp. 21-48), *De Virginate,* and *De Octo Principalibus Vitiis* (pp. 50-167). Followed by a Latin-German glossary (pp. 247-252) and Ambrose, *Expositio Evangelii secundum Lucam* (incomplete) (pp. 253-268). On pp. 269-272 there is a fragment of I Kings.
Other information: Several manuscripts of various dates (s. viii-xi) bound together. PC divided into five books (1+4). Extensive interlinear glossing, but not on pp. 194-200. Used by Huemer (S). Seen in person. Microfilm acquired.
Bibliography: Bergmann, p. 27; Bischoff, *MS,* vol. 1, pp. 95-6; Bischoff, "FHH," 312; Brauer, same as above, 47, 74, and 86; Bruckner, vol. 3, p. 85; *CLA,* vol. 7, p. 20, no. 900; *CSEL,* vol. 10, pp. xviii-xix; L.M. De Rijk, "On the Curriculum of the Arts of the *Trivium* at St. Gall from c. 850-c. 1000," *Vivarium* 1 (1963), 55; R. Ehwald, *Aldhelmi Opera, MGH AA,* vol. 15, p. 335; Halm, same as above, 157; Scherrer, same as above, pp. 88-90; Steimeyer & Sievers, vol. 2, p. 622 and vol. 4, pp. 445-6.

SANKT GALLEN, Stiftsbibliothek, 873
s. xvi (before 1508); 228 pages, quarto; written by Jodocus Nötgersegger; paper.

Contents: On pp. 141-213: PC, H1. Preceded by Aldhelm, *De Virginitate* (pp. 25-139). Followed by an anonymous *Meditatio* (pp. 213-222).

Other information: PC divided into four books.
Bibliography: Scherrer, same as above, p. 302.

SANKT GALLEN, Stiftsbibliothek, 877
s. ix; 470 pages (misnumbered as 370); 223 x 142 mm.; S. Gallen.

Contents: On pp. 124-203: fragment of PO (up to Huemer's page 177, line 18), E1, PC, H2 (with doxology), H1 (first 14 lines). Subscription, Asterius' epigram, and prose preface on pp. 131-2. Preceded by Marius Victorinus, *Ars Grammatica* and a confession of sins (pp. 3-32); treatises on medicine, orthography, et al. (pp. 33 ff.); and *Disticha Catonis* (pp. 111-115). Followed by Donatus, *Ars Minor* (pp. 204-225); Donatus, *Ars Maior* (pp. 226-289); and a dialogue about Donatus between student and teacher (pp. 290-354).
Other information: Miscellany volume. PC divided into five books. Index on pp. 117-123 (three-book format). PC 3.87 to 5.438 written in a different hand. Little glossing. Used by Huemer (P). Seen in person. Microfilm acquired.
Bibliography: Beccaria, pp. 390-1; Bergmann, p. 32; Bernhard Bischoff, *Lorsch im Spiegel seiner Handschriften* (München, 1974), pp. 23 and 118-9; Boas, p. lx; Brauer, same as above, 47 ff., 79, and 86; Bruckner, vol. 2, p. 81; *CSEL*, vol. 10, pp. xiii-xiv; Halm, same as above, 157; Bengt Löfstedt, *Bonifatii, Ars Grammatica, Accedit Ars Metrica, CCSL*, vol. 133B, p. 105; Munk Olsen, vol. 1, pp. 78-9; Pellegrin, p. 351; Scherrer, same as above, pp. 305-6; Steinmeyer & Sievers, vol. 4, p. 454-5 [s. x].

STUTTGART, Württembergische Landesbibliothek, Cod. Poet. et Phil. 4° 2
s. xv (1479-81); 286 leaves; 210 x 160 mm.; written in southwest Germany (Schwaben?); paper.

Contents: On ff. 111r-155r: E1, PC (missing 3.60 to 4.270; ff. 136v-139v blank), H2. Subscription and Asterius' epigram on f. 114r-v. Preceded by Henry of Settimello, *Elegia de Diversitate Fortunae et Philosophiae Consolatione* (ff. 2r-22v); elegies of Maximianus (ff. 23r-37r); Prudentius, *Psychomachia* (38r-65r) and *Dittochaeon* (65v-70v); *Floretus* (70v-101v); and a fragment of Johannes Abbas, *De Septem Vitiis et Virtutibus* (ff. 102r-104r). Followed by *Ecloga Theoduli* (ff. 155v-165r); Alan of Lille, *Anticlaudianus* with commentary (ff. 165v-263r); and *Ilias Latina* (ff. 264r-286r). The leaves immediately preceding

Sedulius (ff. 104v-110v) are blank, as is f. 286v.

Other information: PC apparently divided into six books (last book begins with 5.261). Interlinear glossing throughout. Microfilm acquired.

Bibliography: Wolfgang Irtenkauf and Ingeborg Krekler, *Codices Poetici et Philologici,* vol. 2 *(erste Reihe)* in *Die Handschriften der Württembergischen Landesbibliothek Stuttgart* (Wiesbaden, 1981), pp. 71-3.

TORINO, Biblioteca Nazionale Universitaria, E. IV. 42 (735)
s. vii; 28 leaves (numbered 1-27 and 36); 235 x 212 mm.; probably written at Bobbio.

Contents: On ff. 1r-28r: E1, PC, H1 (PC 1.1-16 on f. 28r). E1 begins with Huemer's page 6, line 5. Subscription *(Robeo. Incipit sacrum opus....)* on f. 28r.

Other information: Once bound with E. IV. 43 (Cerealis, *Libellus contra Maximinum Arianum* on ff. 28-35). Written in rustic capitals (ff. 1-18) and uncials. Divided into five books. Numerous corrections by later hands (s. ix-x). Used by Arevalo *(Taur.)* and Huemer (T). Seen in person. Microfilm acquired.

Bibliography: Carlo Cipolla, *Codici bobbiesi della Biblioteca Nazionale Universitaria di Torino* (Milano, 1907), pp. 80-5 [includes edition of ff. 7v-8r, 11v, and 12v]; *CLA,* vol. 4, p. 13, no. 447; *CSEL,* vol. 10, pp. v-vii; Huemer, *De Sedulii,* pp. 9, 31, 38, and 41; Giuseppe Ottino, *I codici bobbiesi nella Biblioteca Nazionale de Torino* (Torino-Palermo, 1890), pp. 4-5; Federico Patetta, *Studi sulle fonti giuridiche medievali* (Torino, 1967), pp. 690-1; Renato Raffaelli, "La pagina e il testo" in *Atti del convegno internazionale: Il libro e il testo* (Urbino, 1984), p. 20, n. 44; August Reifferscheid, *"Bibliotheca Patrum Latinorum Italica IV:* Die Bibliotheken Piemonts," *Sitz. Wien* 68 (1871), 502-3; Traube, vol. 1, pp. 171 and 244; Fabio Troncarelli, "I codici di Cassidoro: Le testimonianze più antiche," *Scrittura e civiltà* 12 (1988), 51.

TORTOSA, Archivo Capitular de Tortosa, 161
s. xii; 141 leaves; 212 x 130 mm.

Contents: On ff. 56r-98v: E1, PC, H1 (1-61; breaks off at bottom of f. 98v). Subscription and Asterius' epigram on f. 59r. Preceded by Bede, *De Arte Metrica* (ff. 2r-39v); Servius, *De Centum Metris* (ff. 39v-47v); and Priscian, *Partitiones XII Versuum Aeneidos Principalium* (ff.

48r-55v). Followed by Donatus, *Ars Minor* (ff. 99r-102r); an epitaph for Adelaide (f. 102r); Priscian, *Partitiones* (same as above) (ff. 103r-134v); *Liber Hymnorum* (ff. 135r-137v); *Registrum Ephemeridum* (f. 139r); translations of Biblical names, cities, valleys, and mountains in Hebrew into Latin (ff. 139v-140v); and a fragment of a liturgical hymn (f. 141r-v).

Other information: PC divided into five books.   Some glossing. Microfilm acquired.

Bibliography: E. Bayerri Bertomeu, *Los códices medievales de la Catedral de Tortosa: Novísimo inventario descriptivo* (Barcelona, 1962), p. 327; Lisardo Rubio Fernández, *Catálogo de los manuscritos clásicos latinos existentes en España* (Madrid, 1984), pp. 550-1; Passalacqua, p. 291.

TRIER, Bibliothek des Priesterseminars, 61 (R. III. 13)
s. xi$^{ex.}$ (ff. 1-38); 137 leaves; 265 x 188 mm.; S. Matthias, Trier.

Contents: On ff. 1r-38v: E1, PC, H1 (1-6).   Order of PC confused: ff. 4r-8v=PC 1.1-240; ff. 9r-16v=PC 2.263 to 4.23; ff. 17r-24v=PC 1.241 to 2.262; ff. 25r-38v=PC 4.24 to 5.438.   Followed by C. Julius Solinus, *Collectanea Rerum Memorabilium* (ff. 39r-100r); notes on forecasting the weather and the seasons (ff. 100v-102v); a Latin-German glossary (ff. 102v-114r); notes on Ss. Dionysius, Rusticus, and Eleutherius (ff. 114v-115r); Marbod, *Liber Lapidum* (ff. 116r-121v); and Peter Riga, *Aurora* (incomplete) (ff. 122r-137v).

Other information: Volume consists of four parts dating from the eleventh to the fourteenth century, of which ours is the first.   Latin and German glosses in text of Sedulius.   Variant reading of PC 4.8 (*Quod natura negat totum se iudice praestat*) identical with München, Bayerische Staatsbibliothek, Clm 14693.   Seen in person.   Microfilm copy acquired.

Bibliography: Bergmann, p. 103; idem, *Mittelfränkische Glossen. Studien zu ihrer Ermittlung und sprachgeographischen Einordnung* = Rheinisches Archiv 61 (2nd ed.; Bonn, 1977), pp. 160-9; R. Bruch, *GlossariumEpternacense. Spätalthoch-deutsche Glossen aus Echternach. Tatsachen und Quellen, Wörter und Namen* = Publications nationales du Ministère des Affaires Culturelles, 1964, pp. 54 f.; R. Derolez, *Runica Manuscripta. The English Tradition* = Rijksuniversiteit te Gent. Werken uitgegeven door de Faculteit van de Wijsbegeerte en Letteren 118 (Brugge, 1954), pp. 102 ff.; W. Jungandreas, "Die Runen des Codex Seminarii Trevirensis R. III. 61," *Trierer Zeitschrift* 30 (1967), 161-9;

Pekka Katara, *Die Glossen des Codex Seminarii Trevirensis R. III. 13* (Helsinki, 1912); Ker, *Cat.*, p. 483; J. Marx, *Handschriftenverzeichnis der Seminar-Bibliothek zu Trier*, vol. 4 in *Veröffentlichungen der Gesellschaft für Trierische Geschichte und Denkmalpflege* = Trierisches Archiv. Ergänzungsheft 13 (Trier, 1912), pp. 50-1; Munk Olsen, vol. 2, p. 516; H.V. Sauerland, "Aus Handschriften der Trierer Seminarbibliothek," *Neues Archiv* 17 (1892), 606; W. Schröder, "Kritisches zu neuen Verfasserschaften Walahfrid Strabos und zur althochdeutschen Schriftsprache," *Zeitschrift für deutsches Altertum und deutsche Literatur* 87 (1956-7), 196; Steinmeyer & Sievers, vol. 2, p. 622 and vol. 4, pp. 620-1.

TRIER, Stadtbibliothek, 1694/1464 (1093)
s. xi (1048); 246 leaves; 515 x 338 mm.; Echternach.

Contents: On ff. 169r-195r: E1, PC, H1 (1-100). *Accessus* on f. 169r. Subscription, Asterius' epigram, and prose preface on ff. 170v-171r; acrostic poems in praise of Sedulius (in Huemer's order) on f. 195r-v. Preceded by Prudentius, *Cathemerinon, Peristephanon, Apotheosis, Hamartigenia, Psychomachia, Contra Symmachum, Dittochaeon,* with the commentary of Remigius of Auxerre (ff. 1r-114r), and Boethius, *Philosophiae Consolatio* (ff. 115v-168r), also with Remigius' commentary. Eugenius of Toledo, *Carm.* 42 on f. 168v. Followed by Arator, *Historia Apostolica* (ff. 198v-231v); the fables of Avianus (ff. 232r-240r); and *Disticha Catonis* (ff. 241r-245r).
Other information: Book division lacking after beginning of PC 2; five-book format added by later hand. Extensive glossing in E1. Index for first two books on f. 171r-v. Given to the library by J.P.J. Hermes (1765-1833). Used by Huemer (D). The *Stadtbibliothek* also has eight pages of Sedulian fragments (s. xi?) with PC 2.66-109 and PC 2.295-342 on four pages and PC 2.201-246 and PC. 3.222-266 on another four pages. Microfilm acquired.
Bibliography: Werner Bach, *Die althochdeutschen Boethiusglossen und Notkers Übersetzung der Consolatio* (Würzburg, 1934), p. 7; Bergmann, p. 104; idem, *Mittelfränkische Glossen. Studien zu ihrer Ermittlung und sprachgeographischen Einordnung* = Rheinisches Archiv 61 (2nd ed.; Bonn, 1977), pp. 134-141, 311-313, and 315; Ludwig Bieler, *Anicii Manlii Severini Boethii, Philosophiae Consolatio, CCSL,* vol. 94, p. xxvii; Boas, p. lx; idem, "De Librorum Catonianorum Historia atque Compositione," *Mnemosyne* 42 (1914), 25; *CSEL,* vol. 10, pp. xviiii-xx; Henning von Gadow, *Die althochdeutschen Aratorglossen der Hand-*

schrift Trier 1464 = Münstersche Mittelalter-Schriften 17 (München, 1974), passim; Glauche, pp. 55-6, 67, and 95-6; Guaglianone, p. xvii; Huemer, *De Sedulii*, p. 32; Gottfried Kentenich, *Die philologischen Handschriften der Stadtbibliothek zu Trier* = Beschreibendes Verzeichnis der Handschriften der Stadtbibliothek zu Trier 10 (Trier, 1931), pp. 22-6; McKinlay, pp. 36-7; G. Müller and Th. Frings, *Germania Romana II. Dreissig Jahre Forschung. Romanische Wörter* = Mittelhochdeutsche Studien 19.2 (1968), p. 103; Munk Olsen, vol. 1, p. 79; Sanford, 214; J. Schroeder, "Bibliothek und Schule der Abtei Echternach," *Publications de la Section Historique de l'Institut Grand-ducal de Luxembourg* 91 (1977), 239-43; Steinmeyer & Sievers, vol. 4, pp. 622-5.

UDINE, Biblioteca Arcivescovile e Bartolina, Qt. 10. I. 23
s. xi; 41 leaves; 208 x 128 mm.

Contents: On ff. 1r-39r: E1, PC (missing 1.17-28), H1, H2 (missing lines 1-2 and 25-29). H1 followed by epigram beginning *Haec tua perpetuae*. Fragment from Prudentius, *Dittochaeon* on ff. 40r-41v (s. xiii).
Other information: PC divided into five books. Some glossing. Several elaborate initials (at beginning of books) and one illustration (f. 31r). Two initials have been removed (on f. 4 and f. 38). Microfilm acquired.
Bibliography: Mazzatinti, vol. 3, p. 228; Cesare Scalon, *La Biblioteca Arcivescovile di Udine* = Medioevo e umanesimo 37 (Padova, 1979), pp. 95-6.

UTRECHT, Bibliotheek der Rijksuniversiteit, 1661
s. xii; 36 leaves; 174 x 115 mm.

Contents: On ff. 1r-39v: PC, H1. Subscription and Asterius' epigram on ff. 37v-38r.
Other information: PC originally divided into four books (no division between PC 3 and 4); later changed to five-book format. Given to the library by J.A. Grothe. Used by Arntzenius for his 1761 edition. Microfiche acquired.
Bibliography: P.A. Tiele and A. Hulshof, *Catalogus Codicum Manu Scriptorum Bibliothecae Universitatis Rheno-Traiectinae* (Utrecht, 1887-1909), vol. 2, p. 110.

VATICANO (Città del), Biblioteca Apostolica Vaticana, Barb. Lat. 429

s. xiii; 36 leaves; octavo; Venezia?; paper and parchment.

Contents: On ff. 1r-36v: E1, PC, H1, H2. Dedicatory preface to Proba's cento on f. 4r-v (in a later hand).

Other information: PC not divided into books. The paper leaves (ff. 4-5), which include the first 54 lines of PC 1, are written in a more recent hand. Extensive glossing, interlinear and marginal. Microfilm acquired.

Bibliography: *Inventarium Codicum Manuscriptorum Bibliothecae Barberinae Redactum et Digestum a D. Sancte Pieralisi,* vol. 4, p. 107; Jeudy, "Remi," p. 497.

VATICANO, Biblioteca Apostolica Vaticana, Ottob. Lat. 35
s. ix^{in}?; 81 leaves; quarto; written at Fleury?; later at S. Denis, Paris.

Contents: On ff. 1r-35r: E1, H2, PC, H1. Subscription, Asterius' epigram, and prose preface on f. 3r-v; acrostic poem in praise of Sedulius (Bellesarius') on f. 33r; biographical notice *(Incipit ars....)* on f. 35r. Followed by Juvencus, *Evangeliorum Libri Quattuor* (ff. 36v ff.).

Other information: PC divided into five books (1+4). Extensive glossing throughout. Some glosses in small Celtic hand (Bischoff). Used by Arevalo and Huemer (O). Microfilm acquired.

Bibliography: Bischoff, *MS,* vol. 3, p. 40, n. 4; *CSEL,* vol. 10, p. xx; Huemer, *De Sedulii,* p. 32; *Inventarii Codicum Manuscriptorum Latinorum Bibliothecae Vaticanae Ottobonianae,* part 1, p. 7; Mostert, p. 254; *PL,* vol. 19, cols. 29-30.

VATICANO, Biblioteca Apostolica Vaticana, Ottob. Lat. 36
s. xv (1473); 60 leaves; 235 x 165 mm.; Napoli.

Contents: On ff. 1r-59r: PC, H1, H2. Acrostic poems in praise of Sedulius on ff. 58r-59r; followed by verses beginning *Qualiter adfixus ligno iam Christus in alto* (as in the Edinburgh manuscripts, Adv. 18. 4. 7 and Adv. 18. 7. 7).

Other information: Written by Antonio Sinibaldi. PC book division inconsistent. Elaborately decorated border surrounding PC 1.1-13. Title: *Liber Sedulii de Actibus Prophetarum et Toto Christi Salvatoris Cursu.* Used by Arevalo and Huemer *(Ottob. 2).* Seen in person.

Bibliography: *CSEL,* vol. 10, p. xx; Tammaro De Marinis, *La biblioteca napoletana dei re d'Aragona* (Milano, 1947), vol. 2, p. 149;

PL, vol. 19, col. 469.

VATICANO, Biblioteca Apostolica Vaticana, Reg. Lat. 29
s. xvi (c. 1523-1527); 302 leaves; 312 x 218 mm.; paper.

Contents: On ff. 275v-300r: PC, H1, H2 (subscription on f. 298r;
epigram beginning *Haec tua perpetuae* on f. 300r). Preceded by Peter
Riga, *Aurora* (ff. 4v-173v); Johannes Florentinus, *Theotocon* (ff. 174r-
223v); Aeneas Silvius Piccolomini (Pius II), *De Passione Christi* (ff.
273v-275r); et al. Followed by an assortment of short poems. For a
complete description of contents, see Wilmart, below.
Other information: Microfilm copy seen. Used by Arevalo *(Reg. 5).*
Bibliography: G. Morelli, "Manoscritti d'interesse abruzzese della
Biblioteca Vaticana," *BDA* 63 (1973), 59; Manfred Oberleitner, "Die
handschriftliche Überlieferung der Werke des Heiligen Augustinus 1.1,"
Sitz. Wien 263 (1969), 399; André Wilmart, *Codices Reginenses Latini,*
vol 1, in *Bibliothecae Apostolicae Vaticanae Codices Manu Scripti
Recensiti Iussu Pii XI Pontificis Maximi* (Roma, 1937), pp. 73-80.

VATICANO, Biblioteca Apostolica Vaticana, Reg. Lat. 300
s. xi$^{in.}$; 78 leaves; 310-320 x 210-215 mm.; written in northern France,
possibly at Corbie.

Contents: On ff. 40r-77r: E1, PC, H1, H2. Subscription and Asterius'
epigram on f. 41v; acrostic poems in praise of Sedulius (in Huemer's
order) on f. 77r-v. Hymn beginning *In circuitu tuo, Domine* on f. 77r.
Preceded by Arator, *Historia Apostolica* (ff. 1r-39v). Followed by Ps.-
Cato, *Monosticha* (ff. 77v-78r) and Eugenius of Toledo, *Carm.* 38 (on
the ten plagues) (f. 78v).
Other information: Volume consists of two contemporaneous parts (ff.
1-39 and 40-78). PC divided into five books. Extensive interlinear
glossing and marginal notation. Used by Arevalo and Huemer *(Reg. 2).*
Photostatic copy acquired.
Bibliography: Emil Baehrens, *Poetae Latini Minores,* vol. 3 (Leipzig,
1881), p. 212; Henry Bannister, *Monumenti vaticani di paleografia
musicale latina* = Codices e Vaticanis Selecti Phototypice 12 (Leipzig,
1913), pp. 82-3; Boas, p. lxiii; *CSEL,* vol. 10, p. xxi; Huemer, *De
Sedulii,* pp. 39 and 41-2; idem, "Zu *Anthologia Latina* 716 R," *WS* 4
(1882), 172; McKinlay, p. 58; *MCLBV,* vol. 2.1, pp. 58-9; Munk Olsen,
vol. 1, p. 80 and vol. 3.1, p. 89; *PL,* vol. 19, col. 466; Yves-François
Riou, "Quelques aspects de la tradition manuscrite des *Carmina*

d'Eugène de Tolède: Du *Liber Catonianus* aux *Auctores octo morales*,"
RHT 2 (1972), 11-44, esp. 23 and 25; Sanford, 220; Wilmart, *Codices*,
same as above, vol. 2 (1945), pp. 140-3.

VATICANO, Biblioteca Apostolica Vaticana, Reg. Lat. 333
s. ix^{med.}; 163 leaves; 237 x 182 mm.; written in the Loire region,
possibly at Fleury; later probably at Cluny.

Contents: On ff. 101v-162v: E1, PC. Subscription; Asterius' epigram;
biographical notice (attributed to Jerome); and acrostic poems in praise
of Sedulius (in Huemer's order) on f. 163r. Leiden, Bibliotheek der
Rijksuniversiteit, Voss. Lat. Q. 86 (ff. 1-15) "fits on to gathering sixteen
of Reg. 333." The original manuscript was disjoined by Alexander
Petau (1610-72). Preceded by Juvencus, *Evangeliorum Libri Quattuor*
(ff. 1r-101v).
Other information: PC divided into five books (1+4). Used by
Arevalo and Huemer *(Reg. 1).* Microfilm copy acquired.
Bibliography: Beeson, p. 86; *CSEL,* vol. 10, pp. xx-xxi; Grace Frank,
"Vossianus Q 86 and Reginensis 333," *AJP* 44 (1923), 67-70; Glauche,
pp. 33-5; Huemer, *De Sedulii,* pp. 10, 22, and 32; Kurz, 266; McKin-
lay, pp. 58-9; Mostert, p. 264; Munk Olsen, vol. 1, pp. 80-1; *PL,* vol.
19, cols. 465-6; E.K. Rand, "Note on the Vossianus Q 86 and Regi-
nenses 333 and 1616," *AJP* 44 (1923), 171-2; Sanford, 206; Wilmart,
same as above, pp. 244-6.

VATICANO, Biblioteca Apostolica Vaticana, Urb. Lat. 584 (828)
s. xv^{ex.}; 71 leaves; 233 x 151 mm.

Contents: On ff. 1r-48r: PC, H1. The latter is described as *paracteri-*
um. Followed by *Martyrologium Bedae* (ff. 49r ff.); *Anth. Lat.* 488 (f.
69r); et al.
Other information: Used by Arevalo *(Urb.).* Microfilm copy seen.
Bibliography: Cosimus Stornajolo, *Codices Urbinates Latini*, vol. 2, in
Bibliothecae Apostolicae Vaticanae Codices Manu Scripti Recensiti Iussu
Pii X Pontificis Maximi (Roma, 1912), pp. 87-8; *PL,* vol. 19, col. 470.

VATICANO, Biblioteca Apostolica Vaticana, Vat. Lat. 1665
s. xi; 70 leaves; 255 x 158 mm.; Lorsch.

Contents: On ff. 39v-70v: PC, H1, H2, E1 (up to page 10, line 2).
Epigram beginning *Haec tua perpetuae* on f. 68r. Preceded by Arator,

Historia Apostolica (ff. 1r-39r).
Other information: PC divided into five books (1+4). Some glossing and marginal commentary (s. xii). Used by Arevalo *(Vat. 1)* and Huemer (V). Microfilm acquired.
Bibliography: *CSEL,* vol. 10, p. xxi; McKinlay, pp. 56-7; Bartholomeus Nogara, *Codices Vaticani Latini,* vol. 5, in *Bibliothecae Apostolicae Vaticanae Codices Manu Scripti Recensiti Iussu Pii X Pontificis Maximi* (Roma, 1912), pp. 139-40; *PL,* vol. 19, col. 465.

VATICANO, Biblioteca Apostolica Vaticana, Vat. Lat. 3178
s. xv; 29 leaves; 295 x 120 mm.

Contents: On ff. 1r-27r: E1, PC, H1.
Other information: Used by Arevalo and Huemer *(Vat. 2).* Seen in person.
Bibliography: *CSEL,* vol. 10, p. xxi; *PL,* vol. 19, col. 465.

VATICANO, Biblioteca Apostolica Vaticana, Vat. Lat. 9658
s. xiii; 99 leaves; 210 x 125 mm.; S. Francesco, Assisi; parchment and paper.

Contents: On ff. 1r-33v: PC, E1 (only up to Huemer's page 2, line 10). Followed by Prudentius, *Psychomachia* (ff. 34r-56v); *Hymnarium Expositum* (ff. 59r-86r); et al.
Other information: PC originally divided into two books (five-book format added by later hand). Some interlinear glosses. Photostatic copy acquired.
Bibliography: Cesare Cenci, *Bibliotheca Manuscripta ad Sacrum Conventum Assisiensem,* vol. 1 (Assisi, 1981), p. 186; Giovanni Mercati, "Codici del Convento di S. Francesco in Assisi nella Bibli. Vat." in *Miscellanea Francesco Ehrle: Scritti di storia e paleografia,* vol. 5 (Roma, 1924), p. 90; G.E. Mohan, "Initia Operum Franciscalium (XIII-XV S.)," *Franciscan Studies* 36 (1976), 149.

VENDÔME, Bibliothèque Municipale, 165
s. xv; 182 leaves; 216 x 148 mm.; paper.

Contents: On ff. 155r-182v: PC, H1. Dedicatory preface to Proba's cento *(Romulidum doctor....)* (attr. Sedulius) on f. 181r. Preceded by Peter Riga, *Aurora* (ff. 1r ff.); *De Libris Testamenti* (ff. 92r ff.); and Juvencus, *Evangeliorum Libri Quattuor* (ff. 97r ff.).

Other information: Microfiche acquired.
Bibliography: Cat. gen. octavo, vol. 3, pp. 447-8.

VENEZIA, Biblioteca Nazionale Marciana, Lat. XII. 7 (4160)
s. xii?; 36 leaves; 225 x 145 mm.

Contents: On ff. 1v-36r: E1, PC (missing original leaves after 14v
[=PC 1.334 to 3.294]), H1. Biographical notice *(Sedulius primus
laicus....)* and *accessus* on 4v. Acrostic poem in praise of Sedulius
(Liberatus') on f. 5r. Dedicatory preface to Proba's cento, Asterius'
epigram, and prose preface on f. 5v.
Other information: PC apparently divided into five books. Extensively
glossed. Microfilm acquired.
Bibliography: CSEL, vol. 10, p. xxiii; Huemer, *De Sedulii,* pp. 5, 15-
16, and 45; Pietro Zorzanello, *Catalogo dei codici latini della Biblioteca
Nazionale Marciana di Venezia non compresi nel catalogo di G.
Valentinelli,* vol. 2 (Trezzano sul Naviglio, 1981), pp. 80-2.

VOLTERRA, Biblioteca Communale Guarnacci, 6150 (281)
s. xvi; 244 leaves; paper.

Contents: On ff. 1r-43r: PC, H1. Followed by Juvencus, *Evangeli-
orum Libri Quattuor* (ff. 50-119); Proba, *Cento* (ff. 121-137); Jacobus
Bracelleus, *De Illustribus Viris Genuensibus* (ff. 138-145); Antonius
Panormita, *Oratio ad Genuenses contra Venetos* (ff. 145-152); and
Dictys Cretensis, *Ephemeris Belli Troiani* (ff. 153-243). On f. 152v:
fragment of Aurispa's preface to Lucian.
Other information: On f. 244r: *Ans. Falconcinius Volaterranus huius
libri exemplator....* Microfilm acquired.
Bibliography: Kristeller, *Iter,* vol. 2, p. 309; Mazzatinti, vol. 2, p. 237.

WIEN, Österreichische Nationalbibliothek, 85 (Univ. 1013)
s. xii[1] (ff. 1-42); 134 leaves; 282 x 205 mm.; written in Austria
(probably at Lambach).

Contents: On ff. 2v-42v: E1, PC, H1, H2. An assortment of notices
on Sedulius and his writings (including *accessus)* on ff. 1r-2r. Followed
by verses on birds, animals, and trees (f. 42v); Persius, *Satires* (ff. 43v-
57v); a Latin *"glossarium"* (f. 58r); and the comedies of Terence (ff.
58v-134v).
Other information: Volume consists of two parts: ff. 1-42 (s. xii[1]) and

ff. 43-134 (s. xi$^{in.}$). PC divided into five books (1+4). Heavy interlinear glossing and marginal notation. Used by Huemer (d). Microfilm acquired.

Bibliography: J. Andrieu, "Nouveaux manuscrits de Térence," *REL* 18 (1940), 54-6; Wendell V. Clausen, *A. Persi Flacci, Saturarum Liber. Accedit Vita* (Oxford, 1956), p. xiii; *CSEL,* vol. 10, pp. xxii-xxiii; Glauche, p. 52; Hermann Julius Hermann, *Die deutschen romanischen Handschriften,* in *Beschreibendes Verzeichnis der illuminierten Handschriften in Österreich. Die illuminierten Handschriften und Inkunabeln der Nationalbibliothek in Wien* 8.2 (Leipzig, 1926), pp. 1-2 and pp. 182-3; Huemer, *De Sedulii,* pp. 15, 21, 31, 41, and 43; idem, "Zur Bestimmung der Abfassungszeit und Herausgabe des *Carmen Paschale* des Sedulius," *ZÖG* 27 (1876), pp. 500-5; Jeudy, "Remi," p. 497; Munk Olsen, vol. 2, pp. 213-4; Piacentini, p. 121; Sesto Prete, "Manoscritti preumanistici delle commedie di Terenzio nella Biblioteca Nazionale di Vienna," *Codices Manuscripti* 7 (1981), 109-20; Reynolds, pp. 416-7; Sanford, 221; *Tabulae Codicum Manu Scriptorum praeter Graecos et Orientales in Bibliotheca Palatina Vindobonensi Asservatorum* (11 volumes; Wien, 1864-1912), vol. 1 (1864), pp. 13-4; Franz Unterkircher, *Inventar der illuminierten Handschriften, Inkunabeln und Frühdrucke der Österreichischen Nationalbibliothek, Teil 1: Die abendländischen Handschriften* = Museion. Veröffentlichungen der Österreichischen Nationalbibliothek, n. F., 2.2 (Wien, 1957), p. 5.

WIEN, Österreichische Nationalbibliothek, 233 (Philol. 249)
s. xii; 26 leaves; octavo.

Contents: On ff. 3r-26r: PC, H1 (lines 1-86). Preceded by Prudentius, *Dittochaeon* (ff. 1r-3r).
Other information: PC divided into five books (1+4). Some interlinear glosses. Microfilm acquired.
Bibliography: Huemer, *De Sedulii,* p. 39, n. 1; *Tabulae,* same as above, pp. 32-3.

WIEN, Österreichische Nationalbibliothek, 246 (Univ. 517)
s. xii (ff. 87-111); 111 leaves; quarto; written in Austria or Germany.

Contents: On ff. 87r-111r: E1, PC 1.1 to 3.262 (one leaf missing=1.154-99) and 5.396-438, H1. Preceded by *Anti-Priscianus* (ff. 1r-8r); Walter of Châtillon, *Alexandreis* (ff. 9r-42r); *Ars Epistolandi* (ff. 43r-45r); Matthew of Vendôme, *Ars Versificatoria* (ff. 45v-50v); Bernard

Silvester, *Tractatus de Dictamine* (ff. 51r-57v); grammatical excerpts (ff. 58r-64v); Matthew of Vendôme, same as above (ff. 65r-68v); poem by student from Paris asking his mother for money [Walther 16818] (f. 68r); Serlo of Wilton, *Versus de Generibus Nominum* (ff. 68v-69r); Horace, *Odes* (sel.) (ff. 71r-78r) and *Epistles* (*lib.* 2) (ff. 79r-83r); a treatise on Horace's metrics (ff. 83r-84r); and a treatise on the hexameter (ff. 85r-86v).

Other information: On f. 111v: *Iste liber est Sancti Petri in Münster.* Interlinear glosses, some in Old High German. Microfilm acquired.

Bibliography: Bergmann, p. 106; Marvin L. Colker, *Galteri de Castellione Alexandreis* = Thesaurus Mundi Bibliotheca Scriptorum Latinorum Mediae et Recentioris Aetatis 17 (Padova, 1978), p. xxxiii; Huemer, *De Sedulii*, p. 41; Munari, pp. 114-5; Munk Olsen, vol. 1, p. 512; Jan Öberg, *Serlon de Wilton, poèmes latins* = Acta Universitatis Stockholmiensis. Studia Latina Stockholmiensia 14 (Stockholm, 1965); Steinmeyer & Sievers, vol. 2, p. 622 and vol. 4, pp. 631-2; *Tabulae*, same as above, p. 34.

WIEN, Österreichische Nationalbibliothek, 307 (Theol. 708)
s. xi[1]; 59 leaves; quarto.

Contents: On ff. 1r-54v: E1, PC, H1, H2 (followed by doxology). Subscription, Asterius' epigram, and prose preface on f. 54v. Followed by an explanation of the Lord's Prayer for catechetical instruction (ff. 55r-59v) and a treatise on the etymology of words used in tragedy and comedy (frag.) (ff. 59v ff.).

Other information: PC divided into six books (1+5; last book begins with PC 5.261). Used by Huemer (c). Microfilm acquired.

Bibliography: Bergmann, p. 107; *CSEL*, vol. 10, p. xxii; Huemer, *De Sedulii*, pp. 13, 15, 32, 41, 43, 48, and 51; Sanford, 221; Steinmeyer & Sievers, vol. 2, p. 621 and vol. 4, p. 633; *Tabulae*, same as above, p. 42.

WIEN, Österreichische Nationalbibliothek, 3265 (Philol. 345)
s. xiv; 94 leaves; quarto.

Contents: On ff. 37r-60v: PC. Preceded by Alan of Lille, *De Planctu Naturae* (ff. 1r-34r), and an explanation of the Lord's Prayer, mostly excerpted from the writings of Thomas Aquinas (ff. 34r-36v). Followed by *Liber Quinque Clavium Sapientiae* (ff. 61r-70v); Ps.-Boethius, *De Disciplina Scholarium* (ff. 71r-90v); and a meditation by Bernard of

Clairvaux on *Salve Regina* (ff. 91r-94v).
Other information: Extensive interlinear glossing and marginal commentary. Microfilm acquired.
Bibliography: *Tabulae,* same as above, vol. 2 (1868), p. 246; A. Vidmanová-Schmidtová, *Quinque Claves Sapientiae* (Berlin, 1965), p. xii; Olga Weijers, *Pseudo-Boèce, De disciplina scolarium. Édition critique, introduction et notes* = Studien und Texte zur Geistesgeschichte des Mittelalters 12 (Leiden, 1976), p. 87.

WOLFENBÜTTEL, Herzog August Bibliothek, 62.18 Aug. 8° (3697)
s. xiv (1319); 33 leaves; 160 x 108 mm.

Contents: On ff. 1r-33r: PC, H1.
Other information: Written by Otto de Reyken. PC divided into five books (1+4). Some interlinear glossing. Seen in person. Microfilm acquired.
Bibliography: Otto von Heinemann, *Die augusteischen Handschriften* (5 volumes; 1890-1903 = vols. 4-8 of *Kataloge der Herzog August Bibliothek Wolfenbüttel),* vol. 5 (8), p. 120.

WOLFENBÜTTEL, Herzog August Bibliothek, 79 Gud. Lat. 2° (4383)
s. xi; 97 leaves; 290 x 190 mm.; perhaps written in France; prov. Paris.

Contents: On ff. 77v-89v: E1, PC, H2, H1. Biographical notice (*Ars Sedulii....*) and dedicatory preface to Proba's cento on f. 77v. Acrostic poems in praise of Sedulius (in Huemer's order) on f. 89v. Preceded by Latin sequences (ff. 1r-20v); *Rudimenta Grammaticae* (ff. 21r-29v); *Martyrologium de Circulo Anno* (ff. 31r-38v); Bede, *De Arte Metrica* (ff. 39r-56r); *De Schematibus et Tropis* (ff. 56r-61v); Marius Victorinus, *Ars Grammatica (de accentibus)* (ff. 61v-62v); and Arator, *Historia Apostolica* (ff. 63r-77v). Followed by Persius, *Satires* (ff. 89v-93v) and a fragment from a breviary (ff. 94r-97v).
Other information: PC divided into five books (some divisions added later). Used by Artzenius for his edition of Arator. Seen in person. Microfilm acquired.
Bibliography: C.B. Kendall and M.H. King, *Bedae Venerabilis Opera, Pars VI. Opera Didascalia I, CCSL,* vol. 123A, p. 72; Franz Köhler and G. Milchsack, *Die gudischen Handschriften,* in *Kataloge der Herzog August Bibliothek Wolfenbüttel,* vol. 9 (1913), pp. 128-9; Laistner, p. 134; McKinlay, p. 38; Munk Olsen, vol. 2, p. 214; Piacentini, p. 124;

Reynolds, p. 295; Sanford, 217; Rudolf Schützeichel, *Addenda und Corrigenda (II) zum althochdeutschen Wortschatz* = Studien zum Althochdeutschen 12 (Göttingen, 1991), p. 262.

WOLFENBÜTTEL, Herzog August Bibliothek, 109 Gud. Lat. 4° (4413)

s. xii; 80 leaves; 271 x 170 mm.; Werden.

Contents: On ff. 13r-39v: PC, H1, E1 (missing last few lines at bottom of f. 39v). Acrostic poems in praise of Sedulius (in Huemer's order) on ff. 37v-38r. Preceded by Prudentius, *Psychomachia* (ff. 1r-12v). Followed by Arator, *Historia Apostolica* (ff. 40r-61v); the epigrams of Prosper (ff. 62r-80v); and *Magistri Petri de Simonia* (f. 80v).

Other information: No book divisions originally in PC (five-book format added in later hand). Extensive marginal notes. Owned by Bernhard Rottendorff. Seen in person. Microfilm acquired.

Bibliography: Glauche, pp. 67-8 and 124, n. 43; *Gud. Handschr.*, same as above, pp. 144-5; Lehmann, vol 4, pp. 112 and 126; McKinlay, pp. 38-9.

WOLFENBÜTTEL, Herzog August Bibliothek, 191 Gud. Lat. 4° (4495)

s. ix[1]; 62 leaves; 230 x 150 mm.; S. Denis, Paris.

Contents: On ff. 1r-40v: E1, PC 1.1 to 5.424 (missing original leaf after f. 31v [=PC 4.252-304]; ff. 29-30 [=4.99-200] written by a different hand). Followed by Juvencus, *Evangeliorum Libri Quattuor* (ff. 41r-56v); fragment of Sulpicius Severus on S. Martin of Tours (f. 57r-v); six poems addressed to S. Martin (ff. 58r-60v); and explanatory notes on the mass (ff. 61r-62v).

Other information: PC divided into six books (1+5; last book begins with 5.261). Some interlinear glosses, especially in first book. Index for first two books on ff. 5v-6r. Manuscript damaged, according to the catalogue, *"mit dem Messer eines wahrscheinlich noch jugendlichen Barbaren."* Seen in person. Microfilm acquired.

Bibliography: Bischoff, *MS,* vol. 3, pp. 303 and 305; Ernst Dümmler, "Mitteilungen aus Handschriften," *Neues Archiv* 11 (1885-6), 460-6 [s. x]; *Gud. Handschr.*, same as above, pp. 185-6 [s. x-xi]; Donatella Nebbiai-Dalla Guarda, *La Bibliothèque de l'Abbaye de Saint Denis en France* (Paris, 1985), p. 233.

WROCŁAW (BRESLAU), Biblioteka Uniwersytecka, I. Q. 51 (868)
s. xiv¹; 102 leaves; 202 x 155 mm.

Contents: On ff. 1r-8v and 67r-102v: PC. On ff. 9r-66v: Matthew of Vendôme, *Tobias.*
Other information: On f. 1r: *Ecclesiae Collegiatae B.V. Glogoviae Maioris.* Belonged to Heinrich Rantzou (d. 1598).
Bibliography: Otto Günther, "Spuren verschollener Bibliotheken...," *Zentralblatt für Bibliothekswesen* 40 (1923), 485-94; Munari, p. 125; Stegmüller, vol. 3, p. 550, no. 5541.

WROCŁAW (BRESLAU), Biblioteka Zakładu Narodowego im. Ossolińskich (Ossolineum), 819
s. xv; 280 leaves; quarto; paper.

Contents: On ff. 219r-280v: PC *("Sedulius de rebus novi veterisque testamenti. Versus cum glossis et commentario").* Preceded by Peter Riga, *Aurora* (ff. 2r-214v) and "Augustinus doctor," *De Fuga Mulierum* (ff. 215r-216r).
Bibliography: Wojciech Kętrzyński, *Catalogus Codicum Manuscriptorum Bibliothecae Ossolinianae Leopoliensis* (3 volumes; Lwów, 1881-98), vol. 3 (1898), p. 270.

WÜRZBURG, Universitätsbibliothek, M. Ch. Q. 18. Misc.
s. xv (1474); 454 leaves; 205 x 150 mm.; written at Leipzig; later at Ebrach; paper.

Contents: On ff. 174r-259v: PC. Preceded by *Ars Rhetorica* (ff. 2r-84v) and Ps.-Boethius, *De Disciplina Scholarium* (ff. 88r-172r). Followed by Antonius Hankron (Haneron) of Louvain, *De Epistolis Brevibus Edendis* (ff. 267r-299v), with a German version on ff. 332v-341r, and other works on rhetoric and style. See Thurn, below, for a full description.
Other information: Written at the University of Leipzig by Johannes Senff (later at Bamberg). Includes commentary. Microfilm copy acquired.
Bibliography: Bursill-Hall, p. 292; Nikolaus Henkel, *Deutsche Übersetzungen lateinischer Schultexte. Ihre Verbreitung und Funktion im Mittelalter und in der frühen Neuzeit* = Münchener Texte und Untersuchungen zur deutschen Literatur des Mittelalters 90 (München, 1988), p. 258; Kristeller, *Iter,* vol. 3, p. 742; Hans Thurn, *Die Handschriften*

der Zisterzienserabtei Ebrach, in *Die Handschriften der Universitätsbibliothek Würzburg* (4 volumes; Wiesbaden), vol. 1 (1970), pp. 123-6; Olga Weijers, *Pseudo-Boèce, De disciplina scolarium. Édition critique, introduction et notes* = Studien und Texte zur Geistesgeschichte des Mittelalters 12 (Leiden, 1976), pp. 26 and 87-8.

YORK, Minster Library, XVI. Q. 14 (42)

s. xiii$^{in.}$; 141 leaves; 320 x 225 mm.; written in England.

Contents: On ff. 31r-41v: E1, PC (incomplete at end), H1 (15 ff.), H2. *Accessus* on f. 30v; Asterius' epigram and dedicatory preface to Proba's cento on f. 31v. Preceded by Laurence of Durham, *Hypognosticon* (ff. 3v ff.) and Arator, *Historia Apostolica* (ff. 18r-30v). Followed by Prudentius, *Dittochaeon* and *Psychomachia* (ff. 41v-48v); Bede, *De Die Iudicii* (ff. 48v-49r); miscellaneous poems (ff. 49v-55v); Alexander of Ashby, *Brevissima Comprehensio Historiarum* (ff. 55v-58v); Ps.-Methodius, *Revelationes* (ff. 58v-59v); Richard of S. Victor, *De Tabernaculo Federis* (ff. 59v-61v); Peter Pictor, *Carmina* (ff. 61v-64v); Venantius Fortunatus, *Carm.* 8.3 (f. 64r-v); Laurence of Durham, *Consolatio de Morte Amici* (ff. 65r-69v); idem, *Dialogi* (ff. 69v-80r); Matthew of Vendôme, *Ars Versificatoria* (ff. 80r-82v); Alan of Lille, *Anticlaudianus* (ff. 83r-105v); Geoffrey of Vinsauf, *Poetria Nova* (ff. 106r-111v); Geoffrey of Monmouth, *Vita Merlini* (ff. 112r-115v).
Other information: May have come from Durham. Written in double columns.
Bibliography: Margaret T. Gibson and Nigel F. Palmer, "Manuscripts of Allan of Lille, *Anticlaudianus* in the British Isles," *Studi medievali* (3. ser.) 28.2 (1987), 994-7; N.R. Ker and A.J. Piper, *Medieval Manuscripts in British Libraries. IV* (Oxford, 1992), pp. 777-83; Udo Kindermann, *Laurentius von Durham, Consolatio de Morte Amici. Untersuchungen und kritischer Text* (Erlangen, 1969), p. 121; Munari, pp. 127-8; Schenkl, no. 3829.

ZÜRICH, Zentralbibliothek, C 68 (384)

s. ix/x; 127 leaves; 248 x 160 mm.; S. Gallen.

Contents: On ff. 71r-110v: PC (1.1-16 on f. 80r). H1 (lines 39-110) and Ps.-Cyprian, *Carmen ad Flavium Felicem de Resurrectione Mortuorum* (first 16 lines) on f. 1r-v. On ff. 125v-126r: lines omitted in text above (PC 5.104-176 and 196-201) supplied by same hand responsible for H1 (f. 1). Three inserts on f. 79r-v: *Anth. Lat.* 640; *Anth. Lat.*

488; and Alcuin's epitaph *(Carm.* 123). Dedicatory preface to Proba's cento on f. 110v. Preceded by Juvencus, *Evangeliorum Libri Quattuor* (ff. 3r-71r) and followed by Proba, *Cento* (ff. 111r-124v); *Acrostichon Johannis Celse* (ff. 124v-125r); Avianus, *Fabulae* 5 and 9 (ff. 126v-127r).

Other information: PC divided into five continuously numbered books. Lines numbered by later hand. Used by Huemer (Z). Microfilm acquired.

Bibliography: Bruckner, vol. 3, p. 125; *CSEL,* vol. 10, pp. xii-xiii; Guaglianone, p. xvii; Leo Cunibert Mohlberg, *Mittelalterliche Handschriften,* in *Katalog der Handschriften der Zentralbibliothek Zürich,* vol. 1 (Zürich, 1932-52), p. 39; Reynolds, p. 30; Steinmeyer & Sievers, vol. 2, p. 622 and vol. 4, p. 669.

ZÜRICH, Zentralbibliothek, Rh. 77
s. x; 53 leaves; 232 x 160 mm.; Rheinau.

Contents: On ff. 2r-52v: E2, PO (*"prologus metricus"* [PC 1.1-16] on f. 3r-v; subscription and Asterius' epigram on f. 52v). *"Rheinauer Paulus"* on f. 1r. Followed by the mass of King Sigismund for those suffering from fever (ff. 52v-53r); continuation of *"Rheinauer Paulus"* on f. 53v.

Other information: PO divided into five books. Includes indices. Used by Ludwig (t) and Huemer (R). Microfilm acquired.

Bibliography: *CSEL,* vol. 10, p. xxxvii; Huemer, *De Sedulii,* p. 32; Ludwig, pp. 2-3; Mohlberg, same as above, p. 193; *Zeitschrift für deutsches Altertum* 3 (1843), 519-23.

II. MANUSCRIPTS CONTAINING SEDULIAN
FRAGMENTS, HYMNS, ET AL.

AMIENS, Bibliothèque Municipale, 25
s. x; 184 leaves; 300 x 237 mm.; Corbie.

Contents: Evangeliary (missing conclusion of John's Gospel); on ff.
28v, 69r, and 98v: PC 1.355, 356, and 357 respectively.
Bibliography: J.J.G. Alexander, *Insular Manuscripts: 6th to the 9th
Centuries* = A Survey of Manuscripts Illuminated in the British Isles,
vol. 1 (London, 1978), figures 19-22; *Cat. gen. octavo*, vol. 19, p. 16.

AMIENS, Bibliothèque Municipale, 131
s. xi; 100 leaves; 205 x 140 mm.; Corbie.

Contents: Benedictine hymnal; on ff. 28r-29v: *A Solis Ortus Cardine*
and *Hostis Herodes*.
Bibliography: *Cat. gen. octavo*, vol. 19, pp. 61-2; Jullien, 128-9;
Mearns, pp. xv, 1, and 39.

ANGERS, Bibliothèque Municipale, 277 (268)
s. ix; 120 leaves; 170 x 115 mm.; probably written at S. Aubin, Angers.

Contents: On f. 120r-v: PC 5.188 ff. Preceded by *De Primo Adventu
Christi* (ff. 85v ff.).
Other information: Sedulius passage written in Tironian notation. Seen
in person.
Bibliography: Beeson, pp. 72 and 94; Jean-Paul Bouhot, "Explications
du rituel baptismal à l'époque carolingienne," *REAug* 24 (1978), 295-6;
idem, "Le Manuscrit Angers, B.M. 277 (268) et l'opuscule *De spe et
timore* d'Agobard de Lyon," *REAug* 31 (1985), 227-41; *Cat. gen.
octavo*, vol. 31, pp. 276-7; Legendre, p. 588; L. van Acker, *Agobardi
Lugdunensis Opera Omnia, CCCM*, vol. 52, p. 42.

ANTWERPEN, Musaeum Plantin-Moretus Bibliotheek, M. 312 (62)
s. ix; 29 leaves; 265 x 202 mm.

Contents: On f. 1r-v: H1 (beginning with line 91), H2. Followed by

Juvencus, *Evangeliorum Libri Quattuor* (ff. 1v-28r).
Other information: On f. 1: *Collatus cum impresso a Theod. Pulmanno anno 1500....* Seen in person.
Bibliography: J. Denucé, *Musaeum Plantin-Moretus. Catalogue des manuscrits* (Antwerpen, 1927), pp. 55-6.

ARRAS, Bibliothèque Municipale, 466 (574)
s. xiii$^{ex.}$; 344 leaves; 423 x 280 mm.; probably written at S. Vaast, Arras.

Contents: On f. 292r: extracts from PC, beginning with 2.214 ff. and ending with 2.109. Preceded by excerpts from Ovid, *Metamorphoses;* Horace, *Epistles;* Juvenal, *Satires;* and Lucan, *Bellum Civile* (ff. 290r-292r). Followed by excerpts from the elegies of Maximianus and Prudentius, *Psychomachia* (f. 292r-v).
Bibliography: Cat. gen. quarto, vol. 4, pp. 183-5; J.N. Hillgarth, "El *Prognosticum futuri saeculi* de San Julián de Toledo," *AST* 30 (1958), 40, n. 153; Jeudy & Riou, pp. 102-23, esp. p. 113; Jeudy & Riou, "Notes," 314; Stegmüller, vol. 6, no. 8428-30.

AUGSBURG, Staats- und Stadtbibliothek, 2° Cod. 139
s. xv (1419); 271 leaves; 270 x 205 mm.; written in Schwaben; prov. Hl. Kreuz, Augsburg; paper.

Contents: On f. 1r (top of page): first two lines of H1. Volume includes *Commentarius in Eberhardi Bethuniensis Graecismum* (ff. 1r-8r); *Vocabularius ex quo* (ff. 9r-194r); et al.
Bibliography: Herrad Spilling, *Die Handschriften der Staats- und Stadtbibliothek Augsburg 2° Cod. 101-250,* in *Handschriftenkataloge der Staats- und Stadtbibliothek Augsburg* (Wiesbaden, 1974 ff.), vol. 3 (1984), pp. 63-5.

AUGSBURG, Staats- und Stadtbibliothek, 4° Cod. 21
s. xv; quarto; paper.

Contents: Miscellany volume containing many *accessus.* The *accessus* to Sedulius is preceded by others to Horace, Virgil, Sallust, Avianus, Boethius, Arator, Ovid, Juvenal, Prudentius, and Prosper. Followed by *accessus* to Maximianus, Claudian, Statius, Persius, Dares Phrygius, Aesop, Cicero, Juvencus, Martianus Capella, Gregory, and Donatus.
Bibliography: Kristeller, *Iter,* vol. 3, p. 455.

AUGSBURG, Staats- und Stadtbibliothek, 8° Cod. 35
s. xv (1487); 370 leaves; 150 x 105 mm.; written in Germany; prov. S. Ulrich and Afra, Augsburg; paper.

Contents: On f. 15r: PC 2.63-69 (concluding with: *Affer opem nobisque adsis pede, diva, secundo*). Preceded by poem beginning *Grata domus genitor* (f. 14v) and followed by Ps.-Bernard, *Sermo de Miseria Humana* (ff. 16r-23r).
Bibliography: Sottili, vol. 1, p. 29.

AUTUN, Bibliothèque Municipale, 4 (S. 3)
s. viii² (ff. 6-24); 247 leaves; 325 x 238 mm.; written at Flavigny-sur-Ozerain.

Contents: "The Flavigny Gospels;" includes PC 1.355-8, accompanying illustrations of the four evangelists.
Bibliography: *Cat. gen. quarto*, vol. 1, pp. 9-11; Émile Chatelain, "Les Plus vieux manuscrits d'Autun mutilés par Libri," *Journal des savants*, 1898, 380; *CLA*, vol. 6, p. 6, no. 717b; McGurk, pp. 52-3.

AVIGNON, Bibliothèque Municipale, 343 (anc. 388)
s. xvᵉˣ·; 135 leaves; 229 x 155 mm.; paper.

Contents: *Liber hymnorum* beginning on f. 14r; *A Solis Ortus Cardine* and *Hostis Herodes* on ff. 34r-35r. Preceded by hymn beginning *Christe redemptor omnium* and followed by hymn beginning *Nuncium vobis fero*.
Bibliography: *Cat. gen. octavo*, vol. 27, pp. 262-4.

BAMBERG, Staatsbibliothek, Msc. Patr. 133
s. xii/xiii; 8 leaves; 178 x 101 mm.

Contents: On ff. 1r-8r: PC 2.123 to 4.41 (missing 3.30-32, 65-66, 100-101, and 133-134).
Other information: Seen in person.
Bibliography: Friedrich Leitschuh (and Hans Fischer), *Katalog der Handschriften der königlichen Bibliothek zu Bamberg* (Bamberg, 1887-1912), vol. 1, part 1.3 (1903), *Kirchenväter und ältere Theologen, bis zum Ende des XIII. Jahrhunderts*, p. 520.

BAMBERG, Staatsbibliothek, Patr. 17 (B. II. 10)
s. x-xi; 162 leaves; 380 x 304 mm.; Michelsberg, Bamberg.

Contents: On ff. 133r-162r (s. x): *florilegium* in four books *("De laude Dei")* compiled by Alcuin. Includes excerpts from Sedulius on ff. 151v-152r: PC 1.60-102, 282-290, 312-319, and 334-363. Followed by excerpts from works of Juvencus, Arator, Prosper, Venantius Fortunatus, Bede, Aldhelm, and Dracontius. On ff. 1-108: sermons of Augustine. On ff. 157-162: *Miracula Niniae Episcopi.*
Other information: Seen in person.
Bibliography: Radu Constantinescu, "Alcuin et les *Libelli Precum* de l'époque carolingienne," *Revue d'histoire de la spiritualité* 50 (1974), 17; Glauche, p. 11; Michael Lapidge, "The Present State of Anglo-Latin Studies" in *Insular Latin Studies: Papers on Latin Texts and Manuscripts of the British Isles: 550-1066,* ed. Michael W. Herren = Papers in Medieval Studies 1 (Toronto, 1981), p. 53; Leitschuh, *Katalog,* same as above, pp. 363-6; Fidel Rädle, "Bedas Hymnus über das Sechstagewerk und die Weltalter" in *Anglo-Saxonica. Beiträge zur Vor- und Frühgeschichte der englischen Literatur. Festschrift für Hans Schabram zum 65. Geburtstag* (München, 1993), p. 55; F. Vollmer, *Fl. Merobaudis Reliquiae, Blossii Aemilii Dracontii Carmina, Eugenii Toletani Episcopi Carmina et Epistulae, MGH AA,* vol. 14, pp. xiv ff.

BERLIN, Staatsbibliothek zu Berlin-Preussischer Kulturbesitz, Phillipps 1710
s. x; 22 leaves; 180-190 x 100 mm.

Contents: On f. 1r-v: E1 (only to Huemer's page 3, line 2). Followed by a collection of glosses on books of the Old Testament.
Other information: Elaborately decorated initial "P" at beginning of E1. Seen in person.
Bibliography: Valentin Rose, *Verzeichniss der lateinischen Handschriften der königlichen Bibliothek zu Berlin* (Berlin, 1893-1919), vol. 1, *Die Meerman-Handschriften des Sir Thomas Phillipps* (1893), pp. 99-100.

BERLIN, Staatsbibliothek zu Berlin-Preussischer Kulturbesitz, Phillipps 1827
s. xiii*med.*; 73 leaves; 190 x 110 mm.; probably written in Germany.

Contents: On ff. 60r-62r: PC 1.3 ff. (*"Proverbia Sedulii"*). Preceded by *Comedia Babionis* (ff. 55v-60r). Followed by *"Proverbia Prosperi"* (ff. 62v ff.).
Bibliography: Franz G. Becker, *Pamphilus. Prolegomena zum Pam-*

philus (De Amore) und kritische Textausgabe = Beihefte zum MlatJb 9 (Düsseldorf, 1972), pp. 94-5; Rosemary Burton, *Classical Poets in the Florilegium Gallicum* = Lateinische Sprache und Literatur des Mittelalters 14 (Frankfurt, 1983), pp. 60-2; A. Dessì Fulgheri, "Babio," *Commedie latine del XII e XIII secolo* 2 (1980), 216-9; Johannes Hamacher, *Florilegium Gallicum. Prolegomena und Edition der Excerpte von Petron bis Cicero, De Oratore* = Lateinische Sprache und Literatur des Mittelalters 5 (Frankfurt and Bern, 1975), pp. 84-5; Jill Mann, *Ysengrimus. Text with Translation, Commentary, and Introduction* = Mittellateinische Studien und Texte 12 (Leiden, 1987), p. 189; Rose, same as above, pp. 430-3.

BERN, Burgerbibliothek, AA 90. 17
s. x; 4 leaves; octavo.

Contents: E1 (missing last nine lines).
Other information: AA 90 is a widely varied collection consisting of 30 parts, of which ours is the 17th. Seen in person.
Bibliography: Hermann Hagen, *Catalogus Codicum Bernensium (Bibliotheca Bongarsiana)* (Bern, 1875), pp. 111-8, esp. p. 115.

BERN, Burgerbibliothek, 455
s. ix$^{med.}$; 44 leaves; 215 x 167 mm.; written in France (Paris area); later at Laon.

Contents: Collection of hymns; on ff. 1v-2r: *A Solis Ortus Cardine* and *Hostis Herodes;* on ff. 23r-24r: H1.1-30 and 109-110. The latter is preceded by the first lines of Juvencus, *Evangeliorum Libri Quattuor* (f. 22v) and followed by the first lines of Virgil's first *Eclogue* (f. 24r).
Other information: Used by Huemer (ß'). Corrections and additions made by Adelelm of Laon (c. 865-93). Seen in person.
Bibliography: Contreni, pp. 44, 64, 67, and 159-61; *CSEL,* vol. 10, p. 155; Gneuss, *Hymnar,* pp. 49 and 117; Hagen, *Catalogus,* same as above, pp. 396-400; B. Hauréau's review of L. Delisle, *Notice sur les manuscrits disparus de la bibliothèque de Tours pendant la première moitié du XIXe siècle,* in *Journal des savants,* 1883, 521; B. Hauréau, "Sur les poèmes latins attribués à Saint Bernard," *Journal des savants,* 1882, 174; Huemer, *De Sedulii,* p. 44; Ewald Jammers, "Grundsätzliches zur Erforschung der rhythmischen Neumenschriften. Randbemerkungen zu den Cod. St. Gallen 381 und Bern 455," *Buch und Schrift,* n.F., 5-6 (1942-3), 97-100; Jullien, 157; Mearns, pp. xiv, 1, and 39;

Mostert, p. 78; Munk Olsen, vol. 1, p. 66 and vol. 2, p. 707; Dag Norberg, *L'Oeuvre poétique de Paulin d'Aquilée. Édition critique avec introduction et commentaire* (Stockholm, 1979), pp. 83-4.

BERN, Burgerbibliothek, 546
s. xi-xii; 61 leaves; octavo; Fleury?

Contents: On ff. 54r-61v: E1, PC 1.1-99. Preceded by Old Testament excerpts (ff. 1r-34v); hymn beginning *Popule meus quid feci tibi* (ff. 35r-36v); *Kyrie eleison* (ff. 36v-38v); and excerpts from the Old and New Testament (ff. 39r-53v).
Other information: Used by Huemer (ß). Microfilm acquired. Seen in person.
Bibliography: CSEL, vol. 10, p. xxii; B. Grémont, "Les Anciens manuscrits de Fleury," *Bulletin trimestriel de la Société Archéologique et Historique de l'Orléanais* 2 (1962), 276; Hagen, *Catalogus,* same as above, p. 452; Mostert, pp. 80-1.

BOLOGNA, Biblioteca Universitaria, 170 (182)
s. xv; 148 leaves; 205 x 150 mm.; paper.

Contents: On f. 135r: PC 2.63-9. Preceded by *Missa contra Pestem* (of Pope Clement VI) (ff. 132r ff.). Followed by *Errores ex Libro Galeoti Narnensis.*
Bibliography: Lodovico Frati, "Indice dei codici latini conservati nella R. Bibliotheca Universitaria di Bologna," *SIFC* 16 (1908), 174-81.

BOULOGNE-SUR-MER, Bibliothèque Municipale, 20
c. 1000; 231 leaves; 356 x 310 mm.; S. Bertin, at S. Omer.

Contents: "St. Odbert-Psalter;" on ff. 207v-208r: *A Solis Ortus Cardine* and *Hostis Herodes.*
Bibliography: Magda von Bàràny-Oberschall, "*Baculus Pastoralis.* Keltisch-irische Motive auf mittelalterlichen beingeschnitzten Bischofsstäben," *Zeitschrift für Kunstwissenschaft* 12 (1958), 32-3; Helmut Boese, *Die alte Glosa Psalmorum ex Traditione Seniorum* = Vetus Latina. Die Reste der altlateinischen Bibel. Aus der Geschichte der lateinischen Bibel 9 (Freiburg, 1982), p. 19; *Cat. gen. quarto,* vol. 4, pp. 584-5; Jullien, 110-11; Leroquais, *Psautiers,* vol. 1, pp. 94-101; Mearns, pp. xiv, 1, and 39; Joseph Smits van Waesberghe, et al., *The Theory of Music from the Carolingian Era up to 1400* = Répertoire internationale

des sources musicales 1 (München and Duisburg, 1961), 82.

BRUXELLES, Bibliothèque Royale Albert 1er, 8860-8867
s. x; 76 leaves; 150 x 118 mm.; S. Gallen?

Contents: Collection of hymns; includes H2 (ff. 23v-24v). Preceded by hymn beginning *Age Deus causam meam* (ff. 22r-23v) and followed by hymn beginning *Apparebunt ante summum* (ff. 24v-26v).
Other information: From the library of the Bollandists. Seen in person.
Bibliography: Ernst Dümmler, "Die handschriftliche Überlieferung der lateinischen Dichtungen aus der Zeit der Karolinger," *Neues Archiv* 4 (1878-9), 155-8; Joseph van den Gheyn, et al., *Catalogue des manuscrits de la Bibliothèque Royale de Belgique* (Bruxelles, 1901-48), vol. 2 (1902), pp. 289-92; L. Whitbread, "After Bede: The Influence and Dissemination of his Doomsday Verses," *Archiv für das Studium der neueren Sprachen und Literaturen* 204 (1967), 262-3.

BURY ST. EDMUNDS, Grammar School, No press mark
s. xv (c. 1405); erratic pagination.

Contents: Benedictine psalter, etc.; includes *A Solis Ortus Cardine* and *Hostis Herodes*.
Other information: Now deposited at West Suffolk Record Office.
Bibliography: Gneuss, *Hymnar*, pp. 81 and 249; M.R. James, "Bury St. Edmunds Manuscripts," *English Historical Review* 41 (1926), 251-60, esp. 259; Ker, *Med.*, p. 16 and *Suppl.*, p. 5; Mearns, pp. xii, 1, and 39.

CAMBRIDGE, Corpus Christi College, 286
s. vi (late); 265 leaves; 251 x 196 mm.; written in Italy, perhaps Rome; later at S. Augustine's, Canterbury.

Contents: Evangeliary; on f. 129v: PC 1.357; on f. 207v: PC 1.358.
Other information: Written in uncials. Probably brought to England by missionaries from Rome.
Bibliography: Samuel Berger, *Histoire de la Vulgate pendant les premiers siècles du Moyen Âge* (Paris, 1893), pp. 35 and 379; Julian Brown, "The Origin and Date of the Inscriptions which Accompany the Miniatures in 'St. Augustine's Gospels'" in G.D. Henderson, *Losses and Lacunae in Early Insular Art* = University of York Medieval Monograph Series 3 (York, 1982), Appendix B, pp. 41-5; *CLA*, vol. 2 (2nd ed.), p. 4, no. 126; Gamber, vol. 1, p. 228, no. 404; Gneuss, "List," no. 83;

Montague Rhodes James, *A Descriptive Catalogue of the Manuscripts in the Library of Corpus Christi College Cambridge,* vol. 2 (Cambridge, 1912), pp. 52-6; Carol F. Lewine, *"Vulpes Fossa Habent* or the Miracle of the Bent Woman in the Gospels of St. Augustine, Corpus Christi College, Cambridge, Ms. 286," *The Art Bulletin* 56 (1974), 489-504; McGurk, pp. 25-6; Kurt Weitzmann, *Late Antique and Early Christian Book Illumination* (New York, 1977), pp. 22, 112, 115, and plates 41-2; Francis Wormald, *The Miniatures in the Gospels of St. Augustine, Corpus Christi College MS. 286* (Cambridge, 1954), pp. 3-5; idem, *Collected Writings I: Studies in Medieval Art from the Sixth to the Twelfth Centuries* (Oxford, London, and New York, 1984), pp. 13-35.

CAMBRIDGE, Corpus Christi College, 391
s. xi² (c. 1065); 724 pages; 225 x 135 mm.; Worcester.

Contents: "Portiforium of Oswald;" hymns on pp. 277 ff. include *A Solis Ortus Cardine* (stanzas 1-5) and *Hostis Herodes.*
Bibliography: Christine Franzen, *The Tremulous Hand of Worcester. A Study of Old English in the Thirteenth Century* (Oxford, 1991), pp. 69-70; Gamber, vol. 2, p. 611, no. 1693; James, same as above, pp. 241-8; Gneuss, *Hymnar,* pp. 106-8 and passim; Gneuss, "List," no. 104; Anselm Hughes, *The Portiforium of Saint Wulstan* = Henry Bradshaw Society 89-90 (London, 1958-60); Jullien, 137-8; Ker, *Cat.,* pp. 113-5; Ker, *Med.,* p. 206; Dame Laurentia McLachlan, "St. Wulstan's Prayer Book," *Journal of Theological Studies* 30 (1929), 174-7; Mearns, pp. xi, 1, and 39.

CAMBRIDGE, Gonville and Caius College, 144/194
s. ix/x; 43 leaves (paginated 1-86); 248 x 184 mm.; written in England?; prov. S. Augustine's, Canterbury.

Contents: On pp. 1-73: the commentary of Remigius of Auxerre on Sedulius. Followed by glosses on *Disticha Catonis;* a sermon on fasting; et al.
Other information: Bishop suggests that the manuscript was written at Auxerre.
Bibliography: T.A.M. Bishop, "Notes on Cambridge Manuscripts, Part II," *TCBS* 11.2 (1955), 187-9; Marcus Boas, "Näheres zur Überlieferung der sogenannten *Monosticha Catonis,"* *Berliner philologische Wochenschrift* 47 (1927), 316-20; Esposito, 168; Glauche, pp. 52 and 56; Gneuss, "List," no. 120; Montague Rhodes James, *A Descriptive*

Catalogue of the Manuscripts in the Library of Gonville and Caius College (Cambridge, 1907-8), vol. 1, pp. 161-3; Jeudy, "Remi," p. 496; Ker, *Med.* p. 41; Lapidge, "Latin Texts," p. 114 and n. 36; Munk Olsen, vol. 1, p. 67; Sanford, 205; Schenkl, no. 2745.

CAMBRIDGE, Jesus College, 21 (Q. B. 4)
s. xiii; 96 leaves; 257 x 187 mm.

Contents: Augustinian psalter, etc.; hymns include *A Solis Ortus Cardine* and *Hostis Herodes*.
Bibliography: Montague Rhodes James, *A Descriptive Catalogue of the Manuscripts in the Library of Jesus College, Cambridge* (London, 1895), pp. 22-3; Mearns, pp. xii, 1, and 39.

CAMBRIDGE, Jesus College, 23 (Q. B. 6)
s. xii*in.*; 141 leaves; 270 x 191 mm.; Durham.

Contents: Benedictine psalter, etc.; hymns include *A Solis Ortus Cardine* and *Hostis Herodes*.
Bibliography: Frere, no. 907; Gneuss, *Hymnar,* pp. 141, 249, and 253; James, *Descriptive Catalogue,* same as above, pp. 24-8; Ker, *Med.,* p. 61; Mearns, pp. xii, 1, and 39.

CAMBRIDGE, Magdalene College, 10 (F. 4. 10)
s. xiv-xv; 362 leaves; 254 x 178 mm.; Peterborough.

Contents: Benedictine antiphonal, etc.; includes *A Solis Ortus Cardine* and *Hostis Herodes*.
Bibliography: Gneuss, *Hymnar,* pp. 81 and 249; Montague Rhodes James, *A Descriptive Catalogue of the Manuscripts in the College Library of Magdalene College, Cambridge* (Cambridge, 1909), pp. 17-20; Ker, *Med.,* p. 151; Mearns, pp. xii, 1, and 39.

CAMBRIDGE, Queen's College, 17 (H. 29)
s. xiii; 217 leaves; 197 x 133 mm.; Worcester?

Contents: Benedictine psalter, etc.; includes *A Solis Ortus Cardine* and *Hostis Herodes*.
Bibliography: Gneuss, *Hymnar,* p. 249; Montague Rhodes James, *A Descriptive Catalogue of the Manuscripts in the Library of Queen's College, Cambridge* (Cambridge, 1905), pp. 19-22; Ker, *Med.,* p. 215

[rejects Worcester provenance]; Mearns, pp. xii, 1, and 39.

CAMBRIDGE, St. John's College, 262 (Tt. I. 22)
s. xiv*in.*; 96 leaves; 321 x 229 mm.; S. Augustine's, Canterbury.

Contents: Benedictine hymnal; includes *A Solis Ortus Cardine* and *Hostis Herodes* (f. 39r).
Bibliography: Montague Rhodes James, *A Descriptive Catalogue of the Manuscripts in the Library of St. John's College, Cambridge* (Cambridge, 1913), pp. 302-10; Ker, *Med.,* p. 41; Mearns, pp. xiii, 1, and 39.

CAMBRIDGE, University Library, Add. 3322
s. xiv; 321 leaves; 160 x 110 mm.; written in France.

Contents: Cistercian breviary; hymnal beginning on f. 309r includes *A Solis Ortus Cardine.*
Bibliography: Frere, 777; Mearns, pp. xv and 1.

CAMBRIDGE, University Library, Dd. 1. 20
s. xv (c. 1420); 111 leaves; large folio volume; Abingdon.

Contents: Benedictine psalter, etc.; hymns (at end) include *A Solis Ortus Cardine* and *Hostis Herodes.*
Bibliography: *A Catalogue of the Manuscripts Preserved in the Library of the University of Cambridge* (Cambridge, 1856-67), vol. 1 (1856), p. 27; Gneuss, *Hymnar,* p. 249; Mearns, pp. xiii, 1, and 39.

CAMBRIDGE, University Library, Mm. 2. 9
s. xiv; 291 leaves; folio.

Contents: Sarum antiphonary; hymns (at end) include *A Solis Ortus Cardine* and *Hostis Herodes.*
Bibliography: *Cat.,* same as above, vol. 4 (1861), pp. 129-30; Mearns, pp. xiii, 1, and 39.

CLERMONT-FERRAND, Bibliothèque Municipale 74 (67)
s. xiv; 81 leaves; 275 x 200 mm.

Contents: Hymnal on ff. 46v-76v includes *Hostis Herodes.*
Bibliography: *Cat. gen. octavo,* vol. 14, pp. 24-5; Stäblein, p. 156.

COLMAR, Bibliothèque Municipale, 465 (51)
s. xv; 272 leaves; 270 x 210 mm.; Murbach; paper.

Contents: On ff. 213v-214r: *A Solis Ortus Cardine* ("followed by notes on the life of the poet"). Preceded by verses beginning *Se ipse ad quis omne quod posse pro saluto.* Followed by notes from *De Natura Rerum.*
Bibliography: Cat. gen. octavo, vol. 56, pp. 174-5.

DOUAI, Bibliothèque Municipale, 285
s. xii²; 134 leaves; 320 x 230 mm.; written in northern France; prov. Anchin.

Contents: "*Florilegium Duacense;*" on f. 123r: extracts from PC, beginning with 2.214 ff. and ending with 2.109. Preceded by excerpts from the epigrams of Prosper. Followed by excerpts from the elegies of Maximianus.
Bibliography: Cat. gen. quarto, vol. 6, pp. 151-2; Ph. Delhaye, "*Grammatica* et *Ethica* au XIIe siècle," *RTAM* 25 (1958), 89-90; R.B.C. Huygens, *La Tradition manuscrite de Guibert de Nogent* = Instrumenta Patristica 21 (Brugge, 1991), pp. 13-4; Jeudy & Riou, pp. 521-6; Munk Olsen, vol. 2, p. 848; idem, "Les Classiques latins dans les florilèges médiévaux antérieurs au XIIIe siècle I," *RHT* 9 (1979), 84-7; idem, "Note sur quelques préfaces de florilèges latins du XIIe siècle," *Revue romane* 8 (1973), 191-3; Reynolds, p. 377, n. 8; idem, *The Medieval Tradition of Seneca's Letters* (Oxford, 1965), p. 105, n. 8; Henri-Marie Rochais, "Florilèges spirituels latins," *Dictionnaire de spiritualité,* vol. 5, cols. 455-6.

DOUAI, Bibliothèque Municipale, 352
s. xii; 144 leaves; 350 x 240 mm.; Anchin.

Contents: On ff. 147 ff.: E1. Preceded by works of St. Anselm as well as a life of the same by Eadmer (ff. 115 ff.).
Bibliography: "Catalogus Codicum Hagiographicorum Latinorum Bibliothecae Publicae Duacensis," *Analecta Bollandiana* 20 (1901), 372; *Cat. gen. quarto,* vol. 6, pp. 186-7; R.W. Southern, *The Life of St. Anselm, Archbishop of Canterbury, by Eadmer* (Oxford, 1962), p. xvii.

DUBLIN, Trinity College Library, 93
s. xv² (after 1461); 115 leaves; 293 x 200 mm.; written in England.

Contents: Hymnal on ff. 96-113v includes *A Solis Ortus Cardine* and *Hostis Herodes* (f. 113r-v).   Preceded by hymn beginning *Christe redemptor omnium.* Followed by hymn beginning *Sancte Dei preciose* (for S. Stephen).

Bibliography: Marvin L. Colker, *Trinity College Library Dublin: Descriptive Catalogue of the Medieval and Renaissance Latin Manuscripts* (Dublin, 1991), vol. 1, pp. 168-76, esp. p. 175; Frere, no. 727.

DUBLIN, Trinity College Library, 106

s. xv[2]; 177 leaves; 164 x 116 mm.; written in Italy.

Contents: Hymnal on ff. 133v-177v includes *A Solis Ortu [sic] Cardine* and *Hostis Herodes* (ff. 141v-142r).   Preceded by hymn beginning *Christe redemptor omnium.*   Followed by hymn beginning *Ave maris stella.*

Bibliography: Colker, *Catalogue,* same as above, vol. 1, pp. 218-230, esp. 221.

DUBLIN, Trinity College Library, 270

s. xiii-xiv; 213 leaves; 170 x 115 mm.; written in England.

Contents: Hymns on ff. 185r-192r (s. xiii[med.]) include *A Solis Ortus Cardine* (f. 191r-v). Preceded by hymn beginning *Christe redemptor omnium.* Followed by hymn beginning *Nuncium vobis de supernis.*

Bibliography: Bursill-Hall, p. 59; Colker, *Catalogue,* same as above, vol. 1, pp. 482-97, esp. 491; idem, "New Evidence that John of Garland Revised the *Doctrinale* of Alexander de Villa Dei," *Scriptorium* 28 (1974), 68-71; R.W. Hunt, *The Schools and the Cloister: The Life and Writings of Alexander Nequam (1157-1217)* (Oxford, 1984), p. 126.

DUBLIN, Trinity College Library, 921

s. xv[med.]; 174 (+ 7 blank) leaves; 219 x 142 mm.; written in England; paper and parchment.

Contents: Hymns on ff. 82v-107v include *A Solis Ortus Cardine* and *Hostis Herodes* (ff. 84v-85r). Preceded by hymn beginning *Christe redemptor omnium.* Followed by hymn beginning *Sancte Dei preciose* (for S. Stephen).

Bibliography: Bursill-Hall, p. 60; Colker, *Catalogue,* same as above, vol. 2, pp. 1179-92, esp. 1185.

DURHAM, Cathedral Library, B. III. 32
s. xi; 127 leaves; 237 x 152 mm.; Canterbury (prob. Christ Church).

Contents: Benedictine hymnal on ff. 2r-43r includes *A Solis Ortus Cardine* and *Hostis Herodes* (f. 15r-v). Interlinear Anglo-Saxon glossing. Collection of proverbs in Latin and Anglo-Saxon on ff. 43v-45v. Bound with another volume (ff. 56-127), which contains Aelfric's Grammar.
Bibliography: Olof Arngart, "The Durham Proverbs," *Speculum* 56 (1981), 288-300; idem, *The Durham Proverbs* = Lunds Universitets Årsskrift 1.52.2 (Lund, 1956); Gneuss, *Hymnar,* pp. 85-90 and passim; Gneuss, "List," no. 244; Jullien, 133-4; Mearns, pp. xii, 1, and 39; R.A.B. Mynors, *Durham Cathedral Manuscripts to the End of the 12th Century* (Oxford, 1939), pp. 28-9; J. Stevenson, *The Latin Hymns of the Anglo-Saxon Church* = Publications of the Surtees Society 23 (London, 1851), pp. 50-2; Francis Wormald, "Two Anglo-Saxon Miniatures Compared," *British Museum Quarterly* 9 (1934-5), 113-5.

DURHAM, Cathedral Library, C. IV. 10
s. xii[in.]; 103 leaves; 193 x 114 mm.; Durham.

Contents: On ff. 22v-23v: beginning of Remigius' commentary on Sedulius.. Preceded by Marbod of Rennes' *Liber Lapidum* (ff. 1r ff.); a commentary on the Athanasian Creed (ff. 3r ff.); two explanations of Prudentius, *Psychomachia* (ff. 5r ff. and ff. 13r ff.) and notes on *Versus Sibillae* (f. 22r). Followed by a commentary on Boethius, *Philosophiae Consolatio.*
Bibliography: Esposito, 169; Ker, *Med.* (suppl.), p. 27; Mynors, *Durham,* same as above, p. 59; Schenkl, no. 4472.

EDINBURGH, National Library of Scotland, Adv. 18. 5. 10
s. xii[1]; 39 leaves; 195 x 120 mm.; written in Germany.

Contents: On ff. 12v-14r: beginning of Remigius' commentary on Sedulius. Preceded by notes on Juvenal (ff. 1r-5r); Lucan (ff. 5v-7v); and Persius (ff. 8r-12v). Followed by notes on Horace (ff. 14r-22r); Virgil (ff. 22r-30r); Prudentius (ff. 30r-33v); Thebaldus (ff. 34r-39r); and definitions of technical terms (f. 39v).
Other information: Glossing in Latin and German.
Bibliography: Bergmann, p. 14; Ian C. Cunningham, "Latin Classical Manuscripts in the National Library of Scotland," *Scriptorium* 27 (1973), 79-80 [s. xi]; Esposito, 169; Stephen A. Hurlbut, "A Forerunner of

Alexander de Villa-Dei," *Speculum* 8 (1933), 258-63; Jeudy, "Remi," p. 496; Kristeller, *Iter,* vol. 4, p. 17; Munk Olsen, vol. 1, pp. 515-6; Sanford, 217; Klaus Siewert, *Die althochdeutsche Horazglossierung* = Studien zum Althochdeutschen 8 (Göttingen, 1986), pp. 351-63; Erika Tiemensma-Langbroek, "Die althochdeutschen Glossen des Codex Adv. Ms. 18. 5. 10 der National Library of Scotland, Edinburg," *Amsterdamer Beiträge zur älteren Germanistik* 11 (1976), 1-36; Schenkl, no. 3020.

EINSIEDELN, Stiftsbibliothek, 83
s. xii; 462 leaves; 355 x 255 mm.

Contents: Benedictine breviary with hymns on ff. 362v-373r; includes *A Solis Ortus Cardine* and *Hostis Herodes.*
Bibliography: Bruckner, vol. 5, p. 171; Mearns, pp. xvi, 1, and 39; Gabriel Meier, *Codicum Manu Scriptorum Qui in Bibliotheca Monasterii Einsidlensis O.S.B. Servantur* (Einsiedeln, 1899), vol. 1, pp. 74-6.

EINSIEDELN, Stiftsbibliothek, 366
s. xii^1-xiii^1; 58 pages; 267 x 195 mm.

Contents: Fragments of sequences; *A Solis Ortus Cardine* and *Hostis Herodes* on p. 39.
Bibliography: Meier, same as above, pp. 331-2; Stäblein, pp. 261-301 and 581-9.

ENGELBERG, Stiftsbibliothek, 8 (1. 9)
s. xiv; 223 leaves; 375 x 272 mm.

Contents: Benedictine psalter, etc.; on f. 177r: *A Solis Ortus Cardine;* on f. 179v: *Hostis Herodes.*
Bibliography: Benedictus Gottwald, *Catalogus Codicum Manu Scriptorum Qui Asservantur in Bibliotheca Monasterii O.S.B. Engelbergensis in Helvetia* (Freiburg, 1891), pp. 22-7.

ENGELBERG, Stiftsbibliothek, 40 (2. 10)
s. xiv; 168 leaves; 290 x 214 mm.

Contents: Psalter, etc.; on f. 134r: *A Solis Ortus Cardine;* on f. 137r: *Hostis Herodes.*
Bibliography: Gottwald, same as above, pp. 60-3.

ENGELBERG, Stiftsbibliothek, 42 (2. 22)
s. xii; 346 leaves; 283 x 205 mm.

Contents: Benedictine breviary; on f. 305r-v: *A Solis Ortus Cardine* and *Hostis Herodes*.
Bibliography: Gottwald, same as above, pp. 63-8; Mearns, pp. xvi, 1, and 39.

ENGELBERG, Stiftsbibiothek, 140 (6. 21)
s. xii; 135 leaves (last 7 leaves paper); 164 x 98 mm.

Contents: Prayerbook; *"Hymnarius S. Ambrosii"* (ff. 69-87) includes *A Solis Ortus Cardine* (f. 75r) and *Hostis Herodes* (f. 76v).
Bibliography: Bruckner, vol. 8, p. 128; Gottwald, same as above, pp. 142-4; Mearns, pp. xvi, 1, and 39.

ERFURT, Wissenschaftliche Allgemeinbibliothek, Amplon. 8° 8
s. xii*med.*-s. xiv*med.*; 127 leaves; octavo.

Contents: On f. 117r-v: *accessus* to Sedulius and commentary up to PC 1.46. Preceded by notes on the virtues and vices (f. 116r-v) and followed by excerpts from the *Physiologus* (f. 117v).
Bibliography: Colette Jeudy, "Le Florilège grammatical inédit du manuscrit 8° 8 de la Bibliothèque d'Erfurt," *ALMA* 44-45 (1983-5), 91-128, esp. 92; Wilhelm Schum, *Beschreibendes Verzeichniss der amplonianischen Handschriften-Sammlung zu Erfurt* (Berlin, 1887), pp. 674-7.

ERFURT, Wissenschaftliche Allgemeinbibliothek, Amplon. 8° 17
s. xiii-xiv; 121 leaves; octavo.

Contents: On ff. 77r-81r: PC 1.1-249. Preceded by Geoffrey of Vinsauf, *Poetria Nova* with commentary (ff. 1r-57r); commentary on Walter of Châtillon, *Alexandreis* (ff. 57r-75v); et al. Followed by another commentary on *Poetria Nova* (ff. 82r-93r); the homilies of Origen on the Song of Songs (set to meter by Peter Riga) (ff. 94v-115v); et al.
Other information: Note on f. 77r describes our author as: *Sedulius versificator egregius*.
Bibliography: Marvin L. Colker, *Galteri de Castellione Alexandreis* = Thesaurus Mundi. Bibliotheca Scriptorum Latinorum Mediae et Recen-

tioris Aetatis 17 (Padova, 1978), pp. xxx and xxxvi; Schum, *Verzeichniss,* same as above, pp. 684-5.

ERLANGEN, Universitätsbibliothek Erlangen-Nürnberg, 2112. 26
s. xi; 1 leaf; 165 x 120-105 mm.

Contents: On the verso: PC 3.26-87. *Sphaera Pythagorae* on the recto.
Bibliography: Elias von Steinmeyer, *Die jüngeren Handschriften der Erlanger Universitätsbibliothek* (Erlangen, 1913), p. 145.

ESCORIAL, EL, Real Biblioteca de San Lorenzo, Lat. B. II. 1
s. xiv; 501 leaves; 337 x 240 mm.

Contents: Roman breviary with hymns beginning on f. 498; includes *Hostis Herodes.*
Bibliography: Guillermo Antolin, *Catálogo de los códices latinos de la Real Biblioteca del Escorial,* vol. 1 (Madrid, 1910), p. 144.

ÉVREUX, Bibliothèque Municipale, 70
s. xii[1]; 180 leaves; 220 x 140 mm.; written in Rouen; later at Lyre.

Contents: Benedictine psalter, etc.; hymns on ff. 141v-165r include *A Solis Ortus Cardine* and *Hostis Herodes.*
Bibliography: Cat. gen. octavo, vol. 2, p. 440; Gneuss, *Hymnar,* p. 82; Leroquais, *Psautiers,* vol. 1, pp. 196-7; Mearns, pp. xv, 1, and 39; Geneviève Nortier, *Les Bibliothèques médiévales des abbayes bénédictines de Normandie* (Caen, 1966), p. 141.

FIRENZE, Biblioteca Medicea Laurenziana, Conv. Soppr. 524
s. xi-xii; 208 leaves; 250 x 160 mm.; S. Fidele, Strumi

Contents: Cluniac breviary; includes *A Solis Ortus Cardine* and *Hostis Herodes.*
Bibliography: Owen Blum, "Authenticity of Sixteen Medieval Latin Poems Attributed to St. Peter Damian (1007-1072)," *APS Yearbook* 1956, 378-81; Réginald Grégoire, "Repertorium Liturgicum Italicum," *Studi medievali* (3. ser.) 9 (1968), 505-6; Jullien, 151-2; Lokrantz, pp. 26-7; Mearns, pp. xviii, 1, and 39.

FIRENZE, Biblioteca Medicea Laurenziana, Plut. 29. 1

s. xiii$^{med.}$; 476 leaves; 232 x 157 mm.; written in Paris.

Contents: Anthology of religious and secular music (monodic and polyphonic); on f. 242v: *A Solis Ortus Cardine.*
Bibliography: Rebecca A. Baltzer, "Thirteenth-Century Illuminated Miniatures and the Date of the Florence Manuscript," *Journal of the American Musicological Society* 25 (1972), 1-18; Angelus Maria Bandinius, *Catalogus Codicum Latinorum Bibliothecae Mediceae Laurentianae* (Firenze, 1774-78), vol. 2, pp. 1-4; Léopold Victor Delisle in *Annuaire-Bulletin de la Société de l'Histoire de France* 22 (1885), 100-39; Peter Dronke, *Medieval Latin and the Rise of European Love Lyric* (2nd ed.; Oxford, 1968), vol. 2, *Medieval Latin Love-Poetry,* pp. 553-4; S.J.P. van Dijk, *Sources of the Modern Roman Liturgy. The Ordinals of Haymo of Faversham and Related Documents (1243-1307),* in *Studia et Documenta Franciscana* (Leiden, 1963), vol. 1, p. 114.

FREIBURG (BREISGAU), Universitätsbibliothek, 154
s. xv/xvi; 105 leaves; 150 x 110 mm.; paper and parchment.

Contents: On f. 1v: PC 2.63-69. Followed by works of Franz Wiler (died in 1514).
Other information: Miscellany volume consisting of five parts, of which ours (ff. 1-64) is the first (c. 1493-6).
Bibliography: Winfried Hagenmaier, *Die lateinischen mittelalterlichen Handschriften der Universitätsbibliothek Freiburg im Breisgau (Hss. 1-230),* in *Kataloge der Universitätsbibliothek Freiburg im Breisgau: Die Handschriften der Universitätsbibliothek und anderer öffentlicher Sammlungen in Freiburg im Breisgau und Umgebung,* vol. 1.1 (Wiesbaden, 1974), pp. 125-8.

GÖTTINGEN, Niedersächsische Staats- & Universitätsbibliothek, Luneb. 1
s. xvi (c. 1500); 292 leaves; 285 x 210 mm.; S. Michael, Lüneburg.

Contents: On ff. 167r f.: H1. Preceded by Mantuan, *Contra Amorem Insanum* (ff. 164r ff.). Followed by Ps.-Virgil, *De Venere et Baccho* (f. 169r-v).
Other information: Manuscript contains many fragments of poetry, almost all with commentary.
Bibliography: Wilhelm Meyer, *Verzeichniss der Handschriften im preussischen Staate I. Hannover. Teil 2. Die Handschriften in Göttingen*

2. *Universitätsbibliothek* (Berlin, 1893), p. 493; Piacentini, pp. 53 and 138.

HEILIGENKREUZ, Stiftsbibliothek, 227
s. xii²; 110 leaves; 263 x 185 mm.; written in Germany or Austria.

Contents: On ff. 73r-107v: *"Florilegium Santicrucianum,"* which includes excerpts from Sedulius (ff. 98v-100v). Preceded by excerpts from the works of Ovid (ff. 73r-83v); Horace (ff. 83v-90r); Virgil (ff. 90r-91v); Lucan (f. 91v); Persius (f. 92r); Maximianus (f. 92r-v); Juvenal (ff. 92v-95v); Juvencus (f. 95v); and Boethius (ff. 95v-98v). Followed by excerpts from the works of Prudentius (ff. 100v-103v); Arator (ff. 103v-104r); Avitus (ff. 104r-105v); Venantius Fortunatus (ff. 105v-107r); and Sulpicius Severus (f. 107v).

Bibliography: Bergmann, p. 36; Hartwig Gerhard, *Der Liber Proverbiorum des Godefrid von Winchester* (Würzburg, 1974), p. 31; Glauche, p. 106; idem, "Einige Bemerkungen zum 'Florileg von Heiligenkreuz'" in *Festschrift Bernhard Bischoff zu seinem 65. Geburtstag* (Stuttgart, 1971), pp. 295-306; Benedict Gsell, "Verzeichniss der Handschriften in der Bibliothek des Stiftes Heiligenkreuz" in *Die Handschriften-Verzeichnisse der Cistercienser-Stifte 1* = Xenia Bernardina 2.1 (Wien, 1891), pp. 178-9; Johannes Huemer, "Zur Geschichte der classischen Studien im Mittelalter," *ZOG* 32 (1881), 415-6; Birger Munk Olsen, "The Cistercians and Classical Culture," *Cahiers de l'Institut du Moyen-Âge Grec et Latin* 47 (1984), 94; idem, "Les Classiques latins dans les florilèges médiévaux antérieurs au XIIIe siècle I," *RHT* 9 (1979), 115-7; idem, "Note sur quelques préfaces de florilèges latins du XIIe siècle," *Revue romane* 8 (1973), 191; idem, "Vergil i middelalderen: Vergil-håndskrifter og Vergil-florilegier fra det 9. til begyndelsen af det 13. århundrede," *MT* 32-3 (1978), 110; Reynolds, p. 282, n. 1; Steinmeyer & Sievers, vol. 4, p. 468.

HILDESHEIM, Dombibliothek, J. 73a
s. xiii-xiv; 6 leaves; octavo; written in Germany?

Contents: Fragments from PC 1 (160 lines) and 2 (80 lines). Collected with fragments from the works of Justinus, Juvenal, Virgil, Ovid, and Sallust.

Bibliography: Kristeller, *Iter,* vol. 3, p. 576; Jos. Godehard Müller, *Nachricht über die Bibliothek des Gymnasii Josephini und die auf derselben vorhandenen Handschriften und alten Druck* (progr. Hildesheim, 1876), p. 3 [frag. 4. g]; Munk Olsen, vol. 3.2, p. 82.

KARLSRUHE, Badische Landesbibliothek, St. Peter Perg. 87
s. xi; 106 leaves; 340 x 235 mm.; Lorsch?

Contents: On ff. 82v-94r: *Glossarium de diversis;* includes *De Sedulio* (ff. 93v-94r).
Bibliography: Felix Heinzer and Gerhard Stamm, *Die Handschriften von St. Peter im Schwarzwald,* vol. 10.2 in *Die Handschriften der Badischen Landesbibliothek in Karlsruhe: Die Pergamenthandschriften* (Wiesbaden, 1994), pp. 179-81; A. Holder, "Die althochdeutschen Glossen aus Sanct Peter," *Germania* 22 (1877), 392-406; Steinmeyer & Sievers, vol. 2, p. 619 and vol. 4, pp. 409-10.

KLOSTERNEUBURG, Stiftsbibliothek, 1000
s. xiv (1336); 126 leaves; 210 x 155 mm.; S. Maria Magdalena, Klosterneuburg.

Contents: Hymnal on ff. 1-117 includes *A Solis Ortus Cardine* and *Hostis Herodes.*
Bibliography: Handwritten inventory (copy in Bayerische Staatsbibliothek), vol. 6, p. 526; Stäblein, pp. 209-47 and 565-78.

KLOSTERNEUBURG, Stiftsbibliothek, 1095
s. xiii[in.]; 31 leaves; 250 x 190 mm.; written in Bavaria or Austria.

Contents: Florilegium includes excerpts from Sedulius (ff. 24r-25v). Preceded by excerpts from the works of Ovid (ff. 1r-10v); Horace (ff. 10v-16r); Virgil (ff. 16r-17r); Lucan (ff. 17r-v); Persius (ff. 17v-18r); Maximianus (ff. 18r-19r); Juvenal (ff. 19r-22r); Juvencus (f. 22r); and Boethius (ff. 22r-24r). Followed by excerpts from Prudentius (ff. 25v-28r); Arator (ff. 28v-29r); Avitus (ff. 29r-30r); Venantius Fortunatus (ff. 30r-31v); and Sulpicus Severus (f. 31v).
Bibliography: Günter Glauche, "Einige Bemerkungen zum 'Florileg von Heiligenkreuz'" in *Festschrift Bernhard Bischoff zu seinem 65. Geburtstag* (Stuttgart, 1971), pp. 295-306; Handwritten inventory (same as above), vol. 6, pp. 739-42; Johannes Huemer, "Iter Austriacum I," *WS* 9 (1887), 52; Alphons Lhotsky, *"Studia Neuburgensia.* Beiträge zur Grundlegung einer Geschichte der Wissenschaftspflege im spätmittelalterlichen Niederösterreich," *Jahrbuch des Stiftes Klosterneuburg* 1 (1961), 69-103, esp. 82.

KØBENHAVN, Kongelige Bibliotek, Gl. Kgl. S. 1346 4°
s. xi; 13 leaves; 261 x 155 mm.; probably written in Germany; prov. Hamburg (cathedral).

Contents: On ff. 6v-13r: Remigius' commentary on Sedulius (up to PC 4.290). Preceded by commentary on Prudentius, *Psychomachia* (ff. 1r-6v).
Bibliography: Jeudy, "Remi," p. 496; Ellen Jørgensen, *Catalogus Codicum Latinorum Medii Aevi Bibliothecae Regiae Hafniensis* (København, 1926), pp. 47-8; Kristeller, *Iter,* vol. 3, p. 175.

KØBENHAVN, Kongelige Bibliotek, Ny Kgl. S. 223b 4°
s. x; 94 leaves; 195 x 140 mm.; S. Jacques, Liège.

Contents: On ff. 1r-94v: *"Commentarius super Carmen Paschale Sedulii."*
Other information: Codex missing leaves at beginning and end.
Bibliography: Jørgensen, *Catalogus,* same as above, pp. 335-6.

KÖLN, Historisches Archiv der Stadt, GB 8° 96
s. xv^1/3; 152 leaves; 145 x 100 mm.; Köln (Kreuzbrüder); paper and parchment.

Contents: On f. 28v: H1 (first four stanzas; entitled *"In miraculis beatae Mariae"*). Included in a collection of ascetic writings (ff. 10v-50v).
Bibliography: Joachim Vennebusch, *Die theologischen Handschriften des Stadtarchivs Köln. Teil 3. Die Oktav-Handschriften der Gymnasial-bibliothek* = Mitteilungen aus dem Stadtarchiv von Köln 3 (Köln-Wien, 1983), pp. 93-9.

KÖLN, Historisches Archiv der Stadt, Hss-Fragm. A 13
s. x-xi; 2 double leaves; 235 x 165 mm.

Contents: On ff. 1r-2v: PC 3.141-259; on ff. 3r-4v: PC 4.38-157.
Other information: Glossing in Latin and Old High German. Microfilm acquired.
Bibliography: Klaus Siewert, *Glossenfunde. Volkssprachiges zu lateinischen Autoren der Antike und des Mittelalters* = Studien zum Althochdeutschen 11 (Göttingen, 1989), pp. 52-60; Joachim Vennebusch,

Die theologischen Handschriften des Stadtarchivs Köln.   Teil 5. Handschriften des Bestandes W* und Fragmente (Köln-Wien, 1989), pp. 83-4.

KÓRNIK, Biblioteka Kórnicka Polskiej Akademii Nauk, 26
s. xiv; 161 leaves; 135 x 95 mm.

Contents: Breviary with hymns on ff. 116 ff.; includes *A Solis Ortus Cardine* (f. 125r) and *Hostis Herodes* (f. 128r).
Bibliography: Jerzy Zathey, *Catalogus Codicum Manuscriptorum Medii Aevi Bibliothecae Cornicensis* (Wrocław, Warszawa, Kraków, 1963), pp. 56-73.

KÓRNIK, Biblioteka Kórnicka Polskiej Akademii Nauk, 40
s. xviii; 640 pages; 165 x 195 mm.

Contents: On pp. 109-110: *A Solis Ortus Cardine.*
Bibliography: R. Marciniak, et al., *Catalogus Codicum Manuscriptorum Saec. XVI-XVIII Bibliothecae Cornicensis*, vol. 1 (Wrocław, Warszawa, Kraków, 1971), p. 76.

KRAKÓW, Biblioteka Jagiellońska, 320 (AA 1. 18)
s. xv (before 1452); 574 pages; 318 x 110 mm.; written by Johannes de Calisia; paper.

Contents: On f. iiir-v: *A Solis Ortus Cardine; Hostis Herodes* (in a fragment of a fourteenth-century hymnal with neums).   Peter Riga, *Aurora* on pages 1-546.
Bibliography: Władysław Wisłocki, *Catalogus Codicum Manuscriptorum Bibliothecae Universitatis Jagellonicae Cracoviensis* (Kraków, 1877-81), vol. 1, pp. 108-9; Sophia Włodek, Georgius Zathey, and Marianus Zwiercán, *Catalogus Codicum Manuscriptorum Medii Aevi Latini Qui in Bibliotheca Jagellonica Cracoviae Asservantur*, vol. 1 (Kraków, 1980), pp. 409-12, esp. p. 411.

KREMSMÜNSTER, Stiftsbibliothek, CC 309
s. xi$^{ex.}$-xii$^{ex.}$; 243 leaves; 267-275 x 190-197 mm.; written in Bavaria or Austria.

Contents: Collection of hymns on ff. 218r-242v; on ff. 221r-222v: H2 (followed by a doxology). Preceded by Prudentius, *Cath.* 9 (ff. 218r-

221r) and followed by Peter Damian, *Purificatio Beatae Mariae Virginis* (ff. 222v-224r).

Bibliography: Hauke Fill, *Katalog der Handschriften des Benediktiner-stiftes Kremsmünster. Teil 1: Von den Anfängen bis in die Zeit des Abts Friedrich vom Aich (ca. 800-1325)*, vol. 3 in *Verzeichnisse der Hand-schriften österreichischer Bibliotheken* = Österreichische Akademie der Wissenschaften, Phil.-Hist. Klasse, Denkschriften 166 (Wien, 1984), pp. 403-15, esp. p. 414.

LAON, Bibliothèque Municipale, 113
s. ix; 85 leaves; 270 x 209 mm.; Notre-Dame, Laon.

Contents: On f. 59r-v: H2. Preceded by Facundus, *Epistola Fidei Catholicae in Defensione Trium Capitulorum*. Followed by Ps.-Jerome, *Epist.* 42 *(ad Oceanum de vita clericorum)*.

Other information: This appears to be the manuscript used by Huemer (L') for his edition of H2, which he described as Laon 468 (the latter does not contain H2). Seen in person.

Bibliography: Cat. gen. quarto, vol. 1, pp. 97-9; J.-M. Clément and R. Vander Plaetse, *Facundi Episcopi Ecclesiae Hermianiensis Opera Omnia*, *CCSL*, vol. 90A, pp. xv-xvi; *CSEL*, vol. 10, p. 163; Hörmann, p. xx; Huemer, *De Sedulii*, p. 43; G. Morin, *Études, textes, découvertes. Contributions a la littérature et a l'historie des douze premiers siècles* (Maredsous and Paris, 1913), vol. 1, pp. 151 ff.; idem, "Un traité priscillianiste inédit sur la Trinité," *RB* 26 (1909), 255-7.

LAON, Bibliothèque Municipale, 263
s. xii; folio; Notre-Dame, Laon.

Contents: Hymns, etc.; includes *A Solis Ortus Cardine*.
Bibligraphy: Cat. gen. quarto, vol. 1, p. 155; Stäblein, p. 143.

LAON, Bibliothèque Municipale, 468
s. ix$^{med.}$; 61 leaves; 307 x 227 mm.; written in France; prov. Notre-Dame, Laon.

Contents: On ff. 52r-61r: Glosses on E1 and PC (not Remigius' commentary). Preceded by commentary on Virgil (ff. 18r-51r).
Other information: Exemplar from Soissons. On f. 11r: *Istum librum dederunt Bernardus et Adelelmus Deo et sanctae Mariae Laudunensis ecclesiae. Si quis abstulerit offensionem Dei et sanctae Mariae incurrat.*

Bibliography: Cat. gen. quarto, vol. 1, pp. 250-1; Contreni, pp. 37-9 and passim; idem, *Codex Laudunensis 468: A Ninth-Century Guide to Virgil, Sedulius, and the Liberal Arts* = Armarium Codicum Insignium, vol. 3 (Turnhout, 1984); idem, "A propos de quelques manuscrits de l'école de Laon au IXe siècle: Découvertes et problèmes," *MA* 78 (1972), 14-28; idem, "Le Formulaire de Laon: Source pour l'histoire de l'école de Laon au début du Xe siècle," *Scriptorium* 27 (1973), 27, n. 23; S. Martinet, "Les Arts libéraux à Laon au IXe siècle" in *Actes du 95e Congrès National des Sociétés Savantes. Section de philologie et d'histoire jusqu'à 1610* (Paris, 1975), pp. 55-62; Rosamond McKitterick, "Script and Book Production" in *Emulation and Innovation in Carolingian Art* (Cambridge, 1994), p. 226; Munk Olsen, vol. 2, p. 807.

LEIDEN, Bibliotheek der Rijksuniversiteit, B.P.L. 191E
s. xii²; 180 leaves; 229 x 142 mm.; Hardehausen.

Contents: On f. 1v (after index): PC 5.188-195. Ivo of Chartres, *Epistulae* on ff. 1r-57v.
Bibliography: Bergmann, p. 47; Laistner, p. 137; Paul Lehmann, "Encore Albert de Siegburg," *RB* 27 (1910), 235-6; *Bibliotheca Universitatis Leidensis. Codices Manuscripti, III. Codices Bibliothecae Publicae Latini* (Leiden, 1912), pp. 98-100; Passalacqua, pp. 122-3; Steinmeyer & Sievers, vol. 4, pp. 475-7; W.E. van Wijk, "Un comput de la fin du XIIe s.," *Arch. Int. d'Hist. des Sciences* 17 (1951), 870-1; P. Wessner, "Fabii Planciadis Fulgentii Expositio Sermonum Antiquorum," *Commentationes Philologicae Ienenses* 6.2 (1899), 75.

LEIDEN, Bibliotheek der Rijksuniversiteit, Voss. Lat. F. 114
s. ix/x; 196 leaves; 273 x 240 mm.; written in western France.

Contents: On f. 196v: PC 1.1-3. Ps.-Jerome, *Epist. ad Praesidium* on ff. 195r-196v. Works of Augustine (and excerpts) on ff. 1r-194r.
Other information: Owned by Alexander Petau.
Bibliography: K.A. De Meyier, *Codices Vossiani Latini I. Codices in Folio,* vol. 13 in *Bibliotheca Universitatis Leydensis. Codices Manuscripti* (Leiden, 1973), pp. 245-7; M.M. Gorman, "The Manuscript Tradition of Eugippius' *Excerpta ex operibus Sancti Augustini,*" *RB* 92 (1982), 22; G. Morin in *Bulletin d'ancienne littérature et archéologie chrétienne* 3 (1913), 54-8.

LEIDEN, Bibliotheek der Rijksuniversiteit, Voss. Lat. Q. 86

s. ix*med.*; 150 leaves; 230 x 185 mm.; written in the Loire region, possibly Fleury; later probably at Cluny.

Contents: On ff. 79r-81v: H1, H2 (with doxology). Preceded by Arator, *Historia Apostolica* (ff. 1r-63v) and the epigrams of Prosper (ff. 63v-79r). Followed by "Cyprianus Gallus," *Carmen de Sodoma* (ff. 81v-83r) and *Carmen de Iona* (ff. 83r-84r); *Disticha Catonis* (ff. 84r-86r); Avianus, *Fabulae* (ff. 86v-91v); poems from the *Latin Anthology* (ff. 91v-116r); Alcimus Avitus, *De Spiritalis Historiae Gestis* (ff. 116r-144v); and excerpts from Isidore, *Etymologiae* (ff. 145r-150v).
Other information: Originally connected with Vat. Reg. Lat. 333. Disjoined by Alexander Petau. Used by Huemer (V').
Bibliography: Beeson, p. 86; Boas, p. lxi; K.A. De Meyier, *Codices Vossiani Latini II. Codices in Quarto,* vol. 14 in *Bibliotheca Universitatis Leidensis. Codices Manuscripti* (Leiden, 1975), pp. 197-204; Grace Frank, "Vossianus Q 86 and Reginensis 333," *AJP* 44 (1923), 67-70; Glauche, pp. 33-5; Guaglianone, pp. x-xi; McKinlay, pp. 50-1; Mostert, p. 100; Munk Olsen vol. 1, pp. 80-1; Daniel J. Nodes, *Avitus, The Fall of Man. De Spiritalis Historiae Gestis Libri I-III* = Toronto Medieval Latin Texts 16 (Toronto, 1985), p. 11; E.K. Rand, "Note on the Vossianus Q 86 and Reginenses 333 and 1616," *AJP* 44 (1923), 171-2; idem, "A *Vade Mecum* of Liberal Culture in a Manuscript of Fleury," *Philological Quarterly* 1 (1922), 258-77; Reynolds, pp. 12, 30-1, 240-1, 243, and 298; Morris Rosenblum, *Luxorius: A Latin Poet among the Vandals* = Records of Civilization: Sources and Studies 62 (New York and London, 1961), p. 101; Otto Rossbach, "Handschriftliches zur *Anthologia Latina* aus der Leidener Bibliothek," *Philologische Wochenschrift* 41 (1921), 475-80; Sanford, 206; Willy Schetter, "Scaliger, Cujas und der Leidensis Voss. lat. Q. 86," *Hermes* 111 (1983), 363-71; Jean Vezin, "Une importante contribution à l'étude du *Scriptorium* de Cluny à la limite des XIe et XIIe siècles," *Scriptorium* 21 (1967), 315.

LE MANS, Bibliothèque Municipale, 21
s. xiii; 283 leaves; 225 x 160 mm.

Contents: On f. 283r: PC 1.355-8. Preceded by Peter Riga, *Aurora* (ff. 1-228) and a metrical version of Origen's homilies on the Song of Songs (ff. 229 ff.).
Bibliography: Cat. gen. octavo, vol. 20, pp. 34-5.

LILIENFELD, Stiftsbibliothek, 137

c. 1300; 248 leaves; folio; written in large part by Christan von Lilienfeld.

Contents: On ff. 206-214: a *florilegium* which includes excerpts from Sedulius (f. 214r-v). Preceded by excerpts from the works of Prudentius (f. 206v); Ovid (ff. 208v-210v); Maximianus (ff. 210v-211r); Horace (ff. 211r-212r); Virgil (f. 212r-v); Boethius (f. 212v); Juvenal (ff. 212v-213r); Lucan (f. 213r); Persius (f. 213r); Arator (f. 213r-v); Venantius Fortunatus (ff. 213v-214r); and Alcimus Avitus (f. 214r).

Bibliography: Günter Glauche, "Einige Bemerkungen zum 'Florileg von Heiligenkreuz'" in *Festschrift Bernhard Bischoff zu seinem 65. Geburtstag* (Stuttgart, 1971), 295-306; Conrad Schimek, "Verzeichniss der Handschriften des Stiftes Lilienfeld" in *Die Handschriften-Verzeichnisse der Cistercienser-Stifte* = Xenia Bernardina 2.1 (1891), 524-7.

LONDON, British Library, Add. 16975

s. xiv$^{in.}$; 264 leaves; folio; Lyre.

Contents: Benedictine psalter, etc.; includes *A Solis Ortus Cardine* and *Hostis Herodes.*

Bibliography: *Catalogue of Additions to the Manuscripts in the British Museum in the Years 1846-1847* (London, 1864), pp. 335-6; Gneuss, *Hymnar,* pp. 73 and 82; Mearns, pp. xv, 1, and 39; André Wilmart, *Le Jubilus dit de Saint Bernard: Étude avec textes* (Roma, 1944), pp. 17-18.

LONDON, British Library, Add. 18301

s. xii; 157 leaves; octavo; perhaps written in Bavaria; prov. Georgenberg-Fiecht.

Contents: Psalter, etc.; includes *A Solis Ortus Cardine* and *Hostis Herodes.*

Bibliography: *Catalogue of Additions to the Manuscripts in the British Museum in the Years 1848-1853* (London, 1868), p. 96; Mearns, pp. xvi, 1, and 39.

LONDON, British Library, Add. 23935

s. xiii (1260-75); small folio; written in France.

Contents: Dominican psalter, etc.; includes *A Solis Ortus Cardine* and *Hostis Herodes.*

Bibliography: *British Museum. Guide to the Exhibited Manuscripts,* part 2 (London, 1923), p. 39; *Catalogue of Additions to the Manuscripts in the British Museum 1854-1860* (London, 1875), pp. 920-1; J. Wickham Legg, *Tracts on the Mass* = Henry Bradshaw Society 27 (London, 1904), pp. 71 ff.; Mearns, pp. xv, 1, and 39.

LONDON, British Library, Add. 30844
s. xi$^{in.}$; 177 leaves; 400 x 320 mm.; Silos.

Contents: Offices and masses of the Mozarabic liturgy; includes *A Solis Ortus Cardine* (first three stanzas on f. 33v). Last two stanzas attached to the hymn beginning *Veni redemptor gentium.*
Bibliography: Clemens Blume, *Hymnodia Gotica. Die mozarabischen Hymnen des alt-spanischen Ritus* = Analecta Hymnica 27 (Leipzig, 1897), p. 25 and passim; *Catalogue of Additions to the Manuscripts in the British Museum 1876-1881* (London, 1882), p. 119; Gamber, vol. 1, p. 198, no. 305; Jullien, 148-9; Agustín Millares Carlo, "Manuscritos visigóticos. Notas bibliográficas," *Hispania Sacra* 14 (1961), 369-70; Walpole, p. xxvii.

LONDON, British Library, Add. 30848
s. xi$^{4/4}$; 280 leaves; folio; Silos.

Contents: Mozarabic breviary for the entire year; includes *A Solis Ortus Cardine* and *Hostis Herodes.*
Bibliography: *Catalogue of Additions to the Manuscripts in the British Museum 1876-1881* (London, 1882), p. 120; Manuel C. Díaz y Díaz, *Códices visigóticos en la monarquía leonesa* = Fuentes y estudios de historia leonesa 31 (Leon, 1983), p. 315; Jullien, 149; Mearns, pp. xx, 1, and 39; Millares Carlo, same as above, 370-1; J. Pinell, "Los textos de la antigua liturgia hispánica" in *Estudios sobre la liturgia mozárabe* (Toledo, 1965), 157; W.M. Whitehill, "The Manuscripts of Santo Domingo de Silos" in *Homenaje a Fray Justo Perez de Urbel* (Silos, 1976), vol. 1, p. 288.

LONDON, British Library, Add. 30851
s. xi; 202 leaves; 400 x 310 mm.; Silos.

Contents: "The Mozarabic Psalter;" includes H2. *Hymnus in diem sanctae Mariae Virginis*=first five stanzas (f. 118v) Followed by other hymns (*Fit porta Christi* and *Veni redemptor gentium* on ff. 118v-120r).

Continued on ff. 120r-121v by *Hymnus in natale Domini ad matutinum*=stanzas FG; *Hymnus in apparitione Domini*=stanzas HILN; *Hymnus in allisione infantorum*=stanzas KMOP; *Hymnus de Lazaro ad matutinum*=stanzas QRS; *Hymnus in cena Domini ad matutinum*=stanzas TVXYZ).

Bibliography: Clemens Blume, *Hymnodia Gotica. Die mozarabischen Hymnen des alt-spanischen Ritus* = Analecta Hymnica 27 (Leipzig, 1897), pp. 26-8; Louis Brou, "Le IVe livre d'Esdras dans la liturgie hispanique et le graduel romain *Locus iste* de la messe de la dédicace," *SE* 9 (1957), 82, n. 1; *Catalogue of Additions to the Manuscripts in the British Museum 1876-81* (London, 1882), pp. 120-1; M.C. Díaz y Díaz, *Códices*, same as above, pp. 316-7; Ismael Fernández de la Cuesta, *El Breviarium Gothicum de Silos* = Monumenta Hispaniae Sacra. Serie litúrgica 8 (Madrid and Barcelona, 1965), p. 26; Gamber, vol. 1, p. 211, no. 352; Julius Parnell Gilson, *The Mozarabic Psalter (Ms. British Museum, Add. 30,851)* = Henry Bradshaw Society 30 (London, 1905); Gneuss, *Hymnar*, p. 22; Jullien, 82-3; Mearns, pp. xx, 1, and 39; Millares Carlo, same as above, 371; A.W.S. Porter, "Cantica Mozarabici Officii," *EL* 49 (1935), 126-45; Grégoire M. Suñol, *Introduction à la paléographie musicale grégorienne* (Tournai, 1935), pl. 97; Birgitta Thorsberg, *Études sur l'hymnologie mozarabe* = Acta Universitatis Stockholmiensis. Studia Latina Stockholmiensia 8 (Uppsala, 1962), p. 5; Whitehill, same as above, p. 289; idem, "A Collection of Mozarabic Liturgical Manuscripts Containing the Psalter and *Liber Canticorum*," *JLW* 14 (1934), 95-122.

LONDON, British Library, Add. 34750
s. xiii; 94 leaves; small quarto; west of the Rhine.

Contents: Cistercian hymnal; includes *A Solis Ortus Cardine*.
Bibliography: *Catalogue of Additions to the Manuscripts in the British Museum 1894-99* (London, 1901), pp. 70-1; Mearns, pp. xvii and 1.

LONDON, British Library, Add. 37517
s. x$^{ex.}$ (c. 970); 137 leaves (274 pages); 394 x 275 mm.; Christ Church, Canterbury.

Contents: "The Bosworth Psalter;" includes *A Solis Ortus Cardine (Hymnus ad vesperam in Epiphania Domini)* (f. 113v) and *Hostis Herodes* (ff. 113v-114r).
Bibliography: *Catalogue of Additions to the Manuscripts in the British*

Museum 1906-1910 (London, 1912), pp. 65-7; Gamber, vol. 2, p. 581, no. 1615; Abbot Gasquet and Edmund Bishop, *The Bosworth Psalter: An Account of a Manuscript formerly Belonging to O. Turville-Petre Esq. of Bosworth Hall, Now Addit. Ms. 37517 at the British Museum* (London, 1908); Gneuss, "List," no. 291; Jullien, 112-3; Ker, *Med.*, p. 35; P.M. Korhammer, "The Origin of the Bosworth Psalter," *Anglo-Saxon England* 2 (1973), 173-87; Mearns, pp. xi, 1, and 39; Robert Weber, *Le Psautier romain et les autres anciens psautiers latins* = Collectanea Biblica Latina 10 (Roma, 1953), p. xiv; Gernot R. Wieland, *The Canterbury Hymnal* = Toronto Medieval Latin Texts 12 (Toronto, 1982), esp. pp. 65-7.

LONDON, British Library, Arundel 155
s. xi$^{in.}$ (c. 1012-1023); 193 leaves; 292 x 170 mm.; Christ Church, Canterbury.

Contents: "The Arundel Psalter;" includes *A Solis Ortus Cardine* and *Hostis Herodes*.
Other information: Written by Eadvius Basan. Belonged to William Howard in 1592.
Bibliography: J.J.G. Alexander, *The Decorated Letter* (New York, 1978), pp. 35, 37, and 70-1; M. Förster, "Zu den ae. Texten aus Ms. Arundel 155," *Anglia* 66 (1942), 52-5; J. Forshall, *Catalogue of Manuscripts in the British Museum* (n.s.), vol. 1 (London, 1834), pp. 42-3; Gneuss, *Hymnar,* pp. 171, 176, 182, 183, 185, 189, 241, and 250; Gneuss, "List," no. 306; Ker, *Med.* p. 35; Mearns, pp. xii, 1, and 39; Celia and Kenneth Sisam, *The Salisbury Psalter* = Early English Text Society 242 (Oxford, 1959), pp. 4-5, 48-49, and 62.

LONDON, British Library, Arundel 340
s. xiv; 234 leaves; quarto; Salzburg?

Contents: Hymnal, etc.; includes *A Solis Ortus Cardine* and *Hostis Herodes*.
Bibliography: Cat., same as above, p. 102; Mearns, pp. xvii, 1, and 39.

LONDON, British Library, Cotton Jul. A. VI
s. xi$^{in.}$; 90 leaves; quarto; possibly written at Christ Church, Canterbury; later at Durham.

Contents: Calendar, computistic texts, *expositio hymnorum,* and canticles. Prose versions of Latin hymns on ff. 19-71 with continuous Old English interlinear glosses; includes *A Solis Ortus Cardine* (stanzas 1-5) and *Hostis Herodes.*

Bibliography: A. Boutemy, "Un calendrier illustré du British Museum (ms. Cotton Julius A. VI)," *Bulletin de la Société Nationale des Antiquaires de France* (1970), 79-98; Gneuss, *Hymnar,* pp. 8, 55, 91-7, 122, 197-8, and passim; Gneuss, "List," no. 337; Jullien, 135-6; Ker, *Cat.,* pp. 202-5; Ker, *Med.,* p. 72; Michael Lapidge, "A Tenth-Century Metrical Calendar from Ramsey," *RB* 94 (1984), 344; Lokrantz, pp. 21, 38, and 42; B. Luiselli, "Un interessante codice innologico latino: Il Cotton Julius A. VI (ff. 19-71) del British Museum," *Revista di cultura classica e medioevale* 15 (1973), 297-303; Patrick McGurk, "The Metrical Calendar of Hampson. A New Edition," *Analecta Bollandiana* 104 (1986), 80; Mearns, pp. xi, 1, and 39; R.A.B. Mynors, *Durham Cathedral Manuscripts to the End of the 12th Century* (Oxford, 1939), no. 21; J. Planta, *A Catalogue of the Manuscripts in the Cottonian Library Deposited in the British Museum* (London, 1802), p. 2; Elzbieta Temple, *Anglo-Saxon Manuscripts, 900-1066* = A Survey of Manuscripts Illuminated in the British Isles 2 (London, 1976), p. 80.

LONDON, British Library, Cotton Jul. F. VII
s. xv?; 230 leaves; folio; paper.

Contents: On ff. 22r-23r: PC 1.1-9, 1.17-25, 2.63-73, 5.59 ff. Preceded by *Willielmi Botoner registratio, seu excerptio versuum proverbialium, de libro Ovidii, de arte amandi, de fastis, et de epistolis.* Followed by *Bulla Papae Gregorii, de Hospitali S. Pauli apud Norwicenses.*

Bibliography: Duke Humphrey and English Humanism (Oxford, 1970), p. 58, no. 99; Planta, *Cat.,* same as above, pp. 22-3; A.G. Watson, "Thomas Allen of Oxford and His Manuscripts" in *Medieval Scribes, Manuscripts and Libraries. Essays Presented to N.R. Ker,* ed. M.B. Parkes and A.G. Watson (London, 1978), p. 309.

LONDON, British Library, Cotton Tib. A. II
s. ix (early); Christ Church.

Contents: "The Coronation Gospels." On f. 164v: PC 1.358.
Bibliography: Nicolas Barker, *Treasures of the British Library* (New York, 1989), p. 45; Ker, *Cat.,* pp. 239-40.

LONDON, British Library, Cotton Tib. C. I
s. xii (1122-1135) (ff. 2-42); 203 leaves; 295 x 195 mm.; Peterborough.

Contents: On f. 5v: PC 1.361, 362, 359, 360. Two manuscripts joined together, of which the first is a miscellany of computistic texts, while the second contains pontifical orders, et al.

Bibliography: T.A.M. Bishop, *English Caroline Minuscule* (Oxford, 1971), p. 23; Harry Bober, "An Illustrated Medieval School Book of Bede's *De Natura Rerum*," *The Journal of the Walters Art Gallery* 19-20 (1956-7), 65-97; Gneuss, "List," no. 376; C.W. Jones, *Bedae Opera de Temporibus* (Cambridge, Mass., 1943), pp. 368 and 403; Ker, *Cat.*, pp. 259-60; Ker, *Med.*, p. 151; idem, *"Membra Disiecta,"* *The British Museum Quarterly* 12 (1938), 132; idem, "Three Old English Texts in a Salisbury Pontifical, Cotton Tiberius C I" in *The Anglo-Saxons. Studies in some Aspects of their History and Culture* (Festschrift for Bruce Dickins), ed. Peter Clemoes (London, 1959), pp. 262-79; Claudio Leonardi, "I codici di Marziano Capella," *Aevum* 34 (1960), 71-2; Munk Olsen, vol. 1, p. 333; Planta, *Cat.*, same as above, p. 37; Reynolds, pp. 22-3; Fritz Saxl und Hans Meier, *Verzeichnis astrologischer und mythologischer illustrierter Handschriften des lateinischen Mittelalters III, Handschriften in englischen Bibliotheken,* vol. 1 (London, 1953), p. 129; Jean Sonbiran, *Cicéron, Aratea. Fragments poètiques* (Paris, 1972), pp. 113-4.

LONDON, British Library, Cotton Vesp. D. XII
s. xi$^{med.}$; 155 leaves; octavo; Christ Church, Canterbury.

Contents: Hymnal, *expositio hymnorum,* and canticles; includes *A Solis Ortus Cardine* and *Hostis Herodes.*

Bibliography: Gneuss, *Hymnar,* pp. 55, 98-101, 122, 198-9, 241, and passim; Gneuss, "List," no. 391; Jullien, 134; Ker, *Cat.*, pp. 269-71; Mearns, pp. xi, 1, and 39; Planta, same as above, p. 476; Gernot R. Wieland, *The Canterbury Hymnal* = Toronto Medieval Latin Texts 12 (Toronto, 1982), p. 7.

LONDON, British Library, Harley 2693
s. xv; 203 leaves; paper.

Contents: On f. 152v: *"Prohemia in Sedulium."* Preceded by introductions to *Ilias Latina* and Peter Riga. Followed by introductions to Arator, *Tobias,* Prosper, and Juvenal.

Bibliography: Kristeller, *Iter,* vol. 4, p. 165; R. Nares, et al., *A Catalogue of the Harleian Manuscripts in the British Museum* (London, 1808-12), vol. 2, p. 708.

LONDON, British Library, Harley 2928
s. xii (c. 1135); 12°; Solignac.

Contents: Benedictine psalter, etc.; includes *A Solis Ortus Cardine* and *Hostis Herodes.*
Bibliography: Mearns, pp. xv, 1, and 39; Nares, *Cat.,* same as above, vol. 2, p. 720.

LONDON, British Library, Harley 2951
s. xiii*ex.*; octavo; written in England.

Contents: Hymnal of Sarum type in first part of volume; includes *A Solis Ortus Cardine* and *Hostis Herodes.*
Bibliography: Mearns, pp. xii, 1, and 39; Nares, *Cat.,* same as above, vol. 2, p. 721.

LONDON, British Library, Harley 2961
s. xi*med.* (1046-72); 256 leaves; 215 x 138 mm.; S. Peter's, Exeter?

Contents: "The Leofric Collectar;" hymnal includes *A Solis Ortus Cardine* (f. 226v) and *Hostis Herodes* (f. 230r).
Bibliography: E.S. Dewick, *The Leofric Collectar,* vol. 1 = Henry Bradshaw Society 45 (London, 1914); Gamber, vol. 2, p. 555, no. 1530; Gneuss, *Hymnar,* pp. 55, 108-9, 122, 239, and passim; Gneuss, "List," no. 431; Jullien, 138-9; Ker, *Med.,* p. 83; Mearns, pp. xi, 1, and 39; Nares, *Cat.,* same as above, p. 722.

LONDON, British Library, Harley 3376
s. x/xi; 94 leaves; written in western England?

Contents: Alphabetical glossary of difficult Latin words, some of which are from Sedulius.
Bibliography: Gneuss, "List," no. 436; Michael W. Herren, "Hiberno-Latin Lexical Sources of Harley 3376, a Latin-Old English Glossary" in *Words, Texts, and Manuscripts: Studies in Anglo-Saxon Culture Presented to Helmut Gneuss on the Occasion of his Sixty-Fifth Birthday* (Cambridge, 1992), pp. 371-9; Ker, *Cat.,* pp. 312-3; Herbert Meritt,

"Three Studies in Old English I: The Context for Some Latin Words in the Harleian Glossary," *AJP* 62 (1941), 331-4; Robert Oliphant, *The Harley Latin-Old English Glossary Edited from British Museum MS Harley 3376* = Janua Linguarum. Series Practica XX (The Hague and Paris, 1966); J.D. Pheifer, *Old English Glosses in the Epinal-Erfurt Glossary* (Oxford, 1974), pp. xxxv-xxxvi.

LONDON, British Library, Harley 4664
s. xiii (c. 1270); Durham (or Coldingham); paper.

Contents: Benedictine breviary; hymns include *A Solis Ortus Cardine* and *Hostis Herodes*.
Bibliography: Gneuss, *Hymnar,* pp. 115, 250, and 253; Ker, *Med.,* p. 73; Mearns, pp. xii, 1, and 39; Nares, *Cat.,* same as above, vol. 3, p. 187.

LONDON, British Library, Royal 2 A. X
s. xii (before 1170); 220 leaves; 191 x 127 mm.; written at S. Alban's.

Contents: Benedictine breviary; includes *A Solis Ortus Cardine* and *Hostis Herodes*.
Bibliography: Gneuss, *Hymnar,* p. 250; *Guide to the Exhibited Manuscripts* (London, 1923), part 2, p. 38; Ker, *Med.,* p. 167; Mearns, pp. xii, 1, and 39; Sir George F. Warner and Julius P. Gilson, *Catalogue of Western Manuscripts in the Old Royal and King's Collections* (London, 1921), vol. 1, pp. 29-30.

LONDON, British Library, Royal 2 A. XIII
s. xiii (c. 1220); 147 leaves; 191 x 133 mm.; Gloucester?

Contents: Collectar; includes *A Solis Ortus Cardine* and *Hostis Herodes*.
Bibliography: Mearns, pp. xii, 1, and 39; Warner and Gilson, *Cat.,* same as above, vol. 1, p. 31.

LONDON, British Library, Royal 2 A. XX
s. viii[2]; 52 leaves; 235 x 171 mm.; written in England (North or Mercia); prov. Worcester.

Contents: Prayerbook; on f. 16v: lines 65-68 of H2 (repeated on f. 49r); on f. 50r-v: H2.
Other information: Manuscript contains Anglo-Saxon glosses (two on

the second stanza of H2). Owned by John Theyer. Seen in person.
Bibliography: Edmund Bishop, *Liturgica Historica: Papers on the Liturgy and Religious Life of the Western Church* (Oxford, 1918), pp. 192 ff.; *CLA,* vol. 2 (2nd ed.), p. 28, no. 215; Gamber, vol. 1, p. 150, no. 170; Gneuss, *Hymnar,* pp. 103-4, 117, 122, and 157; Gneuss, "List," no. 450; Hörmann, p. xx; Ker, *Cat.,* pp. 317-8; Ker, *Med.,* p. 207; A.B. Kuypers, *The Prayer Book of Aedelvald the Bishop, Commonly Called the Book of Cerne* (Cambridge, 1902), pp. 201-225 [Royal 2. A. XX edited in an appendix]; Wilhelm Meyer, "Poetische Nachlese aus dem sogenannten Book of Cerne in Cambridge und aus dem Londoner Codex Regius 2 A. xx," *NKGWG,* 1917, 597-625; Kenneth Sisam, *Studies in the History of Old English Literature* (Oxford, 1953), p. 120; Warner and Gilson, *Cat.,* same as above, vol. 1, pp. 33 ff.

LONDON, British Library, Royal 4 B. XIV
s. xii$^{ex.}$; 159 leaves; 298 x 200 mm.; Merton.

Contents: On f. 53v: PC 1.45-46, 66-67, and 79-84. Volume is a theological miscellany collected by William, Prior of Merton (d. 1177).
Bibliography: Ker, *Med.,* p. 130; Peter von Moos, *Hildebert von Lavardin, 1056-1133. Humanitas an der Schwelle des höfischen Zeitalters* = Pariser historische Studien 3 (Stuttgart, 1965), p. 362; H.-M. Rochais, *Enquête sur les sermons divers et les sentences de Saint Bernard* = Analecta Sacri Ordinis Cisterciensis 18 (Roma, 1962), p. 13; H.-M. Rochais and E. Manning, *Bibliographie générale de l'Ordre Cistercien,* vol. 21.10-12 (Rochefort, 1982), no. 4001; Warner and Gilson, *Cat.,* same as above, vol. 1, pp. 86-7.

LONDON, Lambeth Palace, 558
s. xiii$^{ex.}$-xv$^{in.}$; 286 leaves; 130 x 102 mm.; Christ Church, Canterbury.

Contents: Benedictine psalter, etc.; hymns beginning on f. 188r include *A Solis Ortus Cardine* and *Hostis Herodes.*
Bibliography: Frere, no. 4; Gneuss, *Hymnar,* pp. 241 and 250; Montague Rhodes James, *A Descriptive Catalogue of the Manuscripts in the Library of Lambeth Palace* (Cambridge, 1932), pp. 761-5; Ker, *Med.,* p. 37; Mearns, pp. xiii, 1, and 39.

LONDON, Lambeth Palace, 563
s. xiii; 159 leaves; 104 x 76 mm.; S. Neot's, Huntingdonshire.

Contents: Benedictine psalter and hymnal; includes *A Solis Ortus Cardine* and *Hostis Herodes*.
Bibliography: Frere, no. 5; Gneuss, *Hymnar,* p. 250; James, *Descriptive Catalogue,* same as above, pp. 772-6; Ker, *Med.,* p. 170; Mearns, pp. xiii, 1, and 39; Eric G. Millar, *Les Principaux manuscrits à peintures du Lambeth Palace à Londres* = SFRMP 8 (Paris, 1924), pp. 35-8.

LÜNEBURG, Ratsbücherei, Theol. 4° 5

s. xv; 358 leaves; 220 x 155 mm.; Lüneburg (Franciscan cloister); paper.

Contents: On ff. 1r-2v (c. 1200; on parchment): PC 4.116-142 and 272-302.
Other information: Includes German interlinear translation in smaller script.
Bibliography: Nikolaus Henkel, *Deutsche Übersetzungen lateinischer Schultexte: Ihre Verbreitung und Funktion im Mittelalter und in der frühen Neuzeit* = Münchener Texte und Untersuchungen zur deutschen Literatur des Mittelalters 90 (München, 1988), pp. 305-6; Marlis Stähli, *Die theologischen Handschriften II: Quartreihe. Die juristischen Handschriften,* vol. 3 in *Handschriften der Ratsbücherei Lüneburg* (Wiesbaden, 1981), pp. 37 ff.; eadem, "Sedulius: *Carmen Paschale-*Bruchstücke einer frühen deutschen Interlinearversion," *Zeitschrift für deutsches Altertum und deutsche Literatur* 114 (1985), 330-7.

MADRID, Biblioteca Nacional, 10001 (Tol. 35. 1)

s x$^{med.}$; 172 leaves; 360 x 260 mm.; Toledo.

Contents: Mozarabic psalter, etc.; hymnal on ff. 108v-172v includes H2 (as in London, British Library, Add. 30851).
Bibliography: Clemens Blume, *Hymnodia Gotica. Die mozarabischen Hymnen des alt-spanischen Ritus* = Analecta Hymnica 27 (Leipzig, 1897), pp. 21-3 and passim; Louis Brou, "Le IVe livre d'Esdras dans la liturgie hispanique et le graduel romain *Locus iste* de la messe de la dédicace," *SE* 9 (1957), 82; A. Canellas, *Exempla Scripturarum Latinarum,* vol. 2 (Zaragoza, 1966), no. 14; Manuel C. Díaz y Díaz, *Códices visigóticos en la monarquía leonesa* = Fuentes y estudios de historia leonesa 31 (Leon, 1983), pp. 324-5; idem, *Index Scriptorum Latinorum Medii Aevi Hispanorum* (Madrid, 1959); Gamber, vol. 1, pp. 212-3, no. 353; Gneuss, *Hymnar,* pp. 22 and 27; José Janini, *Liber*

Missarum de Toledo y libros místicos, vol. 2 (Toledo, 1983), p. xxiv; José Janini and José Serrano, *Manuscritos litúrgicos de la Biblioteca Nacional* (Madrid, 1969), pp. 120-3; Jullien, 80-1; Mearns, pp. xx, 1, and 39; Agustín Millares Carlo, "Manuscritos visigóticos. Notas bibliográficas," *Hispania Sacra* 14 (1961), 379-81; A.M. Mundó, "La datación de los códices litúrgicos visigóticos toledanos," *Hispania Sacra* 18 (1965), 14 and 21; A.W.S. Porter, "Cantica Mozarabici Officii," *EL* 49 (1935), 126-45; Don Michael Randel, *The Responsorial Psalm Tones for the Mozarabic Office* (Princeton, 1969), p. 7; H. Schneider, *Die altlateinischen biblischen Cantica* (Beuron, 1938), pp. 126-58; W.M. Whitehill, "A Collection of Mozarabic Liturgical Manuscripts Containing the Psalter and *Liber Canticorum,*" *JLW* 14 (1934), 95-122.

MADRID, Biblioteca Nacional, 10029 (Tol. 14. 22)
s. ix/x; 159 leaves; 230 x 160 mm.; written in northern Spain.

Contents: On ff. 51v-52v: H1. Preceded by Corippus, *In Laudem Iustini* (ff. 17-51) and followed by *Versus in Ponte Emeritae* (ff. 52-53) and poetry of Eugenius of Toledo. On f. 143v: PC 2.63-81.
Bibliography: Claude W. Barlow, *Martini Episcopi Bracarensis Opera Omnia* = Papers and Monographs of the American Academy in Rome 12 (New Haven, 1950), pp. 278-9; J. Jiménez Delgado, "Juvenco en el códice matritense 10.029," *Helmantica* 19 (1968), 277-332; Roland Demeulenaere, *Verecundi Iuncensis Opera, CCSL,* vol. 93, p. xvi; Lisardo Rubio Fernández, *Catálogo de los manuscritos clásicos latinos existentes en España* (Madrid, 1984), p. 355; Wilhelm von Hartel, *Bibliotheca Patrum Latinorum Hispaniensis* (Wien, 1887), vol. 1, pp. 284-90; Johannes Huemer, *Gai Vetti Aquilini Iuvenci Evangeliorum Libri Quattuor, CSEL,* vol. 24, p. xxxiii; Janini, *Man. lit.,* same as above, pp. 128-9; Jeudy, "Phocas," 102; E.A. Lowe, *Paleographical Papers,* ed. Ludwig Bieler (Oxford, 1972), vol. 1, p. 49; Nicolò Messina, *Pseudo-Eugenio di Toledo, Speculum per un nobile visigoto* = Monografias de la Universidad de Santiago de Compostela 85 (Santiago de Compostela, 1984), pp. 17-19; Agustín Millares Carlo, "Manuscritos visigóticos. Notas bibliográficas," *Hispania Sacra* 14 (1961), 377-8; idem, *Nuevos estudios de paleografía española* (Mexico City, 1941), pp. 57-8; Munk Olsen, vol. 1, pp. 70-1; Joseph Partsch, *Corippi Africani Grammatici Libri Qui Supersunt, MGH AA,* vol. 3.2, pp. l-lvi; Elisabeth Pellegrin, "Manuscrits des auteurs classiques latins de Madrid et du chapitre de Tolède," *BIRHT* 2 (1953), 7-24; C.M. Sage, *Paul Albar of Cordoba: Studies on His Life and Writings* = The Catholic University of America

Studies in Medieval History (n.s.) 5 (Washington, 1943), pp. 94, 96, and 219-20; Feliciano Speranza, *Blossi Aemili Draconti Satisfactio una cum Eugeni Recensione* = Biblioteca di Helikon. Rivista di tradizione e cultura classica dell'Università di Messina. Testi e studi 9 (Roma, 1978), p. xviii; Ulrich Justus Stache, *Flavius Cresconius Corippus. In Laudem Justini Augusti Minoris. Ein Kommentar* (Berlin, 1976), pp. 30-2; Ludwig Traube in *MGH, PLAC,* vol. 3, p. 125; Manuela Verdrell Peñaranda, "Estudio del códice de Azagra, Biblioteca Nacional de Madrid, MS. 10029," *Revista de archivos bibliotecas y museos* 82 (1979), 655-705; F. Vollmer, *Fl. Merobaudis Reliquiae, Blossii Aemilii Dracontii Carmina, Eugenii Toletani Episcopi Carmina et Epistulae, MGH,* vol. 14, pp. xviii and xxxviii.

MAGDEBURG, Dom-Gymnasium, 253 (Bf. 31)
s. xv/xvi; 21 leaves; folio; paper.

Contents: On ff. 1r-3v: H1. Followed by Mantuan, *Carmen contra Poetas Impudice Loquentes* (ff. 4r-7v), et al.
Bibliography: H. Dittmar, *Die Handschriften und alten Drucke des Dom-Gymnasiums* (Magdeburg, 1878; continued in 1880), pp. 92-3; Walther, no. 2382.

MANCHESTER, John Rylands University Library, Lat. 116 (Crawford 133)
s. ix (after 814); 113 leaves; 420 x 325 mm.; Trier (S. Maximin?).

Contents: Benedictine psalter; hymns beginning on f. 95r include *A Solis Ortus Cardine.*
Bibliography: Bischoff, "FHH," 310; Gneuss, *Hymnar,* pp. 31 and 49; Montague Rhodes James, *A Descriptive Catalogue of the Latin Manuscripts in the John Rylands Library at Manchester,* vol. 1 (Manchester, 1921), pp. 211-7; Jullien, 100-1; Mearns, pp. xvi and 1; L. Whitbread, "After Bede: The Influence and Dissemination of his Doomsday Verses," *Archiv für das Studium der neueren Sprachen und Literaturen* 204 (1967), 262.

METZ, Bibliothèque Municipale, 1168
s. xii; 56 leaves; 310 x 230 mm.; Anchin.

Contents: *Vitae Ss. Dunstani et Aicadri;* on f. 56v: H1 (*Antiphonam sanctum Dunstanum angelus docuit...*).

Bibliography: *Cat. gen. octavo,* vol. 48, p. 398.

MILANO, Biblioteca Ambrosiana, E. 57 Sup.
s. xv (1496-1500); 224 leaves; 220 x 150 mm.; written in central Italy;
paper.

Contents: On ff. 160r-176v: E1, PC 1.1 to 2.193 (breaks off at mid-
page). Preceded by Juvencus, *Evangeliorum Libri Quattuor* (ff. 25r-98r)
and Arator, *Historia Apostolica* (ff. 105r-159v).
Other information: No glossing. Microfilm seen.
Bibliography: Ettore Cuzzi, "I tre codici ambrosiani di Aratore,"
Rendiconti del Reale Istituto Lombardo di Scienze e Lettere (2. ser.) 69
(1936), 248-51; Astrik L. Gabriel, *A Summary Catalogue of Microfilms
of One Thousand Scientific Manuscripts in the Ambrosiana Library,
Milan* (Notre Dame, 1968), p. 218; Louis Jordan, *Inventory of Western
Manuscripts in the Biblioteca Ambrosiana,* part 3 = Publications in
Medieval Studies 22.3 (Notre Dame, 1989), pp. 85-9; Kristeller, *Iter,*
vol. 1, p. 298 and vol. 2, p. 531; Paolo Revelli, *I codici ambrosiani di
contenuto geografico* = Fontes ambrosiani 1 (Milano, 1929), p. 79.

MILANO, Biblioteca Ambrosiana, R. 57 Sup. (S.P. II. 66)
s. vii*ex.*; 23 leaves (46 pages); 255 x 148 mm.; written at Bobbio.

Contents: On ff. 1-23: PC 4.128 to 5.438. Palimpsest of portions of
Cicero's speeches (*Pro M. Aemilio Scauro, Pro M. Tullio, Pro L. Valerio
Flacco, Pro M. Caelio*). Original eleven and a half leaves folded to form
23 leaves.
Other information: Written in uncial and half-uncial script. Published
by A. Mai in 1814. Used by Huemer (M). Microfilm acquired.
Bibliography: *CLA,* vol. 3, p. 28, no. 363; *CSEL,* vol. 10, pp. iv-v; P.
Engelbert, "Zur Frühgeschichte des Bobbieser Skriptoriums," *RB* 78
(1968), 238-40; Mirella Ferrari, "Il Codex Muratorianus e il suo ultimo
inedito," *Italia medioevale e umanistica* 32 (1989), 15; Theodor Gottlieb,
"Über Handschriften aus Bobbio," *Zentralblatt für Bibliothekswesen* 4
(1887), 442-63, esp. 455; Françoise Henry, "Les Débuts de la miniature
irlandaise," *Gazette des beaux-arts* (ser. 6) 37 (1950), 33; Huemer, *De
Sedulii,* pp. 9, 38, and 41; Angelo Paredi, "Il fondo bobbiese dell'Am-
brosiana," *Columba* 5 (1965), 88-9; Alessandro Pratesi, *Frustula
Palaeographica* = Biblioteca di scrittura e civiltà 4 (Firenze, 1992), pp.
184-5; Renato Raffaelli, "La pagina e il testo" in *Atti del convegno
internazionale: Il libro e il testo* (Urbino, 1984), p. 20; August

Reifferscheid, "Die Ambrosianische Bibliothek in Mailand," part 3 of *Bibliotheca Patrum Latinorum Italica,* vol. 2.1 (Wien, 1871), p. 87; Reynolds, pp. 56, 61, 74, 88, and 91; O. Seebass, "Handschriften von Bobbio in der Vatikanischen und Ambrosianischen Bibliothek," *Zentralblatt für Bibliothekswesen* 13 (1896), 57-79, esp. 66; Michele Tosi, "L'*Edictus Rothari* nei manoscritti bobiensi," *Archivum bobiense* 4 (1982), 15 and 35; Traube, vol. 1, p. 165; Fabio Troncarelli, "I codici di Cassiodoro: Le testimonianze più antiche," *Scrittura e civiltà* 12 (1988), 51.

MONTE CASSINO, Archivio e Biblioteca dell'Abbazia, 420
s. xi (c. 1050); 422 pages; 155 x 95 mm.; Monte Cassino.

Contents: Breviary; includes *A Solis Ortus Cardine* and *Hostis Herodes.*
Bibliography: Réginald Grégoire, "Repertorium Liturgicum Italicum," *Studi medievali* (3. ser.) 9 (1968), 535-6; Maurus Inguanez, *Codicum Casinensium Manuscriptorum Catalogus,* vol. 3 (Monte Cassino, 1940-1), pp. 30-1; Jullien, 150; Lokrantz, p. 25; Mearns, pp. xviii, 1, and 39.

MONTE CASSINO, Archivio e Biblioteca dell'Abbazia, 506
s. xi; 216 pages; 205 x 135 mm.; Monte Cassino.

Contents: Hymnal, etc.; includes *A Solis Ortus Cardine* (pp. 46-48) and *Hostis Herodes* (pp. 64-66).
Bibliography: Beneventan, vol. 2, p. 88; Joseph Gajard, *Le Codex VI. 34 de la Bibliothèque Capitulaire de Bénévent (XIe-XIIe siècle). Graduel de Bénévent avec prosaire et tropaire* = Paléographie musicale 15 (Solesme, 1937), p. 78; Réginald Grégoire, "Repertorium Liturgicum Italicum," *Studi medievali* (3. ser.) 9 (1968), 537; Inguanez, *Codicum,* same as above, pp. 151-4; Jullien, 122; A. Lentini and F. Avagliano, "I carmi di Alfano I, Arcivescovo di Salerno," *Miscellanea cassinese* 38 (1974), 22; Lokrantz, p. 28; Mearns, pp. xviii, 1, and 39.

MONTE CASSINO, Archivio e Biblioteca dell'Abbazia, 559
s. xi/xii; 196 pages; 165 x 115 mm.; Monte Cassino.

Contents: Breviary; hymns include *A Solis Ortus Cardine* (p. 164).
Bibliography: Beneventan, vol. 2, p. 90; Gamber, vol. 2, p. 582, no. 1616b; Réginald Grégoire, "Repertorium Liturgicum Italicum," *Studi medievali* (3. ser.) 9 (1968), 539; Inguanez, same as above, pp. 232-5; Lokrantz, p. 29; Mearns, pp. xix and 1.

MÜNCHEN, Bayerische Staatsbibliothek, Clm 1880
s. xvi-xvii; 319 leaves; 205 x 160 mm.; written in Germany; prov. S.
Ulrich and Afra, Augsburg; paper.

Contents: On. ff. 129v-130v: H2 (with extensive notes). On f. 168r:
PC 4.64-81.
Bibliography: C. Halm, G. Laubmann, et al., *Catalogus Codicum
Latinorum Bibliothecae Regiae Monacensis* (München, 1868 ff.), vol.
1.2, p. 300; Sottili, vol. 2, pp. 785-95.

MÜNCHEN, Bayerische Staatsbibliothek, Clm 5594
s. xv$^{ex.}$; 359 leaves; 305 x 210 mm.; written at Leipzig University (later
at Diessen); paper.

Contents: Collection of hymns on ff. 337-359; includes H2 (with
doxology) on ff. 339r-341r.
Other information: Interlinear glosses and marginal commentary. Seen
in person.
Bibliography: Halm, *Catalogus,* same as above, vol. 1.3, pp. 24-5;
Nikolaus Henkel, *Deutsche Übersetzungen lateinischer Schultexte. Ihre
Verbreitung und Funktion im Mittelalter und in der frühen Neuzeit* =
Münchener Texte und Untersuchungen zur deutschen Literatur des
Mittelalters 90 (München, 1988), pp. 162-5.

MÜNCHEN, Bayerische Staatsbibliothek, Clm 14420
s. x-xii; 199 leaves; 245 x 158 mm.; S. Emmeram, Regensburg.

Contents: On ff. 145r-148v (s. xii): Commentary on PC (1.1 up
through 3. 242-50). Preceded by a commentary on Terence (ff. 79r ff.)
and followed by Virgil's *Eclogues* (ff. 149r ff.)
Other information: Miscellany volume. Seen in person.
Bibliography: Bernhard Bischoff, "Das Güterverzeichnis des Klosters
Ss. Faustino e Giovita in Brescia aus dem Jahre 964," *Italia medioevale
e umanistica* 15 (1972), 53-61; Halm, *Catalogus,* vol. 2.2 (1876), p.
170; Munk Olsen, vol. 2, pp. 650 and 739; R. Peiper, *Alcimi Ecdicii
Aviti Viennensis Episcopi Opera Quae Supersunt, MGH AA,* vol. 6.2, pp.
lxxiii-lxxiv.

MÜNCHEN, Bayerische Staatsbibliothek, Clm 14698
s. xv; 331 leaves; 210 x 142 mm.; S. Emmeram, Regensburg.

Contents: Miscellany volume with a collection of hymns on ff. 28r ff. On ff. 35v-36r: *A Solis Ortus Cardine* and *Hostis Herodes* (with doxology). Includes German translation. Preceded by hymn beginning *Christe redemptor omnium* and followed by hymn beginning *Audi benigne conditor.*

Other information: Manuscript of the Franciscan Michael Pfollinger of Regensburg. Over 60 Latin hymns which have been translated into German are included on ff. 28r-45r. Seen in person.

Bibliography: Halm, *Catalogus,* same as above, vol. 2.2 (1876), pp. 219-20; Nikolaus Henkel, *Deutsche Übersetzungen lateinischer Schultexte. Ihre Verbreitung und Funktion im Mittelalter und in der frühen Neuzeit* = Münchener Texte und Untersuchungen zur deutschen Literatur des Mittelalters 90 (München, 1988), pp. 112-17; idem, "Mittelalterliche Übersetzungen lateinischer Schultexte ins Deutsche. Beobachtungen zum Verhältnis von Formtyp und Leistung" in *Poesie und Gebrauchsliteratur im deutschen Mittelalter. Würzburger Colloquium 1978* (Tübingen, 1979), pp. 168-9.

MÜNCHEN, Bayerische Staatsbibliothek, Clm 17027

s. x; 153 leaves; 180 x 140 mm.; written at Freising; later at Schäftlarn.

Contents: Benedictine ritual with hymns on ff. 127v ff.; includes *A Solis Ortus Cardine* (with doxology) on ff. 134r-135r. Preceded by hymn beginning *Te lucis ante terminum.* Followed by hymn for S. Stephen: *Hic primus almo sanguine.*

Other information: Microfilm seen.

Bibliography: Natalia Daniel, *Handschriften des zehnten Jahrhunderts aus der Freisinger Dombibliothek. Studien über Schriftcharakter und Herkunft der nachkarolingischen und ottonischen Handschriften einer bayerischen Bibliothek* = MBMRF 11 (München, 1973), p. 98; Gamber, vol. 2, p. 553, no. 1520; Halm, *Catalogus,* same as above, vol. 2.3 (1878), p. 76; Jullien, 124-5; Mearns, pp. xvi and 1.

MÜNCHEN, Bayerische Staatsbibliothek, Clm 18650

s. xv; 175 leaves; 215 x 150 mm.; Tegernsee.

Contents: On f. 152r-v: H2 and PC 2.63-9 *("Salutat matrem Domini").* Preceded by Bonaventura, *De Quinque Festivitatibus Infantiae Salvatoris* (ff. 126r ff.) and *De Ligno Vitae, alias De Arbore Crucis* (ff. 136v ff.). Followed by *Speculum Mortis* (ff. 153r-158v).

Other information: Seen in person.

Bibliography: Halm, *Catalogus,* same as above, vol. 2.3 (1878), p. 196.

MÜNCHEN, Bayerische Staatsbibliothek, Clm 19456
s. x/xi; 174 leaves; 120 x 105 mm.; Tegernsee.

Contents: On ff. 1v-164r: Remigius' commentary on Sedulius. Followed by glosses on Bede, *De Arte Metrica* (ff. 164r-168v) and *De Schematibus et Tropis* (ff. 169r-174r).
Other information: Used by Huemer for his partial edition of Remigius' commentary (*CSEL,* vol. 10, pp. 316 ff.). Seen in person.
Bibliography: Christine Elisabeth Eder, *Die Schule des Klosters Tegernsee im frühen Mittelalter im Spiegel der Tegernseer Handschriften* (München, 1972), pp. 42-3; J.P. Elder, "Did Remigius of Auxerre Comment on Bede's *De Schematibus et Tropis?" MS* 9 (1947), 141-50; Glauche, pp. 52, 56, and 92; Halm, *Catalogus,* same as above, vol. 2.3, p. 248; Huemer, "Glossen," passim; Colette Jeudy, "Le *Carmen* 111 d'Alcuin et l'anthologie de Martial du manuscrit 522 (502) de la Bibliothèque Municipale d'Angers" in *Scire Litteras. Forschungen zum mittelalterlichen Geistesleben. Festschrift Bernhard Bischoff zu seinem 80. Geburtstag* = Abhandlungen der Bayerischen Akademie der Wissenschaften, Phil.- hist. Klasse, n. F., 99 (München, 1988), p. 225; Jeudy, "Remi," p. 497; Cora E. Lutz, "One Formula of *Accessus* in Remigius' Works," *Latomus* 19 (1960), 778, n. 5.

MÜNCHEN, Bayerische Staatsbibliothek, Clm 19474
s. xii$^{ex.}$; 78 pages; 155 x 105 mm.; Tegernsee.

Contents: Collection of *accessus* on pp. 59-78; includes *accessus ad Sedulium* (pp. 73-4). Preceded by *accessus* to works of "Cato" (pp. 59-60); Avianus (pp. 60-65); Prosper (pp. 65-66); Ovid (pp. 66-67); Cicero (pp. 67-68); Homer (p. 68); Arator (p. 69); Ovid (pp. 70-71); and Theodulus (pp. 72-3). Followed by *accessus* to works of Ovid (pp. 75-76); Prudentius (pp. 76-77); and Maximianus (pp. 77-78).
Other information: Seen in person.
Bibliography: Glauche, pp. 118 and 121; Halm, *Catalogus,* same as above, vol. 2.3 (1878), pp. 248-9; R.B.C. Huygens, *Accessus ad Auctores, Bernard d'Utrecht, Conrad d'Hirsau, Dialogus super Auctores* (Leiden, 1970), pp. 3 and 28-9; Munk Olsen, vol. 1, p. 238 and vol. 2, p. 178; Reynolds, pp. 65-6 and 350-1; Sanford, 229; Steinmeyer & Sievers, vol. 5, pp. 70-1, no. 721.

MÜNCHEN, Bayerische Staatsbibliothek, Clm 19475
s. xii²; 45 leaves; 180 x 124-135 mm.; written in Germany; prov.
Tegernsee.

Contents: Collection of *accessus* on ff. 1r-16r and 31v; on f. 5v:
accessus ad Sedulium.   Preceded by *accessus* to Ovid (f. 1r); Prudentius
(ff. 1v-2v); Cato (f. 2v); Avianus (ff. 2v-4r); Maximianus (f. 4r); Homer
(f. 4r-v); *Physiologus* (f. 4v); Theodulus (ff. 4v-5r); Arator (f. 5r); and
Prosper (f. 5r).   Followed by *accessus* to Ovid (ff. 5v-8r); Lucan (ff. 8r-
9v); Cicero (ff. 9v-12r); Boethius (f. 12r-v); Priscian (ff. 12v-13r);
Horace (ff. 14v-16r); *Pamphilus* (f. 31v); and Thebaldus (f. 31v).
Other information: Seen in person.
Bibliography: Glauche, pp. 118-123; Halm, *Catalogus*, same as above,
vol. 2.3, p. 249; Stephen A. Hurlbut, "A Forerunner of Alexander de
Villa-Dei," *Speculum* 8 (1933), 258-63; Huygens, same as above, pp. 2
and 28-9; Jeudy, "Phocas," 113-4; Munk Olsen, vol. 2, pp. 178-9;
Sanford, 226.

MÜNCHEN, Bayerische Staatsbibliothek, Clm 22307
s. x/xi; 195 leaves; 193 x 137 mm.; Tegernsee and Windberg.

Contents: On ff. 143r-151v: Remigius' commentary on Sedulius (only
up to PC 1.226).   Preceded by treatise beginning *Deus summe atque
ineffabiliter bonus* (ff. 86r ff.) and followed by selections from grammat-
ical treatises (ff. 152r ff.).
Other information: Used by Huemer for his partial edition of Remigius'
commentary in *CSEL,* vol. 10, pp. 316 ff.   Seen in person.
Bibliography: Christine Elisabeth Eder, *Die Schule des Klosters
Tegernsee im frühen Mittelalter im Spiegel der Tegernseer Handschriften*
(München, 1972), pp. 50-1; Glauche, p. 52; Halm, *Catalogus*, same as
above, vol. 2.4 (1881), pp. 41-2; Colette Jeudy, "Le *Carmen* 111
d'Alcuin et l'anthologie de Martial du manuscrit 522 (502) de la
Bibliothèque Municipale d'Angers" in *Scire Litteras. Forschungen zum
mittelalterlichen Geistesleben. Festschrift Bernhard Bischoff zu seinem
80. Geburtstag* = Abhandlungen der Bayerischen Akademie der Wissen-
schaften, Phil.- hist. Klasse, n. F., 99 (München, 1988), p. 225; Jeudy,
"Remi," p. 497; Cora E. Lutz, "One Formula of *Accessus* in Remigius'
Works," *Latomus* 19 (1960), 778, n. 5.

**MÜNCHEN, Bayerische Staatsbibliothek, Clm 29338/1 (formerly
29033a)**

s. viii[1]; 2 leaves; 205 x 140 mm.; written at Luxeuil or in a related house; later at S. Emmeram, Regensburg.

Contents: PC 2.133-162 and 275-300.
Other information: Used as a fly-leaf in Clm 14102. Script is "Luxeuil minuscule of the advanced type...." Seen in person.
Bibliography: Bernhard Bischoff, *Die südostdeutschen Schreibschulen und Bibliotheken in der Karolingerzeit, Teil 1. Die bayrischen Diözesen* = Sammlung bibliothekswissenschaftlicher Arbeiten 49 (2nd corr. ed.; Leipzig, 1940), pp. 256-7; idem, same as above, part 2: *Die vorwiegend österreichischen Diözesen* (Wiesbaden, 1980), p. 246; *CLA,* vol. 9, p. 27, no. 1328; *CSEL,* vol. 10, p. x; Pierre Salmon, *La Lectionnaire de Luxeuil II: Étude paléographique et liturgique suivie d'un choix de planches* = Collectanea Biblica Latina 9 (Roma, 1953) pl. 5; Traube, vol. 3, p. 236.

MÜNCHEN, Bayerische Staatsbibliothek, Clm 29338/3 (formerly 29033c)
s. x/xi; 4 leaves; 210 x 188 mm.; Regensburg (Mittelmünster).

Contents: On ff. 1r-4r: PC 5.221-438, H1. Followed by acrostic poems in praise of Sedulius (in Huemer's order; Liberatus' has only first eight lines); subscription; Asterius' epigram; and biographical notice beginning *Sedulius versificus primo laicus....* Followed by Arator, *Epistola ad Florianum* and *Epistola ad Vigilium* on f. 4v.
Other information: Written in two columns. Some interlinear and marginal glosses. Seen in person.
Bibliography: Armin Schlechter, *Die althochdeutschen Aratorglossen der Handschrift Rom Biblioteca Apostolica Vaticana Pal. Lat. 1716 und verwandte Glossierungen* = Studien zum Althochdeutschen 20 (Göttingen, 1993), pp. 330-6.

MÜNCHEN, Universitätsbibliothek, Frag. 57
s. xv; 2 leaves; 200 x 146 mm.

Contents: PC 1.1-22, 1.48-305, 1.335-367, 2.62-128, 2.263-300, 3.1-29.
Bibliography: Paul Lehmann and Otto Glauning, *Mittelalterliche Handschriftenbruchstücke der Universitätsbibliothek und des Georgianum zu München* = Zentralblatt für Bibliothekswesen, Beiheft 72 (Leipzig, 1940), pp. 43-4.

NAPOLI, Biblioteca Nazionale Vittorio Emmanuele II, VI. E. 43
s. xi/xii (1099-1118); 283 leaves; S. Sophia, Benevento.

Contents: Breviary, etc.; includes *A Solis Ortus Cardine* on f. 189v and *Hostis Herodes* on f. 192v.
Bibliography: Beneventan, vol. 2, p. 101; Hartmut Hoffman, "Der Kalender des Leo Marsicanus," *Deutsches Archiv* 21 (1965), 97-8; Jullien, 120-1; A. Lentini and F. Avagliano, "I carmi di Alfano I, Arcivescovo di Salerno," *Miscellanea cassinese* 38 (1974), 22; Walther Lipphardt, *Lateinische Osterfeiern und Osterspiele* = Ausgaben deutscher Literatur des XV. bis XVIII. Jahrhunderts. Reihe Drama 5, vol. 1 (Berlin and New York, 1975), p. 22; Lokrantz, pp. 21 and 39; Mearns, pp. xviii, 1, and 39.

NAPOLI, Biblioteca Nazionale Vittorio Emmanuele II, VI. F. 2
s. xi/xii; Monte Cassino.

Contents: Benedictine psalter, etc.; includes *A Solis Ortus Cardine* and *Hostis Herodes.*
Bibliography: Beneventan, vol. 2, p. 102; Mearns, pp. xix, 1, and 39.

NEW HAVEN, Yale University Library, MS 316
s. xv$^{ex.}$; 37 leaves; 199 x 143 mm.; written in Germany; paper.

Contents: On f. 37r-v: H2. Preceded by Arator, *Historia Apostolica* (ff. 1r-37r).
Bibliography: Barbara A. Shailor, *Catalogue of Medieval and Renaissance Manuscripts in the Beinecke Rare Book and Manuscript Library, Yale University,* vol. 2 = Medieval and Renaissance Texts and Studies 48 (Binghamton, 1987), p. 119.

ORLÉANS, Bibliothèque Municipale, 155 (132)
s. x$^{ex.}$; 236 pages; 238 x 170 mm.; Fleury.

Contents: On pp. 233-235 (s. xiii): *A Solis Ortus Cardine* and *Hostis Herodes.* Preceded by Augustine on the Lord's Prayer (pp. 215 ff.)
Bibliography: Cat. gen. octavo, vol. 12, pp. 71-2; S. Corbin, *Paléographie musicale* in *École Pratique des Hautes Études, IVe Section, Sciences historiques et philologiques* (Paris, 1973), 385-92; Cyrille Lambot, "L'Authenticité du sermon 369 de S. Augustin pour la fête de Noël" in *Colligere Fragmenta. Festschrift Alban Dold zum 70.*

Geburtstag am 7.7.1952 (Beuron, 1952), pp. 103-112; Lesne, pp. 550-553; Mostert, p. 136; Ch. Samaran and R. Marichal, *Catalogue des manuscrits en écriture latine portant des indications de date, de lieu ou de copiste* (Paris, 1959-84), vol. 7, p. xxxviii.

ORLÉANS, Bibliothèque Municipale, 164 (141)
s. xi; 312 pages; 322 x 256 mm.; Fleury.

Contents: On pp. 310-311 (s. ix$^{in.}$): PC 5.125-181. First part of manuscript contains sermons of St. Augustine. Followed by part of the office of the dead.
Bibliography: Cat. gen. octavo, vol. 12, pp. 77-8; P. Courcelle, "Fragments non identifiés de Fleury-sur-Loire III," *REAug* 2 (1956), 452 [collated against Huemer's text]; Lesne, pp. 552-3; Mostert, p. 139; Samaran and Marichal, same as above, vol. 7, p. 489; P. Verbraken, "Les Deux sermons du prêtre Eraclius d'Hippone," *RB* 71 (1961), 3-21.

OXFORD, Bodleian Library, Ashmole 1523 (SC 8229)
s. xiv; 257 leaves; 330 x 219 mm.; S. Andrew's, Bromholm.

Contents: Cluniac psalter, etc.; includes *A Solis Ortus Cardine* and *Hostis Herodes.*
Bibliography: W.H. Black, *A Descriptive, Analytical, and Critical Catalogue of the Manuscripts Bequeathed unto the University of Oxford, by Elias Ashmole Esq.* (Oxford, 1845), cols. 1430-1; S.C. Cockerell and M.R. James, *Two East Anglian Psalters at the Bodleian Library, Oxford* (Oxford, 1926); Gneuss, *Hymnar,* p. 116; Ker, *Med.,* p. 13; Mearns, pp. xiii, 1, and 39; *Sum. Cat.,* vol. 2, part 2 (1937), p. 1155.

OXFORD, Bodleian Library, Ashmole 1525 (SC 8229)
s. xii/xiii; 180 leaves; large folio volume; Christ Church, Canterbury.

Contents: Benedictine psalter, etc.; includes *A Solis Ortus Cardine* and *Hostis Herodes.*
Bibliography: Black, same as above, cols. 1436-7; Gneuss, *Hymnar,* pp. 241 and 250; Ker, *Med.* p. 37; *Latin Liturgical Manuscripts and Printed Books. Guide to an Exhibition Held during 1952* (Oxford, 1952), p. 30, no. 45; Mearns, pp. xiii, 1, and 39; *Sum. Cat.,* vol. 2, part 2 (1937), p. 1155.

OXFORD, Bodleian Library, Barlow 41 (SC 6481)

s. xiii$^{3/4}$; 355 leaves; 183 x 112 mm.; Evesham.

Contents: Benedictine breviary; hymns on ff. 245v ff. include *A Solis Ortus Cardine* and *Hostis Herodes.*
Bibliography: Frere, no. 99; Gneuss, *Hymnar,* p. 250; Ker, *Med.,* p. 81; *Latin Liturgical Manuscripts and Printed Books. Guide to an Exhibition Held during 1952* (Oxford, 1952), p. 38, no. 69; Mearns, pp. xiii, 1, and 39; *Sum. Cat.* vol. 2, part 2 (1937), p. 1061.

OXFORD, Bodleian Library, Canon. Lit. 370 (SC 19454)
s. xiii (1266); 143 leaves; 337 x 238 mm.; Padova?

Contents: *"Psalterium David"* with canticles, etc.; hymns on ff. 101v ff. include *A Solis Ortus Cardine* and *Hostis Herodes.*
Other information: Written by Johannes de Gaibana.
Bibliography: Mearns, pp. xix, 1, and 39; *Sum. Cat.,* vol. 4 (1897), p. 393.

OXFORD, Bodleian Library, D'Orville 45 (SC 16923)
s. xi (c. 1075); 245 leaves; 327 x 222 mm.; Moissac.

Contents: Psalter, etc., with hymnal on ff. 167r-196v; *A Solis Ortus Cardine* and *Hostis Herodes* on f. 175r-v.
Bibliography: Baroffio, 495; Louis Brou, *The Psalter Collects from V-VIth Century Sources* = Henry Bradshaw Society 83 (London, 1949), pp. 31-5; Jean Dufour, *La Bibliothèque et le scriptorium de Moissac* = Centre de Recherches d'Histoire et de Philologie de la IVe Section de l'École Pratique des Hautes Études V, Hautes études médiévales et modernes 15 (Genève and Paris, 1972), pp. 108-9; idem, "Les Manuscrits liturgiques de Moissac" in *Liturgie et musique IXe-XIVe siècles* = Cahiers de Fanjeaux 17 (1982), pp. 124-5; P.M. Gy, "Collectaire, rituel, processionnal," *RSPh* 44 (1960), 453; Jullien, 130-1; J. Leclercq, "La Rencontre des moines de Moissac avec Dieu," *Annales du Midi* 75 (1963), pp. 410-2; idem, "Méditations d'un moine de Moissac au XIe siècle," *Revue d'ascétique et de mystique* 40 (1964), 197 ff.; A.-G. Martimort, "Répertoire des livres liturgiques du Languedoc antérieurs au Concile de Trente" in *Liturgie et musique IXe-XIVe siècles* = Cahiers de Fanjeaux 17 (1982), 79; Mearns, pp. xv, 1, and 39; *Sum. Cat.,* vol. 4 (1897), pp. 48-9; André Wilmart, *Precum Libelli Quattuor Aevi Karolini* (Roma, 1940), p. 33.

OXFORD, Bodleian Library, Douce 381 (SC 21956)
s. xiii-xv; 184 leaves; 429 x 337 mm.

Contents: Collection of fragments of manuscripts. Hymnal on ff. 33-60 (s. xiii) includes *A Solis Ortus Cardine* and *Hostis Herodes*.
Bibliography: Mearns, pp. xiii, 1, and 39; *Sum. Cat.*, vol. 4, pp. 614-5.

Oxford, Bodleian Library, Junius 25 (SC 5137)
s. viii-ix; 197 leaves; 290 x 200 mm.; Reichenau and Murbach.

Contents: On ff. 158-193: *"Glossarium Junius A"* (s. ix); includes "Commentary on Sedulius" (f. 182v).
Bibliography: Bergmann, pp. 84-5; Walther Bulst, "Zu den Murbacher Hymnen," *Zeitschrift für deutsches Altertum und deutsche Literatur* 80 (1944), 157-62; *CLA,* vol. 2 (2nd ed.), p. 35, nos. 242-3; Esposito, 169; Gamber, vol. 2, p. 603, no. 1670; Gneuss, *Hymnar,* p. 21; idem, "Latin Hymns in Medieval England: Future Research" in *Chaucer and Middle English Studies in Honour of Rossell Hope Robbins,* ed. Beryl Rowland (London, 1974), p. 422, n. 10; Nikolaus Henkel, *Deutsche Übersetzungen lateinischer Schultexte. Ihre Verbreitung und Funktion im Mittelalter und in der frühen Neuzeit* = Münchener Texte und Untersuchungen zur deutschen Literatur des Mittelalters 90 (München, 1988), pp. 68-72; Jullien, 88-9; Schenkl, no. 272; E. Sievers, *Die Murbacher Hymnen nach der Handschrift hrsg.* (Halle, 1874); Steinmeyer & Sievers, vol. 2, pp. 619-20 and vol. 4, pp. 589-60; *Sum. Cat.*, vol. 2.2 (1937), pp. 969-71; C. Vogel, "L'Hymnaire de Murbach contenu dans le manuscrit Junius 25 (Oxford, Bodleian. 5137). Un témoin du cursus bénédictin ou cursus occidental ancien," *Archives de l'Eglise d'Alsace* 25 (1958), 1-42.

OXFORD, Bodleian Library, Lat. Class. D. 7 (SC 31376)
s. xi-xiii; 22 leaves; 305 x 219 mm.

Contents: On ff. 5-6 (s. xi$^{ex.}$): PC 3.292-339 and 4.101-148. Preceded by fragments of the works of Persius, Statius (s. xiii), and Avianus. Leaves 7-22 are blank.
Bibliography: Paul M. Clogan, "A Preliminary List of Anonymous Glosses of Statius' *Achilleid,*" *Manuscripta* 9 (1965), 108; idem, *The Medieval Achilleid of Statius. Edited with Introduction, Variant Readings, and Glosses* (Leiden, 1968), p. 17; *Sum. Cat.*, vol. 6 (1924),

p. 44; Robert Dale Sweeney, *Prolegomena to an Edition of the Scholia to Statius* = Mnemosyne Supplement 8 (Leiden, 1969), p. 43.

OXFORD, Bodleian Library, Lat. Liturg. F. 1 (SC 29740)
s. xiii (c. 1230); 290 leaves; 140 x 95 mm.; written in France?

Contents: Cistercian breviary; hymns on ff. 279r ff. include *A Solis Ortus Cardine.*
Bibliography: Mearns, pp. xv and 1; *Sum. Cat.,* same as above, vol. 5 (1905), pp. 681-2.

OXFORD, Bodleian Library, Lat. Theol. C. 4 (SC 1926)
s. x$^{ex.}$; 4 leaves; 350 x 235 mm.; written at Worcester?

Contents: PC 1.142-79, 180-218, 219-25, and 339-end.
Other information: Formerly binding leaves for Oxford, Bodl. Auct. F. Inf. I. 2. PC 1.315 ff. = *"Prologus quattuor evangelistarum."* Continuous marginal commentary (= *"Expositio Remigii"*) as well as interlinear glosses. Seen in person.
Bibliography: T.A.M. Bishop, *English Caroline Minuscule* (Oxford, 1971), p. 19 and plate xix; Gneuss, "List," no. 652; Ker, *Cat.,* p. 418; Lapidge, "Latin Texts," p. 114 and n. 82; Andy Orchard, *The Poetic Art of Aldhelm* = Cambridge Studies in Anglo-Saxon England 8 (Cambridge, 1994), p. 164; *Sum. Cat.,* vol. 2, part 1 (1922), p. 121.

OXFORD, Bodleian Library, Laud Lat. 5
s. xiii; 200 leaves; folio; Guisborough.

Contents: Augustinian psalter, etc.; hymnal on ff. 165 ff. includes *A Solis Ortus Cardine* and *Hostis Herodes.*
Bibliography: Henry Coxe, *Catalogi Codicum Manuscriptorum Bibliothecae Bodlianae. Pars Secunda Codices Latinos et Miscellaneos Laudianos Complectens* (Oxford, 1858-85), cols. 7-8; Ker, *Med.,* p. 94; Mearns, pp. xiii, 1, and 39; J. Tait, *Chronica Johannis de Reading et Anonymi Cantuariensis 1346-1367* (Manchester, 1914), p. 23.

OXFORD, Bodleian Library, Laud Lat. 95
s. xiii; 149 leaves; folio; Ely.

Contents: Hymnal of Sarum type on ff. 134 ff.; includes *A Solis Ortus Cardine* and *Hostis Herodes.*

Bibliography: Coxe, same as above, cols. 43-4; Ker, *Med.*, p. 78; Mearns, pp. xiii, 1, and 39.

OXFORD, Bodleian Library, Liturg. Misc. 297 (SC 19395)
s. xii (c. 1150); 360 leaves; 225 x 162 mm.; Würzburg?

Contents: Benedictine breviary; hymns on ff. 302r ff. include *A Solis Ortus Cardine* and *Hostis Herodes.*
Bibliography: Mearns, pp. xvii, 1, and 39; *Sum. Cat.*, vol. 4 (1897), pp. 376-7.

OXFORD, Bodleian Library, Liturg. Misc. 407 (SC 29071)
s. xiii-xiv; 255 leaves; 146 x 114 mm.; written in France.

Contents: Psalter, etc. (c. 1237), with Franciscan hymnal (s. xiv) on ff. 223r ff.; includes *A Solis Ortus Cardine* and *Hostis Herodes.*
Bibliography: Frere, no. 178; Mearns, pp. xv, 1, and 39; *Sum. Cat.*, vol. 5 (1905), pp. 552-3.

OXFORD, Bodleian Library, Selden Supra 41 (SC 3429)
s. xvi (1540-50); 402 leaves; 219 x 165 mm.; Norwich, Carmelite convent; paper.

Contents: On f. 38r: PC 1.170-96. Introduced by following: *Sedulius in carmine pascali sequentes versus edidit de sancto Helia Carmelicae religionis primo patriarcha.* Manuscript contains material relating to the Carmelite order.
Other information: Written by John Bale (d. 1563).
Bibliography: Ker, *Med.*, p. 140; Kristeller, *Iter,* vol. 4, p. 261; *Sum. Cat.*, vol. 2, part 1 (1922), pp. 630-2.

OXFORD, Jesus College, 10
s. xii-xiii; 190 leaves; 202 x 140 mm.; Hereford Priory, Gloucester.

Contents: Benedictine antiphonal, etc.; hymns include *A Solis Ortus Cardine* and *Hostis Herodes.*
Bibliography: Henry Coxe, *Catalogus Codicum Manuscriptorum Qui in Collegiis Aulisque Oxoniensibus Hodie Adservantur* (Oxford, 1852), part 2, p. 4 (of section); Frere, no. 537; Gneuss, *Hymnar,* pp. 116 and 250; Ker, *Med.*, pp. 92 and 99; Mearns, pp. xiii, 1, and 39.

OXFORD, Keble College, 31
s. xv¹; 258 leaves; 127 x 96 mm.; written in Venezia or Padova.

Contents: Franciscan breviary; hymns on ff. 117-26 include *A Solis Ortus Cardine* and *Hostis Herodes* (f. 117r-v).
Bibliography: M.B. Parkes, *The Medieval Manuscripts of Keble College, Oxford* (London, 1979), pp. 109-11.

OXFORD, Lincoln College, Lat. 22
s. xv^{in.}; 265 leaves; quarto.

Contents: On f. 1r ff.: E1 (missing page 8, line 9 ff.). Preceded by *"versus ad Theodosium"* (probably the dedicatory preface to Proba's cento). Albertus Magnus, *De Meteoris* on ff. 6r-265v.
Bibliography: Coxe, same as above, vol. 1, p. 25 (of section); Winfried Fauser, *Die Werke des Albertus Magnus in ihrer handschriftlichen Überlieferung. Teil 1. Die echte Werke* (Münster, 1982), p. 60.

OXFORD, St. John's College, 60
s. xv^{ex.}; 118 leaves; folio; Thame.

Contents: Sarum hymnal; includes *A Solis Ortus Cardine* and *Hostis Herodes*.
Bibliography: Coxe, same as above, p. 17 (of section); Mearns, pp. xiii, 1, and 39.

PARIS, Bibliothèque de l'Arsenal, 1008
s. xvii (1684); 639 pages; 345 x 230 mm.; S. Germain-des-Prés, Paris; paper.

Contents: *"Receuil de dom Claude Estiennot;"* on pp. 174-80: E1 (from a Fleury manuscript). Preceded by *rescriptum Leonis Papae VI pro Monasterio Floriacensi* (pp. 173 f.). Followed by *Fundatio Cellae S. Medardi de Chaloto, Monachorum Josaphetensium* (pp. 181 ff.).
Bibliography: Henri Martin, *Catalogue des manuscrits de la Bibliothèque de l'Arsenal* (Paris, 1885-1900), in *Catalogue général des manuscrits des bibliothèques publiques de France. Paris,* vol. 2 (1895), pp. 222-7.

PARIS, Bibliothèque Mazarine, 364 (759)
s. xi^{ex.}(c. 1099-1105); 332 leaves; 207 x 133 mm.; Monte Cassino.

Contents: Benedictine breviary, etc.; hymns include: *A Solis Ortus Cardine* (f. 150r-v) and *Hostis Herodes* (f. 153r-v).

Other information: On f. 137v: ...*pretende super famulum tuum abbatem nostrum Oderisium....* Seen in person.

Bibliography: M. Avery, "The Beneventan Lections for the Vigil of Easter and the Ambrosian Chant Banned by Pope Stephen IX at Monte Cassino," *Studi gregoriani per la storia di Gregorio VII e della riforma gregoriana* 1 (1947), 445 ff.; Peter Baldass, "Die Miniaturen zweier *Exultet*-Rollen (1): London, Add. 30337; Vat. Barb. Lat. 592," *Scriptorium* 8 (1954), 87; Baroffio, 495; P. Batiffol, "Note sur un bréviaire cassinésien du XIe siècle" in *Melanges Julien Havet* (Paris, 1895), pp. 201-9; G. de la Batut, *Les Principaux manuscrits à peinture conservés à la Bibl. Mazarine de Paris* = SFRMP 16 (Paris, 1933), 9-12; *Beneventan,* vol. 2, pp. 112-3; Owen Blum, "Authenticity of Sixteen Medieval Latin Poems Attributed to St. Peter Damian (1007-1072)," *APS Yearbook* 1956, 378-81; A. Boeckler, *Abendländische Miniaturen bis zum Augsgang der romanischen Zeit* = Tabulae in Usum Scholarum X (Berlin and Leipzig, 1930), p. 75; Antoine Chavasse, "Les Plus anciens types du lectionnaire et de l'antiphonaire romains de la messe," *RB* 62 (1952), 9; Klaus Gamber and Sieghild Rehle, *Manuale Casinense (Cod. Ottob. lat. 145)* = Textus Patristici et Liturgici 13 (Regensburg, 1977), p. 8; M. Inguanez, "Il *Quem queritis* pasquale nei codici cassinesi," *Studi medievali* (n.s.) 14 (1941), 142-9; Jullien, 122-3; J. Lemarié, "Textes relatifs au culte de l'archange et des anges dans les bréviaires manuscrits du Mont-Saint-Michel," *SE* 13 (1962), 116 and 126; Leroquais, *Bréviaires,* vol. 2, pp. 398-403; Walther Lipphardt, *Lateinische Osterfeiern und Osterspiele,* vol. 1 = Ausgaben deutscher Literatur des XV. bis XVIII. Jahrhunderts. Reihe Drama 5, vol. 1 (Berlin and New York, 1975), pp. 19-20; Lokrantz, pp. 28-9; Mearns, pp. xviii, 1, and 39; August Molinier, *Catalogue des manuscrits de la Bibliothèque Mazarine,* in *Catalogue général des manuscrits des bibliothèques publiques de France. Paris* (four volumes; Paris, 1885-98), vol. 1 (1885), pp. 132-3; Henri René Philippeau, "Textes et rubriques des *Agenda mortuorum,*" *Archiv für Liturgiewissenschaft* 4 (1955-6), 57-8; Ch. Samaran, R. Marichal, *Catalogue des manuscrits en écriture latine,* vol. 1 (Paris, 1959), p. 233; Hélène Toubert, "Le Bréviaire d'Oderisius (Paris, Bibliothèque Mazarine, Ms. 364) et les influences byzantines au Mont-Cassin," *MEFRM* 83 (1971), 187-261; André Wilmart, *Auteurs spirituels et textes dévots du Moyen Âge latin. Études d'histoire littéraire* (Paris, 1932), pp. 139-41 and 145; idem, "Prières pour la communion en deux psautiers du Mont-Cassin," *EL* 43 (1929),

320-8.

PARIS, Bibliothèque Mazarine, 512 (805)
s. ix²; 142 leaves; 252 x 194 mm.; S. Éloi, Noyon.

Contents: A collection of prayers, et al.; on ff. 132r-133r: H2.
Preceded by Augustine, *Oratio in Librum de Trinitate* (f. 131v).
Followed by Venantius Fortunatus, *Carm.* 2.2 *("In honore sanctae
crucis"),* beginning *Pange lingua gloriosi* (f. 133v).
Other information: Seen in person.
Bibliography: Jean-Baptiste Molin, "Les Manuscrits de la *Deprecratio
Gelasii*: Usage privé des psaumes et dévotion aux litanies," *EL* 90
(1976), 113-48, esp. 135-40; Molinier, *Cat.,* same as above, vol. 1, pp.
198-200; Wickersheimer, p. 50.

PARIS, Bibliothèque Mazarine, 3896 (604)
s. xvi (1535); 267 leaves; 140 x 98 mm.; possibly written in Flanders;
paper.

Contents: Miscellany of verse and liturgical pieces; on ff. 98r-100r:
H2. Followed (as above) by Venantius Fortunatus, *Carm.* 2.2 *("In
honore sanctae crucis"),* beginning *Pange lingua gloriosi* (f. 100v).
Petrarch, *Carmen de Beata Maria Magdalena* on ff. 9r-10r.
Other information: Seen in person.
Bibliography: Molinier, *Cat.,* same as above, vol. 3 (1890), pp. 227-8;
Elisabeth Pellegrin, *Manuscrits de Pétrarque dans les bibliothèques de
France* = Censimento dei codici petrarcheschi 2 (Padova, 1966), vol. 1,
p. 26; eadem, "Manuscrits de Pétrarque en France," *Italia medioevale
e umanistica* 4 (1961), 366.

PARIS, Bibliothèque Nationale, Lat. 103
s. xi$^{in.}$; 165 leaves; 285 x 215 mm.; S. Denis, Paris.

Contents: Benedictine psalter, etc., with hymns on ff. 146r ff. (s. xi$^{in.}$);
A Solis Ortus Cardine and *Hostis Herodes* (the latter begins *Ibant magi*
and is entitled *De innocentibus*) on ff. 151v and 152r. Lines 33-36 and
37-40 are reversed.
Other information: Seen in person.
Bibliography: Gamber, vol. 2, p. 586, no. 1622; Gneuss, *Hymnar,* p.
198; Jullien, 125-6; Philippe Lauer, *Bibliothèque Nationale. Catalogue
général des manscrits latins,* vol. 1 (Paris, 1939), p. 39; Leroquais,

Psautiers, vol. 2, pp. 30-2; Mearns, pp. xiv, 1, and 39; Carl-Allan Moberg, *Die liturgischen Hymnen in Schweden. Beiträge zur Liturgie- und Musikgeschichte des Mittelalters und der Reformationszeit* (Uppsala, 1947), vol. 1, p. 62; E.K. Rand, "Traces de piqûres dans quelques manuscrits du haut Moyen Âge," *Comptes-rendus de l'Académie des Inscriptions et Belles-Lettres* (Paris, 1939), 430; Stegmüller, vol. 7, no. 10230-1.

PARIS, Bibliothèque Nationale, Lat. 1092
s. xi (c. 1000); 159 leaves; 230 x 140 mm.; Narni (or S. Severino, Napoli).
Contents: Benedictine hymnal (very similar to Vat. Lat. 7172); *A Solis Ortus Cardine* on f. 25r; *Hostis Herodes* and remaining lines of H2 on f. 38r-v.
Other information: Seen in person.
Bibliography: F. Avril and Y. Zakuska, *Manuscrits enluminés d'origine italienne (Bibl. nat.),* vol. 1 (Paris, 1980), pp. 28-9 and pl. xv; Guido Maria Dreves, *Das Hymnar der Abtei S. Severin in Neapel. Nach den Codices Vaticanus 7172 und Parisinus 1092* = Analecta Hymnica 14a (Leipzig, 1893); Gamber, vol. 2, p. 604, no. 1673; Edward B. Garrison, "Notes on Certain Italian Medieval Manuscripts 3: Three Manuscripts of Narni," *La bibliofilia* 69 (1967), 1-67 (esp. 5-6); Gneuss, *Hymnar,* pp. 50, 72, and 199; Jullien, 116-7; Lauer, *Cat.* same as above, vol. 1, p. 397; Claudio Leonardi, "L'inno al martire Gregorio" in *La basilica di San Gregorio Maggiore in Spoleto* (Spoleto, 1979), pp. 29-36; idem, "S. Gregorio di Spoleto e l'innario umbro-romano dei codici Par. lat. 1092 e Vat. lat. 7172" in *Lateinische Dichtungen des X. und XI. Jahrhunderts. Festgabe für Walther Bulst zum 80. Geburtstag* (Heidelberg, 1981), pp. 129-48; M.G. Lokrantz, "Una raccolta di inni mariani trovati in un codice di Oxford dell' XI secolo," *Aevum* 41 (1967), 283-5; Ernesto Maurice, "Intorno all collezione d'inni sacri contenuta nei manoscritti Vaticano 7172 e Parigino latino 1092," *ARSR* 22 (1899), 5-23; Mearns, pp. xvii, 1, and 39; Dag Norberg, "Ein Erasmushymnus aus Italien" in *Lateinische Dichtungen des X. und XI. Jahrhunderts. Festgabe für Walther Bulst zum 80. Geburtstag* (Heidelberg, 1981), pp. 154-61; idem, *L'Oeuvre poétique de Paulin d'Aquilé. Édition critique avec introduction et commentaire* (Stockholm, 1979), p. 86.

PARIS, Bibliothèque Nationale, Lat. 1327
s. ix-x; 83 leaves; 160 x 95 mm.; Reims?

Contents: Psalter and hymnal; includes *A Solis Ortus Cardine* (in Tironian notation) on f. 70r.
Other information: Seen in person.
Bibliography: Émile Chatelain, *Introduction à la lecture des notes tironiennes* (Paris, 1900), p. 224; Jullien, 111-12; Lauer, *Cat.* same as above, vol. 1, pp. 497-8; Legendre, p. 54; Leroquais, *Psautiers*, vol. 2, p. 73; Mearns, pp. xiv and 1.

PARIS, Bibliothèque Nationale, Lat. 3417
s. xiv; 79 leaves; 220 x 150 mm.; Notre-Dame de la Grasse.

Contents: On ff. 78v-79v: H1 (*"Versus Sedulii docti viri"*). Preceded by anonymous preface to Juvencus, *Evangeliorum Libri Quattuor*.
Other information: Owned by Charles-Maurice Le Tellier, archbishop of Reims. Seen in person.
Bibliography: *Bibliothèque Nationale. Catalogue général des manuscrits latins* (Paris, 1939 ff.), vol. 5 (1966), pp. 370-3; Hauréau, *Notices*, vol. 1, pp. 208-13; Yves Lefèvre, *L'Elucidarium et les lucidaires. Contribution, par l'histoire d'un texte, à l'histoire des croyances religieuses en France au Moyen Âge* (Paris, 1954), p. 28

PARIS, Bibliothèque Nationale, Lat. 3630
s. xiii; 97 leaves; 245 x 203 mm.; S. Évroult.

Contents: On f. 7r: E1 (fragment: Huemer's p. 4, lines 5-7). Leaves 3-27 are a *florilegium* drawn from the works of Gregory, Augustine, Ambrose, Jerome, Rufinus, Cassiodorus, Cyprian, et al.
Other information: Seen in person.
Bibliography: *Cat. gen.*, same as above, vol. 6 (1975), pp. 390-7; B. Hauréau, "Notice sur les oeuvres authentiques ou supposées de Jean de Garlande," *Not. et extr.* 27.2 (1879), 1-86; Lefèvre, same above, pp. 31-2 [s. xiv].

PARIS, Bibliothèque Nationale, Lat. 3639
s. xv/xvi; 272 leaves; 200 x 135 mm.; paper.

Contents: On f. 222v: PC 2.63-9. Volume is a miscellany of about 300 pieces in praise of the Virgin Mary, beginning with Bernard of Cluny, *Mariale*.
Bibliography: *Cat. gen.*, same as above, vol. 6 (1975), pp. 413-36, esp. p. 430; B. Hauréau, *Des poèmes latins attribués à Saint Bernard* (Paris,

1890), pp. 90-4; idem, "Sur les poèmes attribués à Saint Bernard," *Journal des savants*, 1882, 404, 409, and 412-3.

PARIS, Bibliothèque Nationale, Lat. 7558
s. ix²/⁴; 168 leaves; 230 x 165 mm.; probably from central France.

Contents: On ff. 166v-168v: H1. Preceded by works of Bede *(De Arte Metrica* and *De Schematibus et Tropis),* Claudius Marius Victor, Ausonius, Paulinus of Nola, et al.
Other information: Used by Huemer (π'). Seen in person.
Bibliography: Catalogus Codicum Manuscriptorum Bibliothecae Regiae (four volumes; Paris, 1739-44), vol. 4 (1744), p. 373; Émile Chatelain, *Notice sur les manuscrits des poésies de S. Paulin de Nole* (Paris, 1880), pp. 36-9; *CSEL,* vol. 10, p. 155; Ernst Dümmler, "Die handschriftliche Überlieferung der lateinischen Dichtungen aus der Zeit der Karolinger," *Neues Archiv* 4.2 (1879), 299-301; P.F. Hovingh, "A propos de l'édition de l'*Alethia* de Claudius Marius Victorius, parue dans le *Corpus Christianorum,*" *SE* 11 (1960), 193-211; idem, *Claudii Marii Victorii, Alethia, CCSL,* vol. 128, pp. 117 ff.; G. Jachmann, "Das Problem der Urvariante in der Antike und die Grundlagen der Ausoniuskritik" in *Concordia Decennalis* (Köln, 1944), p. 59; C.B. Kendall and M.H. King, *Bedae Venerabilis Opera, Pars VI. Opera Didascalia I, CCSL,* vol. 123A, p. 63; Laistner, p. 135; Paul Lejay, "Marius Victor. L'Éditeur Morel et le ms. latin 7558 de Paris," *Revue de philologie, de littérature et d'histoire anciennes* (n.s.) 14 (1890), 71-8; Joseph T. Lienhard, "Textual Notes on Paulinus of Nola, *Carm.* 6, 256-330," *VC* 31 (1977), 53-4; Claude Moussy, *Paulin de Pella, Poème d'action de grâces et prière, Sources chrétiennes,* vol. 209, pp. 212 ff.; Sesto Prete, "The Textual Tradition of the Correspondence between Ausonius and Paulinus," *Collectanea Vaticana in Honorem Anselmi M. Card. Albareda* = Studi e testi 220 (1962), pp. 309-30; Reynolds, p. 28.

PARIS, Bibliothèque Nationale, Lat. 8310
s. xiii-xiv; 94 leaves (last unnumbered); 225 x 145 mm.

Contents: On ff. 91v-93v: H2. Preceded by works of Prudentius.
Other information: Seen in person.
Bibliography: Catalogus Codicum, same as above, vol. 4, p. 447.

PARIS, Bibliothèque Nationale, Lat. 8319
s. ix-xii; 89 leaves; 221 x 139 mm.

Contents: On f. 45: Asterius' epigram. Arator, *Historia Apostolica*, et al. on ff. 1-34.
Other information: Miscellany volume consisting of seven different parts.
Bibliography: Beccaria, pp. 316-7; Boas, p. xlviii; Ernst Dümmler in *MGH, PLAC*, vol. 1, p. 442; McKinlay, pp. 17-8; idem, *"Membra Disiecta* of Manuscripts of Arator," *Speculum* 15 (1940), 95-8; *MCLBV*, vol. 2.1, pp. 87-9; Munk Olsen, vol. 2, p. 481; Reynolds, p. 384.

PARIS, Bibliothèque Nationale, Lat. 11347
s. xv-xvi; 246 leaves; 210 x 150 mm.; paper.

Contents: On f. 55r-v: H2. Preceded by poetry of Mantuan (ff. 1r ff.). Followed by works of Raphael Zovenzonius (ff. 56r ff.); Prudentius (ff. 59 ff.); Sebastian Brant (ff. 63v ff.); et al.
Bibliography: Léopold Victor Delisle, "Inventaire des manuscrits conservés à la Bibliothèque Impériale sous les nos. 8823-11503 du fonds latins," *BECh* 24 (1863), 230.

PARIS, Bibliothèque Nationale, Lat. 11550
s. xi (after 1029); 329 leaves; 435 x 325 mm.; S. Germain-des-Prés, Paris.

Contents: Benedictine psalter, etc., with hymnal; on f. 255r-v: *A Solis Ortus Cardine* and *Hostis Herodes*.
Other information: Seen in person.
Bibliography: J.J.G. Alexander, *The Decorated Letter* (New York, 1978), pp. 25 and 30; H. Anglès, *La música a Catalunya fins al segle XIII* (Barcelona, 1935), p. 106; P. Bohigas, "El manuscrit lat. 11550 de la Bibliothèque Nationale," *Estudis Universitaris Catalans* 13 (1928), pp. 235-44; Léopold Victor Delisle, "Inventaire des manuscrits latins de Saint-Germain-des Prés," *BECh* 26 (1865), 186; Yvonne Deslandres, "Les Manuscrits decorés au XIe siècle à Saint-Germain-des-Prés par Ingelard," *Scriptorium* 9 (1955), 3-16; Gamber, vol. 2, p. 586, no. 1622; A. Gastoué, "Musique et musiciens français dans les anciens manuscrits," *Tresors des bibliothèques de France* 5 (1935), 75; Jullien, 127-8; Ph. Lauer, *Les Enluminures romanes des manuscrits de la Bibl. Nat. Paris* (Paris, 1927), pp. 124-6; Leroquais, *Psautiers*, vol. 2, pp. 105-110; Émile Mâle, *L'Art religieux du XIIe siècle en France. Étude sur les origines de l'iconographie du Moyen Âge* (Paris, 1922), pp. 8-9; Mearns, pp. xiv, 1, and 39; Jean-Baptiste Molin, "Les Manuscrits de la

Deprecatio Gelasii," *EL* 90 (1976), 123-4; Charles Niver, "Notes upon an Eleventh-Century Psalter," *Speculum* 3 (1928), 398-401; Ch. Samaran and R. Marichal, *Catalogue des manuscrits en écriture latine portant des indications de date, de lieu ou de copiste*, vol. 3 (Paris, 1974), p. 241; Walpole, p. xxii; André Wilmart, *Precum Libelli Quattuor Aevi Karolini* (Roma, 1940), p. 33.

PARIS, Bibliothèque Nationale, Lat. 13029
s. ix$^{med.}$; 59 leaves; 326 x 240 mm.; written in Brittany; later at Corbie.

Contents: "The Grammar of Smaragdus;" on f. 9v: *accessus* to Sedulius.
Other information: Came to S. Germain-des-Prés in 1638.
Bibliography: Léopold Victor Delisle, "Inventaire des manuscrits latins de Saint-Germain-des-Prés," *BECh* 28 (1867), 549; Glauche, pp. 51-2; Colette Jeudy, "Le *Carmen* 111 d'Alcuin et l'anthologie de Martial du manuscrit 522 (502) de la Bibliothèque Municipale d'Angers" in *Scire Litteras. Forschungen zum mittelalterlichen Geistesleben. Festschrift Bernhard Bischoff zu seinem 80. Geburtstag* = Abhandlungen der Bayerischen Akademie der Wissenschaften, Phil.- hist. Klasse, n. F., 99 (München, 1988), pp. 225-6; Jeudy, "Remi," p. 497; L.W. Jones, "The Scriptorium at Corbie, II. The Script," *Speculum* 22 (1947), 390; B. Löfstedt, L. Holtz, and A. Kibre, *Smaragdus, Liber in Partibus Donati, CCCM,* vol. 68, p. xv; Cora E. Lutz, "One Formula of *Accessus* in Remigius' Works," *Latomus* 19 (1960), 778; Max Manitius, "Zur karolingischen Literatur III. Zu Smaragd von St.-Mihiel," *Neues Archiv* 36 (1911), 60-75; Yves-François Riou, "Quelques aspects de la tradition manuscrite des *Carmina* d'Eugène de Tolède: Du *Liber Catonianus* aux *Auctores octo morales*," *RHT* 2 (1972), 18-25.

PARIS, Bibliothèque Nationale, Lat. 13047
s. viii²; 167 leaves; 272 x 190 mm.; written at Tours; later at Corbie and then at S. Germain-des-Prés, Paris.

Contents: On ff. 115r-122r: PC. 1.17-368. On ff. 161r-163r: H1. Fragment of PC preceded by Ps.-Cyprian, *De Resurrectione* and *De Incarnatione* (ff. 113r ff.). Followed on f. 123r by Augustine, *De Civitate Dei* 18.23.
Other information: "Insular marginal notes" (Ganz) on f. 161r-v. Used by Huemer (π). Seen in person.
Bibliography: Maurice Bévenot, *The Tradition of Manuscripts. A Study*

in the Transmission of St. Cyprian's Treatises (Oxford, 1961), p. 51; Bischoff, *MS*, vol 2, p. 287; *CLA*, vol. 5, p. 37, no. 649; *CSEL*, vol. 10, p. 155; Léopold Victor Delisle, *Le Cabinet des manuscrits*, vol. 2, p. 434, no. 649; idem, "Inventaire," same as above, 550; David Ganz, *Corbie in the Carolingian Renaissance* = Beihefte der Francia 20 (Sigmaringen, 1990), p. 128; G.D. Hobson, "Some Early Bindings and Binders' Tools," *The Library* 19 (1938), 215; Huemer, *De Sedulii*, p. 41; Emil Kroymann, *Quinti Septimi Florentis Tertulliani Opera*, *CSEL*, vol. 70, passim; idem, "Das Tertullianfragment des Codex Parisinus 13047, die sogenannten *Schedae Scoppianae* und die Überlieferung des verlorenen Fuldensis," *RhM* 70 (1915), 358-67; Marcello Marin, "Problemi di ecdotica ciprianea. Per un'edizione critica dello pseudo-ciprianeo *De aleatoribus*," *Vetera Christianorum* 20 (1983), 148-50; H. Omont, "Un manuscrit de Corbie," *Revue de philologie, de littérature et d'histoire anciennes* (n.s.) 4 (1880), 67-8; R. Peiper, *Alcimi Ecdicii Aviti Viennensis Episcopi Opera Quae Supersunt*, *MGH AA*, vol. 6.2, p. lx, n. 85; idem, *Cypriani Galli Poetae Heptateuchos*, *CSEL*, vol. 23, pp. vii-viii; P. Petitmengin, "La Diffusion monastique des oeuvres de Saint Cyprien" in *Sous la règle de Saint Benoît. Structures monastiques et sociétés en France du Moyen Âge à l'époque moderne. Abbaye bénédictine Sainte-Marie de Paris 23-25 Octobre 1980* = Centre de Recherches d'Histoire et de Philologie de la IVe Section de l'École Pratique des Hautes Études V, Hautes études médiévales et modernes 47 (Genève, 1980), p. 411; idem, "Un monument controversé, le *Saint Cyprien* de Baluze et dom Maran (1726)," *RHT* 5 (1975), 100 ff.; Hans von Soden, *Die cyprianische Briefsammlung. Geschichte ihrer Entstehung und Überlieferung* = Texte und Untersuchungen 25 (Leipzig, 1904) p. 3; Hermann Tränkle, *Q.S.F. Tertulliani adversus Iudaeos. Mit Einleitung und kritischem Kommentar* (Wiesbaden, 1964), p. xcv; Jean Vezin, "Les Reliures carolingiennes de cuir à décor estampé de la Bibliothèque Nationale de Paris," *BECh* 128 (1970), 105-6; E. Wölfflin, "Pseudo-Cyprianus (Victor) *De aleatoribus*," *Archiv für lateinische Lexikographie und Grammatik* 5 (1888), 487-99.

PARIS, Bibliothèque Nationale, Lat. 13388
s. ix; 108 leaves; 216 x 166 mm.; written at S. Martin of Tours; later at Corbie and S. Germain-des-Prés, Paris.

Contents: Benedictine collectar; on f. 49r-v: *Hostis Herodes* (to line 52).
Other information: Seen in person.

Bibliography: Léopold Victor Delisle, "Inventaire des manuscrits latins de Saint-Germain-des-Prés," *BECh* 29 (1868), 228; Gamber, vol. 2, p. 613, no. 1698e; Ganz, same as above, p. 65; Gneuss, *Hymnar,* pp. 48-9; Jullien, 106-7; Mearns, pp. xiv and 39; Jean-Baptiste Molin, "Les Manuscrits de la *Deprecatio Gelasii*: Usage privé des psaumes et dévotion aux litanies," *EL* 90 (1976), 113-48, esp. 128-30; E.K. Rand, *A Survey of the Manuscripts of Tours* = Studies in the Script of Tours I (Cambridge, Mass., 1929), vol. 1, p. 169, no. 143A; idem, "Franco-Saxon Ornamentation in a Book of Tours," *Speculum* 4 (1929), 213-5 and pl. 1, 2, and 4; André Wilmart, *Precum Libelli Quattuor Aevi Karolingi* (Roma, 1940), pp. 61-106.

PARIS, Bibliothèque Nationale, Lat. 14193
s. xi-xvi; 164 leaves; 210 x 143 mm.; S. Germain-des-Prés, Paris.

Contents: On ff. 119r-120v: E1 (missing page 10, line 6 ff.). Identified in list of contents as *proemium ... in opus Paschale Juvenci Presbyteri.*
Other information: Volume consists of fragmentary manuscripts dating from the eleventh to the sixteenth centuries.
Bibliography: Martin Camargo, "The English Manuscripts of Bernard of Meung's *Flores Dictaminum,*" *Viator* 12 (1981), 197-219 (esp. 203-4); Delisle, "Inventaire," same as above, 259; Peter Dronke, *Medieval Latin and the Rise of European Love Lyric* (2nd ed.; Oxford, 1968), vol. 2, *Medieval Latin Love-Poetry,* p. 574; B. Hauréau, *Initia Operum Latinorum* (Turnhout; Brepols reprint), vol. 4, p. 352a; idem, *Notices,* vol. 2, pp. 349-62; L. Ott, *Untersuchungen zur theologischen Brief-literatur der Frühscholastik unter besondere Berücksichtigung des Viktoriner-Kreises* = Beiträge zur Geschichte der Philosophie und Theologie des Mittelalters 34 (Münster, 1937), p. 142; L. van Acker, *Petri Pictoris Carmina, CCCM,* vol. 25, pp. xcvii-xcviii; André Wilmart, "Le Florilège de Saint-Gatien. Contribution à l'étude des poèmes d'Hildelbert et de Marbode III," *RB* 48 (1936), 247.

PARIS, Bibliothèque Nationale, Lat. 14758
s. xiii; 96 leaves (numbered 17-112); 360 x 245 mm.; S. Victor, Paris.

Contents: On ff. 17r-19v: PC 5.172-438, H1, H2.   Followed by Arator, *Historia Apostolica* (ff. 19v-35r); the epigrams of Prosper (ff. 35r-43r); Juvencus, *Evangeliorum Libri Quattuor* (ff. 44r-64r); Hilary of Arles, *Metrum in Genesin* (ff. 65r-66r); the cento of Proba (ff. 66r-68r);

Cyprian, *De Sodoma* (ff. 68r-69r); Avitus, *De Spiritalis Historiae Gestis* (ff. 69r-80r); Dracontius, *De Laudibus Dei* (excerpts) (ff. 80r-83v); and Hildebert, *Liber Sacramentorum super Canonem Missae* (ff. 85r-89v). Codex concludes with Matthew of Vendôme, *Liber Regum Metrice* (ff. 91r-112v).

Other information: Originally volume began with works of Prudentius and included all of the *Paschale Carmen*. Seen in person. Microfilm acquired.

Bibliography: *Le Catalogue de la Bibliothèque de l'Abbaye de Saint-Victor de Paris de Claude de Grandrue 1514* (Paris, 1983), pp. 8-9; Léopold Victor Delisle, "Inventaire des manuscrits latins de Saint-Victor conservés à la Bibliothèque Impériale sous les numéros 14232-15175," *BECh* 30 (1869), 46; McKinlay, pp. 21-2; R. Peiper in *CSEL,* vol. 23, p. vi.

PARIS, Bibliothèque Nationale, Lat. 17188
s. xviii; 367 leaves; 244 x 187 mm.; Notre-Dame, Paris; paper.

Contents: On ff. 283-285: E1 (preceded by dedicatory preface to Proba's cento). Preceded by Hrabanus Maurus, *In Jesu Nave* (ff. 216 ff.) and *De Sacramentis Divinis* (ff. 263 ff.). Followed by *Wicbodi Quaestiones in Octateuchum* (ff. 287 ff.).

Bibliography: Léopold Victor Delisle, "Inventaire des manuscrits latins de Notre Dame et d'autres fonds conservés à la Bibliothèque Nationale sous les numeros 16719-18613," *BECh* 31 (1870), 494.

PARIS, Bibliothèque Nationale, Lat. 18104
s. xii$^{ex.}$ (ff. 136-227); 227 leaves (s. ix-xii); 192 x 147 mm.; written in northern France; prov. Notre-Dame.

Contents: On f. 194v: fragment of E1 (Huemer's page 4, lines 5-6) and H1 (lines 43-4). Preceded by glosses on Boethius and followed by excerpts from Cicero, *Tusculan Disputations* and *De Natura Deorum* (f. 195r).

Other information: Seen in person.

Bibliography: Beeson, pp. 40, 96, and 116; Delisle, "Inventaire ... Notre-Dame," same as above, 541; P. Jal, *Florus. Oeuvres,* vol. 1 (Paris, 1967), p. cxxii; Enrica Malcovati, "Studi su Floro," *Athenaeum* (n.s.) 15 (1937), 76; Tadeusz Maslowski and Richard H. Rouse, "Twelfth-Century Extracts from Cicero's *Pro Archia* and *Pro Cluentio* in Paris B.N. Ms. Lat. 18104," *Italia medioevale e umanistica* 22

(1979), 97-122; Munk Olsen, vol. 2, pp. 865-6; idem, "Les Classiques latins dans les florilèges médiévaux antérieurs au XIIIe siècle I," *RHT* 9 (1979), 112-4; Reynolds, pp. 61, 76, 86, 90-1, 98, 114, 160, and 165-6; R.H. Rouse and M.A. Rouse, "The Medieval Circulation of Cicero's *Posterior Academics* and the *De Finibus Bonorum et Malorum*" in *Medieval Scribes, Manuscripts and Libraries. Essays Presented to N.R. Ker*, ed. M.B. Parkes and Andrew G. Watson (London, 1978), pp. 345-8, 351, and 366-7; R.H. Rouse, "*Florilegia* and Latin Classical Authors in Twelfth- and Thirteenth-Century Orléans," *Viator* 10 (1979), 131-60.

PARIS, Bibliothèque Nationale, Nouv. Acq. Lat. 1235
s. xii*in.*; 262 leaves; 280 x 185 mm.; Nevers.

Contents: Gradual, etc., with hymnal (ff. 147r-177v); includes *A Solis Ortus Cardine* and *Hostis Herodes* on ff. 151r-152v.
Other information: Seen in person.
Bibliography: Michel Huglo, et al., *Fonti e paleografia del canto ambrosiano* = Archivio ambrosiano 7 (Milano, 1956), pp. 83 and 94; Michel Huglo, "Un nouveau prosaire nivernais," *EL* 71 (1957), 28-9; Mearns, pp. xv, 1, and 39; B. Opfermann, "*Litania Italica.* Ein Beitrag zur Litaneigeschichte," *EL* 72 (1958), 306-19, esp. 317; E.J. Reier, "The Introit Trope Repertory at Nevers," Ph.D. Diss., Berkeley, 1981, passim; Stäblein, pp. 69-108 and 528-49.

PARIS, Bibliothèque de Sainte-Geneviève, 1186
s. x-xii; 224 leaves; 232 x 191 mm.; S. Denis, Paris.

Contents: Benedictine psalter, with hymns on ff. 196-218 (s. xi); *A Solis Ortus Cardine* and *Hostis Herodes* on f. 205v and f. 206v respectively.
Bibliography: Solange Corbin, *Répertoire de manuscrits médiévaux contenant des notations musicales I. Bibliothèque Sainte-Geneviève in Paris* (by M. Bernard) in École Pratique des Hautes-Études, Sorbonne, IVe Section. Sciences historiques et philosophiques (Paris, 1965), p. 37; Ch. Kohler, *Catalogue des manuscrits de la Bibliothèque Sainte-Geneviève*, in *Catalogue général des manuscrits des bibliothèques publiques de France. Paris* (Paris, 1893-8), vol. 1 (1893), pp. 548-53; Jullien, 126-7; Leroquais, *Psautiers*, vol. 2, pp. 148-52, no. 378; Mearns, pp. xv, 1, and 39; Carl-Allan Moberg, *Die liturgischen Hymnen in Schweden: Beiträge zur Liturgie- und Musikgeschichte des Mittelalters und der Reformationszeit* (Uppsala, 1947), vol. 1, p. 63.

PERPIGNAN, Bibliothèque Municipale, 1 (41)
s. xii²; 155 leaves; 313 x 231 mm.

Contents: "Perpignan Gospels;" on f. 111v: PC 1.358.
Bibliography: A. Boinet, "Notice sur un Evangéliaire de la Bibliothèque de Perpignan," *Congrès archéologique de France, LXXIIIe Session* (1907), pp. 534-51; *Cat. gen. octavo,* vol. 13, pp. 79-81; C.R. Dodwell, *The Pictorial Arts of the West 800-1200* (New Haven and London, 1993), pp. 225-8.

PHILADELPHIA, University of Pennsylvania Library, Lat. 132
s. xvᵉˣ·; 86 leaves; 210 x 150 mm.; written in Germany; paper.

Contents: Collection of hymns and prayers; includes H2 with German translation.
Other information: *Ex dono R.D. Jo. Heussii ... 1603.* Microfilm copy acquired.
Bibliography: Nikolaus Henkel, *Deutsche Übersetzungen lateinischer Schultexte. Ihre Verbreitung und Funktion im Mittelalter und in der frühen Neuzeit* = Münchener Texte und Untersuchungen zur deutschen Literatur des Mittelalters 90 (München, 1988), p. 264; Norman P. Zacour and Rudolf Hirsch, *Catalogue of Manuscripts in the Libraries of the University of Pennsylvania to 1800* (Philadelphia, 1965), p. 30.

PRAHA, Národní Knihovna, VI. G. 3a
s. xiv; 256 leaves; 178 x 130 mm.; S. Georg.

Contents: On ff. 36v-37r: *A Solis Ortus Cardine* (first stanza only) [as in Chev. 31].
Bibliography: Stäblein, p. 337.

RIPON, Cathedral Library
s. xi; written in England.

Contents: Fragment of hymnal (bifolium); contains part of *A Solis Ortus Cardine,* along with Old English glosses.
Bibliography: Gneuss, *Hymnar,* pp. 103 and 122; Ker, *Cat.* p. 443.

ROMA, Biblioteca Casanatense, 1574 (anc. C. IV. 1)
s. xii; 202 leaves; 250 x 155 mm.

Contents: Hymns on ff. 129v-147r include *A Solis Ortus Cardine* (f. 130r-v) and *Hostis Herodes* (f. 131v).
Bibliography: Stäblein, pp. 407-435 and 606-609.

ROMA, Biblioteca Casanatense, 1907 (anc. B. II. 1)
s. xii[in.]; 262 leaves; 385 x 220 mm.; Monte Amiata (near Siena).

Contents: Plenary missal bound with breviary; includes *A Solis Ortus Cardine* (f. 27v) and *Hostis Herodes* (f. 33r).
Bibliography: Adalbert Ebner, *Quellen und Forschungen zur Geschichte und Kunstgeschichte des Missale Romanum im Mittelalter. Iter Italicum* (Freiburg i. Br., 1896), pp. 162-6; Gamber, vol. 2, p. 536, no. 1440; Edward B. Garrison, *Studies in the History of Medieval Italian Painting,* vol. 3 (Firenze, 1957-8), pp. 1107-8; H.J. Graf, *Palmenweihe und Palmenprozession in der lateinischen Liturgie* = Veröffentlichungen des Missionspriestseminars St. Augustin 5 (Sieburg, 1959), p. ix; Réginald Grégoire, "Repertorium Liturgicum Italicum," *Studi medievali* (3. ser.) 9 (1968), 581 and 585; René-Jean Hesbert, "L'*Antiphonale Missarum* de l'ancien rite béneventain," *EL* 52 (1938), 49; S. Marosszeki, *Les Origines du chant cistercien* = Analecta Sacri Ordinis Cisterciensis 8 (Roma, 1952), 98-9; Mearns, pp. xviii, 1, and 39; Guy Oury, *"Psalmum dicere cum alleluia,"* *EL* 79 (1965), 100, n. 12; *Paléographie musicale. Les Principaux manuscrits de chant grégorien, ambrosien, mozarabe, gallican, publiés en facsimilés phototypiques par les Bénédictins de Solesmes* (Tournai, 1889 ff.), vol. 2, pl. 7; Armando Petrucci, "Censimento dei codici dei secoli XI-XII," *Studi medievali* (3. ser.) 9.2 (1968), 1146-7 [entry prepared by Maria Clara Di Franco]; Pierre Salmon, *L'Office divin au Moyen Âge. Histoire de la formation du bréviaire du IXe au XVIe siècle* = Lex Orandi 43 (Paris, 1967), pp. 20, 64, 105, 107, 109-10, and 119; S.J.P. van Dijk and J. Hazelden Walker, *The Origins of the Modern Roman Liturgy* (London, 1960), pp. 135-6 and 531.

ROMA, Biblioteca Corsiniana (Accademia Nazionale dei Lincei), Rossi 228 (36. D. 25)
s. xv[med.]; 59 leaves; 220 x 160 mm.; paper.

Contents: On f. 5r: *Imploratio ad piissimam Virginem Mariam*=PC 2. 63 ff.
Bibliography: Armando Petrucci, *Catalogo sommario dei manoscritti del Fondo Rossi. Sezione Corsiniana* = Indici e sussidi bibliografici della

biblioteca 10 (Roma, 1977), pp. 110-11.

ROMA, Biblioteca Nazionale Centrale, Vittorio Emmanuele II 175 (Farfa 4)
s. xi$^{ex.}$; 144 leaves; 178 x 106 mm.; Farfa (in Umbria).

Contents: Benedictine psalter, etc.; hymns include *A Solis Ortu [sic] Cardine* (f. 101v) and *Hostis Herodes* (f. 103v).
Bibliography: Giorgio Brugnoli, "Catalogus Codicum Farfensium," *Benedictina* 6 (1952), 291-7; Gneuss, *Hymnar,* p. 72; Jullien, 116; Mearns, pp. xviii, 1, and 39.

ROMA, Biblioteca Vallicelliana, B. 79
s. xi$^{ex.}$; 218 leaves; 145 x 95 mm.; S. Eutizio, Valcastoriana.

Contents: Benedictine breviary; includes *A Solis Ortus Cardine* (ff. 59r-60r) and *Hostis Herodes* (ff. 67v-68r).
Other information: "Certainly made for the Ravenna-Rimini region," according to Garrison. Seen in person.
Bibliography: Edward B. Garrison, *Studies in the History of Medieval Italian Painting,* vol. 4 (Firenze, 1960-2), p. 164; Lokrantz, pp. 25 and 52; Mearns, pp. xix, 1, and 39; Armando Petrucci, "Censimento dei codici dei secoli X-XII," *Studi medievali* (3. ser.) 11.2 (1970), 1036 [entry prepared by Lidia Avitabile]; Pierre Salmon, *L'Office divin au Moyen Âge. Histoire de la formation du bréviaire du IXe au XVIe siècle* = Lex Orandi 43 (Paris, 1967), pp. 19, 57, 105, 107, 111, and 183; S.J.P. van Dijk and J. Hazelden Walker, *The Origins of the Modern Roman Liturgy* (London, 1960), p. 540.

ROMA, Biblioteca Vallicelliana, C. 67
s. xii$^{med.}$ (ff. 93-124); 259 leaves (s. xii-xv); 188 x 130 mm.; written in Italy.

Contents: Florilegium on ff. 93r-113v includes excerpts from the works of Sedulius, Prudentius, Arator, and Prosper on ff. 111v-112v.
Bibliography: Munk Olsen, vol. 2, p. 867; idem, "Les Classiques latins dans les florilèges médiévaux antérieurs au XIIIe siècle I," *RHT* 9 (1979), 70; Armando Petrucci, "Censimento dei codici dei secoli X-XII," *Studi medievali* (3. ser.) 11.2 (1970), 1049-50 [entry prepared by Maria Clara Di Franco].

ROUEN, Bibliothèque Municipale, 56 (A. 347)
s. xii (1180-90); 218 leaves; 270 x 188 mm.; Jumièges.

Contents: Hymnal on ff. 182-218 has "practically the same hymns" as
Rouen, Bib. Mun., 57 (see below).
Bibliography: François Avril, *Manuscrits normands XI-XIIeme siècles
(Catal. exposition, Musée des Beaux-Arts)* (Rouen, 1975), p. 80, no. 90;
L.M. Ayres, "A Miniature from Jumièges and Trends in Manuscript
Illumination around 1200" in *Intuition und Kunstwissenschaft. Festschrift
für Hans Swarzenski* (Berlin, 1973), pp. 117-8; *Cat. gen. octavo,* vol. 1,
p. 16; Gneuss, *Hymnar,* p. 82; Leroquais, *Psautiers,* vol. 2, pp. 183-5
[s. xiii¹]; Mearns, pp. xv, 1, and 39; Geneviève Nortier, *Les Biblio-
thèques médiévales des abbayes bénédictines de Normandie* (Caen, 1966),
p. 163; C. Simonnet, *Six siècles d'enluminures (du Xe au XVIe siècle)*
(Rouen, 1973), nos. 11-12.

ROUEN, Bibliothèque Municipale, 57 (A. 431)
s. xii^ex.; 246 leaves; 235 x 168 mm.; Jumièges.

Contents: Benedictine psalter, etc.; hymns on ff. 201 ff. include *A Solis
Ortus Cardine* and *Hostis Herodes.*
Bibliography: *Cat. gen. octavo,* vol. 1, p. 16; Leroquais, *Psautiers,*
vol. 2, p. 185; Mearns, pp. xv, 1, and 39; Nortier, same as above, p.
163.

ROUEN, Bibliothèque Municipale, 231 (A. 44)
s. xi-xii; 210 leaves; 180 x 110 mm.; S. Augustine's, Canterbury; later
at Jumièges.

Contents: Psalter, etc.; hymnal on ff. 149r-197r includes *A Solis Ortus
Cardine* (f. 160v) and *Hostis Herodes* (f. 162r).
Bibliography: Avril, *Manuscrits,* same as above, no. 85; *Cat. gen.
octavo,* vol. 1, pp. 45-6; Gneuss, *Hymnar,* p. 82, n. 18; Jullien, 139-40;
Leroquais, *Psautiers,* vol. 2, pp. 194-6; Mearns, pp. xv, 1, and 39;
Nortier, same as above, pp. 146, n. 29, and 165.

ROUEN, Bibliothèque Municipale, 1382 (U. 109)
s. xi; 199 leaves; 266 x 180 mm.; Jumièges.

Contents: Saints' lives, et al.; on f. 199v: *Hostis Herodes.*
Bibliography: Michel Andrieu, *Les Ordines Romani du haut Moyen*

Âge, vol. 1: *Les Manuscrits* (Louvain, 1931; repr. 1965), p. 325; "Catalogus Codicum Hagiographicorum Latinorum Bibliothecae Publicae Rotomagensis," *Analecta Bollandiana* 23 (1906), 208-9; *Cat. gen. octavo*, vol. 1, pp. 355-6; Gneuss, "List," no. 925; Bruno Krusch, "Reise nach Frankreich im Frühjahr und Sommer 1892," *Neues Archiv* 18 (1893), 613 [s. xii]; Nortier, same as above, p. 171.

SAINT PETERSBURG, Publichnaia Biblioteka im. M. E. Saltykova Shchedrina, Lat. Q. II. 5
s. ix; 56 leaves; 250 x 190 mm.; written at Corbie; later at Reims.

Contents: On ff. 43v-44r: PC 1.248-257. Preceded by various ecclesiastical statutes (ff. 1-43). Followed by Dungalus Hibernicus, *Poema de Hildoardo Episcopo*, et al.
Bibliography: Elena Viktorovna Bernadskaia, Tamara Pavlovna Voronova, and Svetlana Olegovna Vialova, *Latinskie rukopisi V-XII vekov Gosudarstvennoi Publichnoi Biblioteki im. M. E. Saltykova-Shchedrina: Kratkoe opisanie dlia svodnogo kataloga rukopisei, Khraniashchikhsia v SSSR, part 1* (Leningrad, 1983), p. 26; Karl Gillert, "Lateinische Handschriften in St. Petersburg," *Neues Archiv* 6 (1881), 499; Antonio Staerk, *Les Manuscrits latins du Ve au XIIIe siècle conservés à la Bibliothèque Impériale de Saint-Pétersbourg* (Saint Petersburg, 1910), vol. 1, pp. 193 ff.

SALISBURY, Library of the Cathedral Church, MS 134
s. x/xi; written in England; prov. Salisbury Cathedral.

Contents: On ff. 1-53: Remigius' commentary on Sedulius.
Bibliography: A Catalogue of the Library of the Cathedral Church of Salisbury (London, 1880); Esposito, 169; Gneuss, "List," no. 735; Jeudy, "Remi," p. 497; Ker, *Med.*, p. 175; idem, "Salisbury Cathedral Manuscripts and Patrick Young's Catalogue," *The Wiltshire Archaeological and Natural History Magazine* 53 (1949-50), 167, n. 1; Lapidge, "Latin Texts," p. 114 and note 88.

SALZBURG, Stiftsbibliothek St. Peter (Erzabtei), A. V. 41
s. xiii²; 54 leaves; 190 x 120 mm.

Contents: On ff. 1r-53v: a *florilegium* which includes excerpts from Sedulius (ff. 30v-36r). Preceded by excerpts from works of Ovid (ff. 1r-6r); Horace (ff. 6r-19v); Virgil (ff. 19v-23r); Lucan (ff. 23r-24v);

Persius (ff. 24v-25r); Juvencus (f. 25r-v); and Boethius (ff. 25v-30v). Followed by excerpts from works of Prudentius (ff. 36r-43v); Arator (ff. 43v-45r); Alcimus Avitus (45r-48v); Venantius Fortunatus (ff. 48v-53v); and Sulpicius Severus (f. 53v).

Bibliography: Günter Glauche, "Einige Bemerkungen zum 'Florileg von Heiligenkreuz,'" *Festschrift Bernhard Bischoff zu seinem 65. Geburtstag* (Stuttgart, 1971), pp. 295-306; Handwritten inventory of the Stiftsbibliothek (copy in Bayerische Staatsbibliothek), vol. 1, no page number; Johannes Huemer, "Iter Austriacum I," *WS* 9 (1887), 84.

SANKT GALLEN, Stiftsbibliothek, 26

s. xiv; 118 pages; octavo.

Contents: Psalter with canticles and hymns; on p. 93: *A Solis Ortus Cardine.*

Bibliography: Gustav Scherrer, *Verzeichniss der Handschriften der Stiftsbibliothek von St. Gallen* (Halle, 1875), p. 14.

SANKT GALLEN, Stiftsbibliothek, 44

s. viii-ix; 368 pages; 300 x 217 mm.

Contents: On p. 182: PC 1.17-23 (lines 20 and 22 are missing). Preceded by the Old Testament prophets (major and minor) based on a pre-Alcuin text of the Vulgate (pp. 1-181).

Other information: Two codices joined together. Pages 1-184 written at the command of John II, bishop of Konstanz (760-781). Seen in person.

Bibliography: Beccaria, pp. 364-8; Beeson, p. 106; Bischoff, "FHH," 312; Bruckner, vol. 2, p. 58; *CLA,* vol. 7, p. 19, no. 899; Munk Olsen, vol. 2, pp. 482-3; Reynolds, p. xxx; Scherrer, *Verzeichniss,* same as above, pp. 19-20.

SANKT GALLEN, Stiftsbibliothek, 120

s. viii-ix; 230 pages; 280 x 157-162 mm.; S. Gallen.

Contents: On p. 1: PC 3.1-14 (s. x-xi). Jerome's commentary on Daniel on pp. 3-226.

Other information: Seen in person.

Bibliography: Bruckner, vol. 2, p. 62; *CLA,* vol. 7, p. 22, no. 908; Scherrer, *Verzeichniss,* same as above, p. 43.

SANKT GALLEN, Stiftsbibliothek, 292
s. ix-x; 210 pages; 152 x 115 mm.; S. Gallen.

Contents: Glossary (Latin and German); includes glosses on Sedulius (p. 191).
Bibliography: Bergmann, p. 29; Bruckner, vol. 3, p. 93; Scherrer, *Verzeichniss,* same as above, p. 108; Steinmeyer & Sievers, vol. 2, p. 619 and vol. 4, pp. 447-8.

SANKT GALLEN, Stiftsbibliothek, 403
s. xii-xiv; 638 pages; quarto; Disentis.

Contents: Calendar, psalter, etc; hymns (pp. 1-110) include *A Solis Ortus Cardine* (p. 97) and *Hostis Herodes* (p. 98).
Bibliography: Bruckner, vol. 1, p. 91; Iso Müller, "Ein Elsässisch-Westschweizerisches Kalendar im Cod. Sang. 403 aus dem 12. Jahrhundert," *Zeitschrift für schweizerische Kirchengeschichte* 63 (1969), 332-52; idem, "Lektionar und Homiliar im hochmittelalterlichen Brevier von Disentis (Cod. Sang. 403)," *Archiv für Liturgiewissenschaft* 11 (1969), 77-164; Scherrer, *Verzeichniss,* same as above, p. 136.

SANKT GALLEN, Stiftsbibliothek, 410
s. xiv; 286 pages; quarto; paper.

Contents: Collectae, antiphonae, hymni; on p. 227: *A Solis Ortus Cardine.*
Bibliography: Scherrer, *Verzeichniss,* same as above, p. 137.

SANKT GALLEN, Stiftsbibliothek, 413
s. xi$^{2/4}$; 700 pages (pp. 1-2 missing); 258 x 175 mm.; S. Gallen.

Contents: Benedictine breviary or *liber officialis* (Advent to Easter) on pp. 23 ff.; hymns include *A Solis Ortus Cardine* and *Hostis Herodes* (p. 177).
Bibliography: Bruckner, vol. 3, p. 103; Gamber, vol. 2, p. 610, no. 1688; Pierre-Marie Gy, "Les Premiers bréviaires de Saint-Gall (deuxième quart du XIe s.)" in *Liturgie: Gestalt und Vollzug* (a Festschrift for Josef Pascher), ed. W. Dürig (München, 1963), pp. 104-10; Jullien, 153; Mearns, pp. xvi, 1, and 39; Scherrer, *Verzeichniss,* same as above, pp. 137-8.

SANKT GALLEN, Stiftsbibliothek, 414
s. xi²/⁴; 666 pages; 270 x 200 mm.; S. Gallen.

Contents: Breviary *(liber officialis)* (Advent to Easter); hymns beginning on p. 21 include *A Solis Ortus Cardine* (p. 24) and *Hostis Herodes* (p. 31).
Bibliography: Bruckner, vol. 3, p. 103; Gamber, vol. 2, pp. 609-10, no. 1688; Gy, same as above; Jullien, 123-4; Scherrer, *Verzeichniss,* same as above, p. 138.

SANKT GALLEN, Stiftsbibliothek, 418
s. xv; 288 pages (two codices in one volume); folio; paper.

Contents: *Officia. Lectiones cum hymnis;* includes *A Solis Ortus Cardine* (p. 114) and *Hostis Herodes* (p. 116).
Bibliography: Scherrer, *Verzeichniss,* same as above, pp. 138-9.

SANKT GALLEN, Stiftsbibliothek, 438
s. xv; 193 leaves; folio.

Contents: *Psalmi, antiphonae, hymni, sequentiae;* includes *A Solis Ortus Cardine* (f. 137) and *Hostis Herodes* (f. 139).
Bibliography: Scherrer, *Verzeichniss,* same as above, p. 143.

SANKT GALLEN, Stiftsbibliothek, 440
s. xv; unpaginated; folio.

Contents: Psalter, etc.; hymns include *A Solis Ortus Cardine* and *Hostis Herodes.*
Bibliography: Scherrer, *Verzeichniss,* same as above, p. 143.

SANKT GALLEN, Stiftsbibliothek, 503k
s. xiv; 289 leaves; octavo.

Contents: Breviary; includes *Hostis Herodes.*
Bibliography: Scherrer, *Verzeichniss,* same as above, p. 159.

SANKT GALLEN, Stiftsbibliothek, 526
s. xv; 264 pages; small folio; S. Gallen.

Contents: *Liber choralis* (second part of the S. Gallen Breviary);

includes *A Solis Ortus Cardine* (p. 146).
Bibliography: Scherrer, *Verzeichniss*, same as above, p. 161.

SANKT GALLEN, Stiftsbibliothek, 527
s. xv; 282 pages; folio; S. Gallen.

Contents: Psalter, etc.; includes *A Solis Ortus Cardine* (p. 260) and *Hostis Herodes* (p. 261).
Bibliography: Scherrer, *Verzeichniss*, same as above, p. 162.

SANKT GALLEN, Stiftsbibliothek, 528
s. xiv-xv; 332 pages; folio.

Contents: Psalter, etc.; includes *A Solis Ortus Cardine* (p. 262).
Bibliography: Scherrer, *Verzeichniss*, same as above, p. 162.

SANKT GALLEN, Stiftsbibliothek, 529
s. xv; 258 pages; folio.

Contents: *Liber choralis;* includes *A Solis Ortus Cardine* (p. 147) and *Hostis Herodes* (p. 149).
Bibliography: Scherrer, *Verzeichniss*, same as above, p. 162.

SANKT GALLEN, Stiftsbibliothek, 544
s. xvi (c. 1560); 149 leaves; large folio.

Contents: Psalter, etc.; includes *A Solis Ortus Cardine* (f. 133).
Bibliography: Scherrer, *Verzeichniss*, same as above, p. 163.

SANKT GALLEN, Stiftsbibliothek, 870
s. ix^2; 328 pages; 172 x 136 mm.; S. Gallen.

Contents: Excerpt from Sedulius included in a *florilegium* on pp. 6-31, which also contains lines from the works of Arator, Claudian, Ennius, Eucheria, Horace, Isidore, Juvenal, Juvencus, Lactantius, Lucan, Lucretius, Martial, Martianus Capella, Ovid, Persius, Priscian, Prudentius, Serenus, Venantius Fortunatus, and Virgil.
Bibliography: Bruckner, vol. 3, pp. 120-1; Wendell V. Clausen, *A. Persi Flacci, Saturarum Liber. Accedit Vita* (Oxford, 1956), p. xi; McKinlay, pp. 62-3; Munk Olsen, vol. 1, p. 587; idem, "Les Classiques latins dans les florilèges médiévaux antérieurs au XIIIe siècle I," *RHT* 9

(1979), 73-4; idem, "Vergil i middelalderen. Vergil-håndskrifter og Vergil-florilegier fra det 9. til begyndelsen af det 13. århundrede," *MT* 32-3 (1978), 93; Reynolds, pp. 201-2, 220, 241, 263, 293-4, and 382; Sanford, 298; Scherrer, *Verzeichniss*, same as above, p. 301; Chr. Stephan, "Das prosodische Florilegium der S. Gallener Handschrift nr. 870 und sein Werth für die Iuvenalkritik," *RhM* 40 (1885), 263-82.

SANKT GALLEN, Stiftsbibliothek, 1395
s. v-xiii; 473 pages; quarto.

Contents: On pp. 458-465: PC 1.362 to 2.136 (s. x).
Other information: Volume of fragments dating from the fifth to the thirteenth century. Seen in person. Microfilm acquired.
Bibliography: *CLA*, vol. 10, p. 4, no. 984; Pellegrin, p. 346; Scherrer, *Verzeichniss*, same as above, pp. 461-4.

STUTTGART, Württembergische Landesbibliothek, HB. II. 40
s. ix$^{1/3}$; 197 leaves; 340 x 260 mm.; written at Tours; later at Weingarten.

Contents: Gospel book; on ff. 16v, 63v, 95v, 146v: PC 1.355, 356, 357, and 358 respectively.
Other information: Written at Abbey of S. Martin in Tours under Abbot Fridugisus (807-34).
Bibliography: Albert Boeckler, *Abendländische Miniaturen bis zum Ausgang der romanischen Zeit* = Tabulae in Usum Scholarum 10 (Berlin and Leipzig, 1930), pp. 31-4; Helmut Boese, *Codices Biblici (HB II.1-60). Codices Dogmatici et Polemici (HB III. 1-59). Codices Hermeneutici (HB IV.1-36)*, vol. 2.1 in *Die Handschriften der ehemaligen Hofbibliothek Stuttgart*, zweite Reihe, *Die Handschriften der Württembergischen Landesbibliothek Stuttgart* (Wiesbaden, 1975), pp. 44-6; E.K. Rand, *A Survey of the Manuscripts of Tours 1* = Studies in the Script of Tours I (Cambridge, Mass., 1929), p. 149, no. 103.

TOLEDO, Archivo y Biblioteca Capitular, 14. 23
s. xi (1070); 55 leaves; 200 x 160 mm.

Contents: Fragment of PC. Preceded by Elipandus, *Epistulae* and Justus Urgellensis, *Explicatio Mystica in Canticum Canticorum*.
Bibliography: Manuel C. Díaz y Díaz, *Códices visigóticos en la monarquía leonesa* = Fuentes y estudios de historia leonesa 31 (Leon,

1983), p. 49; P. Ewald, *Reise nach Spanien* (Hannover, 1881), p. 360; Agustín Millares Carlo, *Los códices visigóticos de la Catedral Toledana. Cuestiones cronológicas y de procedencia* = Discusos leídos en la recepción de la Academia de la Historia (Madrid, 1935), pp. 24-5; idem, "Manuscritos visigóticos. Notas bibliográficas," *Hispania Sacra* 14 (1961), 410; idem, *Nuevos estudios de paleografía española* (Mexico City, 1941), pp. 58-9; P.A.C. Vega, *Quorumdam Veterum Commentariorum in Cantica Canticorum Antiqua Versio Latina* (Escorial, 1934); Z. García Villada, *Paleografía española*, vol. 1 (Madrid, 1923), p. 124.

TORINO, Biblioteca Nazionale Universitaria, G. V. 38 (1106)
s. x$^{in.}$; 130 leaves; 200 x 140 mm.; Bobbio.

Contents: *Hymni vel cantica secundum regulam sancti Benedicti* on ff. 46r-76v; includes *Hostis Herodes* (ff. 69v-70r).
Bibliography: R. Amiet, "Catalogue des livres liturgiques manuscrits et imprimés conservés dans les bibliothèques et les archives de Turin," *Bollettino storico-bibliografico subalpino* 77 (1979), 630; Wilhelm Gundlach, "Über die Columban-Briefe," *Neues Archiv* 15.2 (1890), 500; Jullien, 95; J. LaPorte, *Le Pénitentiel de saint Columban* = Monumenta Christiana Selecta 4 (Tournai, Paris, Roma, and New York, 1958), pp. 9-10, 12-14, and 91-104; Mazzatinti, vol. 28, p. 114; Mearns, pp. xviii and 39; Costanza Segre Montel, *I manoscritti miniati della Biblioteca Nazionale di Torino*, vol. 1 (Torino, 1980), pp. 127-8; O. Seebass, "Über die beiden Columba-Handschriften der Nationalbibliothek in Turin," *Neues Archiv* 21.2 (1896), 739-46; idem, "Über die Handschriften der Sermonen und Briefe Columbas von Luxeuil," *Neues Archiv* 17.2 (1892), 245-59.

TRIER, Bistumsarchiv, Abt. 95. 16
s. xii-xiii; 187 leaves; 160 x 110 mm.; S. Michael, Hildesheim.

Contents: On ff. 116v-148v: *Glossae Sedulii*. Followed by glosses on Prudentius (ff. 148v-155v).
Other information: Microfilm acquired.
Bibliography: H. Sauerland, *Catalogus Descriptivus Codicum Manuscriptorum Ecclesiae Cathedralis Treverensis* (Trier, 1890-1), vol. 1, pp. 23 ff.

TRIER, Stadtbibliothek, 592/1578
s. ix; 148 leaves; 192 x 147 mm.; S. Maximin, Trier.

Contents: *Hymni de tempore et de sanctis* on ff. 123-129; includes portions of H2.

Bibliography: Gneuss, *Hymnar,* pp. 49-50; Jullien, 101-2; Max Keuffer, *Die ascetischen Handschriften der Stadtbibliothek zu Trier,* in *Beschreibendes Verzeichnis der Handschriften der Stadtbibliothek zu Trier,* 5.1 (Trier, 1900), pp. 46-8; Walpole, p. xxvii.

TROYES, Bibliothèque Municipale, 215

s. xii[ex.]; 135 leaves; 375 x 255 cm,; written in northern France; prov. Clairvaux.

Contents: Miscellany volume containing *"Florilegium Trecense;"* 44°: excerpt from PC beginning with 2.214. Followed by elegies of Maximianus (as in Douai, Bib. Mun., 285).

Bibliography: *Cat. gen. quarto,* vol. 2, pp. 101-13; Francesco Giancotti, *Ricerche sulla tradizione manoscritta delle sentenze di Publilio Siro* = Biblioteca di cultura contemporanea 79 (Messina and Firenze, 1963), pp. 129-30 and 178; J.N. Hillgarth, "El *Prognosticum futuri saeculi* de San Julián de Toledo," *AST* 30 (1958), 43; Jean Leclercq, *Textes et manuscrits cisterciens dans diverses bibliothèques* = Analecta Sacri Ordinis Cisterciensis 12 (Roma, 1956), 296-304; Munk Olsen, vol. 2, pp. 870-1; idem, "Les Classiques latins dans les florilèges médiévaux antérieurs au XIIIe siècle I," *RHT* 9 (1979), 87-9; idem, "Les Classiques latins dans les florilèges médiévaux antérieurs au XIIIe siècle II," *RHT* 10 (1980), 145-6; idem, "Note sur quelques préfaces de florilèges latins du XIIe siècle," *Revue romane* 8 (1973), 191; idem, "The Cistercians and Classical Culture," *Cahiers de l'Institut du Moyen-Âge Grec et Latin* 47 (1984), 64-102, esp. 92; Jan Öberg, *Serlon de Wilton, Poèmes latins. Texte critique avec une introduction et des tables* = Acta Universitatis Stockholmiensis. Studia Latina Stockholmiensia 14 (Stockholm, Göteborg, Uppsala, 1965), pp. 31-2; Reynolds, pp. xxxviii and 377; idem, *The Medieval Tradition of Seneca's Letters* (Oxford, 1965), p. 106, n. 4; L. van Acker, *Petri Pictoris Carmina, CCCM,* vol. 25, p. xciv.

TROYES, Bibliothèque Municipale, 1524

s. xv; 140 leaves; quarto; Clairvaux; paper.

Contents: Miscellany volume; section 7: E1. Followed by subscription; *"quelques vers en honneur de Sedulius;"* and biographical notice *(In Achaia libros suos scripsit...).*

Bibliography: Cat. gen. quarto, vol. 2, pp. 638-9.

TROYES, Bibliothèque Municipale, 1748
s. xiii; 172 leaves; quarto; Clairvaux.

Contents: Miscellany volume, the first section of which consists of hymns, prayers, etc.; on f. 1: *Hostis Herodes.*
Bibliography: Cat. gen. quarto, vol. 2, pp. 735-6.

UPPSALA, Universitetsbiblioteket (Carolina), C. 912
s. xii; 38 leaves; 208 x 136 mm.; written in France or England.

Contents: On f. 36v: excerpts from PC (along with excerpts from Peter Comestor, *Historia Scholastica*). Preceded by *Excerptiones Prisciani* (ff. 1r-32v) and Ps.-Priscian, *De Accentibus* (ff. 32v-35v). Followed by hymn beginning *Sanctarum virginum pangamus* (f. 37r-v); extracts from works of Gregory and Ambrose (f. 38r-v); and a brief geneology of the Carolingian kings up to Charlemagne (f. 38v).
Bibliography: Passalacqua, pp. 294-5; Élisabeth Pellegrin, "Manuscrits d'auteurs latins de l'époque classique conservés dans les bibliothèques publiques de Suède," *BIRHT* 4 (1955), 15-16.

VATICANO (Città del), Biblioteca Apostolica Vaticana, Ottob. Lat. 145
s. xi (c. 1075); 163 leaves; 216 x 135 mm.; S. Sophia, Benevento.

Contents: "*Orationale Cassinense;*" includes *A Solis Ortus Cardine* and *Hostis Herodes.*
Bibliography: Beneventan, vol. 2, p. 165; Gamber, vol. 1, p. 248, no. 465a; Klaus Gamber and Sieghild Rehle, *Manuale Casinense (Cod. Ottob. lat. 145)* = Textus Patristici et Liturgici 13 (Regensburg, 1977); Edward B. Garrison, "Random Notes on Early Italian Manuscripts II," *La bibliofilia* 81 (1979), 2; idem, "Saints Equizio, Onorato and Libertino in Eleventh- and Twelfth-Century Italian Litanies as Clues to the Attribution of Manuscripts," *RB* 88 (1978), 308 and 314; Réginald Grégoire, "Repertorium Liturgicum Italicum," *Studi medievali* (3. ser.) 9 (1968), 591; Jullien, 119-20; O.P. Gy, "Collectaire, Rituel, Processionnal," *RSPh* 44 (1960), 453; Lokrantz, p. 24; Mearns, pp. xix, 1, and 39; Salmon, p. 79; S.J.P. van Dijk and J. Hazelden Walker, *The Origins of the Modern Roman Liturgy* (London, 1960), p. 529.

VATICANO, Biblioteca Apostolica Vaticana, Pal. Lat. 242
s. xii^{ex} (ff. 74-80); 128 leaves; 211 x 84 mm.; written in Germany; prov. Frankenthal.

Contents: Collection of *accessus* on ff. 74v-80v; on f. 78r-v: *accessus ad Sedulium.* Preceded by *accessus* to Prosper (ff. 77v-78r) and followed by *accessus* to Prudentius, *Psychomachia* (f. 78v).
Other information: Miscellany volume with components dating from the ninth to the thirteenth centuries. In gloss: *et a Macedonio presbytero baptizatus in Arcadiam venit.*
Bibliography: Bergmann, p. 94; J.B. De Rossi, *Codices Palatini Latini Bibliothecae Vaticanae*, vol. 1, in *Bibliothecae Apostolicae Vaticanae Codices Manuscripti Recensiti Iubente Leone XIII Pont. Max.* (Roma, 1886), pp. 59-60; Glauche, pp. 118-27; Huemer, *De Sedulii*, p. 28; R.B.C. Huygens, *Accessus ad Auctores, Bernard d'Utrecht, Conrad d'Hirsau, Dialogus super Auctores* (Leiden, 1970), pp. 3 and 28-9; Kurz, 266 ff.; *MCLBV*, vol. 2.2, pp. 29-31; Munk Olsen, vol. 2, p. 181; Sanford, 236; Willy Schetter, *Studien zur Überlieferung und Kritik des Elegikers Maximian* = Klassisch-philologische Studien 36 (Wiesbaden, 1970), p. 6; Steinmeyer & Sievers, vol. 4, p. 607.

VATICANO, Biblioteca Apostolica Vaticana, Reg. Lat. 166
s. xi-xii; 55 leaves (ff. 42-55=s. xi$^{3/3}$); 172 x 125 mm.; written in France, probably Fleury; later possibly at Corbie.

Contents: On ff. 42r-45v: E1, with interlinear glosses (Remigius'). Followed by Prudentius, *Psychomachia* (ff. 46r-49v). On ff. 50r-55v: PC 5.354 ff., H1, H2 (1-36). Acrostic poems in praise of Sedulius (in Huemer's order) on ff. 54v-55r. Ps.-Cato, *Monosticha* on f. 55r-v. Preceded by selected epistles of Sidonius Apollinaris (ff. 1r-26v) and Boethius, *Liber contra Eutychen et Nestorium* (ff. 27r-41r).
Other information: Used by Arevalo and Huemer *(Reg. 3).* Volume consists of three parts of which ours is the third. Probably detached from Orléans, Bibliothèque Municipale, 307. Seen in person. Microfilm acquired.
Bibliography: Boas, p. lxiii; *CSEL*, vol. 10, p. xxi; Huemer, *De Sedulii*, p. 32; *MCLBV*, vol. 2.1, p. 41; Mostert, pp. 258-9; Munk Olsen, vol. 1, p. 80; J. Moncho Pascual, "Note sur l'édition du *De conditione hominis* de Grégoire de Nysse selon la version latine de Denys Le Petit," *Bulletin de philosophie médiévale* 15 (1973), 138-9; Pellegrin, p. 260; A. Wilmart, *Codices Reginenses Latini*, vol. 1, in *Bibliothecae*

Apostolicae Vaticanae Codices Manu Scripti Recensiti Iussu Pii XI Pontificis Maximi (Roma, 1937), pp. 390-3.

VATICANO, Biblioteca Apostolica Vaticana, Reg. Lat. 181
s. xvi (1581); 294 pages; 147 x 96 mm.; paper.

Contents: A collection of hymns and sacred songs; includes *A Solis Ortus Cardine* and *Hostis Herodes* among the hymns *in Nativitatem* (pp. 11-30) and *in Epiphaniam* (pp. 33-41) respectively.
Bibliography: Salmon, pp. 57-8; Wilmart, same as above, pp. 437-9.

VATICANO, Biblioteca Apostolica Vaticana, Reg. Lat. 222
s. xi-xii; 109 leaves; 210 x 130 mm.

Contents: *Mutilum troparium ad sanctorum sollemnitates celebrandas* (ff. 95-102; s. xi); includes *A Solis Ortu [sic] Cardine.*
Bibliography: Eva Odelman, "Comment a-t-on appelé les tropes? Observations sur les rubriques des tropes des Xe et XIe siècles," *Cahiers de civilisation médiévale* 18 (1975), 17-18 and 27-8; Erik Tidner, "In Tropos Liturgicos Studia I," *Eranos* 75 (1977), 57-69; Wilmart, same as above, pp. 524-9.

VATICANO, Biblioteca Apostolica Vaticana, Reg. Lat. 1560
s. x; 147 leaves; 215 x 177 mm.; Auxerre or Fleury.

Contents: On ff. 9r-23v: E1 (starting at Huemer's page 8, line 10), PC 1.121-368 and 2.1-300. Preceded by *Disticha Catonis* (ff. 1r-8v). Followed by Remigius' commentary on Phocas (ff. 24r-34v); *Disticha Catonis* (cont.; f. 35r); Phocas, *Ars de Nomine et Verbo* (ff. 35r-57v); Remigius' commentary on Donatus, *Ars Maior* (ff. 58r-71v and 81v-112r); Persius, *Satires;* Probus' life of Persius; Ps.-Cornutus' commentary on Persius (ff. 72r-81r); and other works of Remigius (ff. 112v-147v).
Other information: Volume consists of seven parts, of which ours is the second. Used by Huemer *(Reg. 4).* Seen in person. Microfilm acquired.
Bibliography: Boas, p. lxi; Bursill-Hall, p. 254; idem, "A Checklist of Incipits of Medieval Latin Grammatical Treatises: A-G," *Traditio* 34 (1978), 466; F. Casaceli, "In margine a Lucano Phars. VI.460," *Bollettino di studi latini* 3 (1973), 349; Michele Cerrati, "Per la classificazione dei codici di Persio," *Rivista di filologia classica* 40

(1912), 113-9; Wendell V. Clausen, *A. Persi Flacci, Saturarum Liber. Accedit Vita* (Oxford, 1956), pp. xi-xii and xxv; idem, "Codex Vat. Reginensis 1560 of Persius," *TAPA* 80 (1949), 238-44; *CSEL,* vol. 10, p. xxi; J.P. Elder, "A Mediaeval Cornutus on Persius," *Speculum* 22 (1947), 243; idem, "Did Remigius of Auxerre Comment on Bede's *De Schematibus et Tropis?*" *MS* 9 (1947), 141-50; idem, "The Missing Portions of the *Commentum Einsidlense* on Donatus's *Ars Grammatica,*" *HSCPh* 56-7 (1947), 129-60; Vittorio Ferraro, *"Semipaganus/semivillanus/semipoeta,"* *Maia* 22 (1970), 139-46; Glauche, pp. 53, 56, and 122-3; Louis Holtz, "Sur trois commentaires irlandais de l'*Art majeur* de Donat au IXe siècle," *RHT* 2 (1972), 50; Colette Jeudy, "Israël le grammairien et la tradition manuscrite du commentaire de Remi d'Auxerre à l'*Ars minor* de Donat," *Studi medievali* (3. ser.) 18.2 (1977), 185; eadem, "Tradition textuelle et commentaire des auteurs classiques latins conservés dans les manuscrits de la Bibliothèque Vaticane III. Le Commentaire de Rémi d'Auxerre au Livre III de l'*Ars maior* de Donat (Ms. Vatican. Reg. lat. 1560)" in *La cultura antica nell'occidente latino dell VII all'XI secolo, 18-24 Aprile, 1974* = Settimane di studio del Centro Italiano di Studi sull'Alto Medioevo 22 (Spoleto, 1975), 217-28; Jeudy, "Phocas," 139-40; C. Marchesi, "Gli scoliasti di Persio," *Rivista di filolologia classica* 40 (1912), 1-5; F. Mariani, "Persio nella scuola di Auxerre e l'*Adnotatio secundum Remigium,"* *Giornale italiano di filologia* 18 (1965), 152-61; *MCLBV,* vol. 2.1, pp. 275-8; Munk Olsen, vol. 1, pp. 82-3; E. Paratore, "Persio e Lucano," *Rivista di cultura classica e medioevale* 5 (1963), 90; *PL,* vol. 19, cols. 466-7; Reynolds, pp. 294-5; Dorothy M. Robathan and F. Edward Cranz, "A. Persius Flaccus" in *Catalogus Translationum et Commentariorum. Medieval and Renaissance Latin Translations and Commentaries,* vol. 3 (Washington, 1976), pp. 237-9; J.E.G. Zetzel, "On the History of Latin Scholia II: The *Commentum Cornuti* in the Ninth Century," *M&H* 10 (1980), 27-31.

VATICANO, Biblioteca Apostolica Vaticana, Reg. Lat. 2078
s. ix$^{1/4}$; 150 leaves; 270 x 160 mm.; written in Reims.

Contents: On ff. 79v-80r: Acrostic poems in praise of Sedulius (in Huemer's order). Preceded by Agroecius, *Ars de Orthographia* (ff. 74v-79v). Followed by *De Habitatione Ruris* (*Anth. Lat.* 26) and *Versus Sibyllae* (f. 80r-v).
Other information: Volume has two parts (ff. 1-80 and 81-150). Used by Arevalo *(Reg. 6).*

Bibliography: Bischoff, "FHH," 314; Boas, pp. xlviii-xlix and lxi; *CSEL,* vol. 10, p. 307; Maurice Cunningham, *Aurelii Prudentii Clementis Carmina, CCSL,* vol. 126, pp. xix and l; Ernst Dümmler, "Die handschriftliche Überlieferung der lateinischen Dichtungen aus der Zeit der Karolinger," *Neues Archiv* 4 (1879), 142-5; R. Ehwald, *Aldhelmi Opera, MGH AA,* vol. 15, p. 50; C.E. Finch, "Symphosius in Codices Pal. lat. 1719, 1753, and Reg. lat. 329, 2078," *Manuscripta* 13 (1969), 4 and 8-11; F. Glorie in *CCSL,* vol. 133, p. 362 and vol. 133A, p. 613; G. Kölblinger, "*Versus Panos* und *De rustico,*" *MlatJb* 8 (1971), 20; *MCLBV,* vol. 2.1, pp. 502-4; R. Peiper, *Alcimi Ecdicii Aviti Viennensis Episcopi Opera Quae Supersunt, MGH AA,* vol. 6.2, p. lxvii; *PL,* vol. 19, col. 469; Yves-François Riou, "Quelques aspects de la tradition manuscrite des *Carmina* d'Eugène de Tolède: Du *Liber Catonianus* aux *Auctores octo morales,*" *RHT* 2 (1972), 14 and 28-9; Sanford, 211; F. Vollmer, *Fl. Merobaudis Reliquiae, Blossii Aemilii Dracontii Carmina, Eugenii Toletani Episcopi Carmina et Epistulae, MGH AA,* vol. 14, p. xli.

VATICANO, Biblioteca Apostolica Vaticana, Reg. Lat. 2120
s. xiii*in.*; 35 leaves; 228 x 135 mm.; written in Orléans (or at S. Victor, Paris).

Contents: Florilegium on ff. 11-35; includes (f. 21r) excerpts from PC: 1.60, 1.66-67, 1.85, 1.242, 1.349, 2.121-122, 4.76-78, and 5.171. Preceded by excerpts from works of Prudentius, Tibullus, Ps.-Virgil, Dracontius, Boethius, Petronius, John of Salisbury, Alan of Lille, John of Hauville, Ovid, and *Ilias Latina.* Followed by excerpts from Propertius, Joseph of Exeter (Iscanus), Ovid, Ps.-Virgil, Ps.-Ovid, Bernard Silvester, Virgil, Valerius Flaccus, Claudian, and Horace.
Other information: Leaves 11-35 once formed part of Paris, Bibliothèque Nationale, Lat. 15155 (ff. 28-38 and ff. 111-122). Seen in person.
Bibliography: Luigi Alfonsi, "Noterelle properziane," *Aevum* 29 (1955), 577-9; B.C. Barker-Benfield, "A Ninth-Century Manuscript from Fleury: *Cato de senectute cum Macrobio*" in *Medieval Learning and Literature. Essays Presented to Richard William Hunt* (Oxford, 1976), pp. 147-9; Franz G. Becker, *Pamphilus. Prolegomena zum Pamphilus (de amore) und kritische Textausgabe* = Beihefte zum MlatJb 9 (Düsseldorf, 1972), pp. 110-2; Th. Birt, *Claudi Claudiani Carmina, MGH AA,* vol. 10, p. cxxvi; Boas, p. lx; idem, "Ein Catoflorilegium," *Historische Vierteljahresschrift* 27 (1932), 601-9; Rosemary Burton, *Classical Poets in the*

Florilegium Gallicum = Lateinische Sprache und Literatur des Mittel-
alters 14 (Frankfurt and Bern, 1983), pp. 79-81; Marvin L. Colker,
Galteri de Castellione Alexandreis = Thesaurus Mundi. Bibliotheca
Scriptorum Latinorum Mediae et Recentioris Aetatis 17 (Padova, 1978),
p. xxviii; Léopold Victor Delisle, "Inventaire des manuscrits latins de
Saint-Victor conservés à la Bibliothèque Impériale sous les numéros
14232-15175," *BECh* 30 (1869), 76; J. Fohlen, "Études recentes sur les
manuscrits classiques latins," *Scriptorium* 34 (1980), 100; Ludwig
Gompf, *Joseph Iscanus. Werke und Briefe* = Mittellateinische Studien
und Texte 4 (Leiden, 1970), p. 52; Johannes Hamacher, *Florilegium
Gallicum. Prolegomena und Edition der Excerpte von Petron bis Cicero,
De oratore* = Lateinische Sprache und Literatur des Mittelalters 5 (Bern
and Frankfurt, 1975), pp. 62-3; Paul Klopsch, *Pseudo-Ovidius, De
Vetula. Untersuchungen und Text* = Mittellateinische Studien und Texte
2 (Leiden, 1967), p. 181; A. La Penna, *Publi Ovidi Nasonis Ibis.
Prolegomeni, testo, apparato critico e commento* = Biblioteca di studi
superiori 34 (Firenze, 1957), p. cxi; Carl Lohmeyer, *Guilelmi Blesensis
Aldae Comoedia* (Leipzig, 1892), pp. 41-2; Munari, pp. 92-5; Pellegrin,
pp. 306 and 328; M.D. Reeve, "Heinsius's Manuscripts of Ovid: A
Supplement," *RhM* 119 (1976), 69; Reynolds, p. 324; Dorothy M.
Robathan, "The Missing Folios of the Paris Florilegium 15155," *CP* 33
(1938), 188-97; R.H. Rouse, "Florilegia and Latin Classical Authors in
Twelfth- and Thirteenth-Century Orléans," *Viator* 10 (1979), 148 and
154; idem, "The *A* Text of Seneca's Tragedies in the Thirteenth
Century," *RHT* 1 (1971), 111 and 114; Sanford, 236; B.L. Ullman,
"Tibullus in the Medieval Florilegia," *CP* 23 (1928), 170; E. Faye
Wilson, "The *Georgica Spiritualia* of John of Garland," *Speculum* 8
(1933), 358-77.

VATICANO, Biblioteca Apostolica Vaticana, Ross. 205 (VIII. 144)
s. xi¹; 107 leaves; 230 x 140 mm.; Moissac.

Contents: Hymnal from Moissac; includes *A Solis Ortus Cardine* (f.
6v).
Bibliography: Guido Maria Dreves, *Hymnarius Moissiacensis. Das
Hymnar der Abtei Moissac im 10. Jahrhundert* = Analecta Hymnica 2
(Leipzig, 1888); Jean Dufour, "Les Manuscrits liturgiques de Moissac"
in *Liturgie et musique (IXe-XIVe siècles)* = Cahiers de Fanjeaux 17
(1982), p. 123; Gamber, vol. 2, pp. 603-4, no. 1672; Jullien, 129-30;
A.-G. Martimort, "Répertoires des livres liturgiques du Languedoc,
antérieurs au Concile de Trente" in *Liturgie et musique (IXe-XIVe siècles)*

= Cahiers de Fanjeaux. 17 (1982), p. 79; Mearns, pp. xiv and 1; Lukas Richter, "Die beiden ältesten Liederbücher des lateinischen Mittelalters," *Philologus* 123 (1979), 68 [s. x-xi]; T.A. Russel, "A Poetic Key to a Pre-Guidonian Palm and the *Echemata*," *Journal of the American Musicological Society* 34 (1981), 109-18; Pierre Salmon, "Livrets de prières de l'époque carolingienne," *RB* 86 (1976), 233; Stäblein, pp. 51-67 and 522-8; idem, "Zur Geschichte der choralen *Pange-lingua*-Melodie" in *Der kultische Gesang der abendländischen Kirche. Ein gregorianisches Werkheft aus Anlass des 75. Geburtstages von Dominicus Johner*, ed. F. Tack (Köln, 1950), pp. 72-75 [c. 1000]; Hans Tietze, *Die illuminierten Handschriften der Rossiana in Wien-Lainz* = Beschreibendes Verzeichnis der illuminierten Handschriften in Österreich, vol. 5 (Leipzig, 1911), p. 26, no. 40.

VATICANO, Biblioteca Apostolica Vaticana, Urb. Lat. 585
s. xi/xii; 262 leaves; 210 x 144 mm.; Monte Cassino.

Contents: Benedictine diurnal, with hymns on ff. 104v ff.; includes *A Solis Ortus Cardine* and *Hostis Herodes* (ff. 114r-115v).
Bibliography: Faustino Avagliano, "Ritrovato il codice cassinese 199," *Benedictina* 19 (1972), 623; idem, "Altri testi della liturgia cassinese per i Ss. Pietro e Paulo," *Benedictina* 15 (1968), 19-44; M. Avery, "The Beneventan Lections for the Vigil of Easter and the Ambrosian Chant Banned by Pope Stephen IX at Monte Cassino," *Studi gregoriani per la storia di Gregorio VII e della riforma gregoriana* 1 (1947), 445 ff.; Peter Baldass, "Die Miniaturen zweier *Exultet*-Rollen (1): London, Add. 30337; Vat. Barb. Lat. 592," *Scriptorium* 8 (1954), 84, 87, and pl. 5c; Giulio Battelli, "L'orazionale di Trani," *Benedictina* 19 (1972), 283; *Beneventan*, vol. 1, p. 73 and vol. 2, pp. 169-70; Owen Blum, "Authenticity of Sixteen Medieval Latin Poems Attributed to St. Peter Damian (1007-1072)," *APS Yearbook* 1956, 378-81; Antoine Chavasse, "Les Plus anciens types du lectionnaire et de l'antiphonaire romains de la messe," *RB* 62 (1952), 9; David Diringer, *The Illuminated Book: Its History and Production* (2nd ed.; London, 1967), p. 295; Ehrensberger, p. 310; Klaus Gamber and Sieghild Rehle, *Manuale Casinense (Cod. Ottob. lat. 145)* = Textus Patristici et Liturgici 13 (Regensburg, 1977), p. 8; Edward B. Garrison, *Studies in the History of Medieval Italian Painting* (Firenze, 1960-62), vol. 4, pp. 389-90 and 395; Hartmut Hoffman, "Studien zur Chronik von Montecassino," *Deutsches Archiv* 29 (1973), 128; Mauro Inguanez, "Il *Quem quaeritis* pasquale nei codici cassinesi," *Studi medievali* (n.s.) 14 (1941), 142-9; Detler Jasper, "Die Papst-

geschichte des Pseudo-Liudprand," *Deutsches Archiv* 31 (1975), 59; A. Lentini and F. Avagliano, "I carmi di Alfano I, Arcivescovo di Salerno," *Miscellanea cassinese* 38 (1974), 17-22; Walther Lipphardt, *Lateinische Osterfeiern und Osterspiele* = Ausgaben deutscher Literatur des XV. bis XVIII. Jahrhundert. Reihe Drama 5, vol. 1 (Berlin and New York, 1975), p. 20; Lokrantz, pp. 24, 39, and 52; Mearns, pp. xix, 1, and 39; Giovanni Mercati, "Due supposte spogliazioni della biblioteca di Monte Cassino" in *Opere minori raccolte in occasione del settantesimo natalizio sotto gli auspicii di s. s. Pio XI*, vol. 3 = Studi e testi 78 (1937), pp. 166-7; Francis Newton, "Leo Marsicanus and the Dedicatory Text and Drawing in Monte Cassino 99," *Scriptorium* 33 (1979), 198; Manfred Oberleitner, "Die handschriftliche Überlieferung der Werke des Heiligen Augustinus 1.1," *Sitz. Wien* 263 (1969), 407 and 267 (1970), 353; Salmon, p. 82; idem, "Livrets de prières de l'époque carolingienne," *RB* 86 (1976), 233; Cosimus Stornajolo, *Codices Urbinates Latini*, vol. 2, in *Bibliothecae Apostolicae Vaticanae Codices Manu Scripti Recensiti Iussu Pii X Pontificis Maximi* (Roma, 1912), pp. 88-94; H. Toubert, "Le Bréviaire d'Oderisius (Paris, Bibliothèque Mazarine, MS 364) et les influences byzantines au Mont-Cassin," *MEFRM* 83 (1971), 193 ff.; Robert Weber, *Le Psautier romain et les autres anciens psautiers latins* (Roma, 1953), p. xv; André Wilmart, "Prières pour la communion en deux psautiers du Mont-Cassin," *EL* 43 (1929), 322, nn. 1-3.

VATICANO, Biblioteca Apostolica Vaticana, Vat. Lat. 2940
s. xv; 170 leaves; 300 x 295 mm.; paper.

Contents: On f. 170v: PC 1.355-8. Preceded by Boccaccio, *Genealogiae Deorum Gentilium* (ff. 1-167) and excerpts from Latin authors, including Lucan, Varro, et al.
Other information: Written by Franciscus de Montepolitiano (vid. f. 167r). Seen in person.
Bibliography: Renato Badalì, "I codici romani di Lucano (III)," *Bollettino del Comitato per la Preparazione dell'Edizione Nazionale dei Classici Greci e Latini* 23 (1975), 63; Filippo Tamburini, "Note diplomatiche intorno a suppliche e lettere di Penitenzieria (sec. xiv-xv)," *Archivum Historiae Pontificiae* 11 (1973), 174.

VATICANO, Biblioteca Apostolica Vaticana, Vat. Lat. 4928
s. xii*in.*; 365 leaves; 227 x 145 mm.; S. Sophia, Benevento.

Contents: Benedictine ordinarium, psalter, etc.; hymns on ff. 214v ff.

include *A Solis Ortus Cardine* and *Hostis Herodes*.

Bibliography: Giulio Battelli, "L'orazionale di Trani," *Benedictina* 19 (1972), 284; *Beneventan*, vol. 2, pp. 149-50; Albert Boeckler, *Abendländische Miniaturen bis zum Ausgang der romanischen Zeit* = Tabulae in Usum Scholarum 10 (Berlin and Leipzig, 1930), p. 104; Virginia Brown, "*Flores Psalmorum* and *Orationes Psalmodicae* in Beneventan Script," *MS* 51 (1989), 424-66; Antoine Chavasse, "Les Plus anciens types du lectionnaire et de l'antiphonaire romains de la messe," *RB* 62 (1952), 9; Ehrensberger, pp. 206-8; Gamber, vol. 1, p. 249, no. 465d; Klaus Gamber and Sieghild Rehle, *Manuale Casinense (Cod. Ottob. lat. 145)* = Textus Patristici et Liturgici 13 (Regensburg, 1977), p. 8; Edward B. Garrison, "Random Notes on Early Italian Manuscripts I," *La bibliofilia* 80 (1978), 214; Réginald Grégoire, "Repertorium Liturgicum Italicum," *Studi medievali* (3. ser.) 9 (1968), 587; Walther Lipphardt, *Lateinische Osterfeiern und Osterspiele* = Ausgaben deutscher Literatur des XV. bis XVIII. Jahrhunderts. Reihe Drama 5, vol. 1 (Berlin and New York, 1975), p. 23; Mearns, pp. xix, 1, and 39; Giovanni Mercati, *Codici latini Pico Grimani Pio e di altra biblioteca ignota del secolo XVI* = Studi e testi 75 (Roma, 1938), pp. 111, 124, and 126; Francis Newton, "Leo Marsicanus and the Dedicatory Text and Drawing in Monte Cassino 99," *Scriptorium* 33 (1979), 198; Salmon, pp. 85-6; idem, "Livrets de prières de l'époque carolingienne," *RB* 86 (1976), 233; H. Toubert, "Le Bréviaire d'Oderisius (Paris, Bibliothèque Mazarine, MS 364) et les influences byzantines au Mont-Cassin," *MEFRM* 83 (1971), 193 ff.; André Wilmart, "Prières pour la communion en deux psautiers du Mont-Cassin," *EL* 43 (1929), 320-8.

VATICANO, Biblioteca Apostolica Vaticana, Vat. Lat. 5776
s. xi$^{ex.}$; 108 leaves; 152 x 102 mm.; written at Tortona?; later at Bobbio.

Contents: Breviary with hymns on ff. 64r-108v, including *A Solis Ortus Cardine* and *Hostis Herodes* (ff. 78r-79r).

Bibliography: M.L. Angrisani, "Materiali per lo studio della produzione libraria latina antica e alto medievale in Italia (1)," *Bollettino del Comitato per la Preparazione della Edizione Nazionale dei Classici Greci e Latini* 24 (1976), 103; Henry M. Bannister, *Monumenti vaticani di paleografia musicale latina* = Codices e Vaticanis Selecti Phototypice Expressi 12 (Leipzig, 1913), vol. 1, p. 93, no. 265; *CLA*, vol. 1, pp. 15-6; no. 48-9; Ehrensberger, pp. 40-1; Gamber, vol. 2, p. 605, no. 1676; Jullien, 114-5; Lokrantz, p. 25; Mearns, pp. xix, 1, and 39; Carl-Allan Moberg, *Die liturgischen Hymnen in Schweden. Beiträge zur*

Liturgie- und Musikgeschichte des Mittelalters und der Reformationszeit (Uppsala, 1947), vol. 1, p. 196; Marco Palma, "Antigrafo/Apografo. La formazione del testo latino degli atti del Concilio Constantinopolitano dell'869-870" in *Atti del Convegno Internazionale: Il libro e il testo* (Urbino, 1984), p. 313, n. 22; Salmon, p. 54.

VATICANO, Biblioteca Apostolica Vaticana, Vat. Lat. 7172
s. xi$^{in.}$; 189 leaves; 217 x 145 mm.; Narni (or S. Severino, Napoli).

Contents: Benedictine hymnal; includes *A Solis Ortus Cardine* (f. 13r) and *Hostis Herodes* (f. 26r).
Bibliography: Bannister, same as above, pp. 124 and 183; Guido Maria Dreves, *Hymnarius Severinianus. Das Hymnar der Abtei St. Severin in Neapel. Nach den Codices Vaticanus 7172 und Parisinus 1092* = Analecta Hymnica 14a (Leipzig, 1893); Ehrensberger, p. 40; Gamber, vol. 2, p. 604, no. 1673; Edward B. Garrison, "Notes on Certain Italian Medieval Manuscripts 3: Three Manuscripts of Narni," *La bibliofilia* 69 (1967), 1-67, esp. 1-3 and 9; idem, "Random Notes on Early Italian Manuscripts 1," *La bibliofilia* 80 (1978), 214; Michel Huglo, "Le Graduel palimpseste de Plaisance (Paris, B.N. lat. 7102)," *Scriptorium* 28 (1974), 31; Jullien, 117-8; Claudio Leonardi, "L'inno al martire Gregorio" in *La Basilica di S. Gregorio Maggiore in Spoleto* (Spoleto, 1979), 29-36; idem, "S. Gregorio di Spoleto e l'innario umbro-romano dei codice Par. lat. 1092 e Vat. lat. 7172" in *Lateinische Dichtungen des X. und XI. Jahrhunderts. Festgabe für Walther Bulst zum 80. Geburtstag* (Heidelberg, 1981), pp. 129-48; M.G. Lokrantz, "Una raccolta di inni mariani trovati in un codice di Oxford dell'XI secolo," *Aevum* 41 (1967), 283-5; Ernesto Maurice, "Intorno alla collezione d'inni sacri contenuta nei manoscritti Vaticano 7172 e Parigino latino 1092," *ARSR* 22 (1899), 5-23; Mearns, pp. xvii, 1, and 39; Dag Norberg, "Ein Erasmushymnus aus Italien" in *Lateinische Dichtungen des X. und XI. Jahrhunderts. Festgabe für Walther Bulst zum 80. Geburtstag* (Heidelberg, 1981), pp. 154-61; Salmon, pp. 54-5.

VATICANO, Biblioteca Apostolica Vaticana, Vat. Lat. 10774
s. xiv$^{ex.}$; 190 leaves; 380 x 280 mm.; Diessenhofen.

Contents: Psalter, with hymnal on ff. 139v ff.; includes *A Solis Ortus Cardine* (f. 139v) and *Hostis Herodes* (f. 141v).
Bibliography: Johannes Bapt. Borino, *Codices Vaticani Latini. Codices 10701-10875*, vol. 12, in *Bibliothecae Apostolicae Vaticanae Codices*

Manu Scripti Recensiti Iussu Pii XII Pontificis Maximi (Roma, 1947), pp. 232-6; A. Dirks, "De Tribus Libris Manu Scriptis Primaevae Liturgicae Dominicanae," *Archivum Fratrum Praedicatorum* 49 (1979), 9 and 26.

VATICANO, Biblioteca Apostolica Vaticana, Vat. Lat. 11441
s. xv (c. 1448-1480); 538 leaves; 195 x 145 mm.; paper and parchment.

Contents: On ff. 536v-537v: PC 1.1-53 and 2.41-69. Preceded by Lactantius, *De Ave Phoenice.*
Bibliography: Duke Humphrey and English Humanism (Oxford, 1970), p. 57, no. 97; P. Hemeryck, "Les Traductions latines du *Charon* de Lucien au quinzième siècle," *MEFRM* 84 (1972), 160 and 164; Colette Jeudy, "La Tradition manuscrite des *Partitiones* de Priscien et la version longue du commentaire de Rémi d'Auxerre," *RHT* 1 (1971), 133; C.H. Lohr, "Medieval Latin Aristotle Commentaries. Authors: Johannes de Kathia-Myngodus," *Traditio* 27 (1971), 318; Giovanna Petti Balbi, "Libri greci a Genova a metà del Quattrocento," *Italia medioevale e humanistica* 20 (1977), 282-3, 290, 292, and 298; José Ruysschaert, *Codices Vaticani Latini: Codices 11414-11709,* vol. 14, in *Bibliothecae Apostolicae Vaticanae Codices Manu Scripti Recensiti Ioannis XXIII Pontificis Maximi* (Roma, 1959), pp. 41 ff.

VERONA, Biblioteca Capitolare, CVIII (101)
s. xiii; 230 leaves; 330 x 212 mm.; Verona.

Contents: Breviary; hymns (ff. 171r-212v) include *A Solis Ortus Cardine* and *Hostis Herodes.*
Bibliography: Réginald Grégoire, "Repertorium Liturgicum Italicum," *Studi medievali* (3. ser.) 9 (1968), 578; Lokrantz, pp. 27, 39-40, and 42; Mearns, pp. xix, 1, and 39; G. Zivelonghi and C. Adami, *I codici liturgici della cattedrale di Verona* (Verona, 1987), pp. 108-9.

VERONA, Biblioteca Capitolare, CIX (102)
s. xi[ex.]; 190 leaves; 220 x 145 mm.; S. Zeno, Verona.

Contents: Hymnal includes *A Solis Ortus Cardine* and *Hostis Herodes.*
Bibliography: Gamber, vol. 2, p. 605, no. 1675; Grégoire, same as above, 578; Michel Huglo, et al., *Fonti e paleografia del canto ambrosiano* = Archivio ambrosiano 7 (Milano, 1956), pp. 90-1; Lokrantz, p. 27; eadem, "Una raccolta di inni mariani trovati in un codice di Oxford dell'XI secolo," *Aevum* 41 (1967), 284-5; Mearns, pp.

xix, 1, and 39; Stäblein, pp. 358-406 and 597-606; Maria Venturini, *Vita ed attività dello 'Scriptorium' veronese nel secolo XI* (Verona, 1930), p. 120; Zivelonghi and Adami, same as above, pp. 106-7.

VORAU, Stiftsbibliothek, V. 33 (CXI)
s. xii$^{4/4}$ (ff. 45-114); 176 leaves; 220 x 162 mm.; written in Austria.

Contents: Excerpts from Christian poets on ff. 63v-66r; on f. 64v: PC 1.60-103. Preceded by excerpts from Maximianus (ff. 63v-64v) and followed by excerpts from Prudentius (ff. 64v-65v); Arator (f. 65v); Alcimus Avitus (f. 65v); and Sulpicius Severus (f. 65v).
Bibliography: Pius Fank, *Catalogus Voraviensis seu Codices Manuscripti Bibliothecae Canoniae in Vorau* (Graz, 1936), pp. 19-22; idem, *Die Vorauer-Handschrift: Ihre Entstehung und ihr Schreiber* (Graz, 1967), pp. 34-5; Hartwig Gerhard, *Der Liber Proverbiorum des Godefrid von Winchester* (Würzburg, 1974); Günter Glauche, "Einige Bemerkungen zum 'Florileg von Heiligenkreuz'" in *Festschrift Bernhard Bischoff zu seinem 65. Geburtstag* (Stuttgart, 1971), pp. 295-306; Munk Olsen, vol. 2, p. 876; idem, "Les Classiques latins dans les florilèges médiévaux antérieurs au XIIIe siècle I," *RHT* 9 (1979), 94-6 and 117; L. van Acker, *Petri Pictoris Carmina, CCCM,* vol. 25, pp. cviii-cix.

WIEN, Österreichische Nationalbibliothek, 2171 (Jur. can. 81)
s. ix; 52 leaves; 287 x 215 mm.; written in southern Germany.

Contents: On f. 1r: Glosses on Sedulius. Followed by *Canon Sancti Silvestri Papae Urbis Rome et CCLXXXIV Episcoporum* (f. 1v); a collection of church canons (ff. 2r-26v); et al.
Bibliography: Bergmann, p. 111; Hermann Julius Hermann, *Die deutschen romanischen Handschriften,* in *Beschreibendes Verzeichnis der illuminierten Handschriften in Österreich. Die illuminierten Handschriften und Inkunabeln der Nationalbibliothek in Wien* 8.1 (Leipzig, 1926), pp. 103-4; Huemer, "Glossen," 540; Steinmeyer & Sievers, vol. 2, p. 620 and vol. 4, p. 646; *Tabulae Codicum Manuscriptorum praeter Graecos et Orientales in Bibliotheca Palatina Vindobonensi Asservatorum* (Wien, 1864-1912), vol. 2, pp. 22-3; Franz Unterkircher, *Inventar der illuminierten Handschriften, Inkunabeln und Frühdrucke der Österreichischen Nationalbibliothek, Teil 1: Die abendländischen Handschriften* = Museion. Veröffentlichungen der Österreichischen Nationalbibliothek, n. F., 2.2 (Wien, 1957), p. 63.

WIEN, Österreichische Nationalbibliothek, 15507 (A.N. 44. D. 13)
s. xvii (1637); 287 leaves; folio; paper.

Contents: On pp. 41-68: *A Solis Ortus Cardine* (setting by Palestrina).
Bibliography: Tabulae, same as above, vol. 9, pp. 2-4.

WIEN, Österreichische Nationalbibliothek, 15765 (A.N. 33. D. 33)
s. xviii (1754); 44 leaves; folio; paper.

Contents: On ff. 36r-40r: *A Solis Ortus Cardine.*
Bibliography: Tabulae, same as above, vol. 9, p. 43.

WIEN, Österreichische Nationalbibliothek, 15807 (A.N. 34. A. 16)
s. xvii (1601); 169 leaves; quarto; paper.

Contents: On ff. 5v-7r: *A Solis Ortus Cardine* and on f. 8r: *Hostis Herodes.*
Bibliography: Tabulae, same as above, vol. 9, pp. 50-2.

WIEN, Österreichische Nationalbibliothek, 15815 (A.N. 33. D. 19)
s. xviii; 56 leaves; folio; paper.

Contents: On ff. 43r-47r: *A Solis Ortus Cardine.*
Bibliography: Tabulae, same as above, vol. 9, pp. 54-5.

WIEN, Österreichische Nationalbibliothek, 15816 (A.N. 33. D. 20)
s. xviii; 58 leaves; folio; paper.

Contents: On ff. 44v-48v: *A Solis Ortus Cardine.*
Bibliography: Tabulae, same as above, vol. 9, pp. 55-6.

WIEN, Österreichische Nationalbibliothek, 15834 (A.N. 33. B. 75)
s. xviii; 6 leaves; folio; paper.

Contents: A Solis Ortus Cardine (setting by Johann Josef Fux between 1711 and 1714).
Bibliography: Tabulae, same as above, vol. 9, p. 58.

WIEN, Österreichische Nationalbibliothek, 16193 (A.N. 44. D. 5)
s. xvii; 298 leaves; 560 x 420 mm.; paper.

Contents: On ff. 19v-31r: *A Solis Ortus Cardine.*
Bibliography: Tabulae, same as above, vol. 9, pp. 111-13.

WIEN, Österreichische Nationalbibliothek, 16197 (A.N. 43. E. 18)
s. xvi; 115 leaves; 550 x 410 mm.; paper.

Contents: On ff. 7v-13r: *A Solis Ortus Cardine;* on ff. 13v-17r: *Hostis Herodes.*
Bibliography: Tabulae, same as above, vol. 9, pp. 116-7.

WIEN, Österreichische Nationalbibliothek, 16202 (A.N. 43. E. 19)
s. xvii; 142 leaves; 550 x 420 mm.; paper.

Contents: On ff. 106v-108r: *A Solis Ortus Cardine.*
Bibliography: Tabulae, same as above, vol. 9, pp. 124-5.

WIEN, Österreichische Nationalbibliothek, 16203 (A.N. 43. E. 16)
s. xvii; 104 leaves; 550 x 410 mm.; paper.

Contents: On ff. 87v-94r: *A Solis Ortus Cardine.*
Bibliography: Tabulae, same as above, vol. 9, pp. 125-6.

WIEN, Österreichische Nationalbibliothek, 16204 (A.N. 43. E. 16)
s. xvii; 134 leaves; 550 x 410 mm.; paper.

Contents: On ff. 103v-110r: *A Solis Ortus Cardine.*
Bibliography: Tabulae, same as above, vol. 9, pp. 126-7.

WIEN, Österreichische Nationalbibliothek, 16697 (A.N. 38. B. 15)
s. xix; 261 leaves; 480 x 310 mm.; paper.

Contents: On ff. 183r-184r: *Hostis Herodes* (setting by Orlando di Lasso).
Bibliography: Tabulae, same as above, vol. 9, pp. 194-7.

WIEN, Österreichische Nationalbibliothek, 16709 (A.N. 43. E. 12)
s. xvii; 224 leaves; folio; paper.

Contents: On ff. 19v-23r: *Hostis Herodes.*
Bibliography: Tabulae, same as above, vol. 9, pp. 220-1.

WIEN, Österreichische Nationalbibliothek, 17459 (A.N. 65. A. 17)
s. xviii (1734); 14 leaves; quarto; paper.

Contents: A Solis Ortus Cardine.
Bibliography: Tabulae, same as above, vol. 9, p. 314.

WOLFENBÜTTEL, Herzog August Bibliothek, 33. 1 Aug. 2°
s. xv (1491-7); 405 leaves; 310 x 210 mm.; paper.

Contents: Hymns on ff. 188r-189r include A Solis Ortus Cardine. On
f. 199v: excerpt from PC, beginning with 2.54. On f. 210r: *Hostis
Herodes.* On f. 216r-v: excerpt from PC, beginning with 2.73.
Bibliography: Otto von Heinemann, *Die augusteischen Handschriften,*
vol. 3, in *Kataloge der Herzog August Bibliothek Wolfenbüttel,* vol. 6
(Frankfurt, 1966), pp. 24-38.

WOLFENBÜTTEL, Herzog August Bibliothek, 404. 1 (6) Novi
s. xiv; 2 leaves; 225 x 135 mm.; written in Germany.

Contents: Fragment of Sedulius: PC 1.97-125 and 173-205.
Other information: Contains illustrations. Seen in person. Microfilm
acquired.
Bibliography: Hans Butzmann, *Die mittelalterlichen Handschriften der
Gruppen Extravagantes, Novi und Novissimi,* vol. 15, in *Kataloge der
Herzog August Bibliothek Wolfenbüttel, neue Reihe* (Frankfurt, 1972), p.
199.

WOLFENBÜTTEL, Herzog August Bibliothek, 78 Weissenb.
s. xi; 83 leaves; 237 x 165 mm.; Weissenburg.

Contents: Psalter with hymns and prayers; includes A Solis Ortus
Cardine (f. 29v) and Hostis Herodes (f. 31r).
Bibliography: Hans Butzmann, *Die Weissenburger Handschriften* in
Kataloge der Herzog August Bibliothek Wolfenbüttel, vol. 10 (Frankfurt,
1964), p. 235.

WORCESTER, Cathedral and Chapter Library, F. 160
s. xiii (c. 1230); 354 leaves; 260 x 180 mm.; Worcester.

Contents: Benedictine antiphonal, etc.; hymns include A Solis Ortus
Cardine and Hostis Herodes.

Bibliography: Gneuss, *Hymnar,* p. 250; Ker, *Cat.,* p. 217; Ker, *Med.,* p. 213; Mearns, pp. xiii, 1, and 39; Stäblein, pp. 169-204 and 559-64.

ZÜRICH, Zentralbibliothek, C 63 (690)
s. xiii; 176 leaves; 268 x 180 mm.

Contents: *"Kopienband liturgischer Bücher des Grossmünsters"* (with hymnal beginning on f. 169v); includes *A Solis Ortus Cardine* (f. 170v) and *Hostis Herodes* (f. 171r).
Bibliography: Leo Cunibert Mohlberg, *Mittelalterliche Handschriften,* vol. 1 in *Katalog der Handschriften der Zentralbibliothek Zürich* (Zürich, 1932-52), p. 35.

ZÜRICH, Zentralbibliothek, Rh. 21
s. xv (1459); 136 leaves; 313 x 237 mm.; Rheinau.

Contents: Psalter and hymnal (ff. 91v-124v); includes *A Solis Ortus Cardine* (f. 99r) and *Hostis Herodes* (f. 101r).
Bibliography: Mohlberg, *Katalog,* same as above, p. 169; Stäblein, passim; J. Werner, *Die ältesten Hymnensammlungen von Rheinau* = Mitteilungen der antiquarischen Gesellschaft 23.2 (Zürich, 1891), p. 78.

ZÜRICH, Zentralbibliothek, Rh. 28
s. xiii-xiv; 321 leaves (pages 2-643); 290 x 195 mm.; not originally from Rheinau.

Contents: Breviary (complete) with calendar, psalter, and hymnal (on pp. 144-175); includes *A Solis Ortus Cardine* (p. 152) and *Hostis Herodes* (p. 154).
Bibliography: Bruno Albers, "Eine Homiliensammlung Benedikts von Aniane?" *Studien und Mitteilungen zur Geschichte des Benediktiner-Ordens und seiner Zweige* 32 (1911), 579-91; Mohlberg, *Katalog,* same as above, p. 172.

ZÜRICH, Zentralbibliothek, Rh. 34
s. ix[in.]; 200 leaves; 280 x 180 mm.; written at S. Gallen or Reichenau.

Contents: Benedictine psalter with hymnal (ff. 198r-200v); includes *A Solis Ortus Cardine.*
Other information: Written around 820 by the scribe Grimalt.
Bibliography: Walther Bulst, *Hymni Latini Antiquissimi LXXV, Psalmi*

III (Heidelberg, 1956), pp. 175-7; Clemens Blume, *Der Cursus S. Benedicti Nursini und die liturgischen Hymnen des 6.-9. Jahrhunderts in ihrer Beziehung zu den Sonntags- und Ferialhymnen unseres Breviers* = Hymnologische Beiträge 3 (Leipzig, 1908), pp. 57-9; Gamber, vol. 2, pp. 586-7, no. 1622; Gneuss, *Hymnar,* pp. 21-2; idem, "Latin Hymns in Medieval England: Future Research" in *Chaucer and Middle English Studies in honour of Rossell Hope Robbins,* ed. Beryl Rowland (London, 1974), p. 422, n. 10; Jullien, 90-1; Mearns, pp. xvi and 1; Mohlberg, *Katalog,* same as above, p. 175; Pierre Salmon, *Les Tituli Psalmorum des manuscrits latins* = Collectanea Biblica Latina 12 (Paris, 1959), pp. 97-113 and 117-131; Werner, *Hymnensammlungen,* same as above, pp. xiv-xv.

ZÜRICH, Zentralbibliothek, Rh. 82
s. xi; 262 pages (131 leaves); 230 x 135 mm.; Farfa.

Contents: Benedictine hymnal, lectionary, and orational; includes *A Solis Ortus Cardine* (p. 27) and *Hostis Herodes* (p. 35).
Bibliography: Baroffio, 490-8; Gneuss, *Hymnar,* p. 72; Jullien, 115; Mearns, pp. xix, 1, and 39; Mohlberg, *Katalog,* same as above, p. 196; G. Morin, "Le Texte des cantiques aux vigiles de Noël d'après l'usage monastique primitif," *RB* 34 (1922), 277; Werner, *Hymnensammlungen,* same as above, p. 84.

ZÜRICH, Zentralbibliothek, Rh. 83
s. xi; 221 leaves; 227 x 178 mm.; Kempten.

Contents: Benedictine hymnal (ff. 19-57), collectar, and *liber capitulorum*; includes *A Solis Ortus Cardine* and *Hostis Herodes.*
Other information: Came from Kempten to Reichenau under Abbot Burchard I (died 1026).
Bibliography: Henry M. Bannister, *Monumenti vaticani di paleografia musicale latina* = Codices e Vaticanis Selecti Phototypice Expressi 12 (Leipzig, 1913), p. xxvi; Bruckner, vol. 4, p. 46; Gamber, vol. 2, pp. 554-5, no. 1525 and vol. 2, p. 604, no. 1674; Jullien, 104-5; Mearns, pp. xvi, 1, and 39; Mohlberg, *Katalog,* same as above, pp. 196-7; Morin in *RB,* same as above, 277; Stäblein, pp. 249-60 and 578-81; Hermann Tüchle, "Das Kalendar von Kempten," *Studien und Mitteilungen zur Geschichte des Benediktiner-Ordens und seiner Zweige* 81 (1970), 7-21; Werner, *Hymnensammlungen,* same as above, pp. 81-4.

ZÜRICH, Zentralbibliothek, Rh. 91
s. xi (c. 1000); 154 leaves; 208 x 147 mm.; Farfa.

Contents: Benedictine hymnal with collects and lessons; includes *A Solis Ortus Cardine* (f. 81r) and *Hostis Herodes* (f. 94r).
Bibliography: Baroffio, 494; Gneuss, *Hymnar,* p. 72; Jullien, 97; Mearns, pp. xviii, 1, and 39; Mohlberg, *Katalog,* same as above, pp. 202-3, no. 459; Werner, *Hymnensammlungen,* same as above, pp. 79-81.

ZÜRICH, Zentralbibliothek, Rh. 97
s. xi-xii; 242 pages; 199 x 130 mm.

Contents: Benedictine hymnal (s. xii) beginning on p. 131; includes *A Solis Ortus Cardine* (p. 159) and *Hostis Herodes* (p. 160).
Other information: Composite volume consisting of three parts, of which ours (pp. 131-242) was written for use in a monastery in Saxony.
Bibliography: Mearns, pp. xvi, 1, and 39; Mohlberg, *Katalog,* same as above, p. 206; Werner, *Hymnensammlungen,* same as above, pp. 84-6.

ZÜRICH, Zentralbibliothek, Rh. 110
s. xiii-xiv; 296 leaves (parch.) + 21 leaves (paper); 178 x 128 mm.; S. Michel, Tréport.

Contents: Benedictine breviary with hymns on ff. 1r-19v; includes *A Solis Ortus Cardine* (f. 5r) and *Hostis Herodes* (f. 5v).
Bibliography: Mohlberg, *Katalog,* same as above, pp. 213-4.

ZÜRICH, Zentralbibliothek, Rh. 111
s. ix^2; 210 pages; 175 x 125 mm.; written in south-western Germany.

Contents: Hymnal on pp. 139 ff.; includes portions of H2.
Bibliography: Jullien, 103-4; Mohlberg, *Katalog,* same as above, p. 214; Walpole, p. xxvii; Werner, *Hymnensammlungen,* same as above, pp. 78-9.

ZÜRICH, Zentralbibliothek, Rh. 129
c. 1100; 70 leaves; 150 x 100 mm.; Rheinau.

Contents: Hymnarium monasticum; includes *A Solis Ortus Cardine* (f. 18v) and *Hostis Herodes* (f. 23r).
Bibliography: Mearns, pp. xvii, 1, and 39; Mohlberg, *Katalog,* same

as above, p. 223; Werner, *Hymnensammlungen,* same as above, p. 86.

ZÜRICH, Zentralbibliothek, Rh. 133
s. xiv; 371 leaves; 145 x 102 mm.; Schaffhausen.

Contents: Benedictine diurnal with hymns on ff. 271v-328v; includes *A Solis Ortus Cardine* (f. 285r) and *Hostis Herodes* (f. 290v).
Bibliography: Mohlberg, *Katalog,* same as above, p. 225.

ZÜRICH, Zentralbibliothek, Rh. 155
s. xiv; 397 leaves; 115 x 85 mm.

Contents: Breviary (diurnal) with hymns beginning on f. 324r; includes *A Solis Ortus Cardine* (f. 336r) and *Hostis Herodes* (f. 340r).
Bibliography: Mohlberg, *Katalog,* same as above, pp. 237-8.

APPENDICES

I. MANUSCRIPTS LOST OR UNTRACED

The following manuscripts were either lost or destroyed in this century
or proved impossible for me to trace.

* * * * *

CHARTRES, Bibliothèque Municipale, 110 (58)
s. x (ff. 40-88); 220 leaves; 240 x 170 mm.; S. Père-en-Vallée,
Chartres.

Contents: On ff. 40r-88r: E1, PC, H1, H2 (1-61). Biographical notice
(Incipit ars Sedulii....) on f. 40r. Preceded by the *Dialogues* of Gregory
and treatise on the four sacraments (ff. 2r ff.). Followed by a life of the
Antichrist (attr. Alcuin); *Sacramentum Iudaeorum contra Christianos;*
Marbod of Rennes, *Mystica seu Moralis Applicatio de Lapidibus;* and
extracts from the writings of Augustine (ff. 89-97). Works of Ps.-
Dionysius the Areopagite, translated by John Scottus Eriugena (ff. 98
ff.), followed.
Other information: Composite volume consisting of four parts, of which
ours, ff. 40-88 (of the tenth century), was the second. The first 39
leaves dated to s. xii, while ff. 89-97 belonged to s. xi and ff. 98 ff. to
s. xi-xii. PC divided into four books (1.1-101 = *"Prologus,"* followed by
index for PC 1; no division between PC 3 and 4). Many glosses in E1
and H1. Used by Huemer (C). Destroyed during World War II (in
1944). To my knowledge, no copy of ff. 40-88 exists.
Bibliography: Cat. gen. octavo, vol. 11, pp. 58-9; *CSEL,* vol. 10, pp.
xvii-xviii; Kurz, 266; *Speculum* 29 (1954), 336-7; D. Verhelst, *Adso
Dervensis, De Ortu et Tempore Antichristi, CCCM,* vol. 45, p. 110.

LEUVEN, Bibliotheek der Katholieke Universiteit, 80

Contents: PC (incomplete). Manuscript destroyed during first World War.
Bibliography: Ed. de Moreau, *La Bibliothèque de l'Université de Louvain 1636-1914* (Louvain, 1918), p. 70; P. Namur, *Histoire des bibliothèques publiques de la Belgique* (Bruxelles, 1840-2), vol. 2, p. 217.

POMMERSFELDEN, Gräflich Schönbornsche Bibliothek, 218 (2840)
s. xiv (1331); 108 leaves; 330 x 240 mm.; Petersberg, Erfurt.

Contents: On ff. 12r-31r: PC. Preceded by Bernardus Gestensis, *Disputatio cum Milite* (ff. 1r-11r). Followed by Prudentius, *Psychomachia* (ff. 32r-43r); Horace, *Epistles* (ff. 44r-60r); Song of Songs paraphrased in verse (ff. 61r-82r); Ovid, *Ars Amatoria* (ff. 83r-108r); and Rupert's commentary on the Apocalypse (s. xii) (f. 108r-v).
Other information: The library's own current catalogue mentions only Rupert's commentary in its description of the contents of manuscript 218. Unfortunately, I was unable to see the manuscript in person.
Bibliography: Sanford, 239; Stegmüller, vol. 5, p. 193; Joseph Theele, *Die Handschriften des Benediktinerklosters S. Petri zu Erfurt* = Zentralblatt für Bibliothekswesen 48 (Leipzig, 1920), pp. 179-80.

WARSZAWA, Biblioteka Narodowa, Lat. F. 1. 49
s. xiv; 226 leaves; 295 x 220 mm.; paper.

Contents: On ff. 105v-151v: PC (described in catalogue as *"Opus Paschale,"* but in the later tradition the *Paschale Carmen* is often assigned this general name) and a commentary on the PC.
Other information: One of a large group of manuscripts taken from Poland to Russia in the 18th century (S. Petersburg).
Bibliography: Jozef Korzeniowski, *Zapiski z Rękopisów Cesarskiej Biblioteki Publicznej w Petersburgu i innych Bibliotek Petersburskich* = Archiwum do Dziejow Literatury i Oświaty w Polsce 11 (Kraków, 1910), p. 19.

II. EARLY PRINTED EDITIONS

Not only did Sedulius' popularity remain undiminished during the later Middle Ages but his works also continued to be read long after the invention of the printing press. The following pages list over 50 printed editions of the *Paschale Carmen*, including the *editio princeps* (printed around 1473), which are to be dated before the end of the 16th century. Sedulius' poetry appears to have been especially popular in Spain, although we have early printed editions from other countries as well: Belgium, France, Germany, Italy, and the Netherlands. Interestingly enough, Sedulius' reputation spread even as far as "the new world." An edition published in Mexico in 1577 of works of Ovid and Gregory Nazianzus also includes a *"hymnus"* of Sedulius (ff. 53-55) *"In Collegio Sanctorum Petri et Pauli. Apud Antonium Ricardum 1577"* (NYPL, KE 1577).

Among the most intriguing early printed editions which contains poetry of Sedulius is the so-called "Large Passion" illustrated by Albrecht Dürer, printed in Nürnberg in 1511 by Hieronymus Hölzel, entitled *Passio Domini Nostri Iesu ex Hieronymo Paduano Dominico Mancino, Sedulio et Baptista Mantuano per Fratrem Chelidonium Collecta cum Figuris Alberti Dureri Norici Pictoris* (München, Bayerische Staatsbibliothek, Rar. 49). Chelidonius (Benedict Schwalbe) was a monk at S. Egidien in Nürnberg who drew freely on the fifth book of the *Paschale Carmen* (over a hundred lines on ff. 1v-10v) for the text of the poetry that accompanies the illustrations of Dürer (on facing pages).

Another interesting printed edition is Bibliothèque Nationale, Lat. Nouv. Acq. 734, a copy of Jean de Tournes' edition of Sedulius (pp. 131-222), printed in Lyon in 1553. (Cf. Henri Auguste Omont, *Bibliothèque Nationale. Nouvelles acquisitions du Département des Manuscrits pendant les années 1898-1899. Inventaire sommaire* [Paris, 1900], p. 16.) This example of an early printed edition is of potential importance for the textual critic because in the 17th century Renatus Vallinus (René Vallin of Nantes) collated a manuscript which belonged to his colleague, Antoine Legraine, against de Tournes' text. The manuscript, which Renatus Vallinus describes as a *"vetus codex"* (p. 178), contains a number of interesting readings not attested by manuscripts listed in Huemer's critical apparatus.

The list of early printed editions which follows is hardly complete. I have made no attempt, for example, to include all of the editions of early printed hymnals which contain Latin or vernacular versions of the popular *A Solis Ortus Cardine* and *Hostis Herodes*. The list will, however, provide the reader with some idea of how widespread Sedulius' readership continued to be after the development of the printing press. I have included an indication of the sources where I located each edition and have marked with an asterisk those which I have been able to see in person. Wherever possible I have also attempted to correlate this list with that of Arevalo's. (Huemer mentions a few of the most important editions, but does not attempt a systematic listing.)

* * * * *

-Nicolaus Ketelaer and Gerardus de Leempt: Utrecht, c. 1473. *Editio princeps*. *Source:* Wolfgang Borm, *Incunabula Guelferbytana: Blockbücher und Wiegendrucke der Herzog August Bibliothek Wolfenbüttel* = Repertorien zur Erforschung der frühen Neuzeit 10 (Wiesbaden, 1990), p. 298; *BM,* vol. 218, col. 295; *BN,* vol. 169, col. 606; Brunet, col. 258; Hélène Büchler-Mattmann, *Inkunabeln der Bodmeriana* (Zürich, 1976), p. 152; Copinger, vol. 2, p. 73; Graesse, p. 339.

-Leonard Hutz and Lope Sanz: Salamanca, c. 1496. *Source:* Bühler, pp. 107-9; Sosa, 767.

-Pedro Giraldi and Miquel de Planes: Valladolid, Aug. 23, 1497. *Source: Biblioteca Nacional. Catálogo general de incunables,* vol. 2 (Madrid, 1990), p. 194; Bühler, pp. 107-9; Haebler, vol. 2, p. 169; *NUC,* vol. 536, p. 219; Sosa, 768.

-*Jakob Thanner: Leipzig, 1499 (=Arevalo's *Editio iv*). Also published H1 in 1499 and 1503. Apparently reissued in 1502, 1504 (Arevalo's *Editio viii*), 1509 (Arevalo's *Editio ix*), 1513 (Vatican Library, rac. gen. miscell. IV. 18, int. 1), and 1517. *Source: BM,* vol. 218, col. 296; Brunet, col. 258; *Bayerische Staatsbibliothek Alphabetischer Katalog (1501-1840),* vol. 46 (München, 1990), p. 124; Graesse, p. 339; Hain, p. 304; Mead, pp. 74-5; *NUC,* vol. 536, p. 219; *PL,* vol. 19, cols. 478-9; Proctor, no. 3078; Stillwell, p. 455.

-J. Le Fèvre: Paris, 1499 (=Arevalo's *Editio v*). Also includes Juvencus, *Evangeliorum Libri Quattuor. Source: PL,* vol. 19, col. 478.

-Georg Coci (Georgius Cocus), Leonard Hutz, and Lupus Appentegger: Caesaraugustae (Saragossa), Feb. 4, 1500. *"Typ. Pauli Huri."* With commentary of Johannes Sobraria (Juan Sobrarias). Reissued in 1502 (June 24), 1515 (=Arevalo's *Editio xii*), and 1530.

Source: Bib. Nac. Cat., same as above, p. 194; Brunet, col. 258; Bühler, pp. 107-9; Graesse, p. 339; Haebler, vol. 2, p. 169; Mead p. 232; Norton, p. 222, no. 601 and p. 251, no. 671; *NUC,* vol. 536, pp. 218-9; Odriozola, 64; *PL,* vol. 19, col. 479; Sosa, 770; Stillwell, p. 455.

-Johann Rosenbach: Tarragona, Feb. 7, 1500. *Source: Bib. Nac. Cat.,* same as above, p. 194; Bühler, pp. 107-9; Haebler, vol. 2, p. 170; Sosa, 771; Stillwell, p. 455.

-Aulo Ciano Parrasio (*"Sumptibus Iani et Catelliani Cottae"*): Milano, 1501 (=Arevalo's *Editio vi*). *Source: BM,* vol. 218, col. 295; *BN,* vol. 169, cols. 606-7; Brunet, col. 258; *CSEL,* vol. 10, p. xxiv; Graesse, p. 339; *NUC,* vol. 536, p. 218; *PL,* vol. 19, col. 478; Proctor, 13522.

-Conrad Hist: Speyer, 1501. *Source: BM,* vol. 218, col. 295; Brunet, col. 258; Graesse, p. 339; *NUC,* vol. 536, p. 218; Proctor, 11191.

-*Aldus Manutius: Venezia, 1501-2, vol. 2 of *Poetae Christiani Veteres* (=Arevalo's *Editio vii*). *Source: BM,* vol. 218, col. 295; *NUC,* vol. 536, p. 218; *PL,* vol. 19, col. 479.   On the dating see Martin Lowry, *The World of Aldus Manutius. Business and Scholarship in Renaissance Venice* (Ithaca, 1979), p. 148.

-Jakob Kromberger: Seville, March 5, 1504. *Source:* Norton, p. 285, no. 754.

-*N. Chappersotus (editor) and Jean Petit (printer): Paris, c. 1505 (=Huemer's and Arevalo's *Editio princeps*). *Source: BM,* vol. 218, col. 295; *BN,* vol. 169, col. 607; *CSEL,* vol. 10, p. xxv; *PL,* vol. 19, col. 477.

-Carlos Amorós: Barcelona, 1508. *Source:* Norton, p. 70, no. 169.

-Georg Richolff: Münster, 1508-9 (*"impensis Laurentii Bornman,"* i.e. Lorenz Bornemann) (=Arevalo's *Editio iii*). *Source: BN,* vol. 169, cols. 607-8; Josef Benzing, *Die Buchdrucker des 16. und 17. Jahrhunderts im deutschen Sprachgebiet* (Wiesbaden, 1982²), p. 338; *PL,* vol. 19, cols. 477-8.

-Jacobus de Breda (Jacob van Breda): Deventer, 1509. *Source: BM,* vol. 218, col. 296.

-Arnao Guillén de Brocar: Logroño, Dec. 16, 1510 (with commentary of Antonio de Nebrija). *Source:* Norton, p. 144, no. 406; Odriozola, 64.

-Juan de Porras: Salamanca, July 16, 1510 (with commentary of Nebrija). *Source: BM,* vol. 218, col. 296; Norton, p. 179, no. 488;

Odriozola, 64.

-Laur. Hayen: Bois-le-Duc, 1510. *Source: BN,* vol. 169, col. 607.

-Hieronymus Vietor (Philovallis) and Johann Singriener (Singrenius): Wien, 1511 (*"Expensis vero Leonhardi Alantse"*). Edited by Joachim von Watt (Vadianus). *Source:* Graesse, p. 339; *NUC,* vol. 536, p. 219.

-Jacques Mareschal: Lyon, 1512 (with Nebrija's commentary) (=Arevalo's *Editio xi*). *Source:* Brunet, col. 258; *PL,* vol. 19, col. 479.

-*Johann Hess: Wittenberg, Jan. 13, 1513; printed by Johann Grünenberg (*"apud Augustinianos"*). H1 only. Addressed to Spalatin, court secretary of Frederick the Wise. *Source: NUC,* vol. 244, p. 82.

-Arnao Guillén de Brocar: Alcalá, April 1, 1514. *Source: BN,* vol. 169, col. 607; Norton, p. 15, no. 29; Odriozola, 64.

-Joannes Robionus: Lyon, March 28, 1514. *Source:* Odriozola, 64.

-Johann Rosenbach: Barcelona, 1515. Ed. Martin Ivarra. *Source:* Norton, p. 53, no. 128.

-Fadrique de Basilea: Burgos, July 1, 1516. For Arnao Guillén de Brocar, with commentary of Nebrija. *Source:* Norton, pp. 104-5, no. 283; Odriozola, 64.

-*Joannes Bremius (ed.), Jo. Angelus, and Bernardinus de Silva: Torino, Sept. 3, 1516 (=Arevalo's *Editio xiii*). *Source:* Graesse, p. 339; *NUC,* vol. 536, p. 219; *PL,* vol. 19, col. 480.

-Arnao Guillén de Brocar: Toledo, Nov. 19, 1520 (with commentary of Nebrija). *Source:* Norton, p. 411, no. 1145.

-Miquel de Eguía: Alcalá, May 25, 1524 and 1531 (with commentary of Nebrija). *Source: NUC,* vol. 536, p. 219; Odriozola, 65.

-*Theodor Poelman (ed.) and G. Cassander: Basel, 1528, according to Arevalo (*Editio xv*) and later in 1534 (Arevalo's *Editio xvi*), 1537 (Arevalo's *Editio xviii*), 1551 (Arevalo's *Editio xxiv*), and 1573 (Arevalo's *Editio xxxi*). Also contains works of Juvencus, Arator, Venantius Fortunatus and dedicatory letter of Reinhard Lorich (Hadamarius), Marburg, 1537. *Source: NUC,* vol. 287, pp. 280-1; *PL,* vol. 19, cols. 480-3.

-Joannes Grapheus: Antwerpen, 1536. *Source: BCNI,* p. 37.

-Eucharius Cervicornus: Köln, 1537 (also includes Juvencus) (=Arevalo's *Editio xvii*) Arevalo also cites a Köln edition of 1538 (=Arevalo's *Editio xix*). *Source: NUC,* vol. 287, p. 281; *PL,* vol. 19, col. 480.

-The widow of Marten de Keyser (Mart. Caesar): Antwerpen, 1538. Arevalo gives a date of 1536 (*Editio xx*). *Source: BM*, vol. 218, col. 296; *NUC*, vol. 536, p. 219; *PL*, vol. 19, col. 481.

-*Bart. Westheimer: Basel: 1541, 1545, and 1561 (with commentary of Nebrija) (=Arevalo's *Editiones xxi, xxii, xxiii*). Also contains Juvencus. *Source: BM*, vol. 218, col. 296; *BN*, vol. 169, col. 608; Carlos Gilly, *Spanien und der Basler Buchdruck bis 1600. Ein Querschnitt durch die spanische Geistesgeschichte aus der Sicht einer europäischen Buchdruckerstadt* = Basler Beiträge zur Geschichtswissenschaft 151 (Basel and Frankfurt, 1985), pp. 518-9; *NUC*, vol. 536, p. 219; *PL*, vol. 19, cols. 481-2; *Catalogue des incunables et livres du XVI siècle de la Bibliothèque Municipale de Strasbourg* (Strasbourg and Zürich, 1948), pp. 707-8.

-*Jean de Tournes (Tornaesius) and Guillaume Gazeau (Gazeius): Lyon, 1553, 1566, and 1588 (also contains Juvencus and Arator) (=Arevalo's *Editiones xxvi, xxix, xxxiii*). Arevalo also mentions a Lyon edition printed in 1551 (*Editio xxv*). *Source: BN*, vol. 169, col. 608; *PL*, vol. 19, cols. 482-3.

-Granada, 1553 (with Nebrija's commentary). *Source: BM*, vol. 218, col. 296; Graesse, p. 339; Odriozola, 65.

-*Georg Fabricius, ed.: Basel (Oporinus), 1564. In volume entitled *Poetarum Veterum Ecclesiasticorum Opera Christiana et Operum Reliquiae ac Fragmenta* (=Arevalo's *Editio xxviii*), reissued in 1566 and 1588. On the printer, Johannes Oporin, see Gilly above, esp. pp. 185 ff. *Source: BM*, vol. 218, col. 296; *CSEL*, vol. 10, p. xxiv; *PL*, vol. 19, col. 482.

-*Georg Fabricius: Leipzig, 1568. *In Paeanas Tres* (includes *A Solis Ortus Cardine*) (=Arevalo's *Editio xxx*). *Source: BM*, vol. 218, col. 297; *PL*, vol. 19, cols. 482-3.

-Francois Juret (Franciscus Iuretus) (=*editio princeps* of *Paschale Opus*) now lost, 1585. *"Ex vetusto cod. P. Pithoei (Pierre Pithou)." Source: CSEL*, vol. 10, p. xxxviii; Graesse, p. 339.

INDICES

INDEX MANUSCRIPTORUM

INDEX OPERUM ANTIQUIORUM

INDEX LOCORUM

INDEX NOMINUM